PIONEERS OF ROCK AND ROLL

PIONEERS OF ROCK AND ROLL

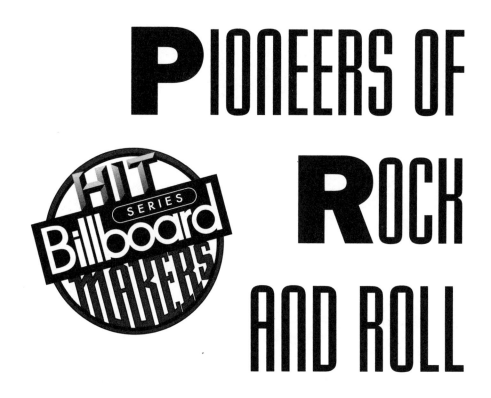

100 ARTISTS WHO CHANGED THE FACE OF ROCK

HARRY SUMRALL

BILLBOARD BOOKS
An imprint of Watson-Guptill Publications/New York

Copyright © 1994 by Harry Sumrall

Edited by Tad Lathrop
Senior Editor: Paul Lukas
Book and Cover Design: Bob Fillie, Graphiti Graphics
Cover Illustration: Paul Rogers
Production Manager: Hector Campbell

First published in 1994 by Billboard books, an imprint of Watson-Guptill
Publications, a division of BPI Communications, L.P., 1515 Broadway,
New York, NY 10036

Library of Congress Cataloging-in-Publication Data
Sumrall, Harry.
    Pioneers of rock and roll : 100 artists who changed the face of rock /
Harry Sumrall.
        p. cm.
    ISBN 0-8230-7628-8
    1. Rock music—Bio-bibliography. I. Title.
ML102.R6S85 1994
781.66'092'2—dc20
    [B]   93-44847
                                               CIP
                                               MN

Manufactured in the United States of America

First Printing, 1994

1 2 3 4 5 6 7 8 9 / 99 98 97 96 95 94

To my grandfather, Harry Allen Sumrall, who loved to read

CONTENTS

CONTENTS

ABOUT "BILLBOARD HITMAKERS"

B*illboard* is the home of the pop charts. For a century, those charts have chronicled the hit songs and albums that have come to represent the pinnacle of commercial achievement in the music industry.

But the charts are not the whole story. Of key importance both in and outside the industry are the artists — the rock and roll bands, soul singers, country musicians, and pop icons who produce the vast body of work from which chart successes emerge.

Billboard Hitmakers is about those artists.

The Hitmakers series presents a broad overview of popular music, with separate volumes devoted to such subject areas as Pioneers of Rock and Roll, Singer-Songwriters, Rhythm and Blues, and Country and Western. Each Hitmakers volume is designed to be enjoyed as a separate reference work dedicated to a distinct segment of the pop spectrum, but the books also complement and reinforce each other. Just as the music scene is constantly changing and growing, the Hitmakers series will expand as new volumes covering new subject areas are published. Taken together, the Billboard Hitmakers series adds up to a growing library of information on pop music's prime movers — with a unique *Billboard* slant.

Each book explores its topic in depth and detail via individual artist profiles arranged alphabetically, with the artists selected for inclusion on the basis of their commercial and/or aesthetic impact on the music scene — including, of course, their history of *Billboard* chart activity.

The artist profiles themselves provide more than just raw chart data, however. Along with biographical facts and career highlights, each profile gives a sense of the artist's impact, offers insights about the music, and places the subject in the grand musical scheme of things. Artists are viewed not as isolated entities but as contributors to an ever-changing soundscape, drawing music from the past, adding to it in the present, and passing it on to musicians of the future. The volumes in the Billboard Hitmakers series chronicle this ongoing evolution, providing a history of popular music as seen from the perspective of the artists who created it.

In addition, each Hitmakers profile lists the artist's significant songs and albums. Titles are chosen first from the top of the *Billboard* charts and are listed chronologically, along with the name of the record's label, its year of release, and its peak chart position. In cases where a profiled artist has no top 40 hits, the titles listed are those generally regarded as the artist's best or most significant recordings.

With rock and roll now moving toward the half-century mark and the originators of blues, gospel, country, and jazz slipping into history, popular music is steadily maturing. Its present-day boundaries encompass an intricate latticework of known genres, nascent movements, as-yet-unlabeled trends, and one-person sonic revolutions. Our intent with the Billboard Hitmakers series is to identify the major players within these diverse yet interrelated musical worlds and present their fascinating stories. And if the books also translate into print some of the musical pleasure these hitmakers have given us over the years, so much the better.

PREFACE

• • • • • • • • • • • • • • • • • •

Rock and roll
wasn't supposed to last.

From the days in 1953 when Bill Haley and His Comets' "Crazy Man Crazy" became the first rock record to enter the *Billboard* charts, through the arrival of Elvis Presley, Chuck Berry, and Little Richard later in the decade, the music and its stars were often dismissed as a passing phase, a garish blip on the screen of constantly changing teen tastes.

In fact, ten years after rock's inception, even the biggest stars of the era downplayed their significance. In 1963, in the first flush of the mania that would be named for them, the Beatles often talked of what they would do "when the bubble burst": at the time, George Harrison mentioned something about becoming an electrician; Ringo Starr said he dreamed of owning a string of ladies' hair salons.

But the bubble didn't burst, for the Beatles or for rock and roll. Rock and roll *did* last. It enters its fifth decade as a multibillion-dollar-a-year industry whose reach extends beyond teenagers to generations who have grown up, and older, with it.

Along the way, it has infiltrated the culture of the world. Its songs have provided the soundtracks for political campaigns and social movements, for wars and revolutions. Its heroes have been at the forefront of constantly evolving tastes, mores, trends, and aesthetics.

From Elvis shaking the Eisenhower years from their secure slumber with a wag of his hips; to Bob Dylan galvanizing the civil rights movement of the 1960s with "Blowin' in the Wind"; to the Beatles changing the look and sound of virtually everything by the sheer power of their presence; to Bob Geldof raising tens of millions of dollars for starving Ethiopians with Band Aid and Live Aid; to the heavy metal of Van Halen, which U.S. military pilots used to pump themselves up for combat in the Gulf War, rock and roll has proved that is has not merely lasted—it has mattered.

That rock has done all this is hardly news. And outlining the role and importance of rock isn't the purpose of this book. Instead, *Pioneers of Rock and Roll* is an examination of artists whose music and careers have defined and redefined rock in the course of its history and, in the process, made it a crucial component of the culture of its time.

"Artists" is the key word in all of this and is used intentionally in place of "performers," "musicians," or "acts." Each of the individuals or groups included in this book has contributed in one or more ways to establishing rock as an art form.

While the latter point—rock as art—could still be open to debate in some aesthetic spheres, the case for such status can certainly be made. If art can be defined as a creative expression of a particular time, for all time, then rock is art. It would be impossible, or at least misleading, to discuss or study or evaluate the social history of the West in the second half of this century without factoring in the impact of rock and roll.

The point of all this as it pertains to this book is that if rock and roll had simply been a commercial device to separate teens (or their parents) from their money, or just another form of entertainment, it would never have lasted. It has lasted because, in its highest forms—in the music of people who are included in this book—it is more than those other aspects. It is art. And this book is about how they have made it thus.

On to practical matters.

The artist entries have several components. Each includes an analysis of music and impact of the individual artist or group that explains why and how they became "pioneers." And each includes a discussion of the artist's career, providing pertinent dates and facts to place the analysis in a historical context.

The discographies included with each entry were

compiled according to a strict formula. Due to space limitations, each list has a maximum of ten entries of albums and/or singles. The lists are based, first, on albums and songs that had the highest ranking in the top 40 of the *Billboard* pop charts. Those albums and songs are listed in chronological order. If the artist had no top 40 singles or albums—or if more then ten charting records were eligible for inclusion—records were chosen to represent a range of styles and/or career phases. Each album or song entry includes, in order, the title, record label, year of release, and peak chart position (if any).

Now, to the artists themselves. For a start, this book is not intended to provide an exhaustive list of rock pioneers. It is, instead, a selective list of artists who have had the greatest impact on the music as an art form.

Before such a list could be drawn up, the title *Pioneers of Rock and Roll* itself had to be defined. The definition of a pioneer seems obvious: an artist whose work had been innovative and influential; an artist who has had an impact on the evolution of the music. And the definition of rock and roll would seem to be self-explanatory.

Neither is as simple as it appears.

While such artists as Presley, Dylan, and the Beatles readily come to mind as influential rockers, there are literally scores of others, major and minor, who have made significant contributions to the art. A line was drawn between those whose work has had a substantive impact on the direction of rock and others whose music has been qualitatively as good but not as "pioneering."

I have tried to be as objective as possible in accomplishing what must be, of necessity, a subjective task. This has, in several cases, forced me to include artists whose work I personally do not abide. It has also necessitated placing musical impact before "name value" or simple commercial success (not that easy a task given the fact that in such a highly commercial form as rock, success can sometimes be as decisive a factor in "pioneering" as aesthetic value). Few of even the most knowledgeable rock fans are familiar with Alexis Korner, yet he was a crucial figure in the development of British blues. He made the list, while Peter Frampton, one of the most successful but musically negligible performers of the late 1970s, did not.

On to the second part of the book's title: "Rock and Roll." What is it? These days, with the "crossover" success of such genres as soul and country and pop, the definition of rock has become diluted, less clear. But even in its fledgling days in the 1950s, the term "rock" was often used to describe artists whose music ranged from hillbilly to straight country and R&B. For the purposes of this book, I have assumed as narrow a definition as possible; to do otherwise would have necessitated a multivolume set.

Thus, the blues masters whose music predated and presaged rock are not included. As important as Muddy Waters, Robert Johnson, Elmore James, and scores of others were in setting the stage for rock and roll, they simply were not rockers. The same could be said of country artists like Waylon Jennings and Johnny Cash. The R&B and soul artists were the most problematic because their music often intersected rock, either as direct competitors on the charts or when their songs and performing styles were borrowed by rockers. A classic case is that of James Brown, George Clinton, and Prince. Musically, Prince is a direct descendant of Clinton, who is a descendant (like many others) of Brown. Prince made the list because he is, all funk aside, intrinsically a rock artist. Brown and Clinton are not. Steve Winwood's glorious vocals would not have been possible without Ray Charles. But Winwood is the rocker; Charles isn't. And while Otis Redding, Sam Cooke, the Temptations, Booker T. and the MG's, and others played major roles in shaping the minds of the likes of the Rolling Stones and an entire generation of '60s rockers, it was those rockers who actually made the rock. To stretch a point—but also to make one—the French classicist Edgar Varèse was a primary influence on the music of Frank Zappa. Zappa made the list, but Varèse didn't.

Finally there is the matter of time. There are few new artists in this book, because at this point in time it is impossible to say who among them might prove to have a historical impact on rock. Groups like Nirvana and Sonic Youth come to mind. Perhaps, as the years pass, they—and who knows who else?—will be seen to have defined their time with their music.

If they last.

HARRY SUMRALL
San Francisco
October 1993

ACKNOWLEDGMENTS

When it comes to this book, I wrote words, but many other very important people had a part in its background and realization.

My wife, Leslie, was there the entire time, with patience and understanding; she also handled all of the computer problems and the printouts, which I, in my technological illiteracy, most certainly would have bungled.

My son, Sam, was there as well, forgoing our usual hikes and afternoons in the park while Dad was sequestered at the keyboard. Then there is the rest of my family: Mom, Dad, Itta, Jonesy, Nin, and Pappy, who wondered and no doubt worried about where rock and roll was leading me. Not to fame and fortune!

Tad Lathrop my indefatigable editor, was a constant source of encouragement and expertise. We shared many thoughts and opinions in our unending, but fascinating, quest for the perfect list of artists.

Miles Hurwitz started the whole thing off when he suggested to Tad that I just might be the person to write this book.

And then there were the people at Billboard Books, who gave me the opportunity to write *Pioneers of Rock and Roll*. Thanks to them all—especially Paul Lukas, who writes a great memo, and Bob Fillie, who executed the fine book design.

My writing career would not have been possible without the support of my great friend Joseph McLellan, who inspired me to become a critic and who gave me my first break. He is also, by the way, the finest music critic, and most agile musical mind, in this country. Thanks, Joe.

Nor would my career have been possible if Shelby Coffey, Chris Williams, and John Walsh hadn't given me a shot in the Style section of the *Washington Post,* long ago.

I am also indebted to my friend and colleague Joel Selvin for many hours of musical discussion on the way to shows and for the photos he provided for the book.

Thanks also to the Brooklyn-based archivist Frank Driggs, who provided most of the remaining photos.

And to my comrade in arms, Zeke Wigglesworth, for Paris, paté—and the PC!

Finally, there are Ron Paras, Robert Goldstein, Allen Perper, Zach Swager, Bill Mayne, and others, with whom I sat up all night, many nights, talking about the music we love.

There are several fine books that I consulted at various points during the writing of this book that were most helpful and that stand as valuable contributions to rock scholarship. They include the books of the king of the charts, Joel Whitburn, most notably *Top Pop Singles 1955–1990* (Record Research) and *The Billboard Book of Top 40 Albums* (Billboard). The various editions of Mike Clifford's *The Harmony Illustrated Encyclopedia of Rock* (Harmony) were a constant source of fact and insight, as was Dafydd Rees and Luke Crampton's *Rock Movers and Shakers* (Billboard). Finally, I also drew upon the many incisive essays by various writers in *The Rolling Stone Record Guide* (Random House).

It was a great help. Thanks to all.

A B B A
. . . .

The songs of Abba rolled out of Sweden in the 1970s like Volvos off an assembly line and promptly parked themselves on the charts of most of the pop-consuming countries of the world.

In time, the sheer volume of those songs, both in numbers made and numbers sold, created an entertainment conglomerate whose annual revenues were said to rival those of the eminent auto maker.

While Agnetha Faltskog, Bjorn Ulvaeus, Benny Andersson, and Anni-Frid Lyngstad—Abba—didn't invent the term Euro-pop, they came to symbolize all that was good and bad about it. Think of American-styled pop melodies retooled to reflect a modernist, continental sense of sleekness and design; think of dance music made in a country without soul (soul music, that is); think of disco and spandex and phonetic English syllables rising in song, and Abba immediately comes to mind.

The music of Abba had more in common with its automotive counterpart than just the bottom line. Like a Volvo, songs such as "Money Money Money" and "Take a Chance on Me" were sturdy, safe pop products churned out by skilled and dedicated craftsmen. *Unlike* a Volvo, they were mostly glitzy and flashy and weren't designed to last.

Not that they had to. Almost as quickly as one Abba hit slid down the charts, there was another on its way up. From 1974 to 1981, the group scored a remarkable nine Number One singles in Britain alone, with another nine songs reaching the top 10. This success was repeated in a vast number of countries worldwide with only the U.S. remaining relatively apathetic to the group's charms (during that time only "Dancing Queen" from 1976 reached the top of the U.S. charts while three other Abba songs made the *Billboard* top 10).

At the core of Abba's success was the group's ability to fuse the simple pop sensibilities of New York's Brill Building masters of the 1950s with the slick, high-tech feel of '70s disco. Songs like "SOS" and "Knowing Me, Knowing You" were pop in the purest melodic sense and they were augmented by sophisticated production flourishes that created a sleek, seamless sound. The vocal harmonies of all four members were equally accomplished, rivalling those of the Beach Boys in their grandiose sound (if not thematic complexity). The result was music that was at once familiar yet distinctly European in feel and flair: hence the title Euro-pop.

At times, the "Euro" threatened to get out of hand. Songs like "Mama Mia" and "Fernando" shamelessly borrowed the worst clichés of Italian and Spanish pop and made Abba sound like a Euro version of a lounge act parody. Not that it mattered. The songs still hit the top of the European charts.

In fact, it was just such a show of pan-European musical personality that seemed to endear the group to the continental pop fans. After decades of idolizing Anglo-American acts, Europe—and much of the rest of the world—seemed to revel in having musical heroes of international status who came from other shores.

Before Abba established itself on the international scene, its members had been part of an active pop movement in their native country. Andersson (b. Goran Bror Benny Andersson, Dec. 16, 1946, Stockholm) was a former pianist of the Hep Cats, a group that had reportedly outsold the Beatles in Sweden in the '60s. Ulvaeus (b. Bjorn Christian Ulvaeus, Apr. 25, 1945, Gothenburg) had performed with the folk group the West Bay Singers. Faltskog (b. Agnetha Ase Faltskog, Apr. 5, 1950, Jonkoping) had a Num-

Abba

ber One hit in Sweden in 1968 with the record "I Was So in Love" and played Mary Magdelene in the Swedish production of *Jesus Christ Superstar*. And Lyngstad (b. Anni-Frid Synni Lyngstad, Nov. 15, 1945, Narvik) had recorded for the EMI label in Sweden and had competed in various song festivals in Japan and Venezuela.

Initially, Andersson and Ulvaeus were brought together in 1969 and dubbed the Hootennany Singers by manager Stig Anderson. In 1971, Faltskog and Lyngstad were recruited to provide vocals for the Singers' upcoming album, *Happiness*. That same year, the foursome performed briefly as a group called the Engaged Couples (Ulvaeus and Faltskog married that year and Andersson and Lyngstad did the same in 1978) but then called it quits.

In 1972, Benny, Bjorn, Agnetha, and Anni-Frid tried again and hit number two on the Swedish charts with the single "People Need Love" released under the aegis of their first names. At this point Andersson hit upon the idea of naming the group after their initials (provoking the ire, then the acquiescence, of the largest fish cannery in Sweden, also named Abba).

But while the group had had a certain success in its homeland, it was hardly at the center of the pop world. This was a decided handicap because, at the time, few if any major pop stars had emerged from outside the pop capitals of the U.S. and Britain. At this point, with nothing else to try, Abba literally took its case to the world. In 1972, Andersson and Ulvaeus entered the song "Better to Have Loved" in the competition for the Swedish entry to the Eurovision Song Contest. It came in third. They did the same in 1973 with the song "Ring Ring," which also came in third.

But in 1974, the third time proved to be charmed when their song "Waterloo" (written with manager Anderson and performed by Abba) was selected to represent Sweden in the Eurovision contest. With the group singing the song in English, "Waterloo" went on to win the contest itself during a broadcast from Brighton, England, that was seen by an estimated 500 million viewers around the world. Abba was on its way. Along the way, the group was lambasted by critics—many of them xenophobic American and British writers who (rightly and wrongly) seemed to look long and hard down their noses at any pop that didn't come from America and Britain.

And the usual pressures of mega-success also took their toll on the group itself. Abba began to break up, literally, when Ulvaeus and Faltskog divorced in

1979 and Andersson and Lyngstad did the same in 1981. But the group continued to perform and record during this time. In 1979, Abba performed six nights at London's Wembley Stadium before a combined audience of 48,000. Also in that year, the group was listed as the biggest-selling act in recording history in the *Guinness Book of World Records*. And, in 1981, the group was honored with the Golden Gramophone award from Polydor Records, an honor usually bestowed on classical artists.

Abba performed its last concert in Stockholm on January 1, 1982. And its last charting single was "Thank You for the Music" in 1983. The group never made an official announcement regarding its breakup. Faltskog and Lyngstad pursued solo careers with modest success, Lyngstad beginning in 1982 with the album *Something's Going On*. Faltskog did the same with 1983's *Wrap Your Arms Around Me*, 1985's *Eyes of a Woman*, and 1988's *I Stand Alone*, which included the single "I Wasn't the One (Who Said Goodbye," a duet with Peter Cetera. Andersson and Ulvaeus teamed with former Andrew Lloyd Webber lyricist Tim Rice on the 1985 musical *Chess*, which yielded the hits "One Night in Bangkok" (recorded by Murray Head) and "I Know Him So Well (recorded by Elaine Paige and Babara Dickson).

The members of Abba reunited in 1985 for a performance on Swedish television's "This Is Your Life" tribute to manager Stig Anderson, who was subsequently sued by Andersson and Ulvaeus in 1991 to recover what they said were unpaid royalties. But its good and bad days notwithstanding, Abba had a major impact on the development of the pop scene. Its combination of synthesizers and vocal harmonies could be heard in the techno-pop of groups like Human League and the Thompson Twins of the early 1980s. And its sleek, studio-perfect sound is also discernible in the confections of the current dance-pop scene of Europe, the U.S., and elsewhere. In that sense, Abba has transcended the Euro-pop sound that it created.

TOP ALBUM

THE ALBUM (Atlantic, '78, *14*)

Additional Top 40 Albums: 4

TOP SONGS

WATERLOO (Atlantic, '74, *6*)
SOS (Atlantic, '75, *15*)
I DO, I DO, I DO, I DO, I DO
  (Atlantic, '76, *15*)
FERNANDO (Atlantic, '76, *13*)
DANCING QUEEN (Atlantic, '76, *1*)
KNOWING ME, KNOWING YOU
  (Atlantic, '77, *14*)
THE NAME OF THE GAME (Atlantic, '77, *12*)
TAKE A CHANCE ON ME (Atlantic, '78, *3*)
THE WINNER TAKES ALL (Atlantic, '80, *8*)

Additional Top 40 Songs: 6

THE ALLMAN BROTHERS

As rock and roll becomes longer of tooth, certain cycles begin to emerge, much as in life itself. There is birth and rebirth as old forms assume new life in newer guises. In 1971, the Allman Brothers were on the cusp of one of those cycles.

A capsule history of rock to that point would reveal that the music began in the American South in the persons of the original blues masters of the late 1940s. By the 1950s, Presley, Berry, and the rest were forging the blues into rock. By the '60s, young British musicians who had drawn their inspiration from their musical forefathers had created, in the process, a new version of blues and rock. Then, just as British blues was running its course at the end of that decade, a new generation of musicians—from the American South—began their own musical journey.

At the head of this generation was the Allman Brothers.

With the release of its eponymously titled debut album in 1969, the group immediately set about establishing a new sound in rock. That sound was a blending of the earthy rock and blues of America with the more stylized blues of the '60s British revisionists.

Vocalist-keyboardist Gregg Allman (b. Dec. 8, 1947, Nashville) sang with a brawling power that could have come straight from a Chicago nightclub. But his vocals also had about them the elegance and articulation of such British giants as Steve Winwood and Jack Bruce. Similarly, the slide guitar of brother Duane (b. Nov. 20, 1946, Nashville) was a distillation of everything from the classic wailings of Elmore James to the eloquent phrasings and riffs of Eric Clapton.

While the brothers Allman were the unquestioned leaders and stars of the group, the rest of the musicians played their roles with panache. Dickie Betts's guitar was the perfect foil for Duane's slide, provid-

ing a delicate but forceful set of counter-leads and instrumental harmonies that gave a distinctive signature to the group's sound. The rhythm section also did its part, with bassist Berry Oakley locking in to the beats of Jai Jimmy Johanson and Butch Trucks—one of the first two-drummer combinations (along with that of the Grateful Dead) in rock history.

The debut album and its follow-up, 1970's *Idlewild South,* established the Allman Brothers' sound as a potent new addition to the rock scene. That same year, Duane's collaboration with Eric Clapton on Derek and the Dominoes' masterpiece, *Layla (And Other Assorted Love Songs),* focused new attention on the Allman Brothers.

But it was 1971's two-record live set, *At Fillmore East,* that truly made the group's reputation. On this record, compact songs gave way to extended improvisations in which Duane's slide slithered and slid through Betts's deft chords and riffs, while Gregg and the rhythm section expanded the sound with jazz-like flourishes. In a sense, these "jams" were the offspring of the lengthy solos and interactions of Cream. But the Allmans took it another step, giving their improvisations a looser, freer-flowing feel; where Cream's solos often seemed to be inspired sparring matches, the Allmans' sounded more like spirited conversations among old friends. The apex of this approach—on *At Fillmore East*—was a grandiose and energetic 22-minute rendering of "Whipping Post" that displayed a complexity and expressive power that were stunning.

Sadly, at the height of its creative power, the group was cut off at the knees when Duane was

The Allman Brothers

killed in a motorcycle crash on October 29, 1971, in Macon, Georgia. A subsequent album, 1972's *Eat a Peach,* featured three cuts that had previously been recorded with Duane; it reached number four on the charts, demonstrating that the group was as popular as ever. But with the death of Oakley (also in a motorcycle crash in Macon, on November 11, 1972) the group began to wander musically even as it became more successful commercially. In 1973, the album *Brothers and Sisters* topped the U.S. charts for five weeks, with the single "Ramblin Man" hitting number two. And in July of that year, the group took part in the biggest rock festival in history, performing with the Grateful Dead and the Band before 600,000 fans at the Watkins Glen Raceway in upstate New York. But by this time, the group's sound—now directed primarily by Betts—had assumed a more mainstream rock approach that had little of the rawness and fervor of the old days. From there, the Allmans degenerated into the usual divisions and conflicts. Gregg was the first to pursue outside interests, releasing a solo album, *Laid Back,* in November 1973. Betts did the same in 1974 with the album *Highway Call.*

The group continued to tour fitfully for a while, and in 1975, the album *Win, Lose or Draw* reached number five, proof of the Allmans' durability. But a low point came in February of that year when Gregg agreed to testify against the group's road manager, John "Scooter" Herring, in a drug case, and the rest of the group consequently severed all ties with him. Gregg went on to marry Cher, becoming something of a media phenomenon in the process (the couple subsequently divorced). And over the next 16 years, the Allmans would disband, regroup, splinter into various offshoots, disband, and regroup again (in 1991, the group was voted Comeback Band of the Year by the readers of *Rolling Stone* magazine).

None of which had much to do with the Allman Brothers' place in the history of rock and roll. That place was secured at the beginning, when the group not only provided a new evolutionary step in the sound of rock but also opened the way, geographically, for a new set of rockers.

The latter point was of crucial importance. Until the Allmans came along, the American South had been dominated less by rockers than by the funky masters of Memphis-based R&B and the legendary Muscle Shoals recording studio. Ironically, Duane had been a part of that scene, performing on records by the likes of Otis Redding, Wilson Pickett, Percy Sledge, and others. In fact, Duane and the other members of the Allman Brothers were brought together by Redding's former manager, Phil Walden, when he set out to form his new Macon-based label, Capricorn Records.

Digressions aside, the Allman Brothers focused attention on the burgeoning scene of new rockers who were emerging in the South at the end of the

1960s. As that decade gave way to the '70s, such groups as the Marshall Tucker Band, Lynyrd Skynyrd, Black Oak Arkansas, and others began to make names of their own. Southern rock became a potent new force in a scene that was otherwise made up mostly of softer, folk-based singer-songwriters and glitzy glam-rockers. While most of the southern rock groups had little of the musical inventiveness and originality of the Allmans, they did display an energy and feel that maintained rock's blues-based roots.

From an evolutionary standpoint, the blues these groups played had less to do with the American original than with the British version from the 1960s. While their sounds differed in specific ways, they were all based on the distorted, high-energy, guitar-based riffs of such British groups as the Yardbirds and Cream. (Tellingly, in an early demo made in the '60s, a fledgling incarnation of the Allmans recorded versions of the former's "Shapes of Things" and the latter's remakes of blues warhorses such as "Spoonful" and "Crossroads.")

In a cultural sense, southern rock also opened up blues-rock to the mainstream of the rock public. While the British blues virtuosos had become rock legends, their music was, for the most part, a phenomenon of the rock press and listening elite (admittedly, a fairly large elite). But the southern rockers took the music to the masses, making it a sound not merely for rock intellectuals, counterculturalists, and such but also for the fan in the street. At southern rock shows, rednecks and their hippie brethren whooped it up side-by-side, united in their affection for high-decibel guitars wailing away on blues riffs.

By the end of the 1970s, a cultural shift was again on the way, with a new rock elite abandoning blues-based rock for the more provocative music of the punks and the new wave. A new cycle had begun—again in London. But it, too, would eventually make its way to another town in Georgia—Athens—where a new southern rock scene would emerge, this one led by a thoroughly idiosyncratic dance band called the B-52's. But that's another story.

TOP ALBUMS

IDLEWILD SOUTH (Atco, '70, 38)
AT FILLMORE EAST (Capricorn, '71, 13)
EAT A PEACH (Capricorn, '72, 4)
BEGINNINGS (Atco, '73, 25)
BROTHERS AND SISTERS (Capricorn, '73, 1)
WIN, LOSE OR DRAW (Capricorn, '75, 5)
ENLIGHTENED ROGUES (Capricorn, '79, 9)
REACH FOR THE SKY (Arista, '80, 27)

TOP SONGS

RAMBLIN MAN (Capricorn, '73, 2)
CRAZY LOVE (Capricorn, '79, 29)

THE ANIMALS

The Rolling Stones have been cited as the leaders of the British R&B movement of the early 1960s. And that was the case. But it was the Animals who first put British R&B on the popular map in the U.S.

The Animals stormed onto the charts in August 1964 with a blues-based rendition of the traditional folk song "House of the Rising Sun." Powered by the rolling arpeggios of organist Alan Price (b. Apr. 19, 1941, Fairfield, Durham) and the belting vocals of Eric Burdon (b. May 11, 1941, Walker, Newcastle, Tyne and Wear), the song went straight to the top of the charts in Britain and America.

To pop fans of the time, the Animals' boiling sound was something of a revolution. Coming, as it did, in the midst of the British Invasion, "House of the Rising Sun" was a resounding slap at the chirping vocal harmonies and pop songs of most of the other invaders. While most British pop groups of the time were busy reinterpreting the rock of such '50s American artists as Little Richard, Buddy Holly, and the Everly Brothers, the Animals drew their sound from the earthy, impassioned music of American blues and R&B masters like Bo Diddley, Muddy Waters, and John Lee Hooker.

Thus, while they were labeled as another long-haired British Invasion group, the Animals were, in fact, another musical animal entirely, one that would transcend, and outlast, the initial British onslaught.

Over the course of the next two years, the Animals climbed the charts with a stunning series of songs that solidified their position as one of the pre-eminent rock groups of the era. "I'm Crying" came with the bluesy chords and bounding rhythms of Hooker's boogies, while Burdon's soulful slant on Nina Simone's classic "Don't Let Me Be Misunderstood" infused it with a raw, unbridled feeling that was remarkable for the pop of the day. "Bring It on Home to Me" had the call-and-response energy of

gospel. And while subsequent hits like "We Gotta Get Outta This Place" and "It's My Life" had a more pop-ish feel, they didn't stray far from the rough-edged blues strut of the group's sound.

The Animals were formed in 1960 (three years before the Stones) in Newcastle-upon-Tyne, England, as the Alan Price Combo. But when Burdon joined two years later, they changed their name to the Animals and soon made their way to London. Collaborating with Mickie Most, a leading pop producer of the time, they created albums that leaned heavily on blues and R&B standards while offering originals that displayed the group's musical derivations.

While guitarist Hilton Valentine, bassist Chas Chandler, and drummer John Steel were a sturdy if unexceptional outfit, it was Burdon and Price who dominated the sound. Price brought a taut, brittle feel to that sound, with keyboard work that was a simplified version of that of American jazz great Jimmy Smith. And Burdon was . . . Burdon.

With his intense, trembling growls and emotional vocal outbursts, Burdon was one of the first of the great British blues stylists, whose ranks would soon be swelled by the likes of Manfred Mann's Paul Jones, Them's Van Morrison, and, later, Rod Stewart, Jack Bruce, Joe Cocker, and others. But in 1964, it was Burdon who held center stage (Mick Jagger and the Rolling Stones would play a less traditional—and a far more revolutionary—role in the evolution and popularization of the British R&B scene).

The Animals were soon beset by defections that changed the group entirely by 1967. Price was the first to depart, in May of 1965, due to musical dif-

TOP ALBUMS

THE ANIMALS (MGM, '64, 7)
THE BEST OF THE ANIMALS (MGM, '66, 6)

Additional Top 40 Albums: 2

TOP SONGS

THE HOUSE OF THE RISING SUN (MGM, '64, *1*)
DON'T LET ME BE MISUNDERSTOOD (MGM, '65, *15*)
WE GOTTA GET OUT OF THIS PLACE (MGM, '65, *13*)
DON'T BRING ME DOWN (MGM, '66, *12*)
 Eric Burdon and the Animals:
SEE SEE RIDER (MGM, '66, *10*)
SAN FRANCISCAN NIGHTS (MGM, '67, *9*)
MONTEREY (MGM, '67, *15*)
SKY PILOT (Part One) (MGM, '68, *14*)

Additional Top 40 Songs: 6

ferences with Burdon and a distaste for flying that had begun to conflict with the group's touring schedule. He went on to form his own group, the Alan Price Set, and was ably replaced by Dave Rowberry. Steel went next, in March of 1966, to open a boutique; Barry Jenkins joined in on drums. The Animals finally called it quits in September of that year. Chandler decided to devote his time to record producing—and promptly made his own mark in rock history when he discovered and nurtured the career of Jimi Hendrix (financing the guitarist's move to England and producing his records).

Burdon was at the center of the decision to disband. At the start of 1966, he had refused to re-sign the group's record deal with producer Most, citing his ambivalence about the group's material. But Burdon was also coming into conflict with the rest of the Animals because of his preoccupation with California's emerging psychedelic sound and his taste for the drug LSD that was fueling that sound.

At the end of 1966, Burdon formed a new outfit with Jenkins staying on as drummer, bassist Danny McCullough, guitarist John Weider, and keyboardist Tom Parker (Vic Briggs and future Police-man Andy Summers would also play guitar with them for a time). The group, billed as Eric Burdon and the Animals, began work on a new record and a new sound.

They relocated to California in January of 1967 and soon proved to be as potent as the original Animals, both musically and commercially. The band's first single, "When I Was Young," was released in the U.S. in April of that year and reached number 15 on the charts. Subsequent releases like "San Francisco Nights," "Monterey" (a tribute to the Monterey Pop Festival), and "Sky Pilot" also charted over the next year. While these songs were far removed from the basic blues sound of the original Animals, they still came with Burdon's impassioned, stirring vocals.

But Burdon had other things on his mind. In December of 1968 he disbanded the New Animals and moved to Los Angeles. Over the next year, he began to perform with Night Shift, a funk band that hailed from Long Beach. Joining the group, he

The Animals

changed its name to War and they began to tour and record. But, again, Burdon changed his mind, quitting the group in 1971 (it went on to become one of the most popular funk bands of the early 1970s). During the next few years, Burdon settled into a somewhat domestic routine, performing at various times with a number of backing groups and recording two albums—1971's *Guilty* and 1976's *Black and White Blues*—with one of his musical heroes, blues great Jimmy Witherspoon.

The original group re-formed in 1976 to record the album *Before We Were So Rudely Interrupted* and again in 1983 to record *Ark*—neither of which achieved the success or acclaim accorded the Animals during their '60s heyday. And in 1986 Burdon bared all in a witty autobiography, amusingly entitled *I Used to Be an Animal, But I'm Alright Now,* which recounted the days when the Animals proved to the world that even British white boys could sing the blues.

THE BAND

The members of the Band stare out from the cover of the group's eponymous 1969 album like a group of Old West outlaws captured in a grainy daguerreotype.

Framed by a dark brown background that accentuates the feeling of oldness, they are a study in crumpled, wrinkled crustiness, their beards and moustaches fuzzing and drooping over faces that seem carved from stone.

In retrospect, the cover photo of the Band does not seem particularly revolutionary. Nor, in fact, does the music that was inside. But at the time, the band's look and sound were crucial components of a vast movement that would be the next evolutionary phase in rock.

By 1969, the rock world was becoming weary of the visual and musical excesses of psychedelia. The frilly, fanciful clothes; the puffy hairdos; the eccentric group names (Electric Prunes, Strawberry Alarm Clock, and such); and the swirling sound of echoed guitars, special effects, and backward tapes had all begun to seem somewhat dated and quaint. Arrayed against this, the Band—the group and the album—seemed an antidote to all the silliness that had pervaded the rock scene.

In the grand scheme of things, the Band represented virtues that were as simple and basic as its name. While the group's look was, in its own way, as contrived as that of the psychedelic era, it was a respite from the visual overload of its predecessors. The jeans and old suit coats of the Band members, along with their wizened expressions and facial hair, seemed to speak of a simpler time, one of simpler attitudes and emotions and, by extension, simpler music.

And the album was loaded with the latter. On songs like "Up on Cripple Creek" and "The Night They Drove Old Dixie Down," Robbie Robertson's guitar was a study in tasteful and tasty conciseness, its wiry phrases ebbing and flowing against the grand organ of Garth Brooks and the lithe piano of Richard Manuel. Bassist Rick Danko and drummer Levon Helm didn't smash and bash and duel rhythmically; they slid and shimmied and shuffled about.

And when they sang, it was like honey dripping off a hive, or like a bear scratching itself against tree

The Band

bark. Helm's vocals were as ornery as his looks on songs like "Rag, Mama, Rag." But when the Band got down to business, they harmonized like a gospel choir, or a group of crooning cowboys, their voices taking on a sublime richness that imbued songs like "Dixie" with a power and eloquence that were sincere and real.

Released in October 1969, *The Band* was an immediate critical and popular success, eventually reaching number nine on the *Billboard* album chart. That album, the group's second, catapulted the Band into the forefront of the rock scene of the day, a position it would build upon in the coming years with albums such as 1971's *Cahoots* (number 21), 1972's two-record live set *Rock of Ages* (number six), and 1973's *Moondog Matinee* (number 28).

But while the Band would prove to be one of the more durable rock acts of the 1970s, several of the most illuminating chapters of its long history had been written much earlier, in fact before the Band was . . . the Band.

The group had been assembled in Canada in 1961 as a backing band for vocalist Ronnie Hawkins. The Hawks, as they called themselves, also included vocalist Bruce Bruno and saxophonist Jerry

Penfound. By 1964, the group had split from Hawkins to become the Levon Helm Sextet, later calling themselves Levon Helm and the Hawks. That same year, without Penfound and Bruno, the group recorded its first record, "Leave Me Alone," changing its name to the Canadian Squires.

As the Hawks, again, the group recorded another single, the Robertson-composed "The Stones I Throw" for Atco Records in 1965. That record came to the attention of Bob Dylan's manager, Albert Grossman. At the time, Dylan was looking for an electric group to back him on an upcoming tour of England. After seeing the group, Dylan and Grossman decided that the Hawks were what he had in mind.

In April of 1965, Dylan and the Hawks began a tour of England, which was documented in the 1966 film *Don't Look Back*. Robertson and Helm, along with keyboardist Al Kooper and bassist Harvey Brooks, also backed Dylan at similar "electric" shows at Forest Hills, New York, and at the Hollywood Bowl.

Having been at the center of the opening volleys of the folk-rock era, the Band continued to work with Dylan in 1966 as he toured England again, this tour culminating in a famous performance at London's Royal Albert Hall in May of that year. Along the way, Helm quit temporarily as a protest against the hard-core folk fans who booed Dylan and the Band during its shows.

In 1967, the group and Dylan moved to Wood-stock, New York, to work on a film of the British tour and to rehearse. With Helm back in the fold, the Band then moved into a large pink house that would become a part of rock and roll lore—a quintessential '60s rock group house that came to be known as Big Pink. Rehearsing with Dylan in the basement of the house, the group recorded the whole process. In time, these recordings became the original rock boot-leg album, *Great White Wonder,* which was subse-quently released commercially by CBS Records in 1975 as *The Basement Tapes.*

At the end of 1967, Gross-man negotiated a recording contract for the Band with Capitol Records, which yield-ed the Band's debut album, *Music from Big Pink,* in 1968. The album came with several Dylan songs, including "Tears of Rage," "This Wheel's on Fire," and "I Shall Be Re-leased." But it was a Robert-son song, "The Weight," that established the group's signa-ture sound and style. As hefty-sounding as its title, the song had a theme line that drew heavily from R&B and a refrain that offered a rock slant on the stately grandeur of country and western. Helm's vocals crackled with down-home fervor, and the Band moved through the song—and the rest of the album—with ease and grace.

Music from Big Pink established the Band with rock's underground movement; "The Weight," on the other hand, was covered by such above-ground artists as Aretha Franklin, the Supremes, and the Temptations (it would also be a featured song in the soundtrack of the 1969 film *Easy Rider*).

The Band was released in 1969, and that year, the group made its live debut—as a distinct performing unit—at the fabled Winterland ballroom in San Francisco. It was at this show that Robertson came down with a mysterious illness attributed to extreme stage fright and was nearly unable to go onstage. At the last moment, producer Bill Graham was forced to call in a hypnotist, who put Robertson "under" and thereby enabled him to perform. The story would become part of the Band's singular legend.

As the 1970s progressed, the Band continued its successful career. The album *Stage Fright* was a play on the rigors of live performance, while *Cahoots* was a somewhat pretentious—not unusual for the time—indictment of the values of American society. In 1971, the group performed three shows at New York's Academy of Music, which were recorded and released in 1972 as the *Rock of Ages* album. There ensued a lengthy period of inactivity while Robertson looked for new musical inspiration. In July of 1973, the Band returned to the stage, performing at the largest rock festival of all time with the Allman Brothers and the Grateful Dead at Watkins Glen in upstate New York.

The group also reestab-lished its relationship with its former mentor, joining Dylan on a tour of the U.S. in 1974. A recording of that tour became the album *Before the Flood.* The Band also went back into the studio with the folk-rock master, providing backing tracks for Dylan's album *Plan-et Waves.* They followed that, in 1975, with a new Band album, *Moondog Matinee,* in which they reveled in the roots of rock and roll. Finally, in 1976, they released the album *Northern Lights—Southern Cross.*

By that time, however, much of the energy and luster had begun to wane, and the Band decided to disband. (The group would release a final album, *Islands,* in 1977, but it was a perfunctory set, record-ed to fulfill the Band's contractual obligations to Capitol Records.) But being the Band, the musicians decided that they would go out with their usual panache. The result was the legendary concert that came to be known as *The Last Waltz.*

On November 25, 1976, the Band returned to Winterland in San Francisco to give their final per-formance. To send themselves off in style, they invit-ed an all-star lineup of musical friends and heroes to join them onstage. The cast included Dylan, Eric Clapton, Ringo Starr, Neil Young, Joni Mitchell, Van Morrison, Paul Butterfield, Muddy Waters, Ronnie Hawkins, Ron Wood, Emmylou Harris, Neil

TOP ALBUMS

MUSIC FROM BIG PINK (Capitol, '68, *30*)
THE BAND (Capitol, '69, *9*)
STAGE FRIGHT (Capitol, '70, *5*)
CAHOOTS (Capitol, '71, *21*)
ROCK OF AGES (Capitol, '72, *6*)
MOONDOG MATINEE (Capitol, '73, *28*)
NORTHERN LIGHTS—SOUTHERN CROSS
  (Capitol, '76, *26*)
THE LAST WALTZ (Warner, '78, *16*)

TOP SONGS

UP ON CRIPPLE CREEK (Capitol, '69, *25*)
DON'T DO IT (Capitol, '72, *34*)

Diamond, Dr. John, Bobby Charles, and the Staples, all of whom took their turns with the Band onstage. Offstage—and onstage—Bill Graham displayed his production genius, employing sets from the San Francisco Opera and supplying a lavish Thanksgiving dinner for the thousands of fans who had come to the show. Director Martin Scorsese was called in to film the event and his efforts yielded *The Last Waltz,* one of the best of all rock concert films. The show also became a three-record set that was released in 1978.

Danko and Helm went on to release undistinguished solo recordings. In 1986, Robertson began his solo career with an excellent eponymous album. Helm and Robertson also pursued film careers, the former landing roles in *Coal Miner's Daughter*

(1980) and *The Right Stuff* (1983) and the latter producing and acting in *Carney* (1980). After several attempted reunions, the group re-formed (without Robertson) in 1986, but its tour came to a tragic end when Manuel hanged himself on March 6th, following a show in Winter Park, Florida. The Band also reunited in 1990 to perform as part of the cast of Roger Waters' production of *The Wall,* which was staged at the site of the Berlin Wall in the city's Potzdammer Platz. That show, which featured various stars, was telecast around the world.

A new version of the Band, with Danko, Helm, Hudson, guitarist James Weider, and keyboardist Stan Szelest, concluded a four-record deal with Columbia Records in 1990; Robertson, in the meantime, continued to pursue his solo career.

BAND AID

In November of 1984, Bob Geldof was a moderately talented vocalist in the moderately successful Irish band the Boomtown Rats. He and the Rats had made a name for themselves with their brash and strutting stage shows and raucous post-punk sound. Then, one night in that month of that year, Geldof sat down, flicked on the telly, and saw a BBC documentary on the famine in Ethiopia.

By 1986, Bob Geldof, Boomtown Rat, had become Bob Geldof KBE, knighted by Queen Elizabeth II. In the press, he was being referred to as Saint Bob. A member of parliament even suggested that he be nominated for the Nobel Peace Prize. And he addressed the United Nations in New York.

What happened in between was Band Aid.

Transfixed by the graphic images of starving Ethiopians on that TV program, Geldof immediately decided, in a display of sheer rock and roll bravura, to do something about the disaster. First, he

enlisted the help of his friend Midge Ure, vocalist of Ultravox, with whom he wrote a song. Then he began to recruit an all-star group of pop stars to record it.

He called the group Band Aid and the song "Do They Know It's Christmas?"

The record was released on December 7, 1984, in conjunction with an Ethiopian benefit show at London's Royal Albert Hall. It entered the U.K. charts at Number One, stayed there for five weeks, and sold more than three million copies, becoming in the process the biggest-selling single in British history. (In the U.S., the record sold more than one million copies and hit number 13 on the charts.)

For the record, the artists who performed as part of Band Aid were Geldof; Ure; Bananarama; Phil Collins; Boy George and Jon Moss of Culture Club; Kool and the Gang's Robert Bell, James Taylor, and Dennis Thomas; Duran Duran; Heaven 17's Glenn Gregory and Martin Ware; Marilyn; George Michael of Wham!; Spandau Ballet; Status Quo's Rick Parfitt and Francis Rossi; Sting; U2's Bono and Adam Clayton; Jody Watley; Paul Weller; and Paul Young.

"Do They Know It's Christmas?" wasn't the best song ever written. It consisted primarily of a simple melody and refrain that were repeated by the vast array of performers. Given the seriousness of its purpose, it was surprisingly upbeat, with a joyous feel that belied the tragedy that had spawned it. Superficially, there was nothing about it that was particularly earthshaking. But it would shake the world of rock.

The success of the song—the very idea of it—immediately created tremors in rock that would grow to an emotional earthquake. It was as if all the forces of ego and self-absorption that had heretofore been directed at careers and hits had been turned outward to the world. Rockers suddenly began to realize that through their immense resources of popularity and drawing power they could literally change the world, or at least have some role in changing it.

By the start of 1985, Band Aid had given rise to USA for Africa, an all-star group of U.S. artists—including Bob Dylan, Ray Charles, Michael Jackson, Lionel Richie, and Bruce Springsteen—who recorded the Jackson-Richie song "We Are the World" for Ethiopian relief. "We Are the World" hit the top of the charts, selling seven million copies and raising a reported $50 million (including revenues from a video and merchandising).

Bob Geldof of Band Aid

Geldof responded with Live Aid, the biggest rock show of all time, unfolding simultaneously in London and Philadelpia on July 13 of that year. The 16-hour show, which came with performances by the likes of Paul McCartney, Dylan, various Rolling Stones, Madonna, the Who, Led Zeppelin, and what amounted to a who's who of the contemporary rock world, drew an estimated two billion viewers in more than 22 countries and generated $70 million in pledged donations directed to the Band Aid Foundation.

Like the group and song that had started it all, Live Aid would be a watershed in rock history, spawning scores of similar benefit shows—of lesser magnitude—directed at raising funds for a variety of causes and/or relief efforts necessitated by natural disasters.

By the close of the decade, such benefit shows had become ubiquitous. Some, like Farm Aid (initiated by Willie Nelson to raise funds for American farmers), became annual events, drawing scores of rock performers. And others came into being following disasters. Thus "It's Everybody's Fault" was a day-long series of shows staged in the Bay Area in November 1989 to benefit victims of the Loma Prieta earthquake that had ravaged northern California. In 1992, singer Gloria Estefan presented an all-star benefit of her own in Florida for the victims of Hurricane Andrew.

There were precedents for these shows that predated Band Aid and Live Aid. In 1971, George Harrison and Ravi Shankar presented "The Concert for Bangladesh" at Madison Square Garden in New York that, with its subsequent film and album, raised an estimated $15 million for the people of that war- and famine-ravaged country. In 1976, the Rolling Stones played a benefit for the victims of an earthquake in Nicaragua.

But these shows, and others like them, were isolated events. While they had a monetary and momentary impact on their specific causes and raised attention to the plight of the victims involved, these shows did not have a broader impact on the world of rock. Band Aid and Live Aid, on the other hand, created a new way of thinking. In an age when rock and its artists had come to exist in a cultural vacuum—one that was bereft of defining causes like the antiwar and civil rights movements of the 1960s—Band Aid provided a *raison d'être* for the

music. The revenues and attention generated by Geldof for the starving Ethiopians inspired other rockers to do the same for causes that they embraced. What ensued was a virtual season of concern in which the rock world began to make its opinions and sensitivities known via shows, tours, and records that were aimed at forcing various agenda onto the public stage.

The range of causes expanded to include social, political, and environmental issues. In December of 1985, 49 artists assembled by former Springsteen sideman Little Steven Van Zandt, collectively going by the name Artists United Against Apartheid, recorded the single "Sun City" to decry the notorious segregationist policies of South Africa. In 1986, U2, Sting, Peter Gabriel, Lou Reed, and Bryan Adams took part in the "Conspiracy of Hope" tour for Amnesty International (which begat a subsequent album and a second tour in 1988). In 1989, Gabriel, U2, Annie Lennox, and the Thompson Twins released *Greenpeace—Rainbow Warriors,* a benefit album for the environmental organization. In 1991, the "Simple Truth" concert, featuring Gabriel, U2, and others, was staged at the Wembley Arena in London as a benefit for Kurdish refugees.

What all of these events and scores of others like them had in common was a shared belief that rock could be used as a force for change and the betterment of the human condition, quite apart from the commercial concerns that no one would or could deny.

The rock world being no more perfect than the rest of the world, it is also likely that the allure of such events had a certain pragmatic cachet for some of the artists involved. The publicity that was invariably generated by these events was good for careers and egos. By 1992, benefit shows had become so prevalent that "Saturday Night Live" produced a scathing parody of USA for Africa, with actors imitating rock stars performing a song for Free Range Chickens. It was hilarious, but not far from the mark.

But excess is the name of the rock game, and even the best of ideas and intentions—like that of Geldof and Band Aid—have a way of becoming just another part of the business in time. However, that does not negate the original idea or intent of Band Aid, or the vast change in rock that it set in motion.

TOP SONG

Do They Know It's Christmas?
(Columbia, '84, *13*)

THE BEACH BOYS

As long as there is a California—the state itself, or, perhaps, simply the state of mind—the music of the Beach Boys will endure as the timeless evocation of the ethos it represents.

The music that the group created in the early years of the 1960s virtually defined the image of surfers, hot rods, sun, beaches, girls, and fun, fun, fun that became the California myth. The titles of their songs said it as well as anything: "Surfin' U.S.A.," "Little Deuce Coupe," "Surfer Girl," "Fun, Fun, Fun," "Dance, Dance, Dance," and "California Girls."

With these hits and others, the group's bassist and songwriter, Brian Wilson, created a new sound in rock and roll. It was called the "surf sound," but in fact it was a combination of older rock verities set in entirely new lyrical and musical contexts. On songs like 1963's "Surfin' U.S.A.," Wilson expropriated the music of Chuck Berry (specifically his '50s "Sweet Little Sixteen"); charged it up with the metallic, "modern," guitar-driven sound of the Ventures; souped it up with his version of producer Phil Spector's wall of sound; added layers of vocal harmonies; slapped on his lyrical paeans to teen life; and came up with a musical revolution.

He didn't accomplish it alone. His brothers Carl (guitar) and Dennis (drums), cousin Mike Love (vocals), and neighbor Al Jardine (guitar) abetted him with lean, rock instrumentals and smooth vocal harmonies that were as clean and young in feel as they were in sound. Beach Boys records were invariably crisp and effervescent; they fairly bubbled with exuberance and energy.

But there was a depth and complexity about those records that belied their innocence and apparent simplicity. The 1963 ballad "In My Room" evoked fears, doubts, and questions that were universal elements of teen life—that showed the other side of the fun, fun, fun mentality. The strutting

lyrics of "I Get Around," on the other hand, were as brash and cocksure as anything written in rock.

On these songs and most of the rest, Wilson devised vocal harmonies that were almost baroque in their intricacy and construction. Such tracks as "Dance, Dance, Dance" and "Help Me Rhonda" were awash in overlapping, interconnected melodies and dense, contrapuntal layers of words and syllables. The result was not unlike a "girl group" by way of a Bach chorale.

But the songs of the early 1960s were only part of the Beach Boys' legacy. During the middle of the decade, Brian Wilson pursued a vastly more ambitious vision that would ultimately yield one of rock and roll's most inspired bodies of work.

Among its key products was the 1966 album *Pet Sounds*. On its songs, from "Wouldn't It Be Nice" and "Caroline No" to "God Only Knows" and others, Wilson displayed an almost classical mastery of composition. His complex productions, with their weaving harmonies and massed instruments, were revolutionary developments in the evolution of rock. While the album was a relative commercial disappointment, it was also vastly influential. Its sound would inspire the Beatles—particularly Paul McCartney—when they began to work on their 1967 masterpiece, *Sgt. Pepper's Lonely Hearts Club Band*.

Wilson then went on to surpass *Pet Sounds* with "Good Vibrations," a brilliantly conceived mass of interconnected voices, instrumental motifs, cellos, harmonies, and a whining theremin.

"Good Vibrations" was the apex of Wilson's genius—and of the Beach Boys' career.

That career began in 1961, when the Beach Boys

The Beach Boys

were formed by brothers Brian Wilson (b. Brian Douglas Wilson, June 20, 1942, Inglewood, California); Dennis Wilson (b. Dennis Carl Wilson, Dec. 4, 1944, Inglewood); Carl Wilson (b. Carl Dean Wilson, Dec. 21, 1946, Hawthorne, California); their cousin, Mike Love (b. Michael Edward Love, Mar. 15, 1941, Baldwin Hills, California); and their friend Al Jardine (b. Alan Charles Jardine, Sept. 3, 1942, Lima, Ohio).

Using various group names, including Carl and the Passions, Kenny and the Cadets, and the Pendle-

tones, they performed at local shows during the year. In September, the Wilsons' father, Murry, who had assumed the role of their manager, secured a deal with the local X label. The debut release was "Surfin'," a Brian Wilson and Mike Love composition. When the single failed, Jardine quit the group and was replaced by another neighbor of the Wilsons, David Marks.

"Surfin' " was subsequently distributed by the Candix label at the beginning of 1962, and it hit number 75 on the charts. At the suggestion of the

Candix executives, the group changed its name to the Beach Boys. When Candix folded in May 1962, Murry Wilson took the group's demos to several labels, one of which, Capitol Records, signed them.

In June, Capitol released the single "Surfin' Safari," which began a slow climb on the charts, peaking at number 14 in October. The Beach Boys had arrived as a major rock act, bringing along the surf sound that they would come to symbolize.

With the release of "Surfin' U.S.A." in 1963, the group began an extended assault on the charts. In May of 1963, Marks was dismissed from the group and Jardine rejoined, forming the classic lineup. The Beach Boys subsequently recorded such hits as "Surfer Girl," "Fun, Fun, Fun," "I Get Around," "Dance, Dance, Dance," "Help Me, Rhonda," "California Girls," "Barbara Ann," and "Sloop John B." From 1963 through September of 1966, the Beach Boys hit the top 40 of the singles charts 20 times and the album chart 12 times.

A major part of the Beach Boys' mystique was the contrast between the sheer joy of its music and the turmoil that was at the group's core. Fissures in the group's joyous facade began to appear in 1964, when Wilson retired from touring after suffering a nervous breakdown. He was temporarily replaced by Glen Campbell, and later by Bruce Johnston (b. June 27, 1944, Peoria, Illinois), who joined the group formally in April 1965 and maintained a role in the Beach Boys over the course of the rest of its career.

Brian continued as the group's producer and songwriter. And while he churned out an increasing number of his usual Beach Boys hits, he also began to sequester himself in the studio and experiment with new sounds and recording processes that were a quantum leap beyond his earlier teen anthems. The result was the 1966 album *Pet Sounds,* which was immediately hailed as a masterpiece and went on to chart at number 10. But Wilson's artistic pursuits began to border on the obsessive. On the group's next single, he spent six months in the studio, recording and rerecording scores of individual tracks. At the end of the year, the resulting "Good Vibrations" became a Number One hit.

TOP ALBUMS

SURFIN' U.S.A. (Capitol, '63, 2)
BEACH BOYS CONCERT (Capitol, '64, 1)
SUMMER DAYS (AND SUMMER NIGHTS!!) (Capitol, '65, 2)
ENDLESS SUMMER (Capitol, '74, 1)

Additional Top 40 Albums: 16

TOP SONGS

SURFIN' U.S.A. (Capitol, '63, 3)
I GET AROUND (Capitol, '64, 1)
HELP ME, RHONDA (Capitol, '65, 1)
BARBARA ANN (Capitol, '66, 2)
GOOD VIBRATIONS (Capitol, '66, 1)
KOKOMO (Elektra, '88, 1)

Additional Top 40 Songs: 29

But again, his mental problems began to intrude on the group's career. While he was recording the followup to *Pet Sounds* (in collaboration with songwriter Van Dyke Parks), Brian's use of drugs combined with his rather nebulous mental state to sabotage completion of the album *Smile.* After months of recording, the album was abandoned.

It proved to be a disaster for the Beach Boys.

By the start of 1967, the group's sound and image were being surpassed by the emerging groups of the San Francisco scene. In July, the Beach Boys declined to perform at the Monterey Pop Festival due to fears that the event's hippie fans might laugh them off the stage. When the group's next album, *Wild Honey,* was released in 1968, it proved to be a disappointment. From that point on, the group ceased to be a consistent commercial or artistic force in rock.

It did press on, however. Over the course of the next 20 years, it released 19 albums (several of which were oldies sets) and numerous singles. The group hit number five on the charts in 1976 with a rendition of Chuck Berry's "Rock and Roll Music." And in 1988, it topped the charts with the single "Kokomo," a song from the soundtrack of the film *Cocktail.*

There were numerous controversies and defections along the way. In 1981, the group made headlines across the U.S. when Secretary of the Interior James Watt refused to allow the Beach Boys to play their annual Fourth of July show at the Washington Monument (the refusal was quickly rescinded when First Lady Nancy Reagan stated she was a fan). At one point or another, each of the original members quit the group to pursue solo careers, only to return when those careers invariably fizzled. The group was also devastated when Dennis Wilson drowned while swimming near his boat in Marina Del Rey on December 28, 1983. Brian Wilson released an eponymous solo album in 1988, but it was a negligible effort that, amid much hype, failed on the charts.

That same year, the Beach Boys were inducted into the Rock and Roll Hall of Fame.

THE BEATLES

The Beatles were more than a rock group. They were a vast cultural phenomenon, an epoch unto themselves.

When the Beatles appeared on "The Ed Sullivan Show," on February 9, 1964, it was as if one door had been slammed shut and another thrust open for an entire generation. As John Lennon, Paul McCartney, George Harrison, and Ringo Starr shook their "mop tops" and played their impossibly new and vital form of rock and roll, the collective consciousness of an entire generation seemed to realize at once that nothing would ever be the same again.

And it wasn't.

Simply stated, the Beatles changed everything.

Over the course of the 1960s, the Beatles dominated the culture in ways that eluded the grasp of politicians, theologians, philosophers, and other rock groups. Their tastes, attitudes, whims, and musical expressions were immediately translated into new trends in hairstyles, clothing, behavior, social beliefs, and rock and roll itself. Everything became "Beatle." There were Beatle boots and Beatle haircuts and Beatle slang: "gear," "fab," and so on. When the Beatles wore a particular coat or shirt or hat, the rest of the rock world did the same. When the Beatles grew moustaches, the rest of the rock world did the same. When the Beatles openly espoused the use of drugs, or questioned religion, or cut their hair, or took a guru (or abandoned one), or gave peace a chance, or did it in the road—Abbey Road—the rock world took its cue and did the same, or tried to, or simply wanted to.

Their impact on rock and roll was similarly overwhelming. When they first emerged with their Mersey sound, they set in motion a British Invasion that conquered America and simultaneously closed the book on all rock that had gone before.

Immediately, the Beatles redefined the concept of a rock group. While Lennon and McCartney wrote most of the songs and provided most of the vocals, particularly in the group's early and middle phases, the Beatles were, in fact, the inspired sum of all four of its members' musical and personal characteristics. Lennon's cynicism and biting wit were complemented by McCartney's lithe pop sensibilities. Harrison's guitar work was sublimely subdued and affecting (as was his personality), while Starr's effervescent presence and drumming grounded the group's more grandiloquent aspects. In short, the Beatles were a four-headed genius that ultimately added up to a singular all-encompassing whole.

This could be heard on the group's records. Each song was a mini-masterpiece that would have been incomplete without any of its parts. Thus, Harrison's solo on "A Hard Day's Night" or Starr's distinctive high-hat cymbal work on "She's a Woman" were as crucial to the end product as Lennon and McCartney's vocals and harmonies: the songs simply would not have been the same without them.

Similarly, the Beatles were the focal point of the inspired work of many of the people who collaborated with them. Their manager, Brian Epstein, who had previously run the record department in his family's store, became an innovative rock businessman, guiding their career through such epochal developments as their performances at Carnegie Hall and Shea Stadium (the first major stadium show in rock history). George Martin had been a relatively obscure record producer at EMI; with the Beatles, he proceeded to revolutionize the use of studio effects and practices in their later music. With director Richard Lester, the Beatles released two films, 1964's *A Hard Day's Night* and 1965's *Help!* that elevated the previously vapid, exploitative form to a new creative cinematic level.

Perhaps the most remarkable aspect of the Beatles' career was the way in which they constantly pursued new sounds and images, always confronting the rock world with new stimuli and possibilities. Up to that point in rock, artists had established their individual musical styles and images and simply stuck with them until they ran dry. The Beatles repeatedly changed their music and themselves and, miraculously, reached new creative pinnacles. In the process, their eclecticism and evolution became salient aspects of the entire '60s generation.

The Beatles' musical innovations were many and manifold: the 1964 single "I Feel Fine" had one of rock's first uses of feedback; the 1965 ballad "Yesterday" employed a string quartet (2,500 versions of the song were subsequently recorded, and it was the first song in history to be performed, in various media, five million times); the song "Norwegian Wood" featured Harrison playing an Indian sitar.

Over time, the Beatles' experimentation grew more complex and expansive. On 1967's "Penny Lane," McCartney provided a time capsule of his boyhood Liverpool that came with an ethereal sound augmented by baroque-inflected trumpet figures. The other side of that single was the revolutionary "Strawberry Fields Forever," on which Lennon employed dense, abstract imagery, reversed tapes, and strings to paint a phantasmagoric musical landscape. And on that year's "All You Need Is Love," the Beatles, backed by a orchestra, created the anthem of the peace-and-love generation.

Each of the Beatles' albums was a masterpiece in its way. But three proved to be more than that. In 1965, *Rubber Soul* introduced levels of musical complexity and lyrical introspection that were virtually unprecedented in rock. In 1966, *Revolver* expanded on that complexity with songs that included abstract expressionistic collages of sound, Harrison's first full-fledged Indian rock composition, a big band, a classical string ensemble, and assorted tape and sound effects.

Those albums were the prelude to the group's defining masterpiece—and what is generally considered to be the greatest rock album of all time—*Sgt. Pepper's Lonely Hearts Club Band*. Released in June 1967, the album became the anthem for the psychedelic era while also establishing rock as an art form of apparently limitless expressive depth.

Sgt. Pepper was the first concept album. While the concept was nebulous, involving the Beatles performing a show of sorts under the title's pseudonym, the songs had a cohesiveness and unity of purpose that gave the album the air of a classical song cycle. From the rocking title cut to the psychedelic sound and imagery of "Lucy in the Sky with Diamonds," the music hall–inflected "When I'm Sixty-Four," and the violent, storming orchestral finale of "A Day in the Life," the album was a tour de force of rock expression that has never been surpassed.

While that album was an artistic apex in the Beatles' career as well as in the history of rock, the group continued to create music that was both innovative and inspired.

The Beatles' formative phase began in 1957 when Lennon (b. John Winston Lennon, Oct. 9, 1940, Liverpool, England) was introduced to McCartney (b. James Paul McCartney, June 18, 1942, Liverpool) following a performance by the former's group the Quarry Men. The two struck up a musical and personal friendship immediately, and McCartney was invited to join the group as a guitarist. In 1958, Harrison (b. Feb. 25, 1943, Liverpool) was also enlisted.

Performing on the local skiffle and rock scene—using group names that changed from the Quarry Men to Johnny and the Moondogs, the Silver Beatles, and, finally, the Beatles—Lennon, McCartney, and Harrison began to accrue a modest local following. In 1960, Lennon's art school friend Stu Sutcliffe was added on bass, as was Pete Best on drums.

That same year, the group journeyed to Hamburg, West Germany, to perform at various clubs, where they played night-long sets and began to develop and refine their stage act.

Over the next three years, they shuttled to and from Liverpool and Hamburg, performing constantly. During one of their trips to Hamburg, Sutcliffe quit the group and McCartney took over on bass. (Sutcliffe died of a brain hemorrhage in 1962.)

On another stay in Hamburg, in 1961, the group made its first recordings with vocalist Tony Sheridan.

They made their debut at the Cavern Club in Liverpool on February 21, 1961, and soon became one of its house acts, eventually eliciting the kind of response that would later mushroom into Beatlemania. It was at the Cavern that Brian Epstein first heard the group, on November 9, 1961.

Impressed, Epstein signed them to a management contract in January of 1962. He immediately set about cleaning up their image, replacing their leather gear with suits and suggesting that they bow after each of their songs.

He began to offer the group to various labels in London. After being turned down by Decca Records, Epstein got in touch with EMI producer George Martin, who agreed to audition the band in May 1962. That audition resulted in a record deal with the label.

During the Beatles' initial sessions, Martin was dissatisfied with Best's drumming. He was sacked, and former Rory Storm and the Hurricanes drummer Ringo Starr (b. Richard Starkey, July 7, 1940, Liverpool) was invited to join.

The Beatles released their debut single, "Love Me Do," in October 1962. It eventually reached number

---

TOP ALBUMS

MEET THE BEATLES! (Capitol, '64, 1)
RUBBER SOUL (Capitol, '66, 1)
REVOLVER (Capitol, '66, 1)
SGT. PEPPER'S LONELY HEARTS CLUB BAND (Capitol, '67, 1)
ABBEY ROAD (Apple, '69, 1)

Additional Top 40 Albums: 22

TOP SONGS

I WANT TO HOLD YOUR HAND (Capitol, '64, 1)
A HARD DAY'S NIGHT (Capitol, '64, 1)
YESTERDAY (Capitol, '65, 1)
HEY JUDE (Apple, '68, 1)
LET IT BE (Apple, '70, 1)

Additional Top 40 Songs: 44

17 on the U.K. charts. Their next single, "Please Please Me," hit number two in February 1963. And when their third single, "From Me to You," topped the charts in May, it was the start of a record-breaking 11 consecutive Number One U.K. hits.

The Beatles soon became a British rock phenomenon. When fans rioted at their performance on the television program "Sunday Night at the London Palladium" in October, the British press coined the term Beatlemania. The group's appearance before the Queen Mother at the Royal Variety Performance in London, in November, was one of the legendary shows in the history of rock.

The group's debut album, *With the Beatles,* was released in the same month and became the first million-selling disc in the history of the British recording industry.

But the biggest rock market in the world was still unaware of the Beatles. That changed in February 1964, when the quartet appeared on "The Ed Sullivan Show."

That same month, the group's single "I Want to Hold Your Hand" topped the U.S. charts, and the Beatles soon dominated those rankings as thoroughly as they had in the U.K. Its debut U.S. album, *Meet the Beatles,* soared to Number One, where it stayed for 11 weeks.

The Beatles' popularity was unprecedented. During the week of April 4, 1964, the Beatles occupied the top five positions of the *Billboard* singles chart with "Can't Buy Me Love" (1), "Twist and Shout" (2), "She Loves You" (3), "I Want to Hold Your Hand" (4), and "There's a Place" (5). *Meet the Beatles* and *Introducing . . . the Beatles* were also at numbers one and two on the album chart.

The Beatles' success, popularity, and artistic achievements continued through 1965 and '66 with the albums *Rubber Soul* and *Revolver* and such Number One hits as "Eight Days a Week," "Ticket to Ride," "We Can Work It Out," and "Paperback Writer."

Along the way, the group starred in the films *A Hard Day's Night* and *Help!* In 1965, the Beatles were awarded MBE's (Member of the British Empire) by Queen Elizabeth II.

They were not above controversy. When Lennon's remarks to a British journalist about the Beatles being more popular than Jesus were printed in the U.S. in 1966, they created a storm of protest that threatened the cancellation of their U.S. tour that year.

Partially as a reaction to that, and also because they were weary of performing their music to screaming Beatlemaniacs, the Beatles retired from concert performances at the end of that tour. Their final concert unfolded at San Francisco's Candlestick Park on August 29, 1966.

Ensconced in the recording studio in 1967, the Beatles proceeded to create songs that would expand the range and depth of rock expression. The culmination of their efforts was *Sgt. Pepper's Lonely Hearts Club Band.*

Shortly after the release of that album, on August 27th, Epstein died in London, apparently from a drug overdose.

Without his presence, the Beatles gradually began to come apart. Their subsequent, self-produced British TV special, "Magical Mystery Tour," proved to be their first failure when it aired in December 1967, although the album of the same name contained several typically striking songs.

During the initial months of 1968, the group journeyed to India to study meditation with the guru Maharishi Mahesh Yogi but returned disillusioned. As they began to record their next album, internal disputes started to emerge, exacerbated by Lennon's relationship with avant-garde artist Yoko Ono. While those recordings yielded the extraordinary eponymous album (often referred to as the White Album) at the end of the year, the rot had set in.

Filming the next album's recording sessions for the documentary *Let It Be* in January 1969, the group was beset by ennui and acrimony. But it rebounded later in the year with *Abbey Road,* which included a suite of songs on its second side that were as evocative and elegant as any music the Beatles had created.

While the film, soundtrack, and single for "Let It Be" were released to the usual success in 1970, the Beatles had virtually ceased to exist as an active entity. On April 9th of that year, McCartney announced that he was leaving the group.

All four Beatles subsequently pursued solo careers, to varying degrees of success.

As a solo artist and with his '70s group Wings, McCartney adhered closely to his Beatles sound on albums ranging from his 1970 eponymous debut to 1982's *Tug of War,* and he carried it into the next decade on releases like 1993's *Off the Ground.*

Lennon recorded various albums, including the 1970 debut, *Plastic Ono Band,* and his final record, 1980's *Double Fantasy.*

Harrison's career began with the exceptional three-record set *All Things Must Pass,* but it faded at the start of the '80s. He made a comeback in 1988 with the album *Cloud Nine* and subsequently teamed with Bob Dylan, Tom Petty, Roy Orbison, and Jeff Lynne in the supergroup known as Traveling Wilburys.

Starr had several singles hits in the 1970s, including "Photograph" and "It Don't Come Easy," among others, but his career, too, faded. At the end of the '80s he made a modest comeback leading a group of musical stars and pals that he called his All Starr Band.

None of them ever came close to approximating the musical grandeur they had achieved with the Beatles.

On December 8, 1980, Lennon was murdered in New York City.

JEFF BECK

For the record, Jeff Beck was born on June 24, 1944, in Wallington, Surrey, England. To judge by the sounds he made with his guitar, however, he might just as easily have come from another planet.

Initially, as the guitarist for the Yardbirds in the mid-1960s, and later as a solo artist, Beck created a lexicon for the guitar that was entirely his own. In the process, with his trademark bouffant hairdo and gum-chewing, devil-may-care presence, he helped to forge—along with other titans like Eric Clapton and Jimmy Page (both also alumni of the Yardbirds) and Jimi Hendrix—the archetypal image of the rock guitar hero.

In that pantheon, Jeff Beck occupied a singular place of originality and virtuosity. While Clapton and Page came out of the blues tradition and Hendrix emerged from, and helped create, the psychedelic era, Beck's approach had few precedents. At its most basic, his playing was an astonishing combination of technical agility and idiosyncratic melodic sensibility. While much of his work was blues-inflected, it also came with clicking, chunky chords that had the feel of Steve Cropper's work with Booker T and the MGs, along with wiry, fleeting phrases that looked back to the work of Les Paul and the country-tinged sound of rockabilly. But in Beck's world, all of this was energized by vast infusions of decibels, altered by distortion boosters and wah-wah pedals, and finally skewed by his own warped musical instincts into a whole new approach to the guitar.

Added to it all was his almost maniacal use of the guitar as a sound source that emitted everything from sitar-like whines ("Heart Full of Soul"), dog-like growls ("Ain't Superstitious"), and the howl of a train whistle ("The Train Kept A-Rollin').

A virtual dictionary of his creative vocabulary came on the song "Jeff's Boogie," which appeared on *Over Under Sideways Down,* the Yardbirds album released in 1966. An instrumental setting for his jewel-like licks, the song was basically a set of repeating chords that would then break to allow Beck to solo for four bars at a time. Improvising like a horn player in a 1930s big band, Beck made each passage a mini tour de force that ranged from dizzying ascending and descending scales to melodic chord-leads; groaning, distorted riffs; chiming, bell-like harmonics; and high, bluesy wails. In stage versions of the song, he expanded these breaks even

Jeff Beck

more, at times quoting the theme from "The Beverly Hillbillies" (picking his guitar like a banjo), at others slamming away at the strings, producing the cacophony of a traffic jam from his fretboard.

In counterpoint to these idiosyncracies, Beck also displayed a penchant for fairly straightforward instrumental interpretations of familiar songs, in the manner of traditional jazz or classical guitarists. Thus, during his initial fling at a solo career in 1967, Beck recorded an instrumental version of "Love Is Blue" (from the Eurovision Song Contest). On the epochal 1968 album *Truth* (with the Jeff Beck Group), he picked out an elegant acoustic rendition of the ancient folk song "Greensleeves." And on *Blow by Blow*, his 1975 debut solo album, he recorded an instrumental version of the Beatles' "She's a Woman."

In combination, the extremes of Beck's musical predilections (which were also augmented by forays into jazz-rock during his solo career) made up a complex, expansive musical vision that remains unparalleled.

After stints with Screaming Lord Sutch, the Nightshifts, and the Tridents during the early 1960s, Beck was recruited by the Yardbirds (on the suggestion of British session master Jimmy Page) in 1965, after the departure of Eric Clapton. While Clapton had left the group because of its turn away from the blues into a more experimental form of rock and pop, this new direction was ideally suited to Beck's roving musical mind.

During his roughly two-year stint with the Yardbirds, Beck recorded a series of songs that would come to define much of the British rock of the era. The group's 1965 hit "I'm a Man" came with a call-and-response section in which Beck 's guitar licks vied with the harmonica wails of the group's vocalist Keith Relf. When the group failed to get the raga sound it wanted from Indian musicians on "Heart Full of Soul," Beck stepped in a provided his own wiry version of a sitar. On one of the group's signature hits, "Shapes of Things," Beck provided a dense, distorted solo whose sound was ominous and futuristic. The title song from *Over Under Sideways Down* was introduced by a lead phrase in which Beck's raspy, reedy lines sounded very much like those of a Middle Eastern zither. And on the menacing 1966 hit "Happenings Ten Years' Time Ago," Beck traded solos with fellow guitarist Page (who joined up that year), opening with a discordant, two-note assault that sounded like the droning of a European police car.

On October 28, 1966, two days into a Dick Clark package tour of the U.S., Beck quit the Yardbirds and went back to Britain to begin a solo career. That career got off to a successful, if uncharacteristic start when Beck released the single "Hi-Ho Silver Lining," on which he sang lead. The song reached number 14 on the U.K. charts and would be re-released in 1972 and 1982, reaching the U.K. charts both times and becoming a staple of the British punk/dance/pub scene.

The vocalist on the B side of that single was a then-obscure British fop named Rod Stewart. By March of 1967, Beck and Stewart teamed up with bassist Ron Wood and drummer Ray Cook (subsequently replaced by Mick Waller) to form the Jeff Beck Group.

After a near-disastrous debut, in March of 1968—when the group was dumped from a Roy Orbison/Small Faces British tour—the Jeff Beck Group regrouped and began a brief but illustrious career. They made their stateside debut at the Fillmore East in June and went on to tour the U.S., establishing themselves as one of the most innovative acts in a constantly innovative era. In August, the group released the album *Truth*, which went to number 15 on the *Billboard* charts. On this record, Beck cut loose with a series of solos and high-powered rock tunes (including an inspired retooling of "Shapes of Things") that set the stage for heavy metal while establishing a level of virtuosity and inventiveness that has rarely been equalled—and never surpassed.

The album also introduced the ebullient Stewart, with his tousled, spiky locks and distinctively raspy vocals. On songs like "Blues Deluxe" and the broiling "Ain't Superstitious," Beck and Stewart sparred with each other constantly, with Beck's guitar imitating Stewart's vocal riffs just as Stewart coaxed and cajoled Beck into new flights of howling, screaming guitar wizardry.

That first U.S. tour and *Truth* enlarged upon Beck's near-mythic reputation and also established Stewart as a new vocal star.

In July of 1968, the group backed Donovan on his hit "Barabajagal," and Beck and Stewart began to toy with the idea of forming a group with drummer Carmine Appice and bassist Tim Bogert of Vanilla Fudge. But those plans were cut short when Beck, an avid hot rod enthusiast, was injured in an auto crash.

By 1969, the group was back in action, this time

joined by pianist Nicky Hopkins (who had provided a burning solo on "Blues Deluxe") and by new drummer Tony Newman (who replaced Waller). In June, the group released the album *Beck-Ola,* which rose to number 15. But internal disputes, particularly between Stewart and Beck, resulted in Stewart's and Wood's departure to join the Small Faces (who changed their name to Faces).

Beck formed a new version of the Jeff Beck Group in 1970 with Cozy Powell (drums), Max Middleton (keyboards), Clive Chaman (bass), and Bob Tench (vocals). The group's two albums, 1971's *Rough and Ready* and 1973's *Jeff Beck Group,* contained funkier, soul-based songs and also provided the first hints of the jazz-rock that Beck would later pursue in the second phase of his solo career.

That phase would begin in 1975, but in the intervening years, Beck finally teamed up with his friends from Vanilla Fudge, forming the group Beck, Bogert and Appice. The trio recorded two albums: an eponymous 1973 debut (which included a version of Stevie Wonder's "Superstition") and a live set recorded in Japan. This group, with its ponderous rock sound, was not a high point in the guitarist's career.

Beck rebounded in 1975 with his first solo album, *Blow by Blow,* in which he finally dropped the distraction of a vocalist and opted for an all-instrumental approach. Produced by George Martin, the album was a concerted foray into jazz-rock in which Beck's playing became more focused on melodic content and (relative) economy and less so on the technical wizardry of the past. The combination proved to be a remarkable success, with the album reaching number four on the charts.

Beck then teamed up with Mahavishnu Orchestra keyboardist Jan Hammer in 1976 and recorded the album *Wired,* which came with a more energetic sound that was closer to rock than jazz. Their collaboration also produced the 1977 jazz-rock blowout *Jeff Beck with the Jan Hammer Group Live.* But after this pairing, Beck retreated to his house in Surrey to rest and work on his hot rods.

He reemerged in 1980 with the album *There and Back,* demonstrating his durability with fans when it

reached number 21 on the *Billboard* charts. But for the most part, Beck's work in the '80s would involve collaborations and live one-offs with old mates. In 1981, he performed a set with Clapton at the Secret Policeman's Other Ball, a benefit for Amnesty International in London (subsequently released on an album of the event). In 1983, he took part in the annual Prince's Trust show at London's Royal Albert Hall with Clapton, Page, the Rolling Stones' Bill Wyman, and others. That same year, he joined those musicians and the likes of Steve Winwood, the Stones' Charlie Watts, and Joe Cocker in a benefit for Ronnie Lane's ARMS (Action for Research into Multiple Sclerosis) organization, the former Small Faces bassist having been afflicted with the disease.

In July of 1985, Beck teamed up with Stewart again for a new version of Curtis Mayfield's classic "People Get Ready." He also released the solo album *Flash* (which was honored with a 1986 Grammy Award for Best Instrumental Rock Performance for its song "Escape"). And he worked with Mick Jagger on the latter's debut solo album, *She's the Boss* (in 1987 he would also work with Jagger on the latter's *Primitive Cool*). He ended the decade with a tour opposite guitarist Stevie Ray Vaughan dubbed "The Fire and the Fury" (although it was tricky deciding who was supposed to be which).

As he entered the 1990s, Beck was becoming increasingly active. He released a new album, *Jeff Beck's Guitar Shop with Terry Bozzio and Tony Hymas,* which won a Grammy in the rock instrumental performance category.

Over the course of his career, Beck established a personal reputation that was as mercurial as his music, his quest for new groups proving to be as active as his search for new ideas. But this tendency to move about, professionally and musically, also made him one of the most creatively expansive members of his rock generation.

And one of the most original. While the other kings of '60s rock guitar spawned legions of ardent and devoted imitators, Beck stood alone in musical sound and vision, probably because no one could imitate him.

TOP ALBUMS

TRUTH (Epic, '68, *15*)
BECK-OLA (Epic, '69, *15*)
JEFF BECK GROUP (Epic, '72, *19*)
JEFF BECK, TIM BOGERT, CARMINE APPICE (Epic, '73, *12*)
BLOW BY BLOW (Epic, '75, *4*)
WIRED (Epic, '76, *16*)
JEFF BECK WITH THE JAN HAMMER GROUP LIVE (Epic, '77, *23*)
THERE AND BACK (Epic, '80, *21*)
FLASH (Epic, '85, *39*)
JEFF BECK'S GUITAR SHOP (Epic, '89)

CHUCK BERRY

While Elvis Presley will forever be the symbol of the rock idol, it is Chuck Berry who defined the music as a creative form. Musically speaking, he is the Rock upon which rock and roll rests.

Berry's songs and instrumental innovations in the early stages of his career in the 1950s laid the groundwork for very nearly all the rock that was to come.

In his music, the rhythmic force and blues inflections of R&B were combined with the song form and melodic content of rockabilly in a sound that was as singular as it was universal.

With songs such as "Maybellene," "School Days," "Roll Over Beethoven," "Carol," and others, Berry virtually created the rock and roll ethos of youthful abandon set to music. Rock's first and foremost storyteller, he articulated its pleasures—cars, girls, dancing, school, sex—with a wry wit and rascally resolve, with vocals that were the aural equivalent of a wink and a nod. His songs became immutable anthems for teenagers of his time and all time.

Berry also established the guitar as the symbol of rock and roll. His signature two-note chords that provided the lead-ins to most of his songs, most notably "Johnny B. Goode," were as distinctive as the songs themselves. And his solos, energized revampings of blues and rockabilly riffs, became the basic building blocks of the rock guitar repertoire. Onstage, his guitar at his hip, hopping about on one leg in what came to be known as his "duckwalk," Berry also changed the role of the rock guitarist from sideman to star.

While he was a central figure in rock's first generation, Berry was also crucial to the development of its second. His songs provided much of the repertoire of the groups of the British Invasion of 1964. His guitar work formed the basis of that of the Rolling Stones' Keith Richards; indeed, the Stones' debut single was a version of Berry's "Come On." The Beatles recorded several Berry songs, including "Roll Over Beethoven" and "Rock and Roll Music." And Berry's compositions were the basis of a number of the Beach Boys' early hits: the group's 1963 surf classic "Surfin' U.S.A." was a retooling of Berry's "Sweet Little Sixteen."

Berry (b. Charles Edward Anderson Berry, Oct. 18, 1926, San Jose, California) began his career in East St. Louis, Missouri, in 1952. Joining a local R&B and blues act, the Johnnie Johnson Trio, he began to perform in the clubs of the teaming St. Louis scene. At one of these, the Cosmopolitan Club, in 1955, he came to the attention of blues master Muddy Waters, who suggested that Berry get in touch with Leonard Chess of the legendary Chicago blues label, Chess Records. Making his way to that city, like scores of aspiring bluesmen before him, Berry made a demo recording for Chess that included a version of the traditional blues song "Ida Red." Revising that song into an original with his own words, Berry retitled it "Maybellene" and promptly began his walk into rock history.

Released as a single by Chess in 1955, "Maybellene" became an immediate hit. Decades before Michael Jackson would be hailed for his crossover success, Berry's song topped the R&B charts and simultaneously went to number five on the pop listings. In November of that year, he was named the Most Promising R&B Artist in the *Billboard* annual deejay poll.

By 1956, Berry was firmly ensconced in the rock scene. In June, he had his second hit when "Roll

Chuck Berry

Over Beethoven" reach number 29 on the charts. At the end of the year, he appeared in the film *Rock, Rock, Rock* performing "You Can't Catch Me" (which would become another staple of the British Invasion).

Over the succeeding two years, Berry hit the charts with several of his signature songs. In 1957, "School Days" sold more than one million copies and reached number three on the charts. "Rock and Roll Music," also released that year, hit number eight. In 1958, "Sweet Little Sixteen" became his biggest hit to that point, selling more than one million copies and hitting number two on the charts. It was succeeded by "Johnny B. Goode," which made number eight, and "Carol," which made it to number 18.

Along the way, Berry appeared in two additional films. In 1957, he performed in *Mr. Rock and Roll* with deejay Alan Freed. And the next year, his revolutionary performance at the Newport Jazz Festival was included in the film *Jazz on a Summer's Day*.

But Berry's career—and life—soon took a turn for the worse. In his youth, Berry had run afoul of the law, serving three years at the Algoa Reform School for a robbery conviction. In 1959, a serious situation flared up when he was charged with a violation of the Mann Act, for illegally transporting a minor across state lines. Convicted of the offense and sentenced to five years in prison, Berry gained an initial reprieve when the judge in the case made racist comments about him, and he was set free pending a retrial. But he was eventually convicted in 1962 and served two years of a three-year sentence at the Indiana Federal Penitentiary in Terre Haute.

While Berry was in prison, Chess reissued his older hits—rerecorded with crowd noise in the background—on the album *Chuck Berry on Stage*. It hit number 29 in 1963, becoming his first charting album.

Released in 1964, Berry resumed his career, which was given a boost by the attention being focused on him by the emerging British groups. His new single, the archetypal Berry song "Nadine (Is It You?)" reached number 23 in the U.S. in March. In June, "No Particular Place to Go" hit number 10; and in September, "You Can Never Tell" made number 14. Berry also toured England that year to great acclaim.

But while his career enjoyed an encouraging restart, it soon began to fade. In 1966, Berry left Chess Records, signing with Mercury Records for a $50,000 advance. But while he would be active during the rest of the 1960s, recording albums like *Live at the Fillmore* with the Steve Miller Band and touring constantly, his records mostly languished on the charts.

In 1970, he re-signed with Chess, and his career seemed to be on the mend. His 1972 album *The London Chuck Berry Sessions,* recorded with members of the Faces, hit number eight on the U.S. charts. A live cut from that album, "My Ding-a-Ling," was released as a single. Surprisingly, it topped the U.S. charts for two weeks. Ironically, given the wry, sexual double entendres that reduced it to the level of a self-parodistic novelty record, it proved to be the biggest hit of his career.

From that point, however, Berry's career faded for good. While he continued to record and tour—his last charting single was "Reelin' and Rockin'," which made number 27 in 1973—Berry was increasingly relegated to the role of golden oldie.

There were a few highlights along the way. In 1978, he played himself in the film *American Hot Wax,* a biography of Alan Freed. In 1979, Berry performed at the White House at the invitation of Jimmy Carter.

But his problems with the law weren't finished. In 1979, he was convicted of income tax evasion and served five months at Lompoc Prison Farm in California. And in 1990, Berry was charged with possession of a controlled substance and three counts of child abuse. While cleared of the abuse charges, he pleaded guilty to one count of marijuana possession and was given a six-month jail term and two years of unsupervised probation.

TOP ALBUMS

THE LONDON CHUCK BERRY SESSIONS (Chess, '72, 8)

Additional Top 40 Albums: 2

TOP SONGS

MAYBELLENE (Chess, '55, 5)
SCHOOL DAY (Chess, '57, 3)
ROCK & ROLL MUSIC (Chess, '57, 8)
SWEET LITTLE SIXTEEN (Chess, '58, 2)
JOHNNY B. GOODE (Chess, '58, 8)
CAROL (Chess, '58, 18)
NO PARTICULAR PLACE TO GO (Chess, '64, 10)
YOU NEVER CAN TELL (Chess, '64, 14)
MY DING-A-LING (Chess, '72, 1)

Additional Top 40 Songs: 5

While his career never reignited successfully after the early 1970s, Berry was increasingly honored and feted by his musical peers. In 1985, he received a Lifetime Achievement Award from the National Academy of Recording Arts and Sciences at the 27th Annual Grammy Awards. In 1986, Berry was inducted into the Rock and Roll Hall of Fame by one of his most illustrious musical offspring, Keith Richards. That same year, Richards organized a star-studded concert in St. Louis to commemorate Berry's 60th birthday; the making of that concert was the subject of the 1988 film *Hail! Hail! Rock 'n' Roll.*

Berry's songs were honored as well. In 1988, "Maybellene" was inducted into the Hall of Fame at the 30th Annual Grammy Awards; "Roll Over Beethoven" received the same honor in 1990. One of the most fitting—and eccentric—honors came in 1989 when Berry was asked to perform at the Jet Propulsion Laboratory when the Voyager 2 spacecraft entered the Neptune system.

A digital recording of Berry's "Johnny B. Goode" had been imprinted on a metal disc aboard the spacecraft (along with a composition by Bach and other cultural and factual data), the idea being that it would communicate a basic picture of humankind to any life forms that might encounter it.

This inspired a spoof on the television program "Saturday Night Live" in which a news report was issued saying that the first words from alien beings have finally reached earth. Those words were "Send more Chuck Berry."

Earthlings had been saying that for years.

THE B-52'S

As far as the B-52's were concerned, when it comes to rock and its culture, nothing ever dies; it merely fades away . . . and comes back later. Which is where the B-52's fade into the grand scheme of things.

Just as punk was going stale on both sides of the Atlantic in 1979, a twerpy, loopy group of loons from Athens, Georgia, made matters interesting once more. That year, the group released its eponymous debut album along with a major label reissue of the single "Rock Lobster" and promptly provided the rock world with a new set of musical and visual stimuli.

The B-52's were an eccentric band of quasi-musicians who had a taste for seemingly every sort of kitschy affectation that had plagued American popular culture since the 1950s.

The name B-52's came from the southern slang for the beehive hairdos affected by the group's female vocalists, Cindy Wilson (b. Feb. 28, 1957, Athens, Georgia) and Kate Pierson (b. Apr. 27, 1948, Weehawken, New Jersey). They also wore miniskirts and go-go boots, while their male counterparts duded themselves up in stovepipe pants and Hawaiian shirts. The resulting look was the visual equivalent of one of those tropical rum drinks with the umbrellas—spiked with LSD.

Musically, the group was hardly less splashy. Their signature song, "Rock Lobster," was a dance-crazed rock blowout, with vocalist Fred Schneider (b. July 1, 1951, Newark, Georgia) declaiming the words like a game show host, while Wilson and Pierson made high-pitched vocal noises that did, in fact, sound like something a rock lobster might make if the creature could make any noise at all.

Against their eccentric vocals, Cindy's brother, guitarist Ricky Wilson (b. Mar. 19, 1953, Athens), clicked out chords and notes like the Ventures on a bad night, while drummer Keith Strickland (b. Oct. 26, 1953, Athens) slapped out simple beats that practically forced one to get out on the nearest floor and do the frug.

All of this was done with tongue firmly in cheek. Or, more to the point, with a calculated sense of irony. There was about the B-52's something of the creative contrivance of the punks, whose sloppiness, boorishness, and musical incompetence were a concerted means to aesthetic ends. The very idiosyncracies, musical and visual, that made the B-52's daffy also gave them a persona that was distinctive.

Not that all of this was contrived. In some ways it seemed to be perfectly genuine, especially given the B-52s' background, which was punctuated by odd former group names and odder personal histories.

Before joining the B-52's, Pierson had been a part of a local Athens folk protest group, the Sun Donuts, while Schneider (a forestry student at the University of Georgia and a waiter at a vegetarian restaurant) had been a member of Bridge Mix and Night Soil.

Ricky Wilson and Strickland worked at the local bus station. And Cindy Wilson made milk shakes at the Whirly-Q Café.

As B-52's lore would have it, the five friends had dinner at a Chinese restaurant in Athens in 1976, shared a tropical drink called a Flaming Volcano, and, on the way home, decided to become the B-52's. That's the way the story went at the time and, given the way the group turned out, it seems plausible.

At any rate, the B-52's began to rehearse and write songs together and made their performing debut on Valentine's Day, 1977, at a party in Athens that was held in a greenhouse.

The group migrated to New York in December 1977 and began performing at the punk–new wave haven, Max's Kansas City. At this time they also independently recorded and released the original version of "Rock Lobster," which came to the attention of Chris Blackwell of Island Records. The album *The B-52's* was issued in 1979, and a re-released version of "Rock Lobster" rose to number 56 on the U.S. charts in 1980.

The B-52's—the group and the album—were without precedent in rock music and the larger rock

The B-52's

scene. Or, more to the point, unprecedented in the way that the group manipulated precedents. Musically, the group's overtly simplistic sound was a throwback of sorts to the surf music of the 1960s, with the trebly chords of Ricky Wilson's guitar conjuring images of everyone from the Telstars to the Ventures. But there was a highly stylized, minimalistic expressiveness to the sound that made it more than merely an imitation of the surf form. This sense of hyperbolic minimalism was augmented by Pierson's beeping keyboard notes, which created a sleek, post-modernist feel. When this sound was combined with the almost cartoonish vocals of Schneider, Cindy Wilson, and Pierson and the group's outlandish visual presence, the overall result was an almost pop art–like deconstruction of rock and its culture.

While the B-52's were not a vast commercial or popular success, at least in the initial part of their career, the group did enjoy a certain countercultural cachet that made its influence wholly disproportionate to its standing in the charts. Its caricatured music begat a new generation of post-punk rockers who thrived on ironic interpretations of various pop forms. Thus, groups like the Go-Go's, with their inspired reworkings of girl-group clichés, were direct musical descendents of the B-52's. Others, like the Butthole Surfers and the Surf Punks, traded on the B-52s' overt references to the surf sound of early 1960s southern California. As the 1980s unfolded, other artists such as Cyndi Lauper and Madonna would create their own images based on the B-52s' penchant for kitschy affectations.

The latter point was particularly significant. While the B-52's were hardly the first rock act to use kitsch as a creative tool—the entire glam-rock scene of the early 1970s positively thrived on it—the group was different in the way it approached tastelessness. For a start, the group actually seemed to like kitsch. When Wilson and Pierson pranced about the stage in go-go boots and Schneider vamped about in his Hawaiian shirts, there was a feeling that this was the way these people really wanted to look. They weren't parodying kitsch as much as embracing and enjoying it and creating with it.

In time, this sensibility would filter through to most of the rest of the culture at large, making itself felt—or, more precisely, seen—in everything from pop fashions to rock videos, interior design, print and television advertising, and the layouts of magazines. While the B-52's were not solely responsible for this pervasive trend—bereft of contemporary symbols to define itself, pop culture had been moving in this direction anyway—the group was a pioneer in drawing from the past to shape present-day image.

Ironically, while artists like Lauper and Madonna would ride this trend to platinum success, the B-52's began to fade as the decade proceeded. Subsequent albums, like 1982's *Mesopotamia* (a mini-album produced by Talking Heads' David Byrne) and 1983's *Whammy* and singles like "Wild Planet" and "Private Idaho" made the middle reaches of the charts. But by 1985, the group began to retreat from the public, in part because of the AIDS-related death that year of Ricky Wilson. In 1986, the group released the album *Bouncing Off the Satellites* and then disappeared from the scene.

But the B-52's made a splashy comeback in 1989 when their new album, *Cosmic Thing*, went platinum on the strength of the million-selling singles "Love Shack" and "Roam." With a new support lineup that included bassist Sara Lee, keyboardist Pat Irwin, and drummer Zach Alford, the group embarked on a 40-city tour of the U.S. in 1990 that drew capacity crowds. The B-52's were more popular than ever. That year, the group was voted Comeback of the Year by *Rolling Stone* magazine, and "Love Shack" was voted the magazine's Best Single of 1989.

But even if the B-52's had never re-formed and had a hit album, they would have secured an affectionate place in rock simply because they were the B-52's. Their unselfconscious display of their very odd tastes and idiosyncracies completely transformed pop culture. Bluntly stated, they made all that was tacky hip.

And while the rest of the pop world has come to dress, act, look, and sound like a caricature of some weird parallel universe, with odd juxtapositions of tastes and trends spanning decades, the B-52's were a central force in making it happen, primarily because, in their case, the weirdness was real.

TOP ALBUMS

WILD PLANET (Warner, '80, 18)
MESOPOTAMIA (Warner, '82, 35)
WHAMMY! (Warner, '83, 29)
COSMIC THING (Reprise, '89, 4)

TOP SONGS

LOVE SHACK (Reprise, '89, 3)
ROAM (Reprise, '89, 3)
DEADBEAT CLUB (Reprise, '90, 30)

BIG STAR

· · · · · · · · · · · · · · · · · ·

At age 17, Alex Chilton
had made a name for himself as a soulful, blue-eyed prodigy
when he rasped out the Box Tops' 1967 hit, "The Letter."
He built on that reputation in 1968, when the group's "Cry Like
a Baby" also reached the upper levels of the charts.

But when the Box Tops disbanded in 1969, Chilton began to pursue a new course that would take him far from the soul sound and success of his youth and, in the process, ultimately deposit him in the ranks of rock's truly innovative figures.

That course would lead him to Big Star.

The group was formed in Memphis in 1972 when Chilton (b. Dec. 28, 1950, Memphis, Tennessee) returned from New York (where he had moved after the breakup of the Box Tops) and promptly teamed up with several old musical friends on the local scene. Guitarist Chris Bell (b. Jan. 12, 1951, Memphis), bassist Andy Hummel (b. Jan. 26, 1951, Memphis), and drummer Jody Stephens (b. Oct. 4, 1952, Memphis) had been performing as a group in that scene since 1971, and they invited Chilton to join. The new group took its name from that of a local supermarket and soon concluded a record deal with the Memphis label Ardent, a fledgling company distributed by soul giant Stax.

In April, Big Star released its debut album, *#1 Record,* a set of crisp and deceptively complex pop songs. Concise and hook-laden, with vocal harmonies and intriguingly melodic theme lines that were derived from the music of the Beatles and the Byrds, other songs came with formidable rock punch and fervor.

It was a thoroughly new sound in rock, but one that had little in common with the bland expressions of the singer-songwriter movement or the long and self-indulgent "jams" that were dominating the rock scene of the time. Because of that, *#1 Record* was mostly ignored by the vast rock marketplace, if not by critics and connoisseurs.

It was a problem that would plague Big Star over the course of its career. Perhaps as a result of the album's commercial failure, Bell left the group in 1973 to pursue a solo career. Chilton then began to perfect the sound on the group's second album, 1974's *Radio City.* Again, the perfectly crafted, ebullient pop songs were the focal point, along with Chilton's expressive vocals and guitar work. But that record was greeted with the same response: rock fans simply didn't want to know, even as the critics were singing its praises.

From the start, the group's label, Ardent, had had difficulties with the group. Given the R&B orientation of its distributor, Ardent had no doubt thought that Chilton would deliver a more soul-based product than what the group was offering. The company seemingly had little idea of what to do with this new rock concoction. When the group's albums failed commercially, the label promptly dropped Big Star from its roster.

In 1974, Hummel quit and was subsequently replaced by Memphis bassist John Lightman. By the end of the year, Lightman had also quit, and Big Star was reduced to the duo of Chilton and Stephens.

They recruited several veterans of the Memphis session scene (including guitarist Steve Cropper), with whom they recorded their third album, *Third,* later retitled *Sister Lovers* (Chilton and Stephens were dating sisters at the time). The darker sensibility at work on the disc may have been due to Big

Big Star

Star's chronic business problems, which continued: with no record label to release it, the album did not appear until 1978, released on the small PVC label. It was subsequently reissued in the U.S. in 1992 on Rykodisc.

But the group was long gone, having folded in 1974. Bell was killed in a car crash in 1978. Hummel became an engineer for General Dynamics. Stephens became involved in record production. Chilton resurfaced in New York in the mid-'70s and began performing in the burgeoning new wave scene. He subsequently released the solo albums *One Day in New York* and *Like Flies on Sherbert*. He also became the subject of a song by the Replacements, one of the scores of groups in the 1980s who openly acknowledged the musical and creative debt they owed him and Big Star.

The group proved to be vastly important to the future evolution of rock. Its seamless blend of rock energy and power and pop

grandeur would subsequently form the basis of a new movement that emerged in the later 1970s and that would become a major rock force in the '80s. That movement was power pop.

One of the first groups to build its sound on that of Big Star was the Raspberries, who affected a Beatles-esque melodicism countered by a raw, basic rock sound. In time, Big Star's approach would prove to be the inspiration for a vast and varied array of groups that emerged from the new wave movement of the late 1970s. A few of these groups, like the Cars, used that sound as a point of departure for their own formidable visions. Others, like the Knack, the Outfield, and scores of others would use it as a means to an end, that end being a crass and vacuous sound that, ironically, achieved the commercial success that had eluded Big Star.

And the group's influence was not confined to power pop. In the 1980s, its edgy but alluring sound insinuated itself into the music of a

> ### TOP ALBUMS
>
> #1 RECORD (Ardent, '72)
> RADIO CITY (Ardent, '74)
> THIRD (PVC, '78)
> BIG STAR LIVE (Rykodisc, '92)

number of groups of the post–new wave era. These included Britain's Aztec Camera, the United States' Hüsker Dü, and, most notably, R.E.M., who co-opted the group's jangly Byrds-tinged characteristics and Chilton's folk-rock vocal inflections to create a sound that would influence the so-called alternative rock scene.

In fact, Big Star's influence was such that its various aspects could be identified in such later, '90s groups as the Bay Area's Jellyfish, the U.K.'s World Party and Teenage Fanclub, and countless others.

For all of its incisiveness and innovation, Big Star was a group that was entirely in the wrong place at the wrong time with the wrong sound. But that did not negate its importance or its impact on the course of rock and roll.

BLIND FAITH

As 1969 began, reports began to circulate in the rock world of a new group that was being formed. It didn't have a name at first, but the names of the musicians involved were enough to create a sensation. As amazing as it seemed to rock fans of the day, Eric Clapton and Ginger Baker of Cream were teaming up with Steve Winwood of Traffic.

At the time, such a collaboration of rock titans was unheard of; for the most part, rock idols of the 1960s either stayed with their groups or went solo, but few combined forces, at least on a formal basis. There wasn't, in fact, a word that would adequately describe such an all-star band, so one was invented: *supergroup*. And Blind Faith was it.

When the formation of Blind Faith was formally announced in February 1969, the rock world was immediately roused into a state a wild anticipation. On guitar was "God" himself, Clapton, the unrivalled virtuoso of electric blues. And there was Baker, the rhythm demon who had virtually defined the role of rock drummer as a lead instrumentalist. And there was the remarkable Winwood, who could sing like Ray Charles and pump the keyboard of a Hammond organ like Jimmy Smith. Few were familiar with the group's bassist, Rick Grech, who had

deserted the group Family in the middle of its U.S. tour to join up. But that didn't matter much, given the others involved. In short, Blind Faith seemed too good to be true.

And as things worked out, that proved to be the case.

Blind Faith spent most of the spring of 1969 in seclusion, writing new songs and rehearsing. By the time it was ready to make its concert debut, English rock fans could barely contain their excitement. When the group finally made it to a stage, for a free show in London's Hyde Park on June 7th, more than 100,000 fans swarmed the place. At the time, it was the biggest crowd in rock history to witness a rock and roll show.

Everything seemed to be "super." A U.S. tour, with a debut show at New York's Madison Square Garden in July, sold out as soon as tickets were made

Blind Faith

available. An eponymous album was released and went to the top of the charts on both sides of the Atlantic. But all was not well, either on record or in the ranks.

While the album was a hit, it was something of a musical disappointment. Songs such as the Cream-like "Had to Cry Today" and the Traffic-like "Sea of Joy" were sturdy numbers, but a tangible feeling of ennui prevailed. "Do What You Like" was a barely disguised revamping of "Toad," the Cream song that was the setup for a Baker drum solo—this one in 5/4 time. Win-

wood's once forceful vocals sounded pale and listless, while Clapton's guitar work was notably subdued. As for Grech, he wasn't Jack Bruce. All in all, the album was, as a wag put it at the time, something of an "anticlimax."

Meanwhile, as the group made its way across the States, there was also talk of increasing tension and mounting disaffection among Blind Faith's virtuosos. It was reported that the band members refused to ride in the same cars or stay in the same hotels. It was as if they were rebelling against the hype and hoopla that surrounded

TOP ALBUM
....
BLIND FAITH (Atco, '69, *1*)

them. When the tour ended, Blind Faith did the same.

By the end of 1969, Baker had formed Air Force (with Grech). Winwood had commenced work on a solo album that would eventually evolve into the Traffic masterpiece *John Barleycorn Must Die*. And Clapton had started devoting some of his formidable solos to Delaney and Bonnie and Friends, the down-home rockers who had opened for Blind Faith on its tour.

But its ultimate failure notwithstanding, Blind Faith proved to be a watershed in rock history. The group opened the floodgates for all-star collaborations. Soon, the once-unassailable '60s idea of the rock group as a distinct unit began to dissolve. Groups like Crosby, Stills and Nash (a combination of members of the Byrds, Buffalo Springfield, and the Hollies); the Faces (members of the Small Faces with Rod Stewart and Ron Wood); and Beck, Bogert and Appice (Jeff Beck with the rhythm section of Vanilla Fudge) began to emerge.

This was a crucial step in the musical evolution of rock, and one that would have its positive and negative aspects.

As to the former, it allowed for a new freedom of expression and the cross-fertilization of ideas and playing styles. Like their counterparts in the jazz world, rock musicians could now move freely among themselves, forming groups, or merely collaborating on recording projects or, perhaps, one-off concerts or tours.

This trend began almost as soon as Blind Faith disbanded. Clapton's association with the "friends" of Delaney and Bonnie (actually the leaders themselves and members of their group) expanded into a host of projects. The seeds of them could be seen on D&B's concert tour of England in 1970, on which they were joined by Clapton, Dave Mason of Traffic, and George Harrison. Soon, various members of the group were appearing on debut solo records by Clapton, Mason, and others. Friends of those "friends," such as American session master Leon Russell, were also invited into the fold, with seemingly everyone joining in on the latter's solo record.

It was, literally, a time of musical chairs. Harrison's first post-Beatles album, the late-1970 *All Things Must Pass,* included various all-star configurations; one of the set's three records came with a "jam" with Clapton, Baker, and others. Even Baker's Air Force had an all-star lineup of English musicians that included Denny Laine (formerly of the

Moody Blues), Traffic's Chris Wood, and a host of other illustrious musicians. Mix-and-match became the order of the day.

What made it all so invigorating for both the musicians and the public was that it was, in fact, public. In the past, rockers had collaborated on various records and projects. But it had usually been done in an almost secretive manner, as with Brian Jones's uncredited saxophone work on the Beatles' "You Know My Name, Look Up the Number," or Donovan's collaboration with the Jeff Beck Group on "Barbajagal." (The *Super Session* record of Stephen Stills, Michael Bloomfield, and Al Kooper, which predated the Blind Faith record in 1968, was a notable exception to the rule.) Additionally, the movement of rock musicians between groups had largely been treated by the parties involved as a creative flirtation, not a full-bore "serious" musical collaboration.

But there was a downside to this new freedom of movement.

As the decades progressed, such collaborations became, for better and worse, commonplace. In the 1960s, it was generally assumed that the sounds heard on any given album by a group were made by that group. The particular sound of a particular musician was an integral part of the identity of a group. But as personnel lists on records began to expand, with guest artists often outnumbering the band members, much of the idea of an identifiable group sound began to diminish. Also, the goal of "artistic" collaboration, as originally envisioned by Blind Faith, was often diluted by the inclusion of artists simply for the purpose of enhancing a record's commercial draw rather than for any creative intent.

Similarly, the supergroup label became devalued over time, employed with the same loose abandon that attended other appellations like "genius" and "virtuoso."

But rock has a habit of overdoing—and sometimes destroying—a good thing. And the collaborative freedom that Blind Faith formally set in motion would prove to be, its excesses notwithstanding, one of those good things. While the group itself did not capitalize on its vast creative possibilities, it showed the way for others. And, in a more general context, it opened up the rock world to myriad new combinations of musicians and sounds.

Blind Faith was the first rock supergroup, but it wouldn't be the last.

BLOOD, SWEAT AND TEARS

Big band music was the rock and roll of its era. During its heyday in the 1930s and '40s, it was at the cutting edge of popular music.

It was brash, energetic, and loud. Its musicians were worshipped by young people. Its lead vocalists—like Frank Sinatra—became pop idols. Its attitudes, style of dress, postures, language, and lifestyle all were embraced by the culture at large to a vast extent. In short, it was the hip—or rather, hep—cultural antecedent of rock.

Thus, when keyboardist Al Kooper began to assemble a big band rock group during the course of 1967, there was a certain symmetry to his vision. By the end of the year that vision had become a reality in the form of the group Blood, Sweat and Tears.

The group's debut album, *The Child Is Father to the Man,* released in April 1968, was an inspired amalgam of jazz and rock. The songs of the album were a combination of rock, pop, and blues idioms, but they were augmented by a complex array of horn and string arrangements that endowed those simpler forms with an instrumental technicality that was revolutionary for the time.

Strictly speaking, the music of Blood, Sweat and Tears wasn't big band jazz in any specific sense. Rather, it was an attempt to fuse the sound of a basic rock group with a horn section in a more expansive manner than that employed by soul and blues groups of the day, most of which used horns as a harmonic and rhythmic underpinning to their sound.

In BS&T's music, Kooper's keyboards, Steve Katz's guitar, Jim Fielder's bass, and Bobby Colomby's drums shared equal creative roles with the horn section, whose members were Fred Lipsius, Jerry Weiss, and Randy Brecker. The result was an ensemble sound that was eclectic, richly varied and textured, and musically sophisticated.

BS&T's sound—and, indeed, the idea of the group itself—would prove to be vastly influential in rock. In the short run, it spawned more overt big band imitators, like the second (and wholly different) version of BS&T, Chicago (originally the Chicago Transit Authority), and others. In the long run, BS&T's musical sophistication and sound would inspire groups such as Steely Dan, whose music would rely on a sleek, professional studio sound buttressed by agile session musicians. And it would be a precursor of the jazz-rock fusion music that would come to prominence at the start of the '70s.

All of that came later, however. In 1968, BS&T was immediately acclaimed by the burgeoning undergound rock scene while *The Child Is Father to the Man* reached number 47 on the charts. But dissension began to appear in the ranks, and by the end of the year, Kooper, Weiss, and Brecker had departed.

Ironically, given its seminal role in the development of rock and jazz, Kooper's version of BS&T would give way to a new edition of the group that would be a vapid musical self-parody of the original—and a vast commercial success.

That new version, fronted by vocalist David Clayton-Thomas (b. David Thomsett, Sept. 13, 1941, Surrey, England) and with a new horn lineup consisting of Chuck Winfield, Lew Soloff, and Jerry Hyman, debuted in March 1969 with an eponymously-titled album that was a gigantic hit. The album topped the charts for seven weeks and sold more than two million copies. In addition, its singles—"You Made Me So Very Happy," "And When I Die," and "Spinning Wheel"—sold three million copies apiece. It was the first album in history to have three gold singles.

Basing its sound on Clayton-Thomas's husky, soul-tinged vocals and on a caricaturish big band approach that Kooper had scrupulously avoided, the new version of BS&T moved to the upper ranks of the pop scene. In 1970, its album won Grammy Awards for Best Album, Best Contemporary Instrumental Performance, and Best Arrangement Accompanying a Vocalist. That same year, its next album, *Blood, Sweat & Tears 3,* topped the charts for two weeks, yielding the single "Hi-De-Ho," which peaked at number 14. And in 1971, *BS&T 4* reached number 10.

At the end of that year, Clayton-Thomas departed to pursue a solo career, and the group, with various new lineups, quickly faded as a commercial

---

TOP ALBUMS

BLOOD, SWEAT & TEARS (Columbia, '69, *1*)
BLOOD, SWEAT & TEARS 3 (Columbia, '70, *1*)
B, S & T; 4 (Columbia, '71, *10*)
BLOOD, SWEAT & TEARS GREATEST HITS
(Columbia, '72, *19*)

Additional Top 40 Albums: 1

TOP SONGS

YOU'VE MADE ME SO VERY HAPPY
(Columbia, '69, *2*)
SPINNING WHEEL (Columbia, '69, *2*)
AND WHEN I DIE (Columbia, '69, *2*)
HI-DE-HO (Columbia, '70, *14*)
LUCRETIA MAC EVIL (Columbia, '70, *29*)
GO DOWN GAMBLIN' (Columbia, '71, *32*)

---

force. In 1974, Clayton-Thomas re-joined temporarily—as he would do again in 1988—but the group stumbled through the rest of the 1970s.

The commercial success of the second version of BS&T notwithstanding, it was Kooper's original lineup that was most important in the history and evolution of rock.

The original group was the culmination of a trend that had been developing for several years. Kooper had been a force in that development as a member of the Blues Project (which also included original BS&T guitarist Katz). One of the first—if not the first—white blues groups on the New York scene, the Blues Project had emerged in 1965, performing rock-inflected renditions of blues standards. But with its second album, *Projections,* released at the end of that year, it began to expand its musical base to include jazz-based songs like "Flute Thing" that were instrumental and came with extended improvi-

sation sections heavily laced with Kooper's keyboards.

One of rock's renaissance men, Kooper (b. Feb. 5, 1944, New York) had a wide range of musical interests that encompassed various disparate projects. He played piano on the Bob Dylan masterpiece "Like a Rolling Stone" and performed with the folk master at the Newport Folk Festival. After departing BS&T, Kooper became involved in one of the first "superstar" collaborations in rock, when he took part in the 1968 *Super Session* album with the Paul Butterfield Blues Band's guitarist Mike Bloomfield and Buffalo Springfield's Stephen Stills.

But BS&T was more than merely an outgrowth of Kooper's eclectic musical sensibilities. It was part of a movement in that direction that began to emerge in 1967 in various quarters. In England that year, blues innovator John Mayall expanded his Bluesbreakers group from its basic four-piece lineup with the addition of a horn section, releasing the album *Crusade* in 1968. Paul Butterfield did the same with his group, recording the album *The Resurrection of Pigboy Crabshaw* that year. While both bands, and their albums, were formidable expressions of the blues, they adhered closely to a traditional blues-based use of horns that was far short of the broad musical experiments that Kooper was contriving with BS&T.

The same could be said, to a lesser extent, of BS&T's closest musical and expressive counterpart, the Electric Flag. In 1967, a competition of sorts had developed between Kooper and Bloomfield, both of whom were forming big band rock groups. Bloomfield actually beat Kooper to the punch when his Electric Flag released the soundtrack album to the Peter Fonda film *The Trip* in 1967. But that album wasn't a formal debut effort and consisted mostly of instrumentals that were used as background music for the film. The group made its debut performance at the Monterey Pop Festival in June 1967.

Electric Flag's debut album, *A Long Time Comin',* was released in April 1968, a month later than BS&T's *The Child Is Father to the Man* and more successful, with a number 31 chart ranking. But while its sound was notably more expansive than that of Butterfield and Mayall—particularly on songs like "Another Country," with its clashing musical layers of sound—it was also based firmly in the blues tradition.

Of all the big band rock groups that came along, the most visible and successful was the Chicago

Transit Authority, also formed in 1967. More rock-than blues-oriented, Chicago (as it would later come to be called) would trade on the big band sound more than any of its counterparts. With its eponymously titled debut album in 1969, the group began a career that would span two decades and more, and yield 19 top-10 singles and 20 albums, five of which topped the charts. But while commercially successful, Chicago was ultimately a musically negligible group that had none of the artistic vision and creative inspiration of Kooper's original Blood, Sweat and Tears.

Blood, Sweat and Tears

DAVID BOWIE

Long before the likes
of Prince and Madonna began to reinvent themselves
as media figures, periodically adapting their image, look,
and sound to fit their latest projects, Bowie became
the master manipulator of his persona and music.

During his career, which began in 1964, Bowie created an astonishing array of public images, replete with constantly changing hairstyles, attire, attitudes, and musical accoutrements, all of which were orchestrated to produce a particular expressive vision.

There was the Major Tom figure of *Space Oddity;* Ziggy Stardust, Alladin Sane, and the Thin White Duke; and such equally defined, if unnamed, incarnations as the cross-dressing glam-queen of the early 1970s, the art rocker of the late '70s, and the Eurodance lizard of the '80s. All were Bowie, and to a remarkable extent, Bowie became, for a time, all of them.

In the process, he developed into one of rock's most enigmatic and charismatic figures.

Along the way, he created some of the most intriguing music of his time, made more so by the sheer range of his artistic vision. There were the brooding, Orwellian themes of *The Man Who Sold the World* (1971); subsequent shifts to flashy rock and, later, the sound of American R&B and soul; a trilogy of albums in collaboration with Brian Eno that delved into the complex, electronic sound of European art rock; and a transition in the 1980s into the emerging fusion of dance, rock, and pop.

As an addendum to his various musical personas, Bowie was also one of the few rock musicians to pursue an acting career as an outlet for his creative urges (as opposed to such commercially based rock actors as Elvis Presley). While that career was hardly noteworthy—with the exception of his critically acclaimed portrayal of John Merrick in the Broad-

way play *The Elephant Man*—it did yield a series of films that were as varied as his musical forays. These included the sci-fi drama *The Man Who Fell to Earth* (1976); the decadent *Just a Gigolo* (1979); the vampire-infested *The Hunger* (1983); the World War II drama *Merry Christmas, Mr. Lawrence* (1983); the dismal, kitschy, pop musical *Absolute Beginners* (1986); and the George Lucas–produced myth *Labyrinth* (1987).

As a whole, these myriad pursuits—the persona, music, and films—differed from those of other rock dilettantes in the way in which Bowie combined all into a unified artistic expression that evolved over the years. Each aspect of Bowie's career was like a stitch in a vast and varied creative tapestry, as opposed to being one in a series of isolated digressions.

These aspects had about them a sense of calculation and inspiration that seemed purposely designed to promulgate both Bowie's career and his artistic aims. When he came onstage in a dress and makeup during his tour of 1970, the theatrical device heightened the decadent feel of the music of *The Man Who Sold the World* while also drawing the attention of the media and the public to that tour and album. Similarly, Bowie's depiction of the star-crazed rocker Ziggy Stardust—with his henna'd, spiky locks; eye patch; stacked heels; and splashy glam attire—was, at once, an affecting and evocative stage contrivance whose outrageousness focused attention on the music, the stage show . . . and Bowie.

It was this fusion of seeming charlatanism and artistic integrity that provoked, intrigued, and fascinated (and, in some cases, repelled) the critics and

David Bowie

public. It often seemed as if Bowie was either the most blatant of public relations hucksters or a truly innovative stage presence, or possibly both.

A case could be made for either, based on Bowie's career. It began in 1964, when Bowie, still using his real name, began performing with such groups as Davie Jones and the King Bees, the Mannish Boys, and the Lower Third. These early efforts met with little success, a trend that continued as the decade progressed and he began to pursue a solo career.

Changing his name to Bowie, because of the popularity of another Davey Jones (this one, a member of the Monkees), he initially secured a contract with the Pye label and later with Decca Records. At this point, he was a typical British pop aspirant, with coiffed locks and the foppish garb of the time. His music, primarily love songs like "The Laughing Gnome," was a pale imitation of the mainstream pop of artists like Anthony Newley and was greeted with apathy by the rock public.

Reacting to this, Bowie dropped out of the music scene in the late 1960s to study Buddhism. He also joined the Lindsey Kemp Mime Company and began to immerse himself in theatre and dance.

He reemerged in the late '60s but was turned down by Apple Records; his new group, Feathers, also proved unsuccessful. Undeterred, Bowie founded the Beckenham Arts Lab, a performance club in south London. He also began work on a television program based on a new song, "Space Oddity," a sprawling and fanciful space-age epic about an astronaut called Major Tom. The program didn't work out, but the song drew the attention of Mercury Records, who released it as a single in 1969.

"Space Oddity" was ignored by the public at first. But when the BBC used it as the theme song for its moon landing coverage, it finally entered the charts in the U.K., where it eventually reached number five. In November of that year, Bowie received the Ivor Novello Award from U.K. Songwriters Guild, in recognition of the song's originality.

But the hit proved to be illusory. "Space Oddity" was generally dismissed as a novelty record, and Bowie's career declined again. In 1971, *The Man*

Who Sold the World was released, but most of the attention that was generated was focused on Bowie's cross-dressing antics, which he employed in promotional tours for the album. At the end of that year, the album *Hunky Dory* was issued but initially languished. However, as 1972 dawned, the single "Changes" provided his U.S. chart debut, eventually making number 66. And by April, *Hunky Dory* had reached number 93 in the U.S. It was Bowie's first foray into the album charts in either the U.S. or the U.K.

Bowie's persistence, along with his imagination, began to pay off in 1972. In July he released *The Rise and Fall of Ziggy Stardust and the Spiders from Mars;* with his new Ziggy look and a smashing band that included guitarist Mick Ronson, bassist Trevor Boulder, and drummer Mick Woodmansey, he began an inexorable rise as a major new force on the rock scene. The Ziggy era marked a new phase in Bowie's artistic development. To that point, his personas—the aspiring young dandy, the spacy Major Tom, the cross-dressing rocker—had had about them a sense of desperation, of someone who would do anything to gain notoriety.

But Ziggy, while equally eccentric and attention-grabbing, was an entirely different device. For the first time in his career—but not the last—Bowie became an artistic chameleon, attaching himself to a new trend in rock and taking on its creative coloration while retaining his individuality.

In the case of Ziggy Stardust, that trend was glam-rock, which had just begun to emerge with such groups as T Rex and the New York Dolls. Like those groups, Bowie/Ziggy had an androgynous look that was countered by a slashing rock sound.

But Bowie wasn't a mere imitator; he distanced himself from his glam counterparts and expanded the boundaries of what they were doing. He added theatrical flourishes and a fallen-rock-idol subtext that amounted to a morality play on the rewards and costs of stardom. In the course of the next few years, Bowie would come to live that role in real life. The rewards came first.

TOP ALBUMS

DIAMOND DOGS (RCA, '74, *5*)
DAVID LIVE (RCA, '74, *8*)
YOUNG AMERICANS (RCA, '75, *9*)
STATION TO STATION (RCA, '76, *3*)
CHANGESONEBOWIE (RCA, '76, *10*)
LET'S DANCE (EMI, '83, *4*)

Additional Top 40 Albums: 10

TOP SONGS

FAME (RCA, '75, *1*)
LET'S DANCE (EMI, '83, *1*)
BLUE JEAN (EMI, '84, *8*)
DANCING IN THE STREET (with Mick Jagger, EMI, '85, *7*)

Additional Top 40 Songs: 9

In 1972, Bowie's star was on the rise. In addition to the success of *Ziggy*—the album hit number five in the U.K. and number 75 in the U.S.—he produced Lou Reed's *Transformer* album and had a hand in the comeback of Mott the Hoople, writing and performing on their hit "All the Young Dudes." He and his wife, Angie Barnet, became media celebrities, with their androgynous look and lifestyle.

His success continued apace in 1973. In May of that year, his new album, *Alladin Sane,* topped the U.K. charts and hit number 17 in the U.S. He and his group toured the world. But cracks also began to appear. At the end of a Ziggy show in London, in July, Bowie abruptly announced that he was retiring from the stage. In fact, it was Ziggy, not Bowie, who was being retired. In November, he threw another curve to the fans and critics when he released the album *Pin-Ups,* which contained a mostly mundane set of covers of '60s British pop hits. But while that album was moderately received, Bowie pursued his successful and singularly enigmatic course.

Over the next two years he would change his direction dramatically. In 1974, he released the menacing album *Diamond Dogs* and presented it onstage with an increasingly theatrical presence. In 1975, he slicked back his hair, dressed up in a sleek suit, and embraced a suave, pseudo-disco image on the R&B-inflected album *Young Americans.* Just as Ziggy had been Bowie's slant on glam-rock, *Young Americans* was his take on the dance-pop scene that was becoming prevalent in the U.K. and U.S. From this album, Bowie scored his most successful U.S. single, "Fame," a collaboration with John Lennon. His persona of the time, the Thin White Duke, took an exit in 1976 when he released the album *Station to Station,* which hinted at new directions to come.

By October of 1976, Bowie had become disenchanted with his life as a rock idol, with its drug culture and entourage of sycophants. Rebelling against this, he moved to Berlin, set himself up in a modest apartment, and began to explore the world of art rock. This new phase in his life and music would last for three years and would produce, arguably, the three finest albums of his career.

Collaborating with the former Roxy Music keyboardist-turned-art-rocker Brian Eno, Bowie began to explore synthesizer music and aleatoric compositional devices that Eno had appropriated from John Cage. Released in January 1977, *Low* came with dense electronic layers of sound, with Bowie declaiming his vocals with an almost operatic intensity.

In October of that year, the album *Heroes* was released; it had a more rock-oriented sound in which Bowie's vocals writhed amid the jagged, angular phrasings of former King Crimson guitarist Robert Fripp and clangorous, cacaphonous collages of sound. *Lodger,* the final installment in the so-called Eno trilogy, was a similarly rock-flavored album that included some of Bowie's most engrossing vocal expressions and lyrical imagery.

He reemerged from art rock semi-seclusion in 1980, taking on the lead roles in *The Elephant Man* on Broadway and Bertolt Brecht's "Baal" for the BBC. He also released the album *Scary Monsters and Super Creeps,* a tentative effort that yielded the hit "Fashion." Over the next two years, he would become involved in numerous film and recording projects of minimal interest.

In 1983, Bowie's career reached a new commercial level. *Let's Dance,* an album that reflected the new amalgam of rock, pop, and dance music that was becoming a major force on both sides of the Atlantic, went to Number One in the U.K. and number four in the U.S. The album's title cut became the first Bowie single to top the charts in both countries. The album also yielded the hits "China Girl" and "Modern Love" and became, in the process, a worldwide smash. As a prelude to his Serious Moonlight '83 tour, Bowie played the U.S. Festival in San Bernadino, California, in June, earning $1 million for his set (the festival's organizer, Apple Computer founder Steve Wozniak, reportedly paid the same amount for an appearance by Van Halen). When the tour commenced in July, it broke records for ticket revenues in various parts of the world.

But 1983 would prove to be the apex of Bowie's career. As the '80s unfolded, his music would become increasingly diffuse and undirected on such albums as 1984's *Tonight* and 1987's *Never Let Me Down.* His film career would also fail to ignite. At the end of the decade, he began to rebel against his solo persona, forming the group Tin Machine, in which he made a point of being one of the band, playing guitar and singing along with bassist Tony Sales, drummer Hunt Sales, and guitarist Reeves Gabriels. But the group's two albums were disappointing, creatively and commercially.

In January of 1990, Bowie announced—shades of Ziggy!—that he was embarking on a new project, the Sound and Vision World Tour 1990, which would be his last global tour. This was—again, like Ziggy—amended: this would be the last tour that would come with performances of his hit songs. By 1993, he was up to his old tricks, releasing the album *Black Tie White Noise,* recalling the dance-oriented music of *Let's Dance.* The album was typical Bowie; it seemed to be a bald attempt on his part to revive his ailing career, but one that included music that was particularly affecting and eloquent.

As usual, Bowie's motives were irrelevant. His work ultimately transcended them, just as it had during the entire length and breadth of his long career. The personas, the songs, the films and plays and looks and sounds all ultimately merged in a single—and singular—artistic product, that product being Bowie himself.

BUFFALO SPRINGFIELD

Buffalo Springfield didn't last long as a group. During its tortuous two-year career, it was beset by defections, realignments, legal problems, and artistic and personal disagreements.

It had but one top 10 hit single. Its first two albums had only a modest impact on the charts, and a third was released after the group had disbanded.

All in all, it was a fairly dismal history for a group that occupies a seminal place in the evolution of American rock.

In its period of activity in the 1960s, the Los Angeles–based quintet created an inspired amalgam of rock, country, folk, soul, and R&B, in the process setting a new course for much of the music of the succeeding decade. What's more, the group became a springboard for the careers of its leading members, guitarists-vocalists Neil Young and Stephen Stills.

The group came to the attention of the vast rock public with its 1967 number seven hit, "For What It's Worth." The song, Stills' lyrical outcry over the police violence at the Sunset Strip riots in Los Angeles that year, became emblematic of the emerging protest movement in rock's counterculture.

With its dry, spare guitar chords, folk harmonies, and Stills' laconic lead vocals and bluesy guitar phrases, "For What It's Worth" hinted at a new way of making rock. The song defied the trends that had prevailed in the pop music of the West Coast to that point. It wasn't a slavish imitation of the British

Invasion (like the Beau Brummels); or a splashy, psychedelic garage barrage (like Strawberry Alarm Clock, Music Machine, or the Seeds); or even a version of the jangling folk-rock of the Byrds. Instead, it provided a hint of the experiments that were being carried out by the next generation of West Coast rockers in Los Angeles and San Francisco.

Those experiments came to fruition on the group's second album, *Buffalo Springfield Again,* arguably one of the finest records in the history of rock. Released in December 1967, *Again* reflected a range of styles derived from American popular music. The songs "Mr. Soul" and "Rock and Roll Woman" combined folk-tinged harmonies with lead vocals that had a lowdown R&B feel; on both, Stills and Young created dense layers of guitar chords and phrases interrupted by furious, dueling solos. "Broken Arrow" and "Expecting to Fly" exhibited an elegiac melodiousness rooted in folk and country music. And on the album's centerpiece, an extended version of the single "Bluebird," the group shifted from a basic rock sound to a section with banjo and folk-based vocal harmonies that offered a new slant on traditional bluegrass.

However, *Again* wasn't as much an exercise in

eclecticism as it was an engrossing expression of various musical forms being blended into a coherent and a sublimely unified sound. That sound would form the basis of much of the California rock that would follow in the 1970s in the music of such artists as the Eagles, Jackson Browne, and Linda Ronstadt. On a more immediate level, it presaged the broad mix of American musical styles that was central to such San Francisco groups as Jefferson Airplane and the Grateful Dead.

Much of Buffalo Springfield's vision was a culmination of the backgrounds of the group's members. Stills (b. Jan. 3, 1945, Dallas, Texas) and guitarist Richie Furay (b. May 9, 1944, Yellow Springs, Ohio) had been members of the New York–based folk group the Au Go Go Singers. Young (b. Nov. 12, 1945, Toronto, Canada) and bassist Bruce Palmer (b. 1946, Liverpool, Canada) had played in the fledgling rock group the Mynah Birds. And drummer Dewey Martin (b. Sept. 30, 1942, Chesterfield, Canada) had previously been a member of the bluegrass band the Dillards. (Oddly, another group made up mostly of Canadians, the Band, would also display a penchant and aptitude for interpreting American musical forms.)

Buffalo Springfield was formed in March 1966 in Los Angeles, initially with a former colleague of Young, bassist Ken Koblun (who soon returned to Canada). Basing its name on that of a steamroller that the members saw on a road construction site, the group signed a recording contract with Atco Records in January of 1967 and released its eponymous debut album, which languished on the charts.

With the success of "For What It's Worth" in March of that year (and its subsequent inclusion on repressings of the debut album), the group began to make a name for itself on the underground rock scene that was emerging on the East and West Coasts. The debut album eventually made it to number 80 on the charts.

But soon, the problems began. In May 1967, Palmer was deported to Canada because of visa violations (he would return to the group at various points during the rest of its career). He was replaced by Koblun and Jim Fielder (later of Blood, Sweat and Tears).

Young left the group that same month, reportedly because of musical disagreements with the others (particularly Stills). He was replaced by Doug Hastings on guitar.

Buffalo Springfield

The disarray was such that in June, when the group appeared at the most important gig of its career, the Monterey Pop Festival, it performed without Young or Palmer. The Byrds' David Crosby was called at the last moment to add his guitar and vocal harmonies to the sound.

Nothing seemed to go right. A second album, *Stampede*, was recorded but not released. Along the way, the excellent singles "Bluebird" and "Rock and Roll Woman" were released but failed to achieve the popular success of "For What It's Worth" (the former charted at number 58 and the latter at number 44).

Young rejoined the group later in the year to work on *Again* along with new bassist Jim Messina. But Young left the group once more, when it began work on its next record. The group disbanded for good in May of 1968 after a show in Los Angeles. A final album of the group's studio efforts, *Last Time Around*, was assembled by Messina and released in September of that year.

Ironically, various members went on to achieve successes that eclipsed that of Buffalo Springfield. Stills and Young recorded solo albums that were imbued with the feel, if not the specific sound, of their original group. Within a year Stills would form a new "supergroup" with the Byrds' Crosby and the Hollies' Graham Nash. And, in 1970, Young would become a fourth member of that group. True to form, he would depart and rejoin it as his sensibilities dictated.

Furay formed the group Poco in October of 1968, and pursued a country rock sound that was also based on the work of Buffalo Springfield. And Messina and his new collaborator, Kenny Loggins, would become a popular rock-based duo in the 1970s.

TOP ALBUMS

BUFFALO SPRINGFIELD (Atco, '66)
BUFFALO SPRINGFIELD AGAIN (Atco, '67)
LAST TIME AROUND (Atco, '68)
RETROSPECTIVE (Atco, '69)

TOP SONGS

FOR WHAT IT'S WORTH (STOP, HEY
   WHAT'S THAT SOUND) (Atco, '67, 7)
BLUEBIRD (Atco, '67)
ROCK AND ROLL WOMAN (Atco, '68)

THE PAUL BUTTERFIELD BLUES BAND

In Britain in the early 1960s, a thriving blues scene existed alongside its rock counterpart, with both sides drawing musical inspiration— and musicians—from each other.

That wasn't the case in the U.S., where the two forms were as segregated as the society at large. Ironically, given the fact that the blues had been central to the development of rock and roll, most young, white rock fans—and musicians—in the U.S. knew little of the genre at the time.

The Paul Butterfield Blues Band changed all that.

While other groups, like the New York–based Blues Project, had begun playing the blues to rock crowds by 1965, it was the Butterfield Band that would, over the course of the decade, do the most to bring the blues to the rock scene in the U.S.

Its leader, Paul Butterfield (b. Dec. 17, 1942, Chicago), had grown up surrounded by the blues.

The Paul Butterfield Blues Band

Entering the city's predominantly black blues scene, he had learned his musical trade at the feet of many of its masters, including Muddy Waters, Little Walter, Willie Dixon, and Buddy Guy.

When he formed his band in 1965, Butterfield enlisted guitarists Mike Bloomfield and Elvin Bishop, keyboardist Mark Naftalin, bassist Jerome Arnold, and drummer Sam Lay. At the time, such a racially integrated group (Arnold and Lay were black) was almost revolutionary. To Butterfield it was simply an outgrowth of his musical background.

Initially, the group played a fairly straightforward interpretation of the urban blues that had been pioneered in the late 1940s and '50s in Chicago by the likes of Waters, Little Walter, and the rest (along with the blues-based R&B of musicians such as Willie Dixon). This sound accrued a substantial local following, which expanded to the rest of the country in July 1965, when the band was invited to perform at the Newport Folk Festival in Rhode Island.

At the festival, the band—the first electric act ever to perform at the festival—was roundly jeered by the many purists who flocked to the event. But Bob Dylan heard their set and invited them to back him when he performed later in the day. The Butterfield Blues Band was literally pushed into history on the coattails of Dylan, whose "electric" performance—and the tumultuous response it generated—became one of the most controversial of the era.

The Butterfield Blues Band's eponymous debut

was released in January 1966 and eventually reached number 123 on the *Billboard* album chart. Basically a reproduction of the group's live act, it came with such blues warhorses as "I Got My Mojo Working," "Shake Your Money Maker," and "Mellow Down Easy," along with band originals that were drawn from the urban blues tradition.

While Butterfield was a more-than-passable vocalist, he was an out-and-out virtuoso on the harmonica, his approach an expressive updating of Walter's epochal style. At the center of the band's sound, along with Butterfield, was the equally impressive playing of Mike Bloomfield (b. July 28, 1944, Chicago), who brought a rock intensity and energy to the traditional electric blues guitar sound pioneered by the '50s Chicago masters. Later in the year, the band appeared on the album *What's Shakin'*, a various-artists record on the Elektra label that also included the group Powerhouse (with Eric Clapton), the Lovin' Spoonful, Tom Rush, and Al Kooper of the Blues Project. In October, the band toured England, appearing with Georgie Fame, Chris Farlowe, Geno Washington, and the Animals. They also recorded with one of Britain's blues masters, John Mayall (the EP *Bluesbreakers with Paul Butterfield* would subsequently be released in England).

While the band's reputation was growing in U.S. rock circles—due to its appearances at such illustrious venues as the Fillmore—it also began to change its personnel and sound. Lay departed to be replaced by Billy Davenport. And as it began to record its second album, the group was being moved in a new direction, away from a strictly Chicago blues-based sound.

The result of this movement was the record *East West*, one of the finest albums in American rock. While songs such as "Walkin' Blues" and "I've Got a Mind to Give Up Living" were primarily blues in derivation, others were a bold new amalgam of various genres. "Get Out of My Life Woman" had an R&B strut, while the band's version of Julian Adderley's "Work Song" was a blues by way of the new R&B-tinged jazz that was emerging at the time. The

album even included a brooding rendition of Monkee Michael Nesmith's pop hit "Mary Mary."

But it was the title cut that elevated the Butterfield Blues Band into the upper ranks of the rock of the day. The 13-minute instrumental came with blues solos by Bishop and Butterfield that were countered by a series of Indian-inspired sections by Bloomfield that built to a crescendo of ensemble improvisation. The song was the Butterfield Blues Band's defining masterpiece.

It was also a seminal moment in American rock history. While the solos and the very structure of "East West" were similar to the new improvisational forays of such West Coast groups as the Jefferson Airplane and the Grateful Dead, the band's intrinsic blues sound was also a primary part of the mix. This combination of rock and blues forms—performed by a group that was moving in rock circles—opened the eyes and ears of a new rock generation to the sound and possibilities of the blues. With this song and album, the Butterfield Blues Band singlehandedly bridged the gap that had existed between the blues and rock in the U.S.

Just as the band was reaching its artistic apex, Bloomfield, who was becoming one of the first great guitar heroes of his rock generation, decided to head in a new, big band direction. He left the group at the end of 1967 to form Electric Flag. (His new group and the Butterfield Blues Band would both appear at the Monterey Pop Festival later in the year).

Butterfield also had new ideas on his mind. With Bloomfield's departure, he revamped the band, moving Bishop to sole lead guitar and adding a horn section of his own. With Gene Dinwiddie on tenor sax, David Sanborn on alto sax, and Keith Johnson on trumpet, along with a new rhythm section comprising drummer Phil Wilson and bassist Bugsy Maugh, the band released the album *The Resurrection of Pigboy Crabshaw* at the start of 1968. With its R&B-based sound, the album was another new direction for the band. But at its core, the Butterfield Blues Band was still making the blues. On songs like "Driftin' and Driftin' " and others, Butterfield and the band displayed a feeling and fervor that were

---

TOP ALBUMS

THE PAUL BUTTERFIELD BLUES BAND (Elektra, '66)

WHAT'S SHAKIN' (with various artists, Elektra, '66)

EAST WEST (Elektra, '66)

THE RESURRECTION OF PIGBOY CRABSHAW (Elektra, '68)

IN MY OWN DREAMS (Elektra, '68)

KEEP ON MOVING (Elektra, '69)

LIVE (Elektra, '71)

SOMETIMES I JUST FEEL LIKE SMILIN' (Elektra, '71)

---

rooted firmly and identifiably in the classic Chicago tradition.

With this album, however, the Butterfield Blues Band's role in rock history effectively came to a close. It would continue to record and tour, with a constantly changing lineup of musicians. In 1969, the group performed at the Woodstock festival (and was included in the three-record set *Woodstock*). The "Crabshaw" lineup released the album *In My Own Dreams,* while subsequent versions of the group, with Butterfield the sole remaining original member, released *Keep on Moving* in 1969, *Live* in 1971, and *Sometimes I Just Feel Like Smilin'* that same year.

In September of 1971, Butterfield disbanded the group and moved to Woodstock in upstate New York. Over the course of the next decade and more, he became involved in various groups and projects.

In 1973, he formed the group Better Days, which recorded two albums. He also collaborated with the Band's Levon Helm and others on his solo album *Put It in Your Ear* in 1976. That same year, he joined a host of rock stars in the Band's farewell concert, "The Last Waltz," in San Francisco (playing harmonica at one point with his idol, Muddy Waters, on the song "Mannish Boy").

In 1981, he and Helms and Rick Danko formed the Danko Butterfield Band, but it came to naught. And after a prolonged illness in mid-decade, he attempted a comeback with the 1986 album *The Legendary Paul Butterfield Rides Again.* Like all of the other records he had released since his heyday in the '60s, it was a failure commercially.

On May 4, 1987, Paul Butterfield was found dead in his apartment in Hollywood.

THE BYRDS

By the spring of 1965 the golden age of '60s rock was in full swing. While the initial wave of the British Invasion had subsided, groups like the Beatles and the Rolling Stones were consolidating their sound and producing music of increasing power and maturity.

In California, the Beach Boys were expanding on the ethos of sun, surf, and fun, fun, fun. And in the East, Bob Dylan was making ready to electrify folk, literally, with his new rock-based sound at the upcoming Newport Folk Festival. At just about every turn, rock seemed to be evolving beyond recognition.

But none of this prepared anyone for the sound of the Byrds. When the opening notes of the group's electric version of Bob Dylan's "Mr. Tambourine Man" first sounded from the speakers of radios and record players in May 1965, it was as if rock had taken a quantum leap forward into a new expressive world.

Those crystalline, chiming notes issuing from the fretboard of Jim McGuinn's Rickenbacker 12-string guitar seemed to fill a vast ocean of aural space. To rock ears accustomed to choppy chords and leads that were picked out in (fairly) linear phrases, his full chordal style was something of a revelation; he seemed to be producing thousands of notes at once in shimmering cascades of sound.

As the breathtaking song shifted into gear, yet another new sound greeted those same rock ears.

The Byrds

This time it came from the vocals of McGuinn (b. James Joseph McGuinn III, July 13, 1942, Chicago), David Crosby (b. David Van Cortland, Aug. 14, 1941, Los Angeles), Gene Clark (b. Harold Eugene Clark, Nov. 17, 1941, Tipton, Missouri), and Chris Hillman (b. Dec. 4, 1944, Los Angeles). The four produced harmonies that were rich and thickly textured, that seemed to soar quite like the group's name. There was a choral-like grandeur to the vocals that, when augmented by McGuinn's latticework of notes, created a sound that was virtually unprecedented.

That sound, which was soon dubbed folk-rock, became a major new force in the rock world. In the short run, it would make the Byrds the most important American rock band of its time; in the long term, it would make them one of the most—if not the most—important American groups of any time.

While none of the other Byrds played their instruments on the single—that task being left (as was often the case in those days) to session musicians—they did participate on the songs for the group's debut album, *Mr. Tambourine Man,* which was released in the summer of 1965. Like the hit single, several of the album's songs were covers of Dylan originals, along with similar-sounding love songs from Clark. All were imbued with the same McGuinn guitar sound and vocal harmonies, which created a wholly new, electric slant on folk music.

Just as the Beatles had fostered a new wave of groups who imitated their sound, the Byrds—who became known as "the American Beatles"—did the same. As 1965 progressed, a tide of folk-rock groups began to emerge with hits of their own, all inspired by the Byrds' revolutionary efforts. The Turtles hit with their version of Dylan's "It Ain't Me Babe." Sonny and Cher scored with Dylan's "I Got You Babe," and Cher, in a solo context, had a hit with her version of Dylan's "All I Really Want to Do." In time, dozens of other groups emerged, like the Grass Roots and the Leaves. And folk-rock began to expand to other areas, with the Mamas and the Papas reinterpreting the sound in a pop context and the Syndicate of Sound opening its 1966 proto-garage-rock classic "Little Girl" with the trademark three-note chordings of McGuinn.

The Byrds' second album, *Turn! Turn! Turn!,* was released in December 1965, and it cemented their stature as the leaders of folk-rock. Its anthem-like title cut, based on folk singer Pete Seeger's interpretation of the Book of Ecclesiastes, came with their by-now signature vocal harmonies and McGuinn's sparkling guitar chords, and it topped the charts in the U.S. The album was the artistic pinnacle of the folk-rock movement.

But while that movement would continue as a major new force in rock over the course of the next year, eventually giving way to the psychedelic groups of the San Francisco scene in 1967, by 1966 the Byrds were evolving in entirely new ways, yielding music that, in breadth and range, would rival that of the Beatles and the Rolling Stones.

TOP ALBUMS

Mr. Tambourine Man (Columbia, '65, 6)
Turn! Turn! Turn! (Columbia, '66, 17)
Fifth Dimension (Columbia, '66, 24)
Younger than Yesterday (Columbia, '67, 24)
The Byrds' Greatest Hits (Columbia, '67, 6)
Byrds (Asylum, '73, 20)

Additional Top 40 Albums: 2

TOP SONGS

Mr. Tambourine Man (Columbia, '65, 1)
Turn! Turn! Turn! (Columbia, '65, 1)
Eight Miles High (Columbia, '66, 14)
So You Want to Be a Rock 'n' Roll Star
   (Columbia, '67, 29)

Additional Top 40 Songs: 3

That year, the group released the single "Eight Miles High," a psychedelic rocker that came with a jagged, dissonant McGuinn guitar solo, whose asymmetrical phrases were a rock reflection of the free-jazz experiments of jazz saxophonist John Coltrane. The song also created a controversy when it was banned by radio stations across the country because of its alleged references to drug use (the Byrds countered that it was really about a ride in an airplane 40,000 feet in the air).

A subsequent album, *Fifth Dimension,* included forays into Indian-tinged music and jazz, all mixed with the group's signature vocal harmonies and melodic sound. From that album, the group released the song "Mr. Spaceman" as a single. With its country-based sound, the song presaged a direction that the group would pursue in a much more pervasive manner in the future.

In March of 1966, Clark departed the group, and it continued as a quartet. When the Byrds began recording their fourth album at the end of the year, they enlisted guitarists Clarence White and Vern Gosdin and South African trumpeter Hugh Masekela.

The result of this collaboration was the 1967 hit single "So You Want to Be a Rock 'n' Roll Star," which reached number 29 on the charts. With its rolling guitar and bass line and Masekela's inspired solos, it was an incisive blend of rock and jazz. The group also looked back to its folk-rock origins with the album *Younger than Yesterday,* with its flowing, folk-based title cut and another electric rendition of a Bob Dylan song, "My Back Pages," which went to number 30 on the *Billboard* singles charts.

In March of 1967, in what would become one of the more baffling footnotes in rock history, McGuinn changed his first name to Roger (a decision that may have had something to with his joining the Subud religious cult). Tensions were mounting in the group at this time, especially between Crosby and McGuinn. By the time the Byrds played the Monterey Pop Festival in June of 1967, the rift was increasing. Crosby—in a hint of his future intentions—performed with Buffalo Springfield during their set at the festival (in 1969, he and the group's Stephen Stills would team up with the Hollies' Graham Nash to form Crosby, Stills and Nash, which would later expand to include the Springfield's Neil Young).

The rift became reality in October 1967; Crosby quit the group when it refused to record his song "Triad" (which would later appear on Jefferson Airplane's 1968 album *Crown of Creation*). Clark was asked to rejoin, but he stayed only three weeks and quit again. At the end of the year, drummer Mike Clarke also departed from the group, leaving McGuinn and Hillman as the remaining members.

A new Byrds' album, *The Notorious Byrd Brothers* (with a cover photo of McGuinn, Hillman, and Clarke peering out from a barn, along with a horse that was reported to represent Crosby), was released in April 1968. Its winsome, folk-flavored rock was an eloquent denouement to the first phase of the group's historic career.

But the Byrds' story was not over. Recruiting a new lineup that would center on McGuinn, Hillman, and new members Gram Parsons (guitars, keyboards, and vocals) and Kevin Kelley (guitar and vocals), the group began a new period of development. McGuinn ceded direction of the music to Hillman and Parsons, who guided the Byrds toward a fusion of country and rock. In February, the group performed at the bastion of country music, the Grand Ole Opry, in Nashville. It also began to record a new country-based album.

But before that album could be released, Parsons quit the Byrds in July, refusing to participate in the group's tour of South Africa. Because of contract problems, his vocals on the new album were re-recorded by McGuinn and Hillman.

When the album was finally released in September, it proved to be yet another watershed for the group—and for rock. Heavily inspired by Parsons, *Sweethearts of the Rodeo* was the first major foray by a rock group into the realm of country music. While everyone from the Beatles to the Rolling Stones, Buffalo Springfield, the Lovin' Spoonful, and scores of other rock acts had flirted with country, the Byrds based their new sound entirely on it. Although the album was a modest commercial success, hitting number 77 on the U.S. charts, it was crucial in the establishment of the country-rock movement that would emerge in the 1970s. The album also predated Dylan's 1969 album, *Nashville Skyline,* which would receive most of the subsequent credit for the country-rock movement.

But with the departure of Parsons, the Byrds' days as one of the preeminent groups in rock were over. Hillman departed in October to form the Flying Burrito Brothers with Parsons and Clarke. Over the next few years, McGuinn would form new versions of the group with various lineups, continuing to tour and release such albums as 1969's *Dr. Byrds & Mr. Hyde,* 1970's *The Ballad of Easy Rider* (whose title cut was part of the soundtrack of the Peter Fonda film of the same title), 1971's *Byrdmaniax,* and 1972's *Farther Along.*

In 1973, the original quintet recorded and released the album *Byrds,* which hit number 20 in the U.S. In February of that year, McGuinn disbanded the final lineup of the group (which, by that time included off-and-on guitarist White, who had worked with the original group on the *Younger than Yesterday* album in 1967). Tragic sidenotes to the group's career occurred later in 1973 when White was struck by a truck and killed and when Parsons died of a drug overdose.

The original members of the group remained active to various degrees during the succeeding decades. Crosby went on to fame and fortune with CS&N and CSN&Y and its various offshoots. McGuinn and Clark pursued solo careers that were musically haphazard and commercially negligible. Hillman became something of a success in the Souther-Hillman-Furay Band and, later, the country group Desert Rose Band.

Although the Byrds would never formally reunite, the original members also got together in various splinter groups from time to time. McGuinn, Clark, and Hillman teamed up in 1979 for a group and album of the same name. In the late 1980s, Clark and Clarke teamed up for a nostalgia-act version of the Byrds. Reacting to this, Crosby, McGuinn, and Hillman performed together at three shows in 1989 in an attempt to establish legal control of the group's name. They would also perform as a group at a star-studded tribute to the late Roy Orbison in Los Angeles later in the year. Clark died in May 1991, four months after the group had been inducted into the Rock and Roll Hall of Fame.

ERIC CLAPTON

In 1965, a new graffiti slogan began to appear, scrawled in tube stations and pub walls across London. It was a simple, declarative statement: "Clapton Is God."

He wasn't, of course. But to rock guitarists of the day he must have seemed as much.

In the dim blues and rock clubs of London, playing with John Mayall's Bluesbreakers, Clapton was single-handedly—one might say, Slowhandedly—reinventing rock guitar.

While Mayall was pursuing his own revolutionary reinterpretations of American blues, Clapton was abetting him with guitar work that had—literally—never been heard before.

For a start, there was the sound. Playing a Gibson Les Paul guitar through a Marshall amplifier—which he ultimately transformed into technological icons of the rock era—Clapton created a thick, distorted guitar tone that was a quantum leap above the tinny, trebly, twangy sound that rock guitarists had employed to that point. He applied that sound to blues riffs and phrasings that had been pioneered by masters such as Muddy Waters, Chuck Berry, and the three Kings of the blues guitar, B.B., Albert, and Freddy. But Clapton did more than simply replicate their innovations. He reworked their lines, inverting them and recasting them with angular rhythmic asides and lithe, sweeping, quasi-lyrical inflections, in the process creating a new lexicon of blues and rock signatures.

He also gave them a new ferocity and energy that were pure rock, in their sound and sensibility. He screamed incredibly high notes; held them suspended in midair with a quivering, warbling vibrato; then resolved them with fleeting phrases that, glued together by the distorted sound, seemed to explode into scores of notes occurring simultaneously. At the end of songs, he didn't simply stop, but slid his fingers down the neck in a saw-toothed glide that ended in a resounding crash.

Clapton's revolutionary sound emerged in all its glory on the 1966 album *Bluesbreakers—John Mayall with Eric Clapton.* On instrumentals like "Hideaway" and "Steppin' Out," he created solos that had the emotional thrust of blues improvisation, but whose eloquent constructions almost seemed scripted (they weren't) to perfection. Backing Mayall's vocals and keyboards on songs like "All Your Love" and the slow blues "Double Crossing Time," he inserted guitar breaks that were endowed with

Eric Clapton

breathtaking articulation and finesse. Simply stated, with the possible exception of B.B. King's *Live at the Regal, Bluesbreakers* was the finest electric blues album of all time . It was also a watershed in the evolution of rock guitar, and by extension, of rock in general. Finally, it represented the crystallization of Clapton's guitar style, which would remain essentially intact—and vastly influential—through the many phases of his distinctive career, from Cream and Blind Faith through solo work.

Clapton (b. Eric Patrick Clapp, Mar. 30, 1945, Ripley, Surrey) got his first guitar in 1962. He began listening to records by blues masters like Son House and Robert Johnson. While studying at the Kingston College of Art, he played in various groups, slowly gaining his blues style.

In 1963, he joined the Roosters, an R&B group whose members included Paul Jones and Tom McGuinness (later of Manfred Mann). When that group disbanded later in the year, he and McGuinness briefly joined the pop group Casey Jones and the Engineers.

In October 1963, Clapton was invited to join the Yardbirds when their guitarist "Top" Topham quit. He took over the role just as the group was embarking on its historic stint at the Crawdaddy Club, which would prove to be the platform for their future move into the rock world. Giorgio Gomelsky, the club's owner and the Yardbirds' manager, astounded by Clapton's guitar work, nicknamed him Slowhand.

With the Yardbirds, Clapton began to make his reputation in the burgeoning rock and R&B scene of London. His work was the focal point of the group's 1964 debut album, *Five Live Yardbirds* (recorded at the Marquee Club). Here his guitar work exhibited a certain power and rock-edged punch, but it still affected the thin, trebly sound that was typical of rock and blues guitarists of the era, while offering modest replications of the work of Waters, King, and the rest.

When the Yardbirds began to record the single "For Your Love" in 1965, Clapton became disgusted with what he considered the group's new pop direction, and he quit in March (although his guitar was heard on *The Yardbirds with Sonny Boy Williamson* and various songs from the group's initial U.S. albums *For Your Love* and *Having a Rave Up with the Yardbirds*).

Clapton was immediately recruited into Mayall's Bluesbreakers, with whom he began to develop the distorted tone and distinctive revisions of the blues masters that would become his signature. Along the way, he became the most revered guitarist on the British rock scene.

In 1966, Clapton also participated in a one-off group, the Powerhouse, recording three songs for the album *What's Shakin'*, which also included the Lovin' Spoonful, the Paul Butterfield Blues Band, and others. The group's members included Jack Bruce and Steve Winwood, whose musical paths would again cross his own.

In June of 1966, Clapton was invited by drummer Ginger Baker to form a trio. They enlisted Bruce on bass and called themselves Cream. Over the course of the next two years, Cream would introduce a new virtuosity in rock and rise to the pinnacle of rock stardom and success.

With Cream, Clapton began to transform his blues derivations into an all-encompassing rock conception.

Cream reveled in a kind of collective musical abandon that approached the improvisational complexity of jazz and the dense interplay of classical Indian music. On the albums *Fresh Cream* and *Disraeli Gears*, this abandon was contained within fairly defined rock song forms. On songs such as "I Feel Free" (*Fresh Cream*), Clapton rolled out lithe solos that came with convoluted phrases and odd harmonic lines, based mostly on sevenths and ninths, that were entirely new to rock. He also continued to expand the sound of his guitar: on "Tales of Brave Ulysses" (*Disraeli Gears*) he became the first guitarist to use the wah-wah pedal. At other times, he dispensed with innovations and simply played, with a mastery that was unparalleled. On the song "Badge," from Cream's final album, *Goodbye,* he

TOP ALBUMS

HISTORY OF ERIC CLAPTON (Atco, '72, 6)
461 OCEAN BOULEVARD (RSO, '74, *1*)
SLOWHAND (RSO, '77, *2*)
BACKLESS (RSO, '78, 8)
JUST ONE NIGHT (RSO, '80, 2)
ANOTHER TICKET (RSO, '81, 7)
UNPLUGGED (Duck/Reprise, '92, *1*)

Additional Top 40 Albums: 12

TOP SONGS

I SHOT THE SHERIFF (RSO, '74, *1*)
LAY DOWN SALLY (RSO, '78, 3)
TEARS IN HEAVEN (Duck/Reprise, '92, 2)

Additional Top 40 Songs: 12

unleashed one of the grandest solos in all of rock and roll.

Onstage, he—and Bruce and Baker—cut loose with extended improvisations in which their instruments seemed to splinter and recombine with an almost telepathic empathy, the rhythms, themes, and solos coalescing in a furious but articulate whole. Clapton's technical prowess reached new levels, as did his expressiveness. On the group's concert version of Robert Johnson's "Crossroads" (from the *Wheels of Fire* album), Clapton created a solo that was at once savage and delicate, lyrical and technically astounding. It was, arguably, the finest individual guitar solo in rock.

With Cream, Clapton revolutionized rock in another way. Not God, per se, he became the symbol of the rock guitar hero. Just as rock guitarists would come to adopt his sound, they also began to assume the commanding presence and role he had created for the guitarist in the rock world.

Ironically, it was a role that Clapton began to rebel against when Cream disbanded at the end of 1968. Bruce pursued a solo career, while Clapton and Baker joined with Winwood and bassist Rick Grech in the first so-called supergroup, Blind Faith. The group's eponymous album was released in June 1969 and topped the charts on both sides of the Atlantic. When the group debuted at a free concert at London's Hyde Park, a crowd of 100,000—the largest in rock history to that point—came out to hear it. A subsequent U.S. tour was also a sellout. But Clapton became disillusioned with the hype and hoopla, and his mostly lackluster work with the group seemed to reflect this. Blind Faith disbanded in October 1969.

Clapton pursued various one-off projects for a time (he had previously recorded with his friend George Harrison, contributing an eloquent solo on the song "While My Guitar Gently Weeps" on the Beatles' White Album in 1968). In September 1969, he joined John Lennon and the Plastic Ono Band for its appearance at the Rock and Roll Revival concert in Toronto. He also began to tour in the U.K. as a guest with Delaney and Bonnie and Friends, the group that had opened for Blind Faith on its U.S. tour. His collaboration with the group yielded the album *Delaney and Bonnie on Tour* in 1970. With the encouragement of Delaney Bramlett, and the help of the "friends," Clapton recorded his eponymous debut album, which was subsequently released in March 1970.

Three of those "friends"—drummer Jim Gordon, bassist Carl Radle, and keyboardist Bobby Whitlock—joined Clapton in the group Derek and the Dominos. The group's classic album, *Layla and Other Assorted Love Songs,* displayed some of Clapton's most agile and inspired solos, along with a title cut that became one of the timeless songs of the rock repertoire. The album's guitar duets with Clapton and Duane Allman were among the defining moments of '70s rock. Released in November 1970, it reached number 16 on the charts.

When that group folded in 1971, Clapton retreated from the scene, beset by increasing drug problems. He remained a recluse for the next two years. But in 1973, he was encouraged by Pete Townshend to reemerge, in a concert the latter staged at London's Rainbow Theatre that included the cream of British rock. That show, which came with a notably below-par performance by Clapton, was captured for posterity on the 1973 album *Eric Clapton's Rainbow Concert.*

Clapton made his formal comeback in 1974 with the album *461 Ocean Boulevard*, which topped the charts, as did its single, a version of the Bob Marley song "I Shot the Sheriff." On that album, Clapton's vocals came to the forefront while his guitar work was relegated to a secondary role, with few of the fiery displays that had made him a legend in his younger days.

It was a course he subsequently pursued over the next 20 years of his career to vast commercial, if modest artistic, success. At times, on albums such as 1985's *Behind the Sun* and 1989's *Journeyman*, he reignited the fire of his older days somewhat. But mostly he seemed content to pursue a mild blues and rock sound. In 1992, he appeared on the MTV program "Unplugged," which yielded an album of the same title that was an unqualified commercial success, selling several million copies. In 1993, that album dominated the Grammy Awards.

While the album had its moments, it never approached the level of power and innovation that Clapton achieved in the 1960s. In fact, it seemed as if the Grammy voters were not so much honoring that record specifically as they were Clapton himself, the awards being a final, formal acknowledgement of the ways in which Clapton had changed the course of rock and roll.

That same year, he was inducted into the Rock and Roll Hall of Fame with his former Cream mates, Baker and Bruce.

THE CLASH

Though the Clash was the musical soul of the punk movement. While the Sex Pistols were the symbol of punk, the key that opened the door to the new rock epoch, the Clash was the boot that kicked and held it open wide for the pop masses to hear.

While the Pistols cavorted about in the glare of the media, the Clash churned out music that stayed true to the cause long after its more illustrious counterpart had self-destructed.

Over the course of its nine-year career, the group created a body of songs that defined and expanded the punk form. From the start, with its debut release, "White Riot," in 1976, the Clash made music that was all the things that punk was supposed to be: brash, rough, raw, and rebellious. Even its pop hits, like "Rock the Casbah" and "Should I Stay or Should I Go?" bristled with punk energy and insouciance, while giving punk a musical weight that counterbalanced its attitude.

The Clash was formed in London at the very dawn of punk, in June of 1976, when guitarist-vocalist Mick Jones (b. June 26, 1955, Brixton, London) teamed up with bassist Paul Simonon (b. Dec. 15, 1955, Brixton). "Bassist" was hardly the word. In true punk style, which thumbed a nose at musicianship, Simonon had never played the instrument, but agreed to give it a go. They were joined by guitarist Keith Levine, drummer Terry Chimes, and former 101ers guitarist-vocalist Joe Strummer (b. John Mellors, Aug. 21, 1952, Ankara, Turkey).

The group began to make a name for itself in the fledgling punk scene with one of its first performances, opening for the Sex Pistols in Sheffield. In September of 1976 it became one of the most prominent groups on that scene when it performed at the Club 101 Punk Festival in London.

But Levine decided to leave the fold, as did Chimes, who was replaced by Topper Headon (b. May 30, 1955, Bromley, Kent). With Headon aboard, the Clash's classic lineup was set.

The group's ties with the Sex Pistols extended to more than sharing a stage in a punk show. Its manager, Bernie Rhodes, had worked at the Sex boutique owned by the Sex Pistols' manager, Malcolm McLaren. Rhodes shared his former employer's unabashed aptitude for creating controversy and parlaying it into an image—and a deal.

In January of 1977, Rhodes negotiated a record contract with CBS. At the time, this was derided in punk circles, with intimations that the Clash and its manager had sold out to the music business. But that was dispelled when the group released "White Riot" in April. With its storming punk sound, the song became, after the Pistols' epochal "Anarchy in the U.K.," one of the foundations of the punk movement and one of its first hits, reaching number 38 on the U.K. charts. The group's eponymous debut album also proved that, major label record deals to the contrary, the Clash was arguably the most potent of the scores of groups emerging on the scene.

The Clash—and its manager—also seemed intent on pushing its image to the public via a series of controversies that generated the attention of the media and the law. In June of 1977, Strummer and Headon were fined five pounds in a London court for spray-painting the group's name on a wall. That same month, they spent a night in jail in Newcastle for the theft of a pillowcase from a Holiday Inn. Rhodes's response was to title the group's upcoming tour, "Out on Parole."

By 1978, the U.K. punk scene was on the wane.

The Clash

In February, the Sex Pistols disbanded after a disastrous U.S. tour. And other leading artists of the scene, such as Siouxsie and the Banshees and Billy Idol, were cutting deals of their own with the industry and moving out into the pop world.

But the Clash was just getting in gear. After two negligible singles, the group assaulted the charts with the song "(White Man) In Hammersmith Palais" and the album *Give 'Em Enough Rope,* both of which were slashing and intense displays of punk power. The former hit number 32 and the latter debuted at number two on the U.K. charts. Tiring of its manager's eccentricities, the group dismissed Rhodes in October (he would subsequently be rehired in 1981).

Like the Sex Pistols before them, the Clash was inevitably drawn to the U.S., where its popularity was growing; in 1978, its debut album had become the biggest-selling import in America. The group's debut U.S. tour, which began in January 1979, was a critical and popular success, as was a second later that year. They would provide the base for the most successful phase of the group's career.

That phase began at the end of 1979, when the group released the album *London Calling* (whose pompous original title, *The New Testament,* was wisely discarded). A two-record set (issued at the price of one), the album was an expansive revision of punk, with traces of rock and pop added to the group's sound. The album's title cut was a stomping rocker with an anthemic melody and a musical adroitness that suggested that the Clash was moving beyond the strict confines of punk's musical tirades. The album eventually reached number 27 on the *Billboard* charts.

The suggestion came to fruition in 1980, when the group released the three-record set *Sandinista!* (issued at the price of two records). While the album was at least one record too long for its own good—there simply weren't enough good songs to warrant such a long set—it did display an expansiveness and sheer bravura that were impressive. It was almost as if the Clash was making the case that punk was more than an attitude, that it could have an expressive depth and power and it could evolve and regenerate itself. The album hit number 24 on the U.S. charts.

TOP ALBUMS

LONDON CALLING (Epic, '80, 27)
SANDINISTA! (Epic, '81, 24)
COMBAT ROCK (Epic, '82, 7)

TOP SONGS

TRAIN IN VAIN (STAND BY ME) (Epic, '80, 23)
SHOULD I STAY OR SHOULD I GO? (Epic, '82, reissued '83)
ROCK THE CASBAH (Epic, '82, 8)

As the new decade began to unfold, punk was co-opted by the music business and the culture at large, merging with the new wave of London, New York, and Los Angeles into a pervasive pop force. The Clash was swept into this vast movement and thrived, while miraculously never relinquishing its punk identity. And with the rehiring of Rhodes, it also continued its controversial antics. In April 1982, the start of a tour in the U.K. was postponed when Strummer disappeared; it was later revealed to be a publicity stunt that Rhodes had staged.

Two months later, the group's album *Combat Rock* achieved a commercial breakout in the U.S., where it reached number seven on the charts and went platinum. At the height of the group's popularity, Headon left because of "political differences" and was replaced by original drummer Chimes (who left the group again in May 1983, with drummer Pete Howard joining). The new lineup promptly left for the U.S. and an opening slot on the Who's "farewell" tour.

With the success of *Combat Rock* and the opening slot on the Who tour—with its implication of a changing of the guard—the Clash was poised to become one of the major acts of its era. This seemed to be confirmed when the single "Rock the Casbah" reached number eight on the U.S. charts in 1983 (another single, "Should I Stay or Should I Go?" made number 50).

In June of 1983, the Clash co-headlined the new wave segment of the three-day US Festival in San Bernadino, California, reportedly earning $500,000 for its performance. While that fee was dwarfed by the $1 million that David Bowie and Van Halen were paid for their performance at the festival, it was unprecedented for a punk act. And it spawned new charges that the Clash had "sold out" to pop success.

But just as the Sex Pistols had been undermined by success, so too the Clash began to come apart. In September 1983, Jones left the group, with Strummer and Simonon issuing a "communique" stating that he had "drifted apart from the original idea of the Clash." In January 1984, a new version of the group was unveiled, with guitarists Vince White and Nick Sheppard. But the rot had set in, and the group curtailed its touring and recording over the next year. At the end of 1985, it released the album *Cut the Crap,* which was lambasted by critics and reached a modest number 88 on the U.S. charts.

At the start of 1986, the Clash disbanded when Strummer and Simonon decided to depart.

By that time, Jones had formed the group Big Audio Dynamite, which enjoyed a modest success in the post–new wave scene. Strummer pursued a solo career that included work in the film *Straight to Hell.* Simonon eventually reemerged in 1991 with the group Havana 3 A.M. The Clash would enjoy one more typically idiosyncratic distinction as a group when "Rock the Casbah" became the first rock record to be broadcast to the troops in the Persian Gulf War in 1990.

Its controversies and posturings notwithstanding, the Clash proved that punk was a musical force to be reckoned with in the grand scheme of rock things. And by its very longevity—and adherence to punk's raw and rebellious stance—the group extended punk's influence and musical significance to succeeding rock generations.

ELVIS COSTELLO

With the release of the album *The Juliet Letters* in 1993, Elvis Costello embarked on an unexpected new course in his career.

The Juliet Letters, a collaboration with the Brodsky Quartet, was a song cycle based on a news report Costello had read about an academic in Verona who responded to letters that had been addressed to the Shakespearean heroine Juliet Capulet. Co-composing a series of musical "letters" with the classically trained members of the Brodsky, Costello created a sublime fusion of rock and classical forms. The songs themselves encompassed a wide range of styles, from dense, dissonant, modern classical forays to R&B-tinged ballads, with references to everyone from the Beatles to Kurt Weill added along the way.

Onstage, during a brief tour to promote the album, Costello stood behind a music stand—with the quartet arrayed about him—declaiming his vocals almost operatically while offering biting, cynical rejoinders about politics, romance, and the world at large. As with the songs, his performance was an inspired amalgam of rock and classical signatures that created a sense of artistic coherence unequalled since the classically based songs of the Beatles in the 1960s.

While *The Juliet Letters* represented a turn off the beaten path, it was hardly surprising. During the course of his career, Costello pursued his expansive musical instincts with a vengeance. From his early, punk-tinged days in the middle 1970s to his side trips into country music and collaborations with such diverse artists as the Dirty Dozen Brass Band, Paul McCartney, and others, Costello displayed a musical voraciousness that was, by turns, idiosyncratic and engrossing.

While Costello didn't alter the course of rock history, he did reaffirm, with his constantly shifting musical forays, its inherent individuality. *The Juliet Letters* typified this brash assertion; at a time when rock was threatening to become a cultural cliché based on a sort of ersatz rebellion, Costello truly rebelled by producing work that was articulate, thought-provoking, and musically valid.

The same could be said of his entire career.

Costello (b. Declan McManus, Aug. 25, 1955, London) emerged in the pub-rock scene of mid-1970s Britain with the group Flip City. While that

Elvis Costello

group was unsuccessful, one of its demos came to the attention of Jake Riviera of the fledgling Stiff label in 1976. Riviera signed Costello—then performing as D.P. Costello (using his mother's maiden name)—and suggested he change his first name to Elvis.

The new name was significant because its obvious reference to the King of rock and roll was a wry counterpoint to Costello's pointedly nerdy appearance. With his razor-cut hair, black horn-rimmed glasses, and penchant for contoured 1950s-styled jackets, Costello was as far from Presley as he was from the safety-pinned, black-leathered punks who were making their entrance into the rock world alongside him. Even at the start, Costello fit no particular rock mold.

That point was confirmed with the release of his debut album, *My Aim Is True,* in August 1977. With its punkish energy and songs that hinted at everything from British Invasion melodies to pub-rock rockabilly, the album was a singular product at a time when the anti-musical posturings of the punks were becoming increasingly dominant.

Initially—and ironically—Costello was identified with that brash movement, touring with such punk acts as Wayne County. In fact, he had more in common with rock artists like Joe Jackson and Graham Parker (with whom he shared a cynical lyrical sensibility and a remarkably similar vocal sound) and former pub-rock leader Nick Lowe (who produced *My Aim Is True*).

Costello's quasi-punk image was heightened in the U.S. in December 1978 when he appeared on the television program "Saturday Night Live" (subbing for the Sex Pistols). Performing live, he halted during "Less than Zero" and said, "I'm sorry, ladies and gentlemen, there's no reason to do this song." He then switched to "Radio Radio," which the show's producers had reportedly asked him not to perform. It was one of the most famous musical moments in the series' history and established the "angry young man" persona that Costello would trade on in succeeding years.

With his group, the Attractions—drummer Pete Thomas, bassist Bruce Thomas, and keyboardist

Steve Nieve—Costello toured the U.S. and U.K. in 1978, gradually building a supportive base of critics and fans. He also released the album *This Year's Model,* which reached number 30 on the U.S. charts.

Over the course of the next two years, Costello's career was on the rise. The album *Armed Forces* reached number 10 in the U.S. in 1979 and he received a Grammy nomination for Best New Artist. In 1980, the album *Get Happy!!* hit number 11 in the U.S.

His reputation as a songwriter was rising in tandem with that of his edgy and intense performances on record and onstage. Songs such as 1977's "Alison" and 1979's "Accidents Will Happen," for all their rock power, displayed a remarkably melodic pop sensibility that elevated them above the thrashing punk and new wave fare of the day. When Linda Ronstadt recorded versions of his songs "Party Girl," "Girls Talk," and "Talking in the Dark" on her 1980 album *Mad Love,* Costello was reportedly displeased. But Ronstadt's covers proved that Costello's songs, like those of classic songwriters before him, could survive and flourish with new interpretations.

In 1981, Costello began his forays outside of rock with the album *Almost Blue,* which came with a markedly country sound. For the first time—but not the last—Costello confounded his fans by displaying his intention to go his own creative way. The album was a modest success, reaching number 50 on the U.S. charts.

That same year, Costello and the Attractions performed with the Royal Philharmonic Orchestra at London's Royal Albert Hall.

Costello returned to brash and bitter rock tirades on albums such as 1982's *Imperial Bedroom* and 1984's *Goodbye Cruel World.* On 1986's *King of America,* be began to widen his musical range with excursions into Tex-Mex, Cajun, and Irish traditional music, collaborating with Tom Waits, Daryl Hall, Los Lobos, and others. With that album, he also reverted to his given name.

Along the way, he appeared in and wrote the theme song for the British television show "Scully" in 1985 and produced the Pogues' album *Rum,*

TOP ALBUMS

My Aim Is True (Columbia, '78, *32*)
This Year's Model (Columbia, '78, *30*)
Armed Forces (Columbia, '79, *10*)
Get Happy!! (Columbia, '80, *11*)
Taking Liberties (Columbia, '80, *28*)
Trust (Columbia, '81, *28*)
Imperial Bedroom (Columbia, '82, *30*)
Punch the Clock (Columbia, '83, *24*)
Spike (Warner, '89, *32*)

Additional Top 40 Albums: 2

TOP SONG

Veronica (Warner, '89, *19*)

Additional Top 40 Songs: 1

Sodomy and the Lash (in 1986, he married the group's bassist, Caitlin O'Riordan).

King of America provided a hint of future musical excursions that came to fruition on the 1988 album *Spike*. In 1986 he had disbanded the Attractions; on *Spike* he enlisted a diverse array of musical collaborators, including the Dirty Dozen Brass Band (with whom he created lusty, earthy songs tinged with New Orleans jazz) and the Byrds' former guitarist Roger McGuinn, among others.

That album also included the song "Veronica," which he had co-written with Paul McCartney. With its flowing pop melodies, "Veronica" was one of the finest songs of his career; released as a single, it went to number 19 on the U.S. charts. His collaboration with McCartney also yielded the songs "My Brave Face," "You Want Her Too," "Don't Be Careless Love," and "That Day Is Done," which were released on the former Beatle's 1989 album *Flowers in the Dirt*. Their partnership would also produce the songs "Mistress and Maid" and "The Lovers That Never Were" on McCartney's 1993 album *Off The Ground*. At the time, McCartney compared Costello's cynical, bitter style with that of his former songwriting mate, John Lennon.

In 1989, Costello was named Best Songwriter in *Rolling Stone* magazine.

While the 1991 album *Mighty Like a Rose* continued the eclectic course pursued on *Spike*, Costello kept on thumbing his nose at what his fans expected of him. At Neil Young's annual benefit show for the Bay Area–based Bridge School in 1990, Costello appeared onstage as a latter-day hippie in flowing locks and wire-rimmed glasses, performing a fiery acoustic set of his hits. He also reportedly began to record his own renditions of pop classics for an album that went unreleased. And he began work on *The Juliet Letters* with the Brodsky Quartet, with whom he shared an affection for the music of the classical composer Dmitri Shostakovich.

Where he would go from there he didn't say, at least not in interviews given at the time. The fact that no one could possibly guess was the true indicator of Costello's creative unpredictability.

THE CRAZY WORLD OF ARTHUR BROWN

With the emergence of the psychedelic era in 1967, rock began to be transformed into a sensory assault of aural imagery.

With the Beatles leading the way with the *Sgt. Pepper's Lonely Hearts Club Band* album, groups began to load up their recordings with myriad extra-musical sound sources that added a quasi-visual presence to their songs.

All of that, however was on record. Onstage, the rock groups of the day were remarkably straightforward in their presentation. The West Coast groups did have their light shows, and the Who and Jimi Hendrix would smash an amplifier or two, but otherwise, rock shows consisted primarily of a musical act getting up on a stage and simply playing their music.

Enter the Crazy World of Arthur Brown.

At the group's shows at the UFO Club in London, Brown would make his entrance by being lowered to the stage by a crane. Dressed in a flowing cape and other psychedelic gear, his face a mask of wildly distorted makeup, Brown would intone his words with a menacing growl, then shriek like a madman, acting out shaman-esque choreography to the songs. At the end of the performance, wearing a helmet of sorts, he would set the device aflame and stagger about deliriously like a human candelabra.

A quarter of a century down the line—in a rock world dominated by dizzying displays of computerized lights, elaborate set designs, and minutely scripted stage business—Brown's act would seem almost quaint. But in 1967, it was quite revolutionary.

With Brown's stage antics, the group offered a new direction for rock shows. His use of theatrical devices to augment the music provided a visual aspect that rock had never enjoyed to that point, short of the more flashy (but nonetheless, primarily musical) performances of everyone from Presley to Jagger and Hendrix.

What made those antics all the more effective was the fact that the music of the Crazy World of Arthur Brown was actually quite good. The songs from the group's sole album, an eponymously titled set of 1968, were a forceful blend of R&B and rock with traces of jazz and the swirling imagery of psychedelia. The group's cover of Screamin' Jay Hawkins's warhorse "I Put a Spell on You" was one of the finest versions of the song ever recorded. And the group's originals, such as "Child of My Kingdom" and "Spontaneous Apple Creation," were instrumentally complex and melodically intriguing pieces that mixed the improvisational forays of keyboardist Vincent Crane with the jazz-tinged rhythms of drummer Drachen Theaker.

Brown's vocals, while histrionic, were also affecting. His rich baritone gave way to hysterical outbursts that thoroughly complemented the songs' manic themes. On the group's signature song, "Fire," Brown's vocals trembled and writhed in horror as the music built to vast crescendos of sound.

In all, the music of the Crazy World of Arthur Brown was as theatrical as its stage presentations.

The group was formed in 1967 by Brown (b. Arthur Wilton, June 24, 1944, Whitby, England), Crane, and Theaker (the latter was succeeded by Carl Palmer, later of Emerson Lake and Palmer). It quickly became a hit in the burgeoning psychedelic scene in London. Signed to the Track label, the group began recording its album in 1968. In September, "Fire" was released as a single and became a major hit, reaching number two on the *Billboard* charts. On the strength of its single, the album also did well, hitting number seven in October.

A U.S. tour ensued at the end of the year (with Fleetwood Mac opening for the group). But it proved to be a disaster, perhaps due to the fact that

The Crazy World of Arthur Brown

the tour technologies of the time were fairly primitive, and the halls in which it was performed were hardly made for rock music of any sort, much less rock with a theatrical presentation.

At any rate, the group never followed up on its initial success and disbanded in 1969.

Brown reemerged in 1970 with Kingdom Come, another group that fused rock music with theatrical shows (during which, from time to time, he would pose on a cross in a depiction of the Crucifixion). That group released three albums, *Galactic Zoo, Kingdom Come,* and *The Journey.* But none were hits, and Brown departed in 1973.

A former philosophy student at Reading University, Brown then headed to the Middle East seeking inspiration; at one point, he ended up performing for the Israeli Army. On his return to Britain in 1975, he then began a study of meditation and faded from the rock scene.

But during its brief career, the Crazy World of Arthur Brown set in motion a new way of thinking about the nature of rock performances. Brown's sense of drama and theatrics opened a new expressive realm for rock music and musicians, one that emphasized visual as well as musical components.

Brown's revolutionary stage shows had an impact on the work of the young David Bowie, whose performances also included extensive use of theatrics and makeup and costumes. Bowie's tours of the early 1970s for the albums *The Rise and Fall of Ziggy Stardust and the Spiders from Mars* and *Diamond Dogs* were augmented by theatrical displays that provided visual accoutrements and themes for the songs. A revolutionary himself, Bowie elaborated on Brown's relatively simple devices, creating whole new stage and public personas.

In the U.S., Brown's work also formed the basis of the new "shock rock" that was being formulated by Iggy and the Stooges and Alice Cooper. In the early performances of the former, in 1970, Iggy would close shows by covering the Stooges in a vast sheet while they were performing. Cooper created full-fledged stage shows, the finale of which culminated in his being placed in a guillotine and getting the chop.

Cooper would expand his visual repertoire over the course of the next two decades, with his shows becoming increasingly self-parodistic and garish, his various stage devices being used as props for music

that (a few decent hits like "Eighteen" and "School's Out" notwithstanding) was mostly a cartoonish take on heavy metal. And Cooper's devices became, in the 1970s, the basis for the vapid and flashy contrivances of the group Kiss. Basically a rock sideshow for the pre-teen set, Kiss's performances came with the musicians cavorting about in black leather sci-fi costumes and mask-like makeup that obscured their faces (one of the group's trademarks was that its members were never seen by their public without that stage makeup). During their shows, the group would also "spit" fire, like the familiar acts in a circus (shades of Brown's flaming helmet!).

In fact, it would all become something of a circus.

As the 1970s proceeded, rock acts increasingly included visual stimuli as part of their stage shows. The Who's 1974 Quadrophenia tour came with intricate displays of laser grids. The focal point of the Rolling Stones' 1973 tour was a gigantic, inflatable phallus. Yes used glop-like sets that glowed. Jethro Tull employed roadies as extras who dressed up in various costumes and cavorted about the stage. Pink Floyd (one of Brown's psychedelic contemporaries at the UFO Club) began the '70s touring with police lights mounted on its amplifiers (and such equally modest devices) and progressed over the course of the decade to stadium shows—like the one in 1977 for the album *Animals*—that included gigantic, inflated barnyard denizens hovering above the crowd.

As the technology of stage shows evolved, so did the shows themselves. The development of computerized lighting systems, sophisticated time-delayed sound, and gigantic video screens all contributed to the possibilities of live performance.

The trend became so pervasive that almost all acts at the arena and stadium level were forced to contrive vast stage shows in which music was often but an extra, albeit important, part. The classic hits of the Rolling Stones—and the Stones themselves—were dwarfed by a 300-foot stage set that was the central focus of its Steel Wheels tour of 1989. In 1992, U2's Zoo TV tour came with a mobile television studio (replete with satellite uplinks) that beamed video images to scores of television monitors that littered the stage (which was flanked by several East German Trabant automobiles suspended above the group).

TOP ALBUM

THE CRAZY WORLD OF ARTHUR BROWN (Track, '68, 7)

TOP SONG

FIRE (Atlantic, '68, 2)

While an argument could be made for the expressive value of such productions, the bottom line from a musical standpoint was that rock acts and their songs were becoming increasingly dominated by the productions that were ostensibly contrived to support them.

Rock shows were giving way to rock spectacles.

While all of this would probably have occurred without the Crazy World of Arthur Brown—the march of technology and rockers' desire to amaze and astound their fans being unstoppable—the group did open up the expressive possibilities of visuals and theatrics to the world of the rock show. That world became crazier and crazier because of it.

CREAM

When drummer Ginger Baker recruited guitarist Eric Clapton and bassist Jack Bruce to form a group in June of 1966, the trio named themselves Cream. It was an arrogant choice, to be sure, but one that proved to be entirely on the mark.

In the course of its brief career, Cream became one of rock and roll's finest and most important groups. It was revolutionary in the truest sense, in that it changed the course of rock, doing so with its unparalleled virtuosity; with its innovations in composition, vocal harmony, and performance practice; and in its redefinition of the roles of guitarist, bassist, and drummer.

It virtually created a new category of rock group —the power trio—that served as a model for scores of imitators (the first, and most important, being the Jimi Hendrix Experience). Its high-decibeled sound and riff-based songs would be cornerstones in the development of heavy metal. And its extended, onstage improvisations would inaugurate an era in which every group worth its weight in Marshall amplifiers would began to engage in instrumental "jams."

Initially, with their painted guitars and drums, bouffant hairdos, and flashy, frilly attire, Clapton (b. Eric Patrick Clapp, Mar. 30, 1945, Ripley, Surrey, England), Baker (b. Peter Baker, Aug. 19, 1939, Lewisham, London), and Bruce (b. John Bruce, May

14, 1943, Glasgow, Scotland) became heroes and symbols of the psychedelic movement. When that image was coupled with the group's enormous commercial success as a recording and touring act, particularly in the U.S., it also had an impact on the rock culture at large. Cream was one of the first rock acts to cross over from the burgeoning '60s underground scene to the pop public as a whole.

Central to the creative method and purpose of Cream was the fact that there wasn't a center. While Clapton had become "God" in England through his epochal work with John Mayall's Bluesbreakers— and thus could have been perceived as the group's leader or focal point—he was, in fact, but one co-equal contributor to the group's sound. Just as he would become the defining virtuoso on his instrument, Baker and Bruce would be the same on theirs—all through their efforts with Cream.

On record, the group blended rock, pop, R&B, and jazz derivations into a wholly new form. Songs such as "I Feel Free" and "Sleepy Time Time" from the group's debut album, *Fresh Cream*, came with jazz-tinged vocal harmonies that were unheard of at the time. Clapton's guitar figures slid through and about those harmonies with solos that amounted to a virtual revamping of traditional blues phrasings (which he had previously revolutionized during his days with the Bluesbreakers). Similarly the traditional rock roles of drums and bass were obliterated by the combined work of Baker and Bruce. Not content to serve as a mere rhythm section to Clapton's solos, they literally elevated their instruments to co-lead status, during solos as well as in the songs themselves.

To make matters even more intriguing, they accomplished this in an instrumental as well as compositional context. Thus, in a song such as the group's signature 1968 hit, "Sunshine of Your Love," Baker's drum breaks during the refrain were almost mini-solos (backing the vocals of Bruce and Clapton) but were so distinctive that they became compositional hooks in and of themselves.

Other groups had hinted at such an instrumental collaboration, most notably the Who. They had first suggested the possibility on songs such as "My Generation" in 1965, in which John Entwistle played the song's lead on his bass guitar.

But Cream was the first to make that possibility a reality. In a rock context—actually in any context—Clapton, Baker, and Bruce were masters of the technical aspects of their instruments. They extended that mastery in various ways, Clapton with his speeded up, lyrical articulations of blues forms; Baker with his rock reinterpretations of the complex polyrhythms of African drumming; and Bruce with bass lines that ranged from the angular phrasings of jazz and the blue-note slurs of the blues to rolling, contrapuntal lines that were similar to those of the baroque master, Bach.

When all of this was combined with riff-based songs that were tempered by a pop sense of melody and form, the result was a sound that was a culmination of the efforts of various preceeding British rock groups, including the Who, the Yardbirds, and others.

Cream also revolutionized rock performance. Borrowing the improvisational methods of jazz musicians, Clapton, Bruce, and Baker reworked the

---

TOP ALBUMS

FRESH CREAM (Atco, '67, 39)
DISRAELI GEARS (Atco, '67, 4)
WHEELS OF FIRE (Atco, '68, 1)
GOODBYE (Atco, '69, 2)
BEST OF CREAM (Atco, '69, 3)
LIVE CREAM (Atco, '70, 15)
LIVE CREAM—VOLUME II
   (Atco, '72, 27)

TOP SONGS

SUNSHINE OF YOUR LOVE
   (Atco, '68, 5)
WHITE ROOM (Atco, '68, 6)
CROSSROADS (Atco, '69, 28)

---

songs from their records, extending them to unprecedented lengths with combined solo sections that lasted 10 to 15 minutes and longer. On such songs as its onstage rendition of the Willie Dixon classic "Spoonful," the group worked its way into dense, turbulent improvisations in which Clapton, Baker, and Bruce engaged in complex interactions of solos and rhythms. "Solos" is perhaps misleading, because, in the jazz tradition, the musicians traded musical ideas, devising new and ancillary motifs that evolved and splintered, finally giving way to the original song.

Some critics of the time, and some later ones, dismissed the group's solo sections as self-indulgent and long-winded. Others extolled their virtuosity. In either case, with these improvisations, as it did in so many other ways, Cream opened a new frontier of expression in rock.

By the time Baker formed the group in June of 1966, the three members of Cream had become leading figures on the burgeoning R&B scene in London. He and Bruce had previously worked together in Alexis Korner's Blues Incorporated in 1963 and the Graham Bond Organization in 1964. And Bruce and Clapton had played in John Mayall's Bluesbreakers in 1965. Bruce had also been a member of Manfred Mann, and Clapton had been a member of the Yardbirds.

Because of their visibility on the R&B scene, their teaming up in Cream was depicted as a sort of musical summit; in various histories of rock they have been referred to as the first "supergroup." In Cream's case, the title was premature, the three members being relatively unknown to the vast rock public. The first real supergroup wouldn't emerge until 1969, when Clapton, Baker, and Steve Winwood (of Traffic)—by then world-famous musicians—formed Blind Faith.

But the formation of Cream was considered something of a musical event at the time. And when the group made its debut at the sixth annual Jazz and Blues Festival in Windsor, in July, it was an immediate hit. The trio went into the studio and recorded its first single, "Wrapping Paper," which was released in November. The song, like many Cream originals, was written by Bruce and lyricist Pete Brown. It was a fairly subdued effort and reached number 34 on the U.K. charts.

With the release of the album *Fresh Cream* in January 1967, the band began to emerge as an artistic and commercial force on the British pop scene. With its instrumental virtuosity, Bruce's emotional vocals, and a revolutionary drum solo by Baker on the song "Toad," the album established the group as one of the leaders of British rock. The album went to number six on the U.K. charts, and its single, "I Feel Free" hit number 11.

The rest of the year saw the consolidation of Cream's stature in England and its emergence as a major draw in the U.S. In March, the group made its U.S. debut, performing as part of disc jockey Murray the K's legendary week-long "Music in the Fifth Dimension" shows at the RKO Theatre in New York (where the Who also made its U.S. debut). Cream toured in the U.K. during the year, appearing as one of the star acts at the seventh annual Jazz and Blues Festival in Windsor. It also toured the U.S. twice, including a fabled performance at the Fillmore West in San Francisco (that was recorded and would yield the live portion of the group's third album, *Wheels of Fire*).

At the end of 1967, the album *Disraeli Gears* was released. Less free-flowing than its predecessor, with a sleeker, more sophisticated sound (via the work of producer Felix Papallardi), the album marked the group's entry into the top levels of rock stardom. Its single, "Sunshine of Your Love," would eventually make number five in the U.S., selling over one million copies, and the album itself would peak at number four. (The album was also notable for its introduction of the wah-wah guitar pedal in rock, used by Clapton on the song "Tales of Brave Ulysses.")

But it was *Wheels of Fire*, released in August of 1968, that truly secured the group's place in rock history. A double-album set, *Wheels of Fire* was divided into studio and concert records, both of which were smashing displays of Cream's mastery of rock. The studio disc came with the hit single "White Room," which went to number six in the U.S. Other high points included the intricate rhythmic interplays of "Politician"; a sublime Clapton solo on the slow blues "Sitting on Top of the World"; Bruce's cello work on "As You Said"; and a classic rendition of the Booker T. Jones warhorse, "Born Under a Bad Sign."

Cream

The live record of *Wheels of Fire* became legendary for its musical wizardry and improvisational grandeur. Clapton's solo on the blues classic "Crossroads" was a tour de force of technique and invention: it is, arguably, the finest solo in the history of rock guitar. Similarly, on his extended solo on "Toad," Baker virtually created a new lexicon of rock drumming with his signature double-bass rhythms on a nearly 15-minute barrage that launched a thousand drum solos—by other and lesser drummers—in the years that followed. Bruce had his moment, storming through a version of "Traintime" on his harmonica, while the tireless Baker smashed against his vocal and harp outbursts with a complex set of cross rhythms.

Wheels of Fire topped the U.S. charts for four weeks in August 1968. It was one of the finest—and pivotal—albums in the history of rock and roll.

But at the very moment when Cream was reaching its artistic apex, it began to break apart. Baker

and Bruce, who had reportedly had an acrimonious relationship during their time with the Bond Organization, began to bicker once again. By the time the group began a U.S. tour in October of 1968, it had already decided to disband. The "farewell" tour—and the group itself—came to an end with a final performance in November at London's Royal Albert Hall. The performance was filmed and was released as the concert-documentary *Farewell Cream* in 1969.

A studio album, *Goodbye,* was released in March 1969. A single-record condensation of the *Wheels of Fire* format, with studio and live cuts, it was mostly a rather disappointing record that illustrated the musical ennui into which the group had descended toward the end. It did yield, however, the memorable song "Badge," which came with yet another classic guitar solo from Clapton (backed by George Harrison recording under the pseudonym L'Angelo Mysterioso).

At the start of 1969, Clapton and Baker formed the group Blind Faith with Traffic's Steve Winwood and bassist Rick Grech of Family, which did indeed become the rock's first supergroup. Clapton would subsequently form the group Derek and the Dominos before pursuing a vastly successful if musically wandering solo career. Baker formed Air Force and, later, the Baker-Gurvitz Army before retreating from the scene to found a studio in Nigeria. He reemerged in the '80s with a solo career and in 1992 joined the Cream-based metal group Masters of Reality. Bruce pursued a long, distinguished and commercially negligible solo career.

Significantly, none of their later efforts approached the power and grandeur of their work with Cream.

In January 1993, the three re-formed for a performance of "Crossroads," "Born Under a Bad Sign," and "Politician" at their induction into the Rock and Roll Hall of Fame.

CREEDENCE CLEARWATER REVIVAL

After nine years of toiling in the trenches—under various names and with various musical approaches—Creedence Clearwater Revival emerged on the rock scene in 1968 with its "swamp rock" sound.

In fact, swamp rock wasn't as much a distinct, definable sound as it was a hook on which the group, its record company, and the press could hang a description of its basic, potboiling version of straightahead rock and roll.

Not that that was necessarily bad, or misleading. CCR came along at a time when rock and roll was scaling back from the excesses of the 1960s, particularly those of the psychedelic era. With its guitar-driven songs, basic beats, and leader John Fogerty's growling vocals, the group was one of the most visible exponents of rock and roll's back-to-the-roots movement.

When the Bay Area–based group's rendition of Dale Hawkins's "Suzie Q" was released in June 1968, its brittle, wiry sound proved a tonic for rock ears that had been deluged with the aural imagery and sound of psychedelia and overwhelmed by the virtuosic displays of groups like Cream and the Jimi Hendrix Experience.

The members of CCR were, at best, competent on their instruments. Fogerty's vocals had a certain passion, but modest range, and his guitar solos (which consumed most of the two-sided "Suzie Q" single) were bare of pyrotechnics. His brother, Tom, was a negligible rhythm guitarist. And bassist Stu Cook and drummer Doug Clifford maintained a steady, if uninspired, rhythmic background.

But as a whole, CCR's sound was sturdy and had a strut and attitude that were at the core of traditional rock and roll.

It was a sound whose time had come—again. Over the course of the next few years, CCR would become one of the most successful groups in rock, and its basic approach would inspire countless imitators.

The group was formed in the Bay Area suburb of El Cerrito in 1959, when John Fogerty (b. May 28, 1945, Berkeley, California), Cook (b. Apr. 25, 1945, Oakland, California), and Clifford (b. Apr. 24, 1945, Palo Alto, California) teamed up in junior high school. That same year, Fogerty's brother Tom (b. Nov. 9, 1941, Berkeley) also joined the group as guitarist and co-lead vocalist.

By 1963, the group was performing on the local scene as Tommy Fogerty and the Blue Velvets. The next year, the group sent an instrumental demo to the Berkeley-based Fantasy label. The group was signed, but at the urging of the label's Hy Weiss, it began to present itself as a "beat group" based on the British Invasion model. It updated its name to the Visions.

It was not to last. When Fantasy released the group's debut single, "Don't Tell Me No Lies," in November 1964, Weiss listed its name as the Golliwogs, supposedly to make it sound more British. The group disliked the new name but went along. It was not the last disagreement the group would have with Fantasy.

Over the succeeding three years, the group released several singles, none of which created a stir. The group was also forced to disband temporarily when John Fogerty and Clifford were drafted in 1966.

But with their return in 1967, the group reunited with a new sense of musical direction and purpose.

Creedence Clearwater Revival

The name was changed again, this time to Creedence Clearwater Revival—Creedence coming from the name of a friend, Clearwater from a beer commercial, and Revival being self-explanatory.

A demo of "Suzie Q" was released to local radio stations in 1968. The response was such that the new head of Fantasy, Saul Zaentz, decided to release it as a single. It was an immediate hit, reaching number 11 on the *Billboard* charts. At the same time, the group's eponymous debut album made it to number 52 and ended up staying on the charts for a very impressive 17 months.

The swamp rock style truly kicked in with the group's 1969 hit "Proud Mary." A boiling rocker with traces of Cajun vocal harmonies and a story line that depicted life on a Mississippi riverboat, the song hit number two on the *Billboard* charts, selling more than one million copies. It would become a rock standard that would be covered by various artists, including Solomon Burke, Sonny Charles & the Checkmates Ltd., and even Elvis Presley. In

1971, Ike and Tina Turner would have a million-selling hit with their version of the song.

CCR then began a lengthy run on the charts that would continue almost to the end of its career, in 1972. Following "Proud Mary," the group's singles "Bad Moon Rising" and "Green River" also hit number two in 1969.

In 1970, chart success continued apace, with the R&B-tinged single "Down on the Corner" reaching number three and its B side, "Fortunate Son," hitting number 14. The double-sided single format worked again when Travelin' Band" b/w "Who'll Stop the Rain" scaled the pop lists, the A side hitting number two and the B side number 13. Subsequent singles were also hits, including "Up Around the Bend," which reached number four in 1970, and "Have You Ever Seen the Rain," which made number eight in 1971. The group's final top 10 hit came with "Sweet Hitch-Hiker," reaching number six in 1971.

Along the way, CCR's albums were equally successful, most selling in excess of one million copies.

The group's second album, *Bayou Country*—replete with swamp rock imagery—went to number seven in 1969. Its successor, *Green River,* topped the U.S. charts for four weeks that same year. In 1970, the album *Willy and the Poorboys* went to number three, and its successor, *Cosmo's Factory,* stayed at Number One for nine weeks.

CCR's stage act was as simple and affecting as its records. The group performed with all the energy and exuberance of the rock masters of the 1950s. It was also one of the biggest concert draws of the time. The group became a staple of the burgeoning

---

TOP ALBUMS

GREEN RIVER (Fantasy, '69, *1*)
WILLY AND THE POORBOYS (Fantasy, '69, *3*)
COSMO'S FACTORY (Fantasy, '70, *1*)

Additional Top 40 Albums: 4

TOP SONGS

PROUD MARY (Fantasy, '69, *2*)
BAD MOON RISING (Fantasy, '69, *2*)
GREEN RIVER (Fantasy, '69, *2*)
DOWN ON THE CORNER (Fantasy, '69, *3*)
TRAVELIN' BAND (Fantasy, '70, *2*)
UP AROUND THE BEND (Fantasy, '70, *4*)
LOOKIN' OUT MY BACK DOOR (Fantasy, '70, *2*)

Additional Top 40 Songs: 6

---

festival scene, performing at pop festivals in Newport, California, Denver, and Atlanta in 1969. It also toured Europe to success and acclaim in 1970.

But its chart and concert success notwithstanding, dissension was surfacing in the group. This was due primarily to John Fogerty's dominance of the group's music; he wrote most of the songs and produced the group's records. At the start of 1971, Tom Fogerty left to spend time with his family and pursue a solo career. His work with the group was included on the subsequent album *Pendulum,* which reached number five on the charts. CCR continued on as a trio.

But by 1972, Cook and Clifford were also demanding more input on the group's music. The result—Fogerty's Revenge, as it came to be called—was the album *Mardi Gras,* released in May 1972. Fogerty ceded much of the creative control of the album to his bandmates, and it proved to be a thorough disaster. While the album reached number 12,

mostly based on CCR's previous reputation, it was a dreary and directionless musical effort. The group disbanded in October 1972.

With the exception of John Fogerty, the members of the group would never come close to repeating the success they had enjoyed with CCR. The debut album by Tom Fogerty was released in June 1972 and promptly languished on the charts; his solo career would prove to be equally disappointing. The same could be said of Clifford and Cook, who recorded from time to time as a rhythm section with various artists before joining the Don Harrison Band in 1976.

John Fogerty's solo career began on an odd note. He commenced work on a new sound that came with bluegrass and country facets, which he attributed to the group the Blue Ridge Rangers. In fact, the "group" was nothing of the sort; Fogerty produced its eponymous 1973 album, wrote the songs, and performed and sang all the parts.

His eponymous debut solo album was released in 1975 and yielded the minor hit "Rockin' All Over the World," which reached chart number 25. But when his subsequent album was pulled from release in 1976, he retreated from the scene for the next nine years, during which he would have an extended creative block.

But he had a successful comeback in 1985 when his album *Centerfield* topped the U.S. charts and sold more than one million copies. The album included the hits "The Old Man Down the Road," which went to number 10, and "Rock and Roll Girls," which hit number 20.

The album also included the song "Zaentz Kan't Dance," a purported lyrical slap at Fantasy head Zaentz, with whom Fogerty had had several disputes about the group's finances. Zaentz responded with a lawsuit that became a test case about copyright infringement; the song was alleged to have borrowed a motif from Fogerty's old "Run Through the Jungle" CCR hit, the rights to which Zaentz owned. In effect, Fogerty was being sued for plagarizing himself. The case would consume much of Fogerty's time and money, although he won the case in 1988.

The success of *Centerfield* was not duplicated on Fogerty's 1986 album *Eye of the Zombie,* which peaked at number 26. But Fogerty continued to be active on the scene, performing at various all-star concerts.

On September 6, 1990, Tom Fogerty died of respiratory failure in Arizona.

CROSBY, STILLS AND NASH

As the 1960s drew
to a close, rock began to move in polar directions.

At one end was a more rock-oriented contingent made up of the back-to-basics movement and the emerging heavy metal scene. At the other was a folk-inflected, semi-acoustic movement that would give rise to the singer-songwriters at the start of the '70s and to the soft rock movement of Fleetwood Mac and others later in the decade.

Leading the way in the latter direction was Crosby, Stills and Nash.

One of the first "supergroup" collaborations in rock, the original trio was made up of David Crosby of the Byrds, Stephen Stills of Buffalo Springfield, and Graham Nash of the British beat group the Hollies. They would later be joined by Neil Young, who also came from Buffalo Springfield.

Over the course of an on-again, off-again career that spanned 25 years, the group's collaboration would yield some of the finest songs and vocal performances of the rock era.

And it was a collaboration in the truest sense. From the start, the group wasn't as much an ensemble like the supergroup Blind Faith as it was a meeting ground and sounding board for its individual members, each of whom brought a singular sensibility to the mix. Crosby wrote songs that were dense, emotionally charged, and folk-based. Stills was more rock oriented, churning out R&B-flavored songs and propelling the sound with his blues and country-tinged guitar solos. Nash contributed a more accessible, pop-oriented approach and lyrics that often came with political and social overtones. And Young was an idiosyncratic presence whose music, vocals, and guitar work gave the group an edge and passion that counterbalanced its softer, more sensitive tendencies.

While these musical differences made for a flourishing collaboration over the years, they also figured in the many conflicts that beset the group during its career. In fact, the recurring breakups, reunions,

bickering, and on- and offstage arguing became a part of the lore of CSN&Y. During one noted reunion attempt in January of 1975, Young reportedly quit the group in the middle of a recording session when Nash and Crosby began arguing over one note of a vocal harmony.

Ironically, such harmonies were at the very core of CSN&Y. On nearly all of its songs, the quartet's sound was defined by the remarkable, luminous vocal harmonies it created. These harmonies, which were often richly textured and delivered with an almost telepathic articulation, gave the music a coherence and uniqueness that were breathtaking.

It was those harmonies that, as the members have recounted it, brought the group together initially.

In June of 1969, Crosby (b. David Van Cortland, Aug. 14, 1941, Los Angeles) and Nash (b. Feb. 2, 1942, Blackpool, England) visited Stills (b. Jan. 3, 1945, Dallas, Texas) at his home in Laurel Canyon. The three decided to "jam" awhile and were immediately struck by the improvised vocal harmonies they were creating. Over the next several months, they began to write songs and rehearse on an informal basis in Los Angeles and London while various contractual problems arising from their former groups and record labels were resolved.

In June of 1968, Crosby, Stills and Nash released their eponymous debut album, which became an immediate hit, eventually selling more than two million copies and reaching number two on the charts (where it would reside for more than two years). The trio's first single, "Marrakesh Express," a pop-flavored romp in the Hollies mode, was also a hit in August, making number 28; "Suite: Judy Blue Eyes," a folkish air with a boisterous Latin refrain (which Stills had written for girlfriend Judy Collins), reached number 21 in November.

Within a month of the album's release, CS&N became CSN&Y with the addition of Young (b.

Nov. 12, 1945, Toronto, Canada). In June, the group made its stage debut at the Fillmore East in New York and was one of the high points of the Woodstock Festival in August. They then began a tour of the U.S., and at the end of the year took part in the Rolling Stones' ill-fated show at the Altamont Speedway in Northern California, which was marred by the stabbing death of a fan.

As 1970 unfolded, the group entered its most successful phase, musically and commercially. In March, it won a Grammy Award for Best New Artist. In May, its rendition of Joni Mitchell's "Woodstock" became its biggest hit, reaching number 11. That same month, CSN&Y's debut album, *Déjà Vu,* sold more than a million copies in one week and topped the charts. It would become one of the classic albums in the history of rock.

In June, Young—furious about the killings at Kent State—wrote "Ohio" in one night, and the group recorded it the next day. Released a week later, it would eventually hit number 14. With Young's scathing, impassioned vocals and slashing guitar, the song became a musical symbol of the torturous Vietnam era.

At the same time, Nash's winsome ballad "Teach Your Children" was also released, rising to number 16 on the charts; in August, that song and "Ohio" were in the top 20 in the same week.

But the individual inclinations that propelled the group also began to divide it. In August, Young quit because of musical and personal differences with the other three. The quartet's final single, Nash's "Our House," was released in October and peaked at number 30.

The other members began to pursue projects of their own, soon proving their individual popularity and creative abilities. In December, Stills released his eponymous debut solo album, an extraordinary record (featuring Eric Clapton, Jimi Hendrix, and others) that charted at number three. In May of 1971, Young's equally remarkable *After the Gold Rush* made number eight and was one of the seminal albums in the singer-songwriter movement. Both came to be considered minor rock classics.

Crosby and Nash were busy as well. In May 1971, Crosby's *If Only I Could Remember My Name* hit number 12; and in July, Nash's debut album, *Songs for Beginners,* reached number 15.

Nash was also the force behind the CSN&Y live compilation album *4 Way Street,* which topped the charts in May and sold more than one million copies.

Over the succeeding two decades, the members would record and tour in various configurations and

TOP ALBUMS

CROSBY, STILLS & NASH (Atlantic, '69, 6)
DÉJÀ VU (Crosby, Stills, Nash & Young, Atlantic, '70, 1)
4 WAY STREET (Crosby, Stills, Nash & Young, Atlantic, '71, 1)
SO FAR (Crosby, Stills, Nash & Young, Atlantic, '74, 1)
CSN (Atlantic, '77, 2)
DAYLIGHT AGAIN (Atlantic, '82, 8)
AMERICAN DREAM (Atlantic, '88, 16)

TOP SONGS

Just a Song Before I Go (Atlantic, '77, 7)
Wasted on the Way (Atlantic, '82, 9)

Additional Top 40 Songs: 6

would unite as a group from time to time. In 1972, the album *Graham Nash/David Crosby* hit number four; in 1976, the Stills/Young Band recorded the album *Long May You Run,* reaching number 26 and selling 500,000 copies.

Myriad combinations of the group surfaced over the years, formally and informally. In 1973, Crosby, Nash, and Young dropped by a performance of Stills's band Manassas at the Winterland ballroom in San Francisco, and a one-hour CSN&Y set ensued. In 1974, the group formally reunited for a sold-out tour of the U.S. That same year, Nash compiled the group's greatest hits on *So Far,* which became CSN&Y's third Number One album. But work on a new CSN&Y recording was halted in 1975 when Young abruptly walked out of the project.

In March of 1977, the original trio re-formed, and its album of new songs, *CSN,* made number two on the charts; the band toured during the year then disbanded. They teamed up again in 1979 for a one-off performance at the MUSE (Musicians United for Safe Energy) concert at New York's Madison Square Garden, captured in the 1980 documentary *No Nukes.* In 1982, the trio recorded another album of new songs, *Daylight Again,* which hit number 8 and sold more than one million copies.

Their activities as a group were curtailed during the mid-1980s because of Crosby's repeated skirmishes with the law on drugs and weapons offenses. He was convicted by a court in Dallas, Texas, in 1983 and served time in the state prison in 1986. But in 1988, Crosby, Stills, Nash, and Young reunited for the album *American Dream,* a potent set of new songs that made number 16. In 1990, CS&N released the new album *Live It Up,* attaining a peak of number 57.

The group performed together several times at Young's annual Bridge School shows in northern California. At one of those, in 1990, the group seemed to magically recreate the sound of its halcyon days, with its timeless harmonies arching and gliding over a capacity crowd of the group's fans.

"It doesn't get much better than this," an ebullient Crosby said from the stage. When Crosby, Stills, Nash, and Young were able to put aside their differences and make music, it didn't.

Crosby, Stills and Nash

BO DIDDLEY

One of the most influential guitarists, vocalists, and songwriters in rock—and one of the music's founding fathers—Bo Diddley was, all that aside, best known for the beat that bears his name.

The "Bo Diddley beat" was a stomping, primal pounding of drums and guitar that propelled his signature songs in the 1950s and '60s. From his debut record, "Bo Diddley," of 1955 through "Who Do You Love" of 1956 and "Mona (I Need You Baby)" of 1964, the beat was the core of his musical onslaught. It set him apart from other rockers of his time, just as it provided the inspiration for scores of artists throughout rock history.

When the Rolling Stones reworked the Buddy Holly song "Not Fade Away"—which would become their first major hit in 1963—they used the beat as the basis of the record. The beat would also figure prominently in the onstage "jams" of everyone from the Yardbirds to Quicksilver Messenger Service and Bruce Springsteen. It became as much a part of rock's lexicon as Presley's vocal grunts and Berry's two-note guitar licks. Simply stated, it was one of the building blocks of rock and roll.

But there was more to Diddley's music than the beat. Diddley's primal energy and sound, his slashing guitar chords, and his witty, earthy songs were all part of a musical bridge from the blues of the Chicago masters of the 1940s and '50s to rock itself. His gruff, exuberant vocals seemed to come straight from the mists of the Mississippi Delta, the birthplace of the rural blues (and Diddley himself), just as his songs reveled in the bluesman's joy of life and love. But what truly separated Diddley from the blues, and made him an epochal rocker in the process, was the way in which he energized blues vocals and guitar figures, via his beat, and transformed them into a wholly new musical language.

On many of his songs, Diddley transferred the sexual intensity of the blues to a rock context, endowing rock with a power and worldliness that few of his contemporaries could equal, much less surpass. While rockers like Berry, Little Richard, Jerry Lee Lewis, Buddy Holly, and the Everly Brothers all brought their own musical personalities to the bubbling rock brew of the 1950s, Diddley gave the music the feel and substance of the blues.

Perhaps that is why his music would play such a crucial role in the subsequent development of rock. His songs would serve, along with Berry's, as a cornerstone of the British beat groups that would revolutionize rock in the 1960s. In Diddley's case, those groups idolized him not on a rock level (as they would with Berry and the others) but more from the standpoint of the bluesman whom they saw as one of their musical forefathers.

Which was as it should have been, given Diddley's background. Diddley (b. Otha Ellis Bates, Dec. 28, 1928, McComb, Mississippi—later changing his surname to McDaniel when he was adopted by his mother's first cousin, Gussie McDaniel) was part of the musical generation that made its way from the rural South to Chicago. In his case, he did it not as a man seeking his musical fortune (like Muddy Waters and others) but in his childhood. Growing up on the south side of Chicago, he cut his teeth on the blues that Waters and others were transforming from a rural to an urban form.

For a time, in his youth, he performed on street corners with the Hipsters, a group that included such future sidemen as drummer Frank Kirkland and maracas player Jerome Green. Playing a guitar his sister had given to him, Diddley graduated from the streets to the 708 Club in 1951 and began making his name on the scene. Along the way, he worked as

Bo Diddley

a construction worker and trained as a Golden Gloves boxer (which yielded the nickname Bo).

In 1955, with Kirkland, Green, Lester Davenport on harmonica, and bluesman Otis Spann on piano, he cut a demo of "Bo Diddley," "I'm a Man," and "You Don't Love Me." Signed to Checker Records, a subsidiary of the legendary Chess label, Diddley became an immediate hit when the double A-sided single "Bo Diddley" b/w "I'm a Man" was released and went to number two on the R&B charts.

With that hit behind him, Diddley began to emerge on the R&B and rock scenes that were coalescing at the time. Later in 1955, he performed at the Apollo Theatre in Harlem and on "The Ed Sullivan Show."

But while a number of his counterparts on that scene, like Berry, would make the quantum leap fully into rock, Diddley would maintain a presence primarily in R&B, flirting with broad pop success but never achieving it to any great extent. His 1956 single "Who Do You Love"—one of the classics of rock and roll—failed to chart. And he didn't have a record on the pop charts until 1959, when "Crackin' Up" hit number 62 and "Say Man" (a novelty song of sorts that came with "the beat" and some jive banter between Diddley and Green) made number 20.

Similarly, songs such as 1960's "Roadrunner" and 1962's "You Can't Judge a Book by Its Cover" were marginal hits, the former hitting a modest number 75 and the latter number 48.

But as is the case sometimes in rock, the ultimate impact of these songs proved to be wholly disproportionate to their standing on the charts.

Their importance—and that of Diddley himself—was acknowledged during a tour on which he performed in England in 1963. The stars of the tour were the Everly Brothers, backed by Diddley and the Rolling Stones (who reportedly declined to perform their trademark renditions of his songs as a show of respect). Significantly, while the Everlys headlined that tour, Diddley was invited to perform at London's R&B club, the Scene.

TOP ALBUMS

HAVE GUITAR WILL TRAVEL
(Chess, '62)
BO DIDDLEY IS A GUNSLINGER
(Chess/Pye, '63)
TWO GREAT GUITARS
(with Chuck Berry, Pye, '64)

TOP SONGS

BO DIDDLEY/I'M A MAN
(Checker, '55)
WHO DO YOU LOVE (Checker, '59)
CRACKIN' UP (Checker, '59)
SAY MAN (Checker, '59, 20)
ROAD RUNNER (Checker, '60)
YOU CAN'T JUDGE A BOOK BY ITS
COVER (Checker, '62)
OOH BABY (Checker, '67)

As the '60s unfolded, Diddley's career reverted to its R&B base. While a presence on the pop charts in the U.K., where albums like *Bo Diddley Is a Gunslinger* made number 20 in 1963, Diddley was largely neglected by the rock masses in his own country. In 1968, "Ooh Baby" reached number 88 on the U.S. charts; it was his first chart single since 1962, and it would be his last.

But the records—good ones, at that—continued nonetheless. He released the album *Two Great Guitars* in 1964, which included inspired duets with Chuck Berry. And in 1968, Diddley recorded the remarkable *Super Blues Band* with Muddy Waters and Little Walter. Along the way, there were notable performances such those at 1965's TNT Awards show and 1969's "Rock 'n' Roll Revival" concert in Toronto.

Other albums were less successful, musically. 1971's *Another Dimension* was a misguided effort to update Diddley's classic sound. And 1973's *The London Bo Diddley Sessions* (with a host of British musicians) was a notably lackluster effort.

But these albums, and his inability to score with the broad pop masses, did nothing to dim Diddley's status in rock. Younger musicians continually made a point of expressing their respect for him and his music. When the Clash began their debut tour of the U.S. in 1979, they rather pointedly invited Diddley to open for them at their shows. And the Rolling Stones' Ron Wood collaborated with Diddley on the one-off group the Gunslingers in 1987, which yielded the album *Live at the Ritz*.

In January of that year, Diddley received his official recognition as a leading member of his musical generation when he was inducted into the Rock and Roll Hall of Fame.

Ironically, a similar recognition by the culture at large came not via music, as it should have, but by a television commercial for Nike that was first broadcast during baseball's all-star game in 1990. The commercial, in which Diddley told baseball/football star Bo Jackson, "You don't know Diddley," made Diddley a household name to the non-musical U.S. public—as he had been in rock all along.

DION AND THE BELMONTS

While rock and roll's roots sprang from the blues of the Mississippi Delta and the country music and rockabilly of the southeastern mountains, the music also came from the more urban sounds of black and white teenagers who harmonized on the streets of the big cities.

In the 1950s, these groups began to create a style of music that would come to be called doo wop. With its sweet melodies and lyrics that were pimply paeans to teen love—usually rendered in rolling, four-part vocal harmonies that came without instrumental backing—doo wop would have a formative impact on much of the rock of its day and on generations of rockers to come.

One of the most popular doo wop groups, and the one that would come to symbolize the genre, was Dion and the Belmonts.

With its signature 1959 hit "A Teenager in Love," the group established the form as a major force in '50s rock and roll. The song was a winning combination of rock energy, youthful yearnings, and theme lines that were firmly in the pop tradition of the Brill Building songwriters of New York. It was a sound that would be imitated by various groups in the 1950s and would provide inspiration for the next generation of rockers that would emerge from England in the '60s; significantly, Dion would be one of two vocalists to be pictured along with the Beatles on the cover of their 1967 masterpiece, *Sgt. Pepper's Lonely Hearts Club Band* (the other being Bob Dylan).

Dion DiMucci (b. July 18, 1939, Bronx, New York) had pursued a singing career at the start of the 1950s, making his debut on Paul Whiteman's "Teen Club" television program in 1951. He later released the single "The Chosen Few" with the Timberlanes in 1957. But tiring of performing and recording with vocalists hired on a one-off basis, he decided to recruit a group from his neighborhood in the Bronx.

The new group, the Belmonts, was made up of tenor Fred Milano (b. Aug. 26, 1940, Bronx), bass vocalist Carlo Mastrangelo (b. Oct. 5, 1939, Bronx), and tenor Angelo D'Aleo (b. Feb. 3, 1941, Bronx), all of whom joined DiMucci in 1957.

The group's name came from Belmont Avenue in the Bronx, an area that would figure prominently in its musical persona. As legend would have it, the Belmonts began to rehearse their songs on the 6th Avenue D train to Manhattan.

Dion and the Belmonts recorded two singles for Mohawk Records in 1958, neither of which proved to be successful. But when the group switched to a new label, Laurie, it hit the charts in June with the single "I Wonder Why," which reached number 22. Later that year, the group performed on "The Biggest Show of Stars for 1958," a tour that included such pop and rock idols as Buddy Holly and the Crickets, Frankie Avalon, Bobby Freeman, and Bobby Darin. And "No One Knows," its next single, hit number 19 in October.

The group was also a part of the ill-fated "Winter Dance Party" tour in January of 1959, which was marred by the deaths of Holly, Richie Valens, and the Big Bopper in an airplane crash.

But it was the release of "A Teenager in Love" in May 1959 that put Dion and the Belmonts—and doo wop—on the broad cultural map. Written by the songwriting team of Doc Pomus and Mort Shuman, the record hit number five and sold one million copies. The success of the record transformed the group into teen idols who would soon be on the covers of the teen fan magazines of the time.

But the group's career would be short-lived. In June 1959, D'Aleo was drafted into the navy. Performing as a trio, the group stormed into the '60s with the hit "Where or When," which sold one million copies and rose to number three. But its next two singles that year didn't make the top 10, and the group disbanded in October 1960, with DiMucci pursuing a solo career.

But during its brief reign on the charts, Dion and the Belmonts established the sound and image of doo wop that would become a part of rock history.

The genre itself had emerged earlier with groups

Dion and the Belmonts

like the Diamonds and the Silhouettes. The former had hit the charts in 1956 with the single "Why Do Fools Fall in Love" and in 1957 with "Little Darlin'." The latter had done the same in 1958 with "Get a Job." The Flamingos had also had a hit with "I Only Have Eyes for You" in 1959, which made the charts a month after Dion and the Belmonts' "A Teenager in Love." While these groups were arguably as musically accomplished as Dion and the Belmonts, it was the Belmonts who would fuse doo wop music with the teen idol persona that would put the genre across to the public at large.

Doo wop would continue to be a force on the charts into the '60s. The Chiffons would have major hits in 1963 with the doo wop–inflected pop songs "He's So Fine" and "One Fine Day." And Dion would record several hits during his ensuing solo career that would become signatures of the doo wop sound.

Those hits began in 1960, when Dion's solo debut single, "Lonely Teenager," was released in December and hit number 12. In 1961, his single "Havin' Fun" stalled on the charts at number 42, but that proved to be only a momentary setback.

In the succeeding two years, Dion recorded two of the finest songs—and biggest hits—of the doo wop era. In October 1961, the strutting rocker "Runaround Sue" topped the charts for two weeks and sold more than one million copies. In March 1962 he hit again with "The Wanderer," which reached number two and also exceeded one million units sold. Both songs were infused with the rolling harmonies and sound of his work with the Belmonts.

The group had re-formed without Dion and, for a time, enjoyed its own charting records. Its single "Tell Me Why" reached number 18 in 1961. And in 1962, "Come on Little Angel" made number 28. But they never equalled Dion's success.

"Runaround Sue" was the first in a line of singles he recorded with girls' names figuring in their titles. In 1962, "Little Diane" reached number eight, while his remake of the Drifters' 1955 hit "Ruby Baby" rose to number two and was another million-selling single in 1963 (this one recorded for his new label,

Columbia). That same year, his old label, Laurie, released his record "Sandy," which hit number 21. Later in 1963, he made the charts again with "Donna the Prima Donna" and "Drip Drop," both ranking at number two. With the latter record, Dion had scored a remarkable 18 Hot 100 hits in three years.

But Dion's career began to fade in 1964, exacerbated by a narcotics problem that would eventually force him to withdraw from the scene for several years. A 1967 reunion with the three original members of the Belmonts yielded the album *Together Again*, but it failed on the charts (he and the group would reunite again in 1972).

Dion made a comeback in 1968 with "Abraham, Martin and John." A musical tribute to Lincoln, King, and Kennedy, the song came with a new folk-rock sound that had little in common with his doo wop past. But it was a hit nonetheless, reaching number four.

But the comeback was fleeting, and Dion increasingly became a "golden oldie" whose early hits were loved and revered but whose new music didn't seem to have a place in contemporary rock. He continued to record over the years, including a 1973 album *Born to Be with You*, a collaboration with legendary producer Phil Spector. And in later years he recorded for the Christian label Dayspring. But his days as one of the preeminent hitmakers in rock were over.

The same could not be said for his influence. Dion and the Belmonts' sound would be a major source of inspiration for countless artists over the years. The Beatles drew much melodic inspiration from the group's songs; in 1968 they would pay tribute to the Belmonts with "Happiness Is a Warm Gun" from their self-titled (so-called White) album, with John Lennon crooning the refrain the way Dion had done it in the '50s. Other artists, like Billy Joel, would base songs on the doo wop sound that Dion and the Belmonts had pioneered and popularized.

In 1989, Dion was invited to perform on a track from Lou Reed's back to basics album, *New York*. That same year, Reed inducted Dion into the Rock and Roll Hall of Fame.

TOP SONGS

A TEENAGER IN LOVE
(Laurie, '59, 5)
WHERE OR WHEN (Laurie, '59, 3)

DION:

RUNAROUND SUE (Laurie, '61, 1)
THE WANDERER (Laurie, '61, 2)
LOVERS WHO WANDER
(Laurie, '62, 3)
LITTLE DIANE (Laurie, '62, 8)
RUBY BABY (Columbia, '63, 2)
DONNA THE PRIMA DONNA
(Columbia, '63, 6)
DRIP DROP (Columbia, '63, 6)
ABRAHAM, MARTIN AND JOHN
(Laurie, '68, 4)

FATS DOMINO

In the 1950s, at the dawn of the rock era, three figures emerged who would provide a crucial bridge between the new form of music and its forefathers in the blues and R&B worlds.

Chuck Berry brought to rock the wry and witty lyrical imagery and guitar phrasings of the urban and rural blues idioms; Bo Diddley provided his epochal "beat" and the sexual intensity of the blues; and Fats Domino imparted to rock the down-home sincerity and soul that was at the core of R&B.

While Berry and Diddley had a more direct influence on the sound of rock, with their distinctive musical signatures being imitated by countless rockers down the line, it was Domino who communicated the feel and the expressive tone of R&B to the rock world. While this feel was less definable or tangible than Diddley's beat or Berry's guitar chords, it was hardly less important in shaping the creative direction rock would subsequently pursue.

There was a warmth and humanity to Domino's music that was a perfect foil to the unabashed energy of his counterparts. With his rolling New Orleans piano chords and lugubrious, slurred vocals, Domino brought to rock and roll an earthiness that tempered the music's exuberant and youthful tendencies. On songs such as 1955's "Ain't That a Shame," 1956's "Blueberry Hill," and 1957's "I'm Walkin'," Domino performed with an expressive depth and weight that would guide and propel rock for decades to come.

Those songs and others were also crucial "crossovers" from the R&B to the rock scenes. Perhaps more than any other artist, it was Domino who cleared the way for R&B's entrance to the broad rock and pop culture at large. He did that with a remarkable series of hits that made him one of the most successful rock artists of the '50s. From 1955 to 1960, he had 10 songs that reached the top 10 of the *Billboard* charts, with scores of others reaching into the Hot 100. This success helped make Domino a seminal figure in rock history.

Domino (b. Antoine Domino, Feb. 26, 1928, New Orleans) was one of nine children in a family that was notably non-musical, given that seemingly everyone in New Orleans had some musical background or feeling. In his teen years, he was taught to play piano by his brother-in-law, Harrison Verrett, and began playing in local clubs. At the time, he was also employed in a bedmaking factory, where his musical career almost ended when he injured his hand on the job.

By 1949, he was performing for three dollars per week at the Hideaway Club in New Orleans with the Billy Diamond band when he was heard by producer and bandleader Dave Bartholomew. Bartholomew, also a talent scout for Imperial Records, immediately signed Domino to the label. The two began to rewrite the traditional blues song "Junker's Blues," turning it into an original called "The Fat Man" (based on Domino's nickname, Fats, which had been given him by Diamond). Released in 1950, it became a Number One hit on the R&B charts (it would sell over one million copies by 1953).

During the succeeding five years, Domino had a series of top 10 R&B hits with songs like "Rockin' Chair," "Goin' Home," "Goin' to the River," and "Please Don't Leave Me," establishing him as one of the leading R&B artists of the time.

With the release of "Ain't That a Shame" in 1955, Domino made the move into the world of rock and roll. With its rolling melody and piano and

Fats Domino

Domino's blues-tinged vocals, the song had an emotional bulk that was the musical equivalent of his five-foot-two-inch, 225 pound frame. It was a major hit, selling more than one million copies and peaking at number 10 on the charts.

Significantly, however, it was outsold and outcharted by a watered-down version by Pat Boone (which reached number two). But the importance of the song resided in the fact that its R&B sound, whether in Domino's or Boone's version, was providing that idiom with a vast, new pop base.

Domino then began to walk a commercial line between R&B and rock and roll with an almost effortless ease. In addition to its broad pop success, "Ain't That a Shame" topped the R&B charts for 11 weeks in 1955. By the end of the year. Domino was voted the Favorite R&B Artist in the *Billboard* annual deejay poll.

At the same time, he was becoming a fixture on the rock scene. In 1956 he was a co-headliner with Frankie Lymon and the Teenagers at deejay Alan Freed's annual rock show at the Paramount Theatre in Brooklyn. His debut chart album, *Fats Domino—Rockin' and Rollin'*, hit chart number 18. By the end of 1956 he was the ninth most-played male vocalist in the U.S. (Elvis Presley topped the list). His crossover success was established when he appeared on "The Ed Sullivan Show" singing "Blueberry Hill."

His version of that R&B standard was his next big hit, reaching number three and selling one million copies in December 1956. Like "Ain't That a Shame," "Blueberry Hill" was an earthy song that came with his pounding, incessant piano chords and barreling vocals.

Domino was also moving into the culture at large

via films. In 1956, he performed in the movie *Shake, Rattle, and Roll*. In 1957, he made his second film appearance, in *The Girl Can't Help It*. That same year, he also appeared on the television program "The Perry Como Show."

The hits continued apace. In 1957, he reached the top 10 with "Blue Monday" (number five) and "I'm Walkin' " (number four). "I'm Walkin' " was a boiling, upbeat song and the most overtly rock and roll hit of his career. (It would later be covered, quite nicely, by Rick Nelson.)

Domino was also the dominant force in R&B. When "I'm Walkin' " finally relinquished the top position on the R&B charts in April 1957, it ended an astounding run at the top of those charts that spanned three singles, including "Blueberry Hill" and "Blue Monday," and lasted 22 weeks.

Over the next three years, Domino continued to chart with a vast array of singles. He had six more top 10 hits during that time, with numerous top 100 singles in between, including "Valley of Tears" and "It's You I Love" (1957), "Whole Lotta Loving" (1958), "I Want to Walk You Home" and "Be My Guest" (1959), and his last top 10 hit, "Walking to New Orleans" (1960).

On all of these songs, his approach was remarkably the same, with his piano and vocals sticking closely to the R&B-based sound that had become his musical signature.

But with the emergence of the British Invasion in 1964, that consistency also made his music seem somewhat dated for the time. Domino continued to release records with waning success, though he made the charts one last time, in 1968, with his cover of the Beatles' "Lady Madonna"—ironically, a song that Paul McCartney had written as a tribute to Domino's piano style.

Ensconced in baronial splendor in New Orleans with his wife and eight children, he toured less and less as the 1960s progressed. By the 1970s, he had become a fixture on the oldies scene, appearing with great success in Las Vegas and in one-off shows in the U.S. and Europe. It was a position he would maintain the rest of his career.

In 1986, Fats Domino was inducted into the Rock and Roll Hall of Fame. In 1987, he received a Lifetime Achievement Award at the 29th Annual Grammy Awards show, and at that same ceremony, the song "Blueberry Hill" was voted into the Hall of Fame of the National Academy of Recording Arts and Sciences.

TOP SONGS

AIN'T THAT A SHAME (Imperial, '55, *10*)

I'M IN LOVE AGAIN (Imperial, '56, *3*)

BLUEBERRY HILL (Imperial, '56, *2*)

BLUE MONDAY (Imperial, '57, *5*)

I'M WALKIN' (Imperial, '57, *4*)

VALLEY OF TEARS (Imperial, '57, *8*)

IT'S YOU I LOVE (Imperial, '57, *6*)

WHOLE LOTTA LOVING (Imperial, '58, *6*)

I WANT TO WALK YOU HOME (Imperial, '59, *8*)

WALKING TO NEW ORLEANS (Imperial, '60, *6*)

Additional Top 40 Songs: 27

THE DOORS

Sex, drugs, rock
and roll...and poetry. The Doors had it all.

The Los Angeles–based group—or more specifically, its leader and vocalist Jim Morrison—symbolized the allure and excess of '60s rock and its surrounding culture. A springboard for Morrison's artistic aspirations, the Doors combined his drug-infused lyrical imagery, sexual posturing, and poetic hyperbole with the distinctive sound of keyboardist Ray Manzarek, guitarist Robbie Krieger, and drummer John Densmore in a provocative package that became a vast commercial success.

Over the course of the late 1960s and early '70s, the Doors hit the charts repeatedly, starting with their signature song, "Light My Fire."

While the group's music was a modestly innovative blend of R&B, jazz, and expansive, psychedelicized rock, it was Morrison's onstage and offstage persona that dominated the group in every way. With his long, wavy locks, black leather pants, and charismatic, overtly sexual presence, he created an image of a rock idol that would inspire countless, disparate imitators over the succeeding decades. His self-contrived role as poetic rock troubadour would be the basis of proto-punk poetess Patti Smith's sound and vision in the 1970s, and his sexual posings and impassioned vocals would serve as a model for INXS's Michael Hutchence in the 1980s and Pearl Jam's Eddie Vedder in the '90s.

Morrison was a singular rock idol in an age of singular rock idols. What set him apart from such contemporaries as Jimi Hendrix, Janis Joplin, Mick Jagger, and others was the way in which he created and established his persona. While their images were derived primarily from the music they made—or from the simple fact that they were rock and rollers—Morrison's employed rock more as means to an end.

That end was the all-encompassing, extramusical image of Morrison himself. In that sense he provid-ed a model for such future media stars as Madonna and Prince, whose exploits and images extended beyond their music into a kind of cult of personality.

In Morrison's case that image was played out in a lifestyle that was saturated in sex, drugs, and alcohol. Onstage, he worked himself up into crescendos of abandon in which he would, by turns, expose himself, simulate various sexual acts, and yell obscenities at security officers and his fans. He was arrested for this behavior at several points, but these brushes with the law merely served to heighten his notoriety and the image he had created for himself.

There was to all of this, however, a sense of contrivance that undercut the reality he was attempting to achieve, that often made him seem like a caricature of an over-the-top rock idol instead of the real thing. There was, for instance, his epic poem/rock song "The End," in which he deliriously depicted the saga of a deranged young man who eventually murders his parents. The song, which was included on the Doors' debut album, became one of the cornerstones of his poet-rocker persona. In real life, Morrison symbolically committed the same offense when he told the press that his parents were dead; the fact that his parents were actually alive and well (his father was an officer in the U.S. Navy) didn't seem to fit into his desired public image.

But in most other aspects, Morrison was as good—or rather, bad—as he set out to be. His sexual exploits, bouts with drugs and alcohol, and generally excessive lifestyle were the stuff of rock legend.

As a result of those antics, Morrison tended to overshadow the other members of the Doors, a relatively quiet lot who seemed content to provide music that was, in effect, the soundtrack to his pop life.

The group was formed by Morrison (b. Dec. 8, 1943, Melbourne, Florida) and Manzarek (b. Feb. 12, 1935, Chicago) in 1965. The latter, who had been a member of Rick and the Ravens (with his brothers Rick and Jim), recruited Densmore (b. Dec. 1, 1945, Los Angeles). The three recorded a demo of Morrison songs before being joined by Krieger (b. Jan. 8, 1946, Los Angeles), who had played with Densmore in the Psychedelic Rangers.

Morrison gave the group its name at the start of 1966. There seems to be some question as to its origin. Some sources cite a passage from William Blake's poem "The Doors: Open and Closed": "there are things that are known and things that are unknown: in between are doors." Other sources claim, however, that the group's name came from a passage in Aldous Huxley's *The Doors of Perception* in which that poem was included: "all the other chemical Doors in the Wall are labelled Dope."

Whichever is the case—if either—both quotations were emblematic of the direction in which Morrison would guide the group.

The Doors began a six-month residency at the fabled Whiskey A-Go-Go in 1966, which eventually ended with the group being sacked because of Morrison's controversial onstage performances of "The End." But the group came to the attention of Arthur Lee, a seminal L.A. rocker and member of the group Love, who directed them to Jac Holzman of Elektra Records, leading to a contract with the label.

The Doors' eponymous debut album was released in January 1967 and was an immediate hit, reaching number two on the charts (during a run that would last 121 weeks). The song "Break on Through" had a surging energy that was augmented by Morrison's rather theatrical vocals, while the group's version of the R&B classic "Back Door Man" was one of the finest renditions ever recorded. But the centerpieces of the album were the two extended cuts, "Light My Fire" and "The End." The former came with an extended improvisational section highlighted by a lithe, scalar solo by Krieger. The latter was Morrison's set piece in which he declaimed the dense, brooding text with a maniacal fervor.

Edited down to a version short enough to be

TOP ALBUMS

THE DOORS (Elektra, '67, 2)
STRANGE DAYS (Elektra, '67, 3)
WAITING FOR THE SUN
  (Elektra, '68, 1)
THE SOFT PARADE (Elektra, '69, 6)
MORRISON HOTEL/HARD ROCK
CAFE (Elektra, '70, 4)
ABSOLUTELY LIVE (Elektra, '70, 8)
L.A. WOMAN (Elektra, '71, 9)

Additional Top 40 Albums: 4

TOP SONGS

LIGHT MY FIRE (Elektra, '67, 1)
HELLO, I LOVE YOU (Elektra, '68, 1)
TOUCH ME (Elektra, '68, 3)

Additional Top 40 Songs: 5

---

played on radio, "Light My Fire" was released as a single in July 1967 and topped the charts for three weeks, selling a million copies in the process. The song elevated the Doors to the first rank of rock acts.

The rest of the year was punctuated by public displays that laid the foundations of the Morrison legend. In September, he created a stir when the group played "Light My Fire" on "The Ed Sullivan Show." Ordered by the program's host to refrain from singing the line "girl we couldn't get much higher," Morrison agreed—then sang it anyway. During the group's tour, in December, Morrison was arrested after a show in New Haven, Connecticut, for taunting police officers. He was charged with a breach of the peace and resisting arrest.

All of this—the success, arrests, and controversy— would be the motifs of the group's career.

The former continued apace with the release of the Doors' second album, *Strange Days,* in November of 1967. A sprawling record that traded the energy and purpose of its predecessor for a contrived, rather pretentious strangeness, *Strange Days* was a musical disappointment. But it hit number three on the charts, and its single, "Love Me Two Times," reached number 25.

As the group made its way through 1968, the provocations continued as well. In May, the Doors made a promo film of the song "The Unknown Soldier" in which Morrison was "shot." That same month he was back to his onstage tricks when he incited a crowd to riot at a Chicago performance.

But in spite of the controversies, or perhaps because of them, the group's records continued to climb the charts. Starting in September 1968, the group's third album, *Waiting for the Sun,* spent four weeks at Number One. Its rather vapid, pop-oriented single "Hello, I Love You" also topped the charts and sold one million copies. The album came with a printed—but not recorded—text of Morrison's rock-poem, "Celebration of the Lizard," which would later be the basis of his decadent visionary persona, "the lizard king."

By 1969, the successes and excesses had become

almost routine. In February, the single "Touch Me" was another million-seller, reaching number three on the charts. Later in the year, the group's fourth album, *The Soft Parade*, hit number six.

But Morrison's growing abuse of drugs and alcohol and his increasingly provocative behavior began to create problems. Arrested in March during a performance in Florida for simulating masturbation and oral sex onstage, he was forced to curtail the group's tours for months pending possible appearances in court. In November, during a drunken incident on an airplane, he was arrested and charged with interfering with the activities of a flight crew—a federal offense.

From there it was all simply more of the same. The group continued to make the top 10 with the albums *Morrison Hotel* (1970), *Absolutely Live* (which included a musical version of "Celebration of the Lizard" in 1970), and *L.A. Woman* (1971). But musically, the Doors never equalled or surpassed their work on their debut album.

Morrison grew increasingly erratic, and the arrests and court appearances continued. In March 1971, he left the group and moved to Paris to write poetry. His first book, *The Lords and the New Creatures,* was a modest success. On July 3rd, he was found dead in his apartment, the police ruling he had died of a heart attack. In keeping with the image he had created, he was buried in Paris's Père-Lachaise cemetery, which was also the final resting place of Oscar Wilde, Frédéric Chopin, and Honoré de Balzac. In the succeeding decades, his grave would become a graffiti-covered shrine for new generations of rock fans who worshipped him and the '60s era which, in many ways, he came to symbolize.

The rest of the Doors tried to keep the group going without him, but their subsequent albums proved to be dull and uninspired. They eventually called it quits in 1972. In 1979, the group re-formed to record musical backgrounds for tapes of Morrison reciting his poetry (in 1970) that became the album *An American Prayer*. And tapes of the group's onstage performances yielded the albums *Alive She Cried* in 1983 and *Live at the Hollywood Bowl* in 1987. Compilations of the Doors' hits were also subsequently released.

In 1991, director Oliver Stone's film *The Doors* generated new interest in the group and its charismatic leader. With Val Kilmer in the role of Morrison, the film was a hyperbolic portrayal of one of the most hyperbolic performers in the history of rock.

DURAN DURAN

In the proverbial case of being in the right place at the right time, Duran Duran came along at the dawn of the age of video rock and parlayed that into becoming the first major teen rock act of the 1980s.

The Birmingham-based group had enjoyed some success in England, soon after it had formed in 1980, with a couple of hit singles and its self-titled debut album. But its records and debut tour in the U.S. had failed to capture much attention.

Enter the fledgling music channel MTV in 1981.

Eager to establish itself as a viable commercial force, and short on videos by major acts with which it could fill out its 24-hour-a-day schedule, MTV began airing videos being produced by obscure, up-and-coming acts . . . like Duran Duran.

It was a marriage made in teen heaven.

Duran Duran

The group had shrewdly invested the revenues from its British hits in a series of dazzling videos that quickly made their way onto the MTV playlist. "Girls on Film" was a black and white study in soft-core decadence, while "Hungry Like the Wolf" featured the group cavorting about in the wilds of Sri Lanka, posing prettily and lip-syncing with outright abandon.

Faster than an electron smashing against a TV screen, Duran Duran became teen idols in the U.S. Affecting a post-punk look that was tempered by a new romantic elegance, vocalist Simon LeBon (b. Oct. 27, 1958, Bushey, Herts), guitarist Andy Taylor (b. Feb. 16, 1961, Tynemouth, Tyne and Wear), keyboardist Nick Rhodes (b. Nicholas Bates, June 8, 1962, Moseley, West Midlands), bassist John Taylor (b. Nigel John Taylor, June 20, 1960, Birmingham), and drummer Roger Taylor (b. Apr. 26, 1960, Castle Bromwich, West Midlands) set young female hearts ablaze.

While critics tended to slam the group's sound, it was a cut above the usual ballad- or dance-based teen fare. Songs like "Rio" and "Is There Something I Should Know" had a techno-pop sleekness bolstered by a new wave edge. It was a homogenized sound, to be sure, and one that the group would churn out on a series of hits. But with Rhodes' sweeping, grandiose layers of synthesized sound and Taylor's propulsive guitar providing a dense backdrop to LeBon's monochromatic vocals, that sound did have a certain distinction.

With the videos—and MTV—constantly reinforcing the group's presence, Duran Duran set out on a major U.S. tour that found them performing to ravenous crowds of hysterical girls. The videos and tour combined to create an insatiable demand for the group's records. From 1983 through its high point in 1985, the group had six top 10 singles on the U.S. charts, culminating with the theme song from the James Bond film *A View to a Kill* in 1985 (the song was the first Bond theme to reach Number One on the charts).

Before the group hooked up with MTV and began its conquest of the crucial U.S. pop market, it was a leading exponent of the "new romantic" movement in the U.K. Initially formed in 1978, in Birmingham, by Rhodes and then-guitarist John Taylor, the group took its name from one of the characters in the 1968 sci-fi film spoof *Barbarella*. Over the next two years, they recruited Andy Taylor, Roger Taylor, and LeBon, and the group began to define its look and sound, which were in line with the fanciful imagery of other new romantic acts like Ultravox and Spandau Ballet. This imagery, which consisted of lush melodic songs, electronic flourishes, and effusive displays of fashion, was a backlash against the punk of the late 1970s.

In Duran Duran's case, this imagery also proved to be the perfect ingredient for the emerging rock video phenomenon. In its videos, the group vamped about in makeup and colorful outfits amid locales that included sailboats and lush jungles and the like, all of which were highly visual and alluring. The songs became soundtracks for this visual seduction, with their stylized new wave/techno-pop veneer. In its way, the entire product was an updating of the photogenic, pretty-boy pop of the late 1950s and early '60s.

In 1981, the group began its run on the U.K. charts with the single "Planet Earth," reaching number 12. The singles "Careless Memories" and "Girls on Film" also appeared on the U.K. singles charts that year, and the group's eponymous debut album hit number three (during a stay on the charts that would last 118 weeks).

The group continued its rise in 1982 with the album *Rio* and the singles "Hungry Like the Wolf" and "Save a Prayer," all reaching the top five. But the group was going nowhere in the U.S. That changed in 1983, when MTV began playing the video of "Hungry Like the Wolf" in heavy rotation. The song went to number three in the U.S., and the album *Rio*, released there in June 1982, rose to number six.

That's when Duran-mania began to explode. As 1983 unfolded, the group's debut album and the singles "Is There Something I Should Know" and "Union of the Snake" all made the upper reaches of the U.S. charts and became hits around the world.

Duran Duran's reign continued in 1984. In June, the single "The Reflex" became the group's first record to reach Number One in the U.S. During the year, the albums *Seven and the Ragged Tiger* and *Arena* went platinum. And, at the end of the year, the film *Sing Blue Silver,* documenting the group's world tour (during which it had played to over 750,000 fans) hit the screens. In November, Duran Duran was invited by Bob Geldof to participate in the all-star group Band Aid to record the song "Do They Know It's Christmas?" for victims of the Ethiopian famine (they would also perform at the Geldof-organized Live Aid concert in London in July 1985).

But the forces of fame and fortune began to exact their typical toll. The group began to splinter in 1985, with Andy and John Taylor joining vocalist Robert Palmer in the group Power Station and the rest of Duran Duran reassembling under the name Arcadia. The former had two top 10 hits with "Some Like It Hot" and "Get It On," while the latter hit with "Election Day."

New Duran Duran albums, like 1986's *Notorious* and 1988's *Big Thing*, continued to be released, to decreasing interest. While the title cut from *Notorious* reached number two and the single "I Don't Want Your Love" (from *Big Thing*) reached number four, the group was on the wane, giving way to a new generation of video stars like Wham!'s George Michael and a host of metal, dance, and rap acts who had learned the ways of success through MTV and video.

In their various ways, each of these groups had followed a path mapped out by Duran Duran. While it could be said that MTV "made" the group, it could also be said that Duran Duran had much to do with establishing the video channel as a new and revolutionary route to rock stardom.

TOP ALBUMS

RIO (Harvest, '83, 6)
ARENA (Capitol, '84, 4)

Additional Top 40 Albums: 4

TOP SONGS

HUNGRY LIKE THE WOLF (Harvest, '82, 3)
IS THERE SOMETHING I SHOULD KNOW (Capitol, '83, 4)
UNION OF THE SNAKE (Capitol, '83, 3)
THE REFLEX (Capitol, '84, 1)
THE WILD BOYS (Capitol, '84, 2)
A VIEW TO A KILL (Capitol, '85, 1)
NOTORIOUS (Capitol, '86, 2)
I DON'T WANT YOUR LOVE (Capitol, '88, 4)

Additional Top 40 Songs: 5

BOB DYLAN

Bob Dylan was the
final piece in the rock puzzle. By the time Dylan's talents
came to fruition, Elvis Presley had given rock its image,
its *raison d'être*. The Beatles had defined its artistic and musical
status. Dylan proved that rock had something to say.

Before Dylan, rock music had been a sound and an attitude, both of which were rebellious and young and forceful in an entirely visceral way. Rock hooked the ears and the rest of the body with its emotional, raucous vocals and twanging guitars and slamming beats, while its words had captured the romantic yearnings, joys, frustrations, and cares of teen life.

Dylan revolutionized the music by elevating the power of words—and the thoughts and feelings they articulated—to a new level of creative importance. His dense, complex, overtly poetic lyrics stimulated the mind, even as his elliptical messages were being rammed home with the power and punch of rock musical signatures.

On such classic songs as "Subterranean Homesick Blues," "Rainy Day Women #12 & 35," "Positively Fourth Street," and "Like a Rolling Stone," Dylan created a new lexicon for rock and roll expression.

These songs and others displayed a new, more reflective aspect of rock and roll and, in the process, redefined its role as an artistic form. Their music made one move, like all good rock songs before them, but their words also made one think.

Thinking along with music, as opposed to simply listening or dancing to it, was a revelation for the rock world. It was a crucial, almost synchronistic development that coincided with rock's emergence from its teen confines into the broader, more sophisticated and complex world outside. In Dylan's music, rock became a force in, and an expression of,

the culture at large. And, in the process, Dylan became a symbol of his time—the 1960s—whose dominance and influence was rivalled only by the Beatles.

But as important as Dylan was for his words and thoughts, he was also a revolutionary musical figure. In the early '60s he had transformed the role and creative substance of folk music with songs that propelled that moribund form, and Dylan himself, into the vanguard of the protest movement. He later extended his expressions, and those of folk music, into an intensely personal, introspective sphere that had, up to that point, usually been the realm of poetry. When he broke with his folk past in 1965 and formally embraced rock, Dylan virtually redefined both musical forms and paved the way for the folk-rock movement that would become a major musical force in the mid-1960s.

While Dylan became the godfather of the movement and one of its biggest stars, his songs would serve as the basis for the music of other groups who reinterpreted those songs in equally revolutionary ways. The Byrds created a new blend of folk and rock with their inspired 1965 version of his song "Mr. Tambourine Man." That single, which topped the charts, begat countless folk-rock groups, including the Turtles, Sonny and Cher, and others, all of whom covered various Dylan songs. Even the Beatles worked that sound into their own music, as on "If I Needed Someone."

But his musical and lyrical innovations aside, Dylan was also one of the most distinctive rock musicians of all time. His whining, nasal vocal raspings were immediately recognizable, as singular in their way as those of Presley, John Lennon, Mick Jagger, or others. His rough, ragged, almost meterless guitar strummings had the feel of the ancient rural blues masters, just as the wheezings of his harmonica were endowed with an expressive power and simplicity that were, at once, supple and direct.

Dylan also symbolized, along with the Beatles, the '60s ethos of change and confrontation. During the decade Dylan consciously and purposefully confounded the expectations that attended him and confronted his fans and critics with his various creative

TOP ALBUMS

HIGHWAY 61 REVISITED (Columbia, '65, 3)
JOHN WESLEY HARDING (Columbia, '68, 2)
NASHVILLE SKYLINE (Columbia, '69, 3)
PLANET WAVES (Asylum, '74, 1)
BEFORE THE FLOOD (Asylum, '74, 3)
BLOOD ON THE TRACKS (Columbia, '75, 1)
DESIRE (Columbia, '76, 1)
SLOW TRAIN COMING (Columbia, '79, 3)

Additional Top 40 Albums: 21

TOP SONGS

LIKE A ROLLING STONE (Columbia, '65, 2)
RAINY DAY WOMEN #12 & 35 (Columbia, '66, 2)

Additional Top 40 Songs: 10

personas. Just as he had conquered folk in the early 1960s and then abandoned it for rock, he also departed from the folk-rock movement later in the decade to pursue more subdued lyrical ruminations and a sound that was a new slant on country and rock. His albums of this period were harbingers of the country rock movement that would come to musical prominence in the 1970s.

Even later, at the start of the 1980s, long after his days as a revolutionary figure had drawn to an end, Dylan continued to be a restless, confrontational artist, embracing Christianity on the albums *Slow Train Coming* and *Saved* (he subsequently abandoned that religion and returned to the Judaism of his early life).

And into the 1990s, Dylan rebelled against his status as musical elder statesman. Refusing to settle into complacent middle age or retire and rest on his

epochal past, he toured and recorded constantly. The results were often mixed at best, but the fact that he was actively attempting to create and perform was perhaps Dylan's ultimate protest.

Much of Dylan's early life is shrouded in mystery (partly the result of the various personas he created at the start of his career). Rock history is littered with tales of Dylan running away from home, Dylan joining a carnival, Dylan roaming the country like an itinerent minstrel.

A fact that is reasonably certain is that in 1960, Dylan (b. Robert Allen Zimmerman, May 24, 1941, Duluth, Minnesota) left his home state and journeyed to New York to visit his ailing hero, folk legend Woody Guthrie.

Having done that, he stayed in New York and began playing around Greenwich Village. His first performance came at the club Gerde's Folk City on April 11, 1961, and over the next several months he began to establish his name on the folk scene. He played harmonica on Harry Belafonte's album *Midnight Special* and did the same on several sessions for folksinger Caroline Hester.

After receiving an effusive review in the *New York Times,* Dylan came to the attention of legendary producer John Hammond, who signed him to a contract with Columbia Records.

In October 1961, his eponymous debut album was released. The set, which included his renditions of traditional folk songs, was mostly ignored by the public, but it did generate attention in the folk milieu.

Around this time, Dylan began a long professional relationship with Albert Grossman, who became his manager and a crucial figure in the initial years of his career.

After a trip to England in early 1963, where he played the role of a folksinger in the BBC radio play "The Madhouse on Castle Street," Dylan returned to the U.S. and began recording his next album. With the release of *The Freewheelin' Bob Dylan* in May 1963, his star began to rise in the folk firmament. The traditional songs of the debut album gave way to originals—"A Hard Rain's Gonna Fall," "Blowin' in the Wind," and "Masters of War"—that placed Dylan squarely at the forefront of the emerging folk-protest movement. The album also became his first charting record, reaching number 22.

As one of the new leading folk figures, Dylan appeared at the Monterey Folk Festival in May. There he met folk siren Joan Baez, with whom he

Bob Dylan

would develop a close personal relationship over the years. Several months later, Dylan's name reached beyond the folk circuit into the broad pop world when Peter, Paul and Mary had a major hit with their version of "Blowin' in the Wind."

As if to confirm his status in the folk-protest scene, Dylan's next album, *The Times They Are A-Changin'*, was loaded with his defiant songs, including the powerful title cut. It charted at number 20 in April 1964.

But in an artistic about-face that would come to personify his music and career, he veered away from protest music on the album *Another Side of Bob Dylan*. Released in October 1964, the album came with dense, brooding, introspective songs that outraged his fans even as it gained new admirers. But the real change came in 1965. After a brief tour of England, where he was hailed as a folk hero, Dylan began recording a new album. In an astonishing move, Dylan, inspired by the new rock scene in Britain, decided to pursue a new, more rock-oriented sound.

That sound emerged on the 1965 album *Bringing It All Back Home*. While the album's second side was devoted to acoustic folk songs (including one of his classics, "Mr. Tambourine Man") the first side came with a set of rolling rockers, replete with electric instruments and drums. One of those songs, "Subterranean Homesick Blues," made the top 40, while the album itself reached number six.

Dylan's folk fans were again outraged, but a new generation of rock musicians and fans embraced him and his music. The confrontation between Dylan's past and present culminated in his performance at the Newport Folk Festival on June 25, 1965, in which, backed by the Butterfield band, he was booed by his old fans.

But Dylan never looked back. As the new folk-rock movement that he inspired began to spread, Dylan outdid his disciples with the single "Like a Rolling Stone." One of his defining masterpieces, the song hit number two on the charts and sold more than one million copies.

Dylan hit the charts again at the end of the year with "Positively Fourth Street" and, in 1966, with "Rainy Day Women #12 & 35." His next album, *Blonde on Blonde*, was released in August and reached number nine. Later in the year, he appeared in the film *Don't Look Back,* a documentary of his 1965 tour of the U.K.

But just as his commercial and artistic powers were at their height, Dylan's career was cut short when he was gravely injured in a motorcycle crash near his home in Woodstock, New York, on July 29, 1966. Amid various rumors that he was dead, Dylan withdrew from the scene for the next 18 months to recuperate.

When he made his comeback in 1968, his sound had changed again. The fury and fire of his rock days gave way to a softer country sound on the albums *John Wesley Harding* and 1969's even more country-inflected Nashville Skyline. The latter yielded his final top 10 hit, "Lay Lady Lay."

Dylan entered the '70s as exhausted—and exhausted of new ideas—as the rest of the rock world. Over the course of the next 20 years he recorded and toured constantly, but he had little to offer that was as revolutionary and inspired as his work in the 1960s.

There were several highlights, however.

On record, Dylan's work became increasingly erratic and uneven. But albums such as 1974's *Planet Waves* and 1975's *Blood on the Tracks* had their moments of interest, as did 1985's *Empire Burlesque*.

Onstage, Dylan proved to be somewhat more inspired, on occasion. In 1971, he appeared at George Harrison's benefit "Concert for Bangladesh" (his performance being one of the high points of the subsequent album and film of the event). In 1974, he teamed with the Band for a ravenously received tour of the U.S. The next year, he and a cast of rock and folk stars embarked on "The Rolling Thunder Revue," a ragtag tour that was his response to the rock spectacles of the era. In 1978, he appeared in the Band's final concert, "The Last Waltz," in San Francisco.

Dylan remained active into the 1980s and '90s. In 1985, he participated in the all-star benefit group USA for Africa and its hit single, "We Are the World." That same year, he performed at Live Aid, the benefit concert for the victims of the Ethiopian famine. During the '80s, he toured with Tom Petty and the Heartbreakers and, intriguingly, with the Grateful Dead.

In 1988, his career and music revived when he joined the Traveling Wilburys, a group that included Harrison, Petty, Roy Orbison, and Jeff Lynne. The group's album, *Traveling Wilburys Volume One,* was a vast hit.

In 1989, Dylan was inducted into the Rock and Roll Hall of Fame.

THE EAGLES

Glenn Frey, Don Henley, Randy Meisner, and Bernie Leadon stare from the cover of the Eagles' 1973 album *Desperado* like a sullen bunch of wild-west outlaws. Dressed in western gear, with guns and bandeleros, their long hair and mustaches drooping, they look dangerous. They weren't.

But they could draw hit records from their holsters faster than almost any other rock group of their time.

The Eagles came out of the wilds of the southern California country rock scene of the early 1970s and promptly established themselves as the leaders of that movement. Over the course of the rest of the decade the group became one of the biggest rock acts in the U.S., selling more than 40 million records worldwide and touring to tumultuous response from its fans.

The Eagles accomplished all that with a sound that was a smooth blend of rock and country styles (which was also true of the music of such other southern California acts as Jackson Browne, Linda Ronstadt, and the Flying Burrito Brothers). But while the movement was often reviled by critics for its middle-of-the-road blandness, the Eagles somehow transcended the more obvious defects of the idiom and emerged as a potent rock act.

The members were all solid musicians. Frey and Leadon traded solos with ease and created dense guitar harmonies. Bassist Meisner and drummer Henley provided a steady rhythmic accompaniment. All four traded lead vocals; their harmonies were country sweet with a raw rock edge.

With the Eagles as its most visible exponent, the country rock movement became one of the most commercially successful rock genres of the 1970s. It paved the way for the adult-oriented rock (AOR) of Fleetwood Mac and other groups later in the decade.

And it was a watershed of sorts in rock history, the point at which the music relinquished its rebellious stance and settled into a non-threatening, non-confrontational, (some would say) non-exciting, overtly commercial existence.

The group—and the movement itself—evolved from the revolutionary musical experiments of the Byrds and Buffalo Springfield in the 1960s. In 1966, the former began to incorporate country forms into its folk-rock sound on the song "Mr. Spaceman." Two years later, encouraged by the group's new member, Gram Parsons, the Byrds released the epochal album *Sweetheart of the Rodeo,* which was a full-fledged amalgam of rock and country music. Similarly, Buffalo Springfield had flirted openly and convincingly with country music as part of its eclectic sound (that also included folk and R&B along with straightahead rock). The culmination of their experiments was the first full-fledged country rock group, the Flying Burrito Brothers, which Parsons formed in 1968.

The difference between these groups and their country rock offspring was that the originals' country-inflected music had been a provocative assault on rock sensibilities of the time. There was an exhilaration and excitement to their musical experiments that were suffused with the edge of the new. The Eagles, Browne, and the rest simply co-opted the work of the Byrds, Buffalo Springfield, and the Flying Burrito Brothers—no doubt out of a true admiration and affection for those groups—and turned it into a sleek, flaccid musical form for the sleek, flaccid '70s.

That said, it must be added that the Eagles never claimed to be more than they were. In fact, the group had an unquestionably polished sound that came with accomplished vocal harmonies and a consistently rocking base. The group's songs, while hardly revolutionary, did fuse country and rock into a persuasive musical expression that was distinctive in its way. Several of those songs, like 1972's "Take It Easy" and "Witchy Woman," drew heavily from Buffalo Springfield's music, with country vocal harmonies countered by propulsive rock guitars and beats. But as the group's sound evolved, its songs became more identifiably their own. Thus, songs like 1975's "One of These Nights" and 1977's "Hotel California" were almost wholly "Eagles" songs, with structures and vocals that were qualitatively different from those of its musical predecessors.

And when Joe Walsh joined the fold as guitarist, vocalist, and songwriter in 1975, he brought with him a gregarious energy and presence that transformed the Eagles into a forceful rock band. The music of the Eagles' later period—songs such as "The Long Run" of 1979 and "Dirty Laundry" of 1982— bore the signature of Walsh's hard rock predilections.

The group was formed in 1971 by Frey (b. Nov. 6, 1948, Detroit, Michigan), Meisner (b. Mar. 8, 1947, Scottsbluff, Nebraska), Henley (b. July 22, 1947, Gilmer, Texas), and Leadon (b. July 19, 1947, Minneapolis, Minnesota).

The musicians' pedigrees were firmly rooted in the country rock scene of southern California. Frey and Henley had been members of Ronstadt's band, Meisner came from Poco, and Leadon from the Flying Burrito Brothers.

Signed by Asylum Records chief David Geffen in April 1972, the group journeyed to London that month to begin recording its eponymous debut album. Released in July, that album was an immediate success, shooting to number 22 on the charts on the strength of the singles "Take It Easy" (number

12) and "Witchy Woman" (number nine). A third single from the album, "Peaceful Easy Feeling," hit number 22 in March 1973.

The Eagles' popularity was based in part on a reaction of rock fans against the prevailing scene. At a time when glam-rock, the flashy pop of Elton John, and the softer, sensitive singer-songwriter movement were besetting the charts, the music of the Eagles— and country rock in general—provided a more rough-hewn, basic rock sound that seemed to speak to the form's simpler virtues.

That sound was furthered and expanded on succeeding albums: 1973's *Desperados,* 1974's *On the Border,* and 1975's *One of These Nights* (which topped the charts for five weeks). During the recording of *On the Border,* slide guitarist Don Felder (b. Sept. 21, 1947, Topanga, California) made significant contributions and was invited to join the group.

During this period, the Eagles' popularity continued to grow, both on record and onstage. In March 1975, its acoustic ballad "Best of My Love" climbed to Number One. In August of that year, the rocking "One of These Nights" did the same. And the archetypal country rock song, "Lyin' Eyes," reached number two in November. The group also toured constantly, becoming, in the process, one of the biggest concert draws of the time.

In December of that year, Leadon quit the group because of musical differences. In a somewhat surprising move, he was replaced by Walsh (b. Nov. 20, 1947, Wichita, Kansas), who had made a name for himself with the James Gang and as a solo artist. Walsh was one of rock's true eccentrics, and his solid guitar solos and funkier instincts provided a new range and harder edge to the Eagles' sound.

Success continued apace. In February 1976, the group won a Grammy Award in the category of Best Pop Performance by a Duo or Group for "Lyin' Eyes." And in March, the compilation album *Their Greatest Hits, 1971–1975* topped the charts for five weeks, selling more than a million copies.

The inclusion of Walsh was felt on the group's

TOP ALBUMS

ONE OF THESE NIGHTS (Asylum, '75, *1*)
EAGLES/THEIR GREATEST HITS 1971–1975 (Asylum, '76, *1*)
HOTEL CALIFORNIA (Asylum, '76, *1*)
THE LONG RUN (Asylum, '79, *1*)

Additional Top 40 Albums: 3

TOP SONGS

BEST OF MY LOVE (Asylum, '74, *1*)
ONE OF THESE NIGHTS (Asylum, '75, *1*)
LYIN' EYES (Asylum, '75, *2*)
NEW KID IN TOWN (Asylum, '76, *1*)
HOTEL CALIFORNIA (Asylum, '77, *1*)
HEARTACHE TONIGHT (Asylum, '79, *1*)

Additional Top 40 Songs: 10

The Eagles

1977 album, *Hotel California,* which came with a harder, more rhythmically charged sound. The album was the group's commercial and artistic high point, hitting Number One at various points for a total of seven weeks and selling over a million units. In 1978, the album won a Grammy for Record of the Year, and its single, "New Kid in Town," was honored in the category of Best Arrangement for Voices.

Tired of touring, Meisner left the group in September 1977 and was replaced by former Poco bassist Timothy B. Schmit (b. Oct. 30, 1947, Sacramento, California).

The group toured off and on during 1978 while recording its next album. That process proved to be arduous, with the group constantly revising its songs and spending a reported one million dollars in the studio.

The result was 1979's *The Long Run.* Released in September, the album was greeted deliriously by the group's fans and topped the charts for eight weeks. Its single, "Heartache Tonight," also hit Number One while the title cut reached number eight. The

group won its fourth Grammy in 1980 when the former single was voted Best Rock Vocal Performance by a Duo or Group.

The group had agreed that it would disband after *The Long Run* and its subsequent tour. It did that in 1980, with all of the members pursing solo careers.

Of these, Henley's proved to be the most successful, musically and commercially. In 1983, his single "Dirty Laundry" charted at number three, and in 1985, "The Boys of Summer" reached number five. The latter won a Grammy for Best Rock Vocal Performance, Male, in 1986. And Henley's 1989 album, *The End of the Innocence,* won a Grammy in the same category in 1990.

The importance of the Eagles in rock history is hotly debated. Some critics dismiss the group as the most prominent exponent of the musically dreary and vapid late country rock movement. Others see the group as a steadying rock force during the mostly dismissable 1970s. But undeniably, the Eagles were one of the most successful and popular rock acts of that decade.

DUANE EDDY

Duane Eddy was the first
guitar hero of rock and roll. With his signature twang
and his hit instrumental records of the late 1950s and early '60s,
Eddy pushed the guitar—and the guitarist—into the spotlight.
It was a development that would alter the future course
of rock music and change the imagery and
iconography of rock culture.

From the start, years before Eddy made his record debut in 1958, the guitar had been the symbol of rock and roll. Rock idols like Elvis Presley and Ricky Nelson posed with it onstage. Musically, the sound of the guitar was the focal point, or basic building block, of a vast number of rock songs by those idols and countless others. And Eddy's hits had actually been preceded by Bill Justis's "Raunchy" and Link Wray's "Rumble," two of the most notable guitar records of the rock era.

But while the importance of the guitar was beyond dispute, guitarists as such were still regarded primarily as sidemen to the stars (or, in the case of Justis and Wray, almost novelty acts). The rock public idolized Presley, while his guitarist, Scotty Moore, toiled in the background. The same could be said of Nelson and his guitarist, James Burton. And other seminal pickers like Bill Haley and the Comets' Frannie Beecher and the Johnny Burnette Trio's Paul Burlison were similarly cast in visibly, if not musically, secondary roles. Even Chuck Berry and Bo Diddley—titans of their instrument and crucial figures in its esthetic development—were singer-guitarists. While they also had an important role in moving the guitar into the spotlight, they did it through their positions as rock stars who also, quite secondarily in the public's mind, just happened to be guitarists.

Eddy changed all that. He made the guitarist a star in his own right. With his vast commercial success, based solely on his role as a guitar (as opposed to a vocal) idol, Eddy paved the way for generations of rock guitarists to come. He provided the model—if, ironically, not the sound—that would be the foundation for the era of the rock guitar hero in the 1960s, when such figures as Jeff Beck, Jimi Hendrix, and Eric Clapton would parlay their guitar skills into unprecedented popular and critical acclaim. They, in turn, would establish the role of the guitar hero as a primary force in the rock world.

Eddy set the ground rules for this development. On hits like "Rebel-'Rouser," "Ramrod," and "Because They're Young," he created his distinctive twang, altering his guitar sound with tremolo effects, whammy-bar whines, and an echo that came from a drainpipe chamber devised for his studio recordings by producer Lee Hazlewood.

Musically, he was hardly revolutionary. Most of his hits were catchy, hook-imbued, boisterous tunes on which he picked out melodies and chords in a song-based manner like that of country master Chet Atkins; to do that, he tuned his strings down an octave and played the theme lines on the bass strings. His solos were similarly derivative, with mostly blues- and R&B-based lines spiced with country and rockabilly flavors, all of which were propelled by rock energy and intensity.

Eddy's importance didn't come from what he

Duane Eddy

played, but how he played it; as the title of one of his 1960 albums put it, *The "Twangs" the "Thang."*

It was a sound that was immediately recognizable and one that was embraced on a vast scale by the record-buying public. In the first five years of his career, Eddy sold more than 12 million records, and he would eventually sell more than 30 million over the course of that career.

Eddy (b. Apr. 28, 1938, Corning, New York) came to the attention of Hazlewood and Lester Sill in 1958, when he was playing with the group the Rebels in Phoenix, Arizona. With their support, he

TOP ALBUMS

HAVE "TWANGY" GUITAR—WILL TRAVEL
   (Jamie, '59, 5)
THE "TWANGS" THE "THANG" (Jamie, '60, 18)
$1,000,000.00 WORTH OF TWANG (Jamie, '60, 11)

Additional Top 40 Albums: 1

TOP SONGS

REBEL-'ROUSER (Jamie, '58, 6)
CANNONBALL (Jamie, '58, 15)
THE LONELY ONE (Jamie, '59, 23)
FORTY MILES OF BAD ROAD (Jamie, '59, 9)
BECAUSE THEY'RE YOUNG (Jamie, '60, 4)
"PEPE" (Jamie, '60, 18)
(DANCE WITH THE) GUITAR MAN (RCA, '62, 12)

Additional Top 40 Songs: 8

recorded the single "Movin' 'n' Groovin'," which was leased to the Philadelphia-based Jamie label and made number 72 on the *Billboard* charts in May of that year.

But it was his next hit, "Rebel-'Rouser," that established the signature twang and—with a notable assist from Ben Demotto's rebel yells—made Eddy a rock guitar hero. The single hit number six in July, and he was invited to perform the song on Dick Clark's "American Bandstand." The record was the first million-seller of his career.

Two additional hits followed in 1958, with "Ramrod" hitting number 27 and the equally aptly titled "Cannonball" reaching number 15. On a number of those records, Eddy's formidable guitar was boosted by the saxophone work of such legendary instrumentalists as Steve Douglas, Plas Johnson, and Jim Horn.

In 1959, the hits continued apace. "The Lonely

One" hit number 23, and Eddy's debut album, *Have "Twangy" Guitar—Will Travel,* made number five. It would remain the biggest selling album of his career.

Over the succeeding five years, Eddy hit the album and singles charts consistently, with "Forty Miles of Bad Road," "Kommotion," and others reaching the Hot 100. While most of these were composed by Eddy and various collaborators, he also borrowed from traditional sources. Thus, 1960's "Bonnie Came Back" was his version of the classic "My Bonnie Lies Over the Ocean"; and in 1963, he recorded a rendition of "Deep in the Heart of Texas."

During that time, he also had hits with songs from movies and television programs. The biggest single of his career was his theme from the film *Because They're Young,* which reached number four in 1960 and sold more than a million copies (he also acted in the film along with James Darren, Tuesday Weld, and Dick Clark). Eddy also recorded a remarkable version of Henry Mancini's theme from the television series "Peter Gunn" and had hits with songs from the films *Pepe* and *Ring of Fire.* In 1962, his version of the "Have Gun Will Travel" TV theme was released as "The Ballad of Palladin" and reached number 33.

By 1964, the British Invasion was pushing most of the rock heroes of the 1950s into the background. That year, Eddy had a final charting record in the U.S. with the album *Lonely Guitar,* which made number 144. He retreated from recording and performing onstage and began to pursue a career in acting, appearing in the films *The Savage Seven* and *Kona* in the mid-1960s.

In the '70s, he played on the B.J. Thomas hit "Rock and Roll Lullaby" and produced a solo album by Phil Everly called *Star-Spangled Springer.* He released the record "Play Me Like You Play Your Guitar" in the U.K., the single making number nine in that country in 1975. Back at home, however, the U.S. single "You Are My Sunshine"—recorded with Waylon Jennings and Willie Nelson in 1978—didn't make the charts.

In 1986, the Art of Noise recruited Eddy for its version of "Peter Gunn," which made number 50 in the U.S. and was honored with a Grammy Award for the Best Rock Instrumental Performance in 1987. That year, Eddy recorded a new, eponymously titled album that included performances by such ardent fans as Paul McCartney and George Harrison.

BRIAN ENO

Eno referred to himself, at one point during his career, as a "non-musician." But another word that comes to mind is provocateur.

During that career, Eno provoked the rock world with ideas, concepts, and new ways of recording and composing and producing—in short, with an all-encompassing creative philosophy that expanded the boundaries of what the music was and could be.

Establishing a role for himself in rock that was similar to that of his hero, John Cage, in modern classical music, Eno became a musical iconoclast, striking down formulaic approaches to making music even as he created new structures and methods in which music—and other art forms, for that matter—could flourish.

TOP ALBUMS

HERE COME THE WARM JETS (Island, '74)
TAKING TIGER MOUNTAIN BY STRATEGY (Island, '74)
ANOTHER GREEN WORLD (Island, '75)
DISCREET MUSIC (Island/Obscure, '76)
BEFORE AND AFTER SCIENCE (EG/Polydor, '77)
MUSIC FOR FILMS (EG/Polydor, '77)
MUSIC FOR AIRPORTS (PVC/Ambient, '79)
NO PUSSYFOOTING (with Robert Fripp, Island, '73)
801 LIVE (with 801, Island, '76)
MY LIFE IN THE BUSH OF GHOSTS
   (with David Byrne, Sire, '81)

Like Cage, to a large extent Eno's importance derived as much from what he didn't play or compose as from any music he actually made. The significance of both came more from the ideas that were embodied in the music.

In Eno's case, those ideas encompassed an astonishing array of sounds and extramusical premises that influenced various schools of rock and numerous groups and artists over two decades. His use of electronics and synthesizers were building blocks of the art rock of the 1970s and presaged the techno-pop movement of the '80s. His early solo albums of the '70s were deconstructions of rock—with intellectual overtones—that inspired the new wave era. His 1976 boxed set of compositional/philosophical writings, Oblique Strategies, served as the basis and background for his collaboration with David Bowie. And his production of albums by Talking Heads and U2 yielded some of the finest recordings of their careers.

Eno (b. May, 15, 1948, Woodbridge, Suffolk, England) first tweaked rock sensibilities with his work in Roxy Music in the early 1970s. A founding member of the group along with vocalist Bryan Ferry, Eno provided much of the impetus for Roxy's

mannered, purposely artificial rock sound. His synthesizer work, with its complex layers of chords and pointilistic flourishes, diverted attention from the usual bass-drums-guitar sound, giving Roxy Music an almost avant-garde musical presence.

It was a sound and approach that conflicted with the more pop-oriented sensibilities of Ferry. The two began to clash over the direction of the group, and in July 1973, Eno left Roxy Music to pursue a solo career.

Eno's interest in fusing rock with more classical influences surfaced in the album No Pussyfooting, his first post-Roxy project. A collaborative effort with King Crimson guitarist Robert Fripp, the 1973 album was a convoluted, brazenly experimental work that blended jagged, distorted rock sound and beats with minimalistic clusters of notes that were similar to those of classicist Terry Riley. Eno and Fripp then continued these experiments on the album Evening Star in 1976. Integrating new visual approaches with the music, the two toured in support of their first album, performing in total darkness with film loops that were the visual equivalent of the repeating figures of Eno's synthesizer.

His artistic aspirations notwithstanding, Eno pursued a more rock-based course with his debut solo album, Here Come the Warm Jets, in 1973. With various Roxy members backing him, he moved in a direction that encompassed everything from the back-to-basics, 1950s-oriented sound of pub rock to Roxy's arch rock posturings and the flashier presence of the emerging glam-rock movement (at this time Eno also affected a glam-rock persona, with makeup and androgynous attire).

While he pursued that sound on later albums like 1974's Taking Tiger Mountain by Strategy and 1975's Another Green World, adding textures of synthesized sound and bleak aural tone-scapes in the process, he was increasingly drawn to the more intellectual rock of the avant-garde New York scene of the mid-1970s. In 1974, he worked with former Velvet Underground member John Cale on the latter's intense and brooding solo albums Slow Dazzle and Helen of Troy. And with Cale, Kevin Ayers, and former Velvet vocalist Nico, he performed at a concert in London that yielded the album June 1, 1974.

While all of these albums, including his own, were intriguing musical efforts and would pave the way for the new wave of the late 1970s and early '80s, there was an intellectual aloofness about them that made them less than satisfying aesthetically. Perhaps for this reason, his solo career failed to generate much enthusiasm from the public at large and was greeted with some ambivalence by most critics of the time.

Not that any of that seemed to deter Eno from pursuing his expansive creative vision.

In January of 1975, Eno was hit by a car and was forced to spend several months in recovery. While he was bedridden, he began thinking about a new form of Muzak, one that would draw on the somnambulistic aspects of that form while employing them to creative ends. The result was his self-coined genre, ambient music, which he introduced on the 1976 album *Discreet Music*. Recorded at barely audible sound levels, the synthesizer-infused instrumental album contained songs that were intended as background music for various activities.

The approach was expanded on 1977's *Music for Films* (ambient music for films that did not exist—in effect, aural dreamscapes) and 1977's remarkable ambient masterpiece *Music for Airports* (music for public spaces). In fact, Eno's ambient music was more than mere background sound; it had an intellectual and even musical allure that elevated them above the level of elevator music.

In addition to his experiments with ambient sound, Eno spent much time in the '70s devising methods of treating instruments via the use of tape loops and electronics. Employing as many as 25 Revox tape decks (which when looped together would elongate or otherwise alter the sounds of guitars, saxophones, and such), Eno performed onstage and on record as a sort of musical effects man, shaping the music that others made. This process was employed on many of his solo records and on those with Fripp and was particularly effective on the *801* album he recorded with former Roxy guitarist Phil Manzanera in 1976.

Eno began to translate this role of sound-shaper into one of record producer as the 1970s progressed. In 1977, he began work with Bowie on the latter's first art rock album, *Low*. While not formally the record's producer, Eno played a crucial role in the development of that album's sound, co-writing songs with Bowie; adding synthesizers, vocal harmonies, and instrumental treatments; and guiding the musical process of the record with instructions from his *Oblique Strategies*. Basically a set of cards with vague directions printed on them, these were shuffled and drawn and used in the composing process (not unlike the way Cage used the I-Ching to guide some of his "chance" compositions).

The result was one of Bowie's greatest albums and one that came with a distinct art rock, Eno-inflected sound, particularly the second side's droning, synthesizer-saturated soundscapes. The collaboration was such an artistic and musical success that Bowie and Eno continued their partnership on the albums *Heroes* (1977) and *Lodger* (1979), the full three being referred to, at times, as the Eno trilogy.

Eno then began to step into a formal producing role that would yield, over the succeeding decade and more, a stunning and diverse array of albums by a wide range of artists. In 1978, he produced Devo's debut album, which was one of the first industrial-rock records. That same year he began a fruitful relationship with Talking Heads and its leader David Byrne, producing their albums *More Songs About Buildings and Food, Fear of Music,* and *Remain in Light*. His work with Byrne became increasingly infused with African influences, and the two collaborated on the 1980 album *My Life in the Bush of Ghosts,* which included a complex interplay of rhythms and "found voices"—Eno's reinterpretation of Cage's use of radio broadcasts, spontaneous noises, and such that were mixed in a collage of sound.

By then an elder statesman of art rock, Eno increasingly became involved in a series of extramusical and intellectual pursuits. While continuing to release albums, primarily of ambient music, like 1982's *On Land,* he also began to create various video and visual projects that were imbued with avant-garde influences—static installations and such. And he was increasingly in demand as a lecturer on art and music and the various creative methods he had used during his career.

While popular and commercial success continued to elude his own work, he did begin to reach the top levels of the charts through albums that he co-produced (with Daniel Lanois) for U2 in the 1980s. The collaboration began in 1984 with the album *The Unforgettable Fire* and culminated with *The Joshua Tree* (named Album of the Year at the 1988 Grammy Awards), and 1991's *Achtung, Baby!* On all of these albums, Eno's distinctive harmonic ideas and treatments of instruments (particularly the Edge's guitar) were primary components in the group's sound.

In 1992, U2 began its "Zoo TV" world tour, for which Eno designed much of the elaborate video imagery that was at the core of its stage production. The tour starred U2, of course, but behind it were many of the musical and video ideas that Eno had pioneered throughout his long and distinguished career.

THE EVERLY BROTHERS

In the pantheon of
1950s rock and roll founders, the Everly Brothers
occupy a singular place of distinction. With their crisp,
two-part harmonies, Don and Phil Everly crafted a vocal sound
that conquered the charts of the late '50s and early '60s
and influenced generations of rockers to come.

On such signature hits as "Bye Bye Love," "Wake Up Little Susie," "Cathy's Clown," and scores of others, the Everly Brothers blended the sweet and simple melodies of country music with the energy and exuberance of rock and finished them off with sibling harmonies that slipped, slid, and glided along effortlessly.

The Everly Brothers' harmonies were something of a revelation in a rock world that was dominated by the solo vocals of artists such as Elvis Presley, Buddy Holly, Chuck Berry, Jerry Lee Lewis, and others. Their vocals also differed greatly from the harmonies of the doo wop groups of the time, who recreated instrumental sections with their vocals and whose music was generally much more pop oriented.

In fact, the Everly Brothers pioneered the tightly defined vocal sound that would inspire everyone from the Beatles to the Beach Boys and much of the first wave of the British Invasion of the 1960s. And with their unabashed use of country derivations, they set the stage for most of the country rock acts of the 1970s, from the Flying Burrito Brothers to the Eagles and beyond.

The Everlys were, in addition, one of the most popular acts in early rock. In the course of the first five years of their career, from 1957 through 1962, they hit the top 10 of the singles chart 12 times, and in the process sold more than 35 million records. With their slicked-back DAs and their trademark black Gibson acoustic guitars (which were subsequently named for them), they became archetypal

rockers of their time—and of all time.

Their career began in 1955, when Don (b. Isaac Donald Everly, Feb. 1, 1937, Brownie, Kentucky) and Phil (b. Jan. 19, 1939, Chicago) performed on their parents' radio show in Knoxville, Tennessee. After signing with Columbia Records in Nashville that year, they released two songs that were virtually ignored. When Columbia dropped them in 1956, they secured a contract as songwriters with a publishing company owned by Roy Acuff and Wesley Rose, through the encouragement of family friend Chet Atkins.

Rose became their manager and offered them to New York–based Cadence Records as a country act. Label head Archie Bleyer suggested they record Felice and Boudleaux Bryant's "Bye Bye Love." With its high-pitched vocal harmonies and acoustic guitar–based sound, the single became a major hit in June 1957, reaching number two on the charts and promptly selling more than one million copies. The single was also a crossover hit, topping the country and western charts and hitting number five on the R&B rankings.

The Everlys were an immediate success. Within months of the single's release, they appeared on Alan Freed's television show "The Big Beat" and on "The Ed Sullivan Show" and most of the major musical variety programs of the time. When their next single, the Bryants' song "Wake Up Little Susie," was released in October, it topped the charts for two weeks and became the duo's second million-selling record.

The Everly Brothers

They continued their chart run in 1958. While their third single was a modest success at number 26, their fourth, the Bryants' "All I Have to Do Is Dream," hit Number One and stayed there for four weeks. Its successor, the rocking "Bird Dog," scored the same rank. "Devoted to You" reached number 10, and "Problems" hit number two at the end of the year.

While the Everlys' songs were lyrically lightweight, dealing primarily with the usual aspects of teen love and lust, their sound was a crisp blend of traditional country music with a rock edge. Their trademark harmonies were based on those of such country "brother" acts as the Louvin Brothers and Jim and Jess McReynolds. But they added a tight rock feel, with staccato syllables and rhythmic flourishes that gave the songs an energy and brashness the country counterparts had never had—or probably wanted, for that matter.

In any case, the Everly Brothers' stirring combination of country and rock made them a hit with fans of both styles and with the pop public at large.

With new hits like "('Til) I Kissed You" in 1959, the Everlys built on the vast popularity they had accrued in the preceeding years. The result of this was an astounding (for the time) $1 million, 10-year deal they concluded with the new label Warner Bros. in February 1960.

Their initial releases for the label seemed to justify the deal. In March, "Cathy's Clown," written by Don and perfected by Phil, hit Number One and sold three million copies worldwide (it was the first entry in the Warner Bros. catalog). It would be their biggest single. In June, their debut album for the label, *It's Everly Time!*, reached number nine, making it the top charting album of their career along with 1961's *A Date with the Everly Brothers*. By the end of 1960, they had reached the top 10 of the singles charts again with "When Will I Be Loved" (number eight) and "So Sad (To Watch Good Love Go Bad)" (number seven).

While their success continued in 1961—with one of their signature songs, "Walk Right Back," hitting number seven—their career began to falter. They

were inducted into the Marine Corps Reserve in November and curtailed their musical activities while serving a six-month tour of duty (during which they briefly reemerged to perform on "The Ed Sullivan Show").

In 1962, they resumed their run on the charts with "Crying in the Rain" making number six and "That's Old Fashioned (That's the Way Love Should Be)" reaching number nine. But those singles would prove to be the final top 10 hits of their career.

Ironically, the Everly Brothers would be overwhelmed, like many of their 1950s counterparts, by the same British Invasion groups they had inspired. Unlike most of those counterparts, the Everlys continued to release records and tour during the rest of the 1960s, remaining particularly popular in the U.K. Their 1967 release "Bowling Green" was the last charting U.S. record they would have for the next 17 years.

In 1972, they recorded the album *Stories We Could Tell* with an all-star team of rockers that included John Sebastian, David Crosby, and Graham Nash; and in 1973, they returned to their country roots with *Pass the Chicken and Listen*, produced by Chet Atkins. Neither charted.

Perhaps it was the strain, or merely the years, but the Everlys' career came to an abrupt and acrimonious end that year. Performing at Knotts Berry Farm in southern California, Phil slammed his guitar against the stage and walked off in mid-set. Don continued the show but announced that the duo was breaking up, telling the crowd the simple truth, that "the Everly Brothers died ten years ago."

The two then pursued solo careers over the next decade. But with the exception of Phil's 1983 duet with Cliff Richard on "She Means Nothing to Me," which made number nine in the U.K., the brothers were far less successful apart than they had been together.

They reunited in 1983 for a concert at London's Royal Albert Hall and released the live double album *Reunion Concert* in 1984, their first charting record in 17 years, at number 164. They also released the single "On the Wings of a Nightingale"—written for

TOP SONGS

BYE BYE LOVE (Cadence, '57, 2)
WAKE UP LITTLE SUSIE (Cadence, '57, 1)
ALL I HAVE TO DO IS DREAM
   (Cadence, '58, 1)
BIRD DOG (Cadence, '58, 1)
PROBLEMS (Cadence, '58, 2)
('TIL) I KISSED YOU (Cadence, '59, 4)
CATHY'S CLOWN (Warner, '60, 1)
SO SAD (TO WATCH GOOD LOVE GO
   BAD) (Warner, '60, 7)
WALK RIGHT BACK (Warner, '61, 7)
CRYING IN THE RAIN (Warner, '62, 6)

Additional Top 40 Songs: 16

them by Paul McCartney—which reached number 50. Encouraged by this modest success, they resumed touring and recording. *EB 84,* an album of new songs, was released at the end of the year and peaked at number 38.

In 1986, the Everly Brothers were among the first set of inductees into the Rock and Roll Hall of Fame. And in 1988, a granite statue of the brothers was unveiled on Everly Brothers Boulevard in Central City, Kentucky.

FAIRPORT CONVENTION

More often than not, the term folk-rock is linked with the musical movement that was spearheaded by Bob Dylan and the Byrds in the U.S. in the mid-1960s. But in fact there were two distinct folk-rock movements, the other originating in Britain in the later years of the decade.

The American version is generally better known because it was so…American. It swept onto the rock scene in 1965 with the Byrds' transcendent rendition of Dylan's "Mr. Tambourine Man," which generated enormous attention and commercial success. And with the momentum provided by a ravenous press and public, the movement proceeded to yield masterpieces like Dylan's "Like a Rolling Stone" and other—if lesser—pop hits by the Turtles, Sonny and Cher, and countless more. American folk-rock lived fast and hard, produced much in the way of music and money, and faded quickly: by 1967 it was being superceded by the groups of the emerging San Francisco scene.

By contrast, its British counterpart was so . . . British. Rarely in the headlines—and rarely in the charts—British folk-rock was a quiet, if remarkable and eloquent, musical force of its own. Its practitioners concerned themselves with revamping their country's ancient folk music traditions in a rock context. Along the way, they assimilated the various forms that had come from those traditions, most of

which, ironically, were American idioms, such as bluegrass, Cajun, and the myriad offshoots of country—even rock itself. Like the musical traditions that spawned it, British folk-rock didn't fade; it continued to thrive and flourish over the decades.

Spearheading this version of folk-rock was Fairport Convention. Over the course of its 12-year career, this seminal group established the folk-rock sound in Britain and defined and guided it. With its constantly evolving array of musicians—20 members in 14 different configurations during those 12 years—Fairport was also the breeding ground of a number of the other groups of the movement.

Given the various lineups that operated under the group's name during its career, it is impossible to define Fairport Convention's sound in any specific way. The dynamics of the group's musical evolution resided in the emphasis that was given at various points—by various members—to its traditional or more rock-based inclinations. Thus, an album such as *What We Did on Our Holidays* from 1968 was

Fairport Convention

more folk-oriented, while a later album like 1973's *Rosie* had a more rock-based sound. Common to all the group's work, however, was a combination of the melodic and lyrical structures of the English folk tradition and the electric-guitar-based rock of the 1960s. It was a combination that was, by turns, winsome and rocking, provocative and entrancing, energetic and softly alluring.

Arguably, the most representative version of Fairport Convention was the lineup of the late '60s that included vocalist Sandy Denny and guitarist Richard Thompson. Denny was more a folk purist, with a rich, lustrous, and notably dramatic voice that could span centuries of folk traditions in a second while making it all sound fresh and new. Thompson was a complex songwriter given to lyrics that were dark and ascerbic. He was also a remarkable guitarist who

brought country, blues, and rock derivations to the group's sound; he also contrived figures from his guitar whose lithe, sinewy harmonies were approximations of the whines of traditional Uilleann pipes. Along with the rest of the group, Denny and Thompson created the wonderful 1969 albums *Unhalfbricking* and *Liege and Lief,* the latter considered by many to be the finest of all British folk-rock recordings.

Fairport Convention was formed in the spring of 1967, its original lineup including Thompson, Simon Nichol (guitar and vocals), Ashley Hutchings (bass), Judy Dyble (autoharp and vocals), and Shaun Frater (drums). The group began rehearsing and performing sporadically—its initial sound based on American folk-rock and original material—until it came to the attention of Joe Boyd, who became its manager and producer.

The group's lineup changed almost immediately, with Frater leaving and vocalist Ian Matthews and drummer Martin Lamble joining for its eponymously titled debut album in 1968. Later in the year, Denny came on board from another fledgling folk-rock group, Strawbs. She brought along a varied repertoire of traditional folk and several originals, including "Who Knows Where the Time Goes."

Thompson's songs also became a prominent part of Fairport's sound—along with the vocals of Denny—on *What We Did on Our Holidays* (which also included incisive covers of songs by Dylan and Joni Mitchell). The group then began to create a rich,

---

TOP ALBUMS

FAIRPORT CONVENTION (A&M/Polydor, '68)
WHAT WE DID ON OUR HOLIDAYS (Island, '69)
UNHALFBRICKING (A&M/Island, '69)
LIEGE AND LIEF (A&M/Island, '69)
ANGEL DELIGHT (A&M/Island, '71)
BABBACOMBE LEE (A&M/Island, '71)
ROSIE (A&M/Island, '73)
NINE (A&M/Island, '73)
RISING FOR THE MOON (Island, '74)
FAIRPORT CHRONICLES (A&M, '76)

---

varied sound on songs such as "A Sailor's Life" (from *Unhalfbricking*), in which Denny's ethereal folk-based refrains gave way to an extended improvisational section with Thompson's guitar cutting a swath across Lamble's primordial poundings. This music was neither folk nor rock but an inspired amalgam of the two.

By January of 1969, Matthews had quit—displeased with this new direction—and was replaced by fiddler-vocalist Dave Swarbrick. Fairport Convention was poised to become the leading group of the folk-rock scene.

But at its creative apex, the group was struck by tragedy. Following a performance in Birmingham in June of 1969, the group's van skidded off a highway and Lamble was killed (as was Thompson's girlfriend). The group very nearly disbanded.

It didn't. Instead, the members regrouped and, inspired by the way the Band had created an intrinsically American form of music on their album *Music from Big Pink,* proceeded to do the same with the music of their own country. The result was *Liege and Lief,* a sublime redefinition of folk and rock that cemented the group's place in rock history.

The artistic success of that album notwithstanding, dissension began to emerge in the ranks. By the end of the year, Denny had departed to found the group Fotheringay. Hutchings also left to form Steeleye Span, which would become one of the better groups of the English folk-rock movement.

Joining up at that point were drummer Dave Mattacks and bassist Dave Pegg. With their steady, understated presence, the two became one of the finest bass and drum combinations in folk-rock—arguably, in all of rock.

The new lineup released the albums *Live at the L.A. Troubadour* in 1969 and the notable *Full House* in 1970, the latter a tour de force by Thompson and Swarbrick.

By 1971, the original group—or what was left of it—was coming apart. In January, Thompson left to pursue a solo career. Following the release of the 1971 albums *Angel Delight* and *Babbacombe Lee,* Nichol, the group's last original member, departed to form the Albion Country Band with Hutchings.

From that point until the group's demise in 1978, numerous musicians joined Fairport Convention. The ensuing lineups were sturdy enough, but the original vision and sound that had established Fairport Convention as a seminal folk-rock group became diluted. The group was reinvigorated by a re-formation with Denny in 1974, which yielded the albums *Fairport Live* and *Rising for the Moon.* But when she left in 1976, the group began to falter. Its last album was *Farewell Farewell* in 1978.

Most of the original and former members of Fairport Convention continued to be active in the folk-rock scene. Hutching's work with the more rock-oriented Steeleye Span was consistently noteworthy, as was Nichols with the Albion Country Band. In 1992, Mattacks and Pegg teamed up as the rhythm section of Jethro Tull in a musical marriage that wedded the stylistic extremes of folk-rock.

Thompson's solo career, interjected with a lengthy collaboration with his then-wife, Linda, produced many remarkable albums that were endowed with an astonishing array of songs and idioms and his sterling guitar and vocals. In the 1990s, his mastery was finally acknowledged with the release of *Watching the Dark,* a three-CD retrospective of his career, including his work with Fairport Convention.

Sadly, the stirring voice of Denny was stilled when she died in 1978 after suffering a brain hemorrhage from a fall in a friend's home.

FLEETWOOD MAC

In the course of its
23-year career, Fleetwood Mac was many groups—or
rather one group with many lineups—that created many
different forms of rock and roll. But only two of them counted.
And those two could hardly have been more different.

In its original form, in 1967, Fleetwood Mac was one of the more authentic and articulate bands on the burgeoning British blues scene. Ten years and assorted lineups later, a vastly different version of the group made musical history when its album *Rumours* sold more than 17 million copies worldwide and established a new, easygoing, adult-oriented brand of rock and roll.

Anchored through all of those years by the rhythm section of drummer Mick Fleetwood (b. June 24, 1942, London) and bassist John McVie (b. Nov. 26, 1945, London)—whose names provided that of the

group—Fleetwood Mac went through musicians and musical styles with an astonishing alacrity (in its first seven years alone, there were 10 different versions of the group).

In fact, it was Fleetwood and McVie's tenacity that enabled Fleetwood Mac to evolve and finally flourish. In the process, the group's career became one of the most convoluted and colorful in rock, with more than the usual share of wild and (in some cases perhaps literally) crazy members acting out their roles while making diverse and, at times, inspired music.

Fleetwood Mac's musical pedigree could not have been better.

Fleetwood, McVie, and guitarist Peter Green (b. Peter Greenbaum, Oct. 29, 1946, London) were members of John Mayall's Bluesbreakers—in fact, Green had been Eric Clapton's replacement in that seminal band. In July of 1967, they were dismissed from the group and were teamed with guitarist Jeremy Spencer by Mike Vernon of the Horizon record label.

The group, with temporary bassist Bob Brunning, made its debut at the Windsor Jazz and Blues Festival (the preeminent showcase for British blues groups of the time) in August 1967. McVie rejoined in the next month and the group released its debut single, "I Believe My Time Ain't Long," in November of that year.

The timing of the single—and of the group itself—was fortuitous. Fleetwood Mac came along at a time when British blues was emerging from its traditional London base, and the group became a prominent part of that musical tidal wave. When its eponymously titled debut album was released in March 1968, it went to number four in the U.K.

While many of the British blues groups were developing along proto-heavy-metal lines, with riff-based songs and garish guitar solos, Fleetwood Mac distinguished itself with fairly faithful renditions of American urban blues. Having established himself as one of the virtuosos of blues guitar during his days with Mayall, Green began to expand his sound with tastefully spare solos and emotional vocals. On the song "Black Magic Woman" he played a Latin-tinged, blues-inflected solo that was lifted almost intact, two years later, by Carlos Santana on his hit version.

To Green's inspired guitar work, Spencer added

delicate, forceful slide riffs that recalled those of the master, Elmore James. And Fleetwood and McVie were developing into one of the sturdier rhythm sections in rock, with stark, straightforward backgrounds that were remarkably disciplined in comparison with the flashy Cream imitators that were common at the time.

The result was a sound that, over the course of the next two years, would yield some of the finest musical moments in British blues. Songs such as the haunting "Albatross" and the rollicking "Oh Well" transcended the genre and moved the group into a broader rock world, while albums such as 1968's *Mr. Wonderful* and 1969's *Then Play On* had an intensity and power that combined the best of both forms. On the former album, Green recruited a third guitarist, Danny Kirwan (b. Mar. 13, 1950, London), who added a set of counter solos to add texture to the group's sound. And keyboardist Christine Perfect (b. July 12, 1943) of the group Chicken Shack became a part-time member in the studio.

But by 1969, the first of Fleetwood Mac's many odd personal problems began to emerge. Green, who had converted from Judaism to Christianity, began to appear onstage in flowing robes and, offstage, to give in to messianic pretensions. In April 1970, he quit the group to pursue a solo career that would yield the excellent album *The End of the Game* before he descended into madness.

Perfect, who by now had married McVie, joined the group. With Spencer now setting the musical direction, Fleetwood Mac released the album *Kiln House* in October 1970. The blues influences gave way to a lower-keyed rock sound that was competent but somewhat ambiguous. It would be a trend that would mar many of the group's albums over the next five years.

During that time, Fleetwood Mac stumbled from one personal and musical crisis to the next. In February 1971, Spencer disappeared while the group was on tour in Los Angeles. It would later be revealed that he had joined the religious cult the Children of God (he would subsequently record the albums *Jeremy Spencer and the Children of God* in

1973 and *Flee* in 1979). He was replaced by L.A. guitarist-vocalist Bob Welch. This version of the group yielded the eloquent album *Bare Trees*, which came with increasing vocal and song contributions from Christine McVie. While the album reached number 70 on the U.S. charts, Fleetwood Mac still seemed to be floundering, in search of a new and defining sound.

That quest became more complicated in 1972 when Kirwan was sacked from the group after refusing to tour. He pursued a solo career for a time and was subsequently admitted to a mental institution. Bob Weston of Long John Baldry's band joined up, as did vocalist Dave Walker, formerly of the British blues-rock band Savoy Brown. The two new members propelled the group into a newer, more rock-oriented sound.

Ensuing albums such as 1973's *Penguin* and *Mystery to Me* and 1974's *Heroes Are Hard to Find* were directionless affairs. Fleetwood Mac was touring and recording constantly during this time, but the group continued to be afflicted with problems. Weston had an affair with Fleetwood's wife and was sacked in 1973. Walker re-joined Savoy Brown that same year. And in 1974, Welch quit to pursue a solo career.

The low point was reached at the end of 1973 when the group's manager formed an ersatz version of the group for touring purposes. Fleetwood Mac was quickly falling apart.

But the group's fortunes were soon to change—beyond anyone's wildest speculations.

In December 1974, Fleetwood was introduced to Lindsey Buckingham at a studio in Los Angeles. Buckingham was part of a duo, Buckingham Nicks, that had recorded a largely ignored eponymous album in 1973. He had subsequently been a guitarist with Don Everly for a time while his partner Stevie Nicks had become a waitress.

Fleetwood and Buckingham hit it off, musically and personally, and Buckingham and Nicks were invited to join Fleetwood Mac. The result of this new lineup was the eponymous album that was released in August 1975.

TOP ALBUMS

FLEETWOOD MAC (Reprise, '75, 1)
RUMOURS (Warner, '77, 1)
TUSK (Warner, '79, 4)
MIRAGE (Warner, '82, 1)

Additional Top 40 Albums: 5

TOP SONGS

DREAMS (Warner, '77, 1)
DON'T STOP (Warner, '77, 3)
SARA (Warner, '79, 7)
HOLD ME (Warner, '82, 4)
BIG LOVE (Warner, '87, 5)
LITTLE LIES (Warner, '87, 4)

Additional Top 40 Songs: 12

Everything suddenly seemed to coalesce for the group. Buckingham and Nicks brought a new sense of energy and direction to Fleetwood Mac's sound. Their flowing, melodic songs were the ideal counterparts to the pop sensibilities that Christine McVie had been pursuing for some time. And the vocals of the three, while vastly different in their individual ways, combined in rich, distinctive harmonies. Buckingham provided intense, bluesy guitar solos. And Fleetwood and McVie rolled along as they always had.

It all made for a subtle, mature sound that seemed right for a rock world that was fast approaching its middle years. Songs like "Over My Head" and "Say You Love Me" had a winsome, melodic sound that was a soothing combination of rock and pop, while "Rhiannon (Will You Ever Win)" was an intriguing ballad that featured an alluring vocal treatment by Nicks.

In fact, Nicks became the focal point of the group's sound and image. She had an overtly sexual presence that was accentuated by flowing, gypsy-like outfits and stacked heels. Her pouting face was framed by long blonde locks. And her raspy voice cut through the soft-sounding songs, giving them an edge that invigorated the band's otherwise easygoing music.

It was a combination that began to insinuate itself into the public consciousness. Over the course of 15 months, the *Fleetwood Mac* album created an avalanche of attention. "Over My Head" went to number 20 while "Say You Love Me" and "Rhiannon" reached number 11. In September 1976, the album went platinum and hit Number One.

Nearly a decade after it had begun, the group had become one of the biggest rock acts in the world.

In 1977, it became the biggest.

In February of that year the album *Rumours* was released. A culmination of the sound that had been pursued on *Fleetwood Mac, Rumours* was the band's masterpiece. It yielded a wide range of emotionally eloquent songs and an expressive middle-of-the-road sound that proved to be an unprecedented commercial success. The rocking "Go Your Own Way" hit number 10 while the anthemic "Don't Stop" made number three. And the album's focal point, "Dreams," topped the charts; it was the group's first Number One single.

Within two months, the album itself was at Number One. In time, it sold more than 17 million copies worldwide, becoming one of the most successful records in the history of rock.

But the group's personal problems continued apace. By the time *Rumours* was released, Buckingham and Nicks had ended their personal relationship and the McVies had separated. Mick Fleetwood's divorce was finalized at that time. As it had always done, the group plugged along, its sound becoming more expressive amid the turmoil.

In 1979, the group released the album *Tusk*. A sprawling, convoluted record, *Tusk* was a blatant attempt by the group to distance itself from the pop conventions of *Rumours*. While it was criticized at the time for its pretensions to art, *Tusk* displayed the group's—particularly Buckingham's—musical voraciousness. The title song was a Beatles-like tour de force that was recorded with the University of Southern California marching band. "Sara" was a sensitive ballad that tempered the forced grandness of the title cut. The former peaked at number eight while the latter made number seven. And the album, a two-record set, rose to number four.

But the centrifugal forces of success began to tear the group apart. While the group continued to tour, the various members began to pursue careers of their own. Fleetwood recorded the African-inflected album *The Visitor* in 1981. That same year, Nicks's solo debut album, *Bella Donna,* topped the charts, and Buckingham's solo *Law and Order* reached number 32.

Over the course of the next few years, this process would continue. The group's album *Mirage* was released in 1982 and went to Number One. Nicks's career blossomed, yielding the albums *The Wild Heart* (1983), *Rock a Little* (1985), and *The Other Side of the Mirror* (1989), all of which made the top 20. Christine McVie's eponymous album reached number 26 in 1984. Buckingham's *Go Insane* reached number 23, also in that year.

In 1987, the group re-formed for the album *Tango in the Night,* which reached number seven. But by that time, Buckingham had become increasingly disenchanted with the group and was dismissed when he refused to tour. He was replaced by Los Angeles session guitarists-vocalists Rick Vito and Billy Burnette (son of '50s rocker Johnny Burnette). With its new lineup, Fleetwood Mac released the rather lackluster album *Behind the Mask* in 1990. Later in the year, Christine McVie and Nicks quit the group at the end of a tour.

As he had done in the past, Fleetwood said that the group would go on.

It didn't.

THE FLYING
BURRITO BROTHERS

Rock and roll had emerged,
in the 1950s, as a revolutionary amalgam of the blues
and country music. But while the blues subsequently provided
a musical platform for numerous artists and yielded the
British blues movement of the 1960s, country music was
mostly neglected as a distinct musical resource
during the first decade and more of rock's history.

The rockabilly artists of the '50s had incorporated various country elements into their music. And groups like the Beatles and the Lovin' Spoonful had released the odd country-inflected single in the '60s. But the first group entirely devoted to fusing country music and rock did not emerge until 1968. That group was the Flying Burrito Brothers.

The father of that group—and of the country rock sound it pioneered—was Gram Parsons.

With the release of their 1969 debut album, *The Gilded Palace of Sin*, Parsons and the Flying Burrito Brothers virtually created country rock. The album was an unprecedented blend of country melodies, vocals, harmonies, and instrumental signatures and the guitar- and beat-based energy and abandon of rock. On songs like "Hippie Boy," an odd rock guitar line is set against vocals and musical motifs that could have come straight from a honky-tonk bar (or a Nashville recording session). On "Burrito #1" and "Hot Burrito #2," Parsons' vocals were delivered with a straight, unadorned country suppleness that was enlivened by a rock and blues-tinged expressivity. Instrumentally, the guitars of Parsons and Chris Hillman played to and against the sinuous lines and whines of "Sneaky" Pete Kleinow's pedal steel, while bassist Chris Ethridge (and various studio drummers) anchored the sound and gave it a rock solidity and force.

On that album, the Flying Burrito Brothers set in motion the country rock movement that would become a major rock force in the 1970s. That movement would include, in time, the likes of Poco, Pure Prairie League, and the Grateful Dead offshoot the New Riders of the Purple Sage. The Burritos' sound would also influence a vast range of artists who were not strictly country rockers, from Dan Fogelberg to Loggins and Messina, the Eagles, and countless others. Even groups like the Rolling Stones, with whom Parsons became acquainted in the early 1970s, would fall under the Burritos' musical spell and influence (Mick Jagger would subsequently state that Parsons had taught him how to sing country music).

The Flying Burrito Brothers was the culmination of the unique musical vision that Parsons had pursued with a remarkable fervor for a number of years.

An enigmatic and elusive figure, Parsons (b. Cecil Connor, Nov. 5, 1946, Winter Haven, Florida) had begun to explore country music in a rock context during the mid-1960s with various musicians in the southern California area. Adopting a role similar to the one that Alexis Korner had played in the development of British blues at the start of the '60s, Parsons became a tireless crusader for the musical merits of his favorite idiom, guiding others in its direction and instructing them in its execution and interpretation. Unlike the British bluesman, however, Parsons

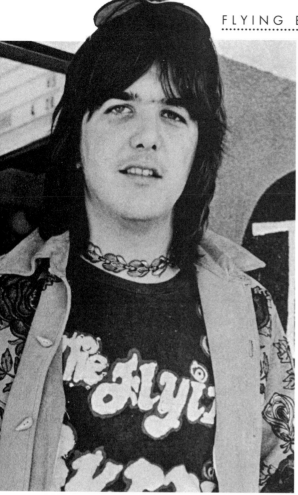
Gram Parsons

While that album was the first country-oriented effort by a major rock group, it was initially viewed as a creative digression in the Byrds' eclectic musical career (in fact, the Byrds—without Parsons—would become a significant exponent of the country rock sound).

But Parsons seemed to sense that a new aggregation was needed to build his music from the ground up. Later in 1968, he split from the Byrds to form the Flying Burrito Brothers. He was soon joined by that group's bassist, Chris Hillman, on guitar and by Kleinow and Ethridge (both of whom had been session musicians in the southern California rock scene). After the release of the group's debut album, Byrds drummer Michael Clarke came aboard.

While *The Gilded Palace of Sin* didn't make the top 40, it earned critical acclaim and turned attention to the group and its country rock sound. The Burritos began to tour constantly during the year, accruing a growing following of fans. But at the end of 1969, Ethridge quit to resume his session work. Hillman moved to bass, and Bernie Leadon was recruited from Dillard and Clark.

Over the course of its fairly brief career, the Burritos not merely established but ultimately expanded Parsons' country rock sound. On its second album, 1970's *Burrito Deluxe,* the group assumed a more rock-based presence, due in part to the playing of guitarist Bernie Leadon (who would take the lessons he had learned and put them to use in his next band, the Eagles).

The new direction conflicted with Parsons' sensibilities and he left in April 1970, to be replaced by guitarist Rick Roberts.

With Parsons' departure, the Flying Burrito Brothers continued to evolve musically, but not necessarily in the best of directions. With Roberts, they increasingly turned to authentic but somewhat innocuous music that, ironically, would also prove to be a hallmark of the country rock movement.

wasn't content to simply replicate that idiom. With his lithe vocals and insightful guitar work, he was intent on creating a revolutionary fusion of country and rock.

His initial attempt in that direction came with the obscure 1967 album *Safe at Home* by the equally obscure group the International Submarine Band. While that album failed to generate much interest, it proved to be a catalyst for his subsequent collaboration with the Byrds. Joining that group in 1968, in the waning days of its epochal folk-rock phase, Parsons began to guide its energies—and songs—in the direction of country music (the Byrds had released the country-flavored hit single "Mr. Spaceman" in 1966). The result of his collaboration with the Byrds was the 1968 album *Sweetheart of the Rodeo,* whose sound was the direct precursor of the music Parsons subsequently pursued with the Flying Burrito Brothers.

TOP ALBUMS

THE GILDED PALACE OF SIN (A&M, '69)
BURRITO DELUXE (A&M, '70)
THE FLYING BURRITO BROTHERS (A&M, '71)
LAST OF THE RED-HOT BURRITOS (A&M, '72)
CLOSE UP THE HONKY TONKS (A&M, '72)
FARTHER ALONG: THE BEST OF THE FLYING
   BURRITO BROTHERS (A&M, '88)

The new lineup lasted nearly a year, during which the group's third album, *The Flying Burrito Brothers,* was released. A bland and mostly negligible record, it hinted at the creative vacuum that had been created by the absence of Parsons.

Perhaps as a result of this, the Burritos began to fall apart. Kleinow departed at the start of 1971, as did Leadon. He was replaced by Al Perkins on guitar.

A new lineup was formed in October 1971 that included fiddler Byron Berline, bassist Roger Bush, and guitarist Kenny Wertz of Country Gazette. They seemed to regain a sense of direction and energy that could be heard on the 1972 bluegrass-inflected album *Last of the Red-Hot Burritos.* But the group, renamed Hot Burrito Revue and Country Gazette, was immediately compromised when Hillman and Perkins left to join Manassas and Clarke retired to his home in Hawaii.

But the new members pressed on, augmented by the Gazette's Alan Munde on banjo and guitar, Don Beck on pedal steel, and Erik Dalton on drums. The outfit toured Europe before finally disbanding in 1973.

But the Flying Burrito Brothers' history was not over. In 1974, Kleinow and Ethridge re-formed the group with Floyd Guilbeau, Joel Scott Hill, and former Byrds drummer Gene Parsons. In 1975, they released the album *Flying Again,* which proved to be a commercial and creative debacle. The same could be said of their final album, *Airborne,* which had none of the energy, excitement, or revolutionary flair that the Flying Burritos had generated in their halcyon days.

It was a somewhat lackluster ending to a group that had virtually pioneered a new rock genre.

The primary importance of Parsons and the Flying Burrito Brothers was defined as much by what they did with their sound as by the sound itself. With country rock, they reintroduced the rock world to one of its basic, formative sources and, in the process, integrated it into the rock mainstream. It was a development that was crucial and one that was long overdue.

On September 19, 1973, Gram Parsons died of heart failure in southern California.

THE FOUR SEASONS

Frankie Valli wasn't the first vocalist in rock and roll to hit a falsetto note. But his signature high-pitched vocals virtually defined the sound of the Four Seasons.

With the release of the single "Sherry" in 1962, Valli's falsetto vocals and the Four Seasons' harmonies went straight to the top of the charts. Over the course of the next five years, the Seasons would become a prominent fixture on those charts and would create some of the finest rock records of its time—and of all time.

The list of those hits was astonishing, both in quality and quantity. In addition to its debut hit, "Sherry," there was "Big Girls Don't Cry," "Walk Like a Man," "Candy Girl," "Dawn (Go Away)," "Rag Doll," "Let's Hang On," and "Working My Way Back to You," among many others. On these and the rest, the Four Seasons created quintessentially American rock that not only survived the British Invasion of 1964, but gave those interlopers a run for their guineas. In fact, before the emergence of the Byrds, the Four Seasons and the Beach Boys were the most successful and visible non-British acts in the rock world.

The Four Seasons

Which was ironic, given the Four Seasons' sound.

In many ways, that sound was a holdover from the rock and roll of the 1950s. Their block-like vocal harmonies were revampings of the doo wop sound of that decade. Its songs, many co-written by vocalist-keyboardist Bob Gaudio, had the melodic pop majesty of the Brill Building masters of '50s Manhattan. And Valli's falsetto vocals had the sturdy, passionate feel of R&B. It was this across-the-board approach that transcended the public's predilection for British rock in the mid-1960s and has made the Four Seasons' records stand up over the succeeding decades.

At the time, the nature of their sound also explained the quartet's crossover success in the pop marketplace; the Four Seasons were one of the first white acts to have major hits on the R&B charts. "Sherry" and "Big Girls Don't Cry" simultaneously topped the rock and R&B listings in 1962.

At the core of their approach was Valli's singing. While his falsetto notes were the group's signature, they were but one aspect of vocal performances that were unsurpassed in their expressive depth and range. Valli pounced on the songs with an intensity and abandon that were, at once, full of teen yearnings and the more mature and worldly expressions of the R&B artists. On "Sherry," Valli was coy and teasing, while on "Walk Like a Man," he was strutting and defiant. On "Rag Doll," he crooned the lyrics with a soulful passion, while on the pounding "Let's Hang On," he rocked with an emotional urgency that was irresistible.

That hit and its follow-up, "Working My Way Back to You," also established a new approach to soul that—along with the more R&B-inflected music of the Righteous Brothers and the Young Rascals— would ultimately pave the way for the "blue-eyed soul" of such acts as Hall and Oates in the 1970s and the dance-oriented pop-soul of the '80s and '90s.

During the course of their career—which was suspended at the end of the 1960s and revived briefly in the mid-'70s—the Four Seasons were one of the most successful acts of the rock era, selling over 80 million records.

Valli (b. Frank Castelluccio, May 3, 1937, Newark, New Jersey) began his career in 1953, recording the single "My Mother's Eyes" for the Mercury label. It promptly flopped. He then performed with various vocal groups in the New Jersey area, one of which, the Variety Trio, included future Four Seasons member guitarist-vocalist Tommy De Vito (b. June 19, 1936, Montclair, New Jersey). The trio changed its name to the Variatones and then the Four Lovers, under which it released the single "(You're the) Apple of My Eye" in 1956. The 'Tones' career was failing when keyboardist-vocalist Bob Gaudio (b. Nov. 17, 1942, Bronx, New York) joined in 1959. That same year, bassist-vocalist Nick Massi (b. Nicholas Macioci, Sept. 19, 1935, Newark) also joined the group, now named Frank Valle and the Romans, completing the Four Seasons' classic lineup.

In 1960, they teamed up with New York producer Bob Crewe and became his vocal session group on various records (including the Freddy Cannon/ Danny and the Juniors' single "Twistin' All Night Long"). Along the way, Gaudio, a protégé of Crewe, began writing songs for the group, many in tandem with the producer. The Four Lovers also changed their name to the Four Seasons, after a bowling alley in New Jersey.

After recording a single for the Gone label, the group was signed by the Chicago-based Vee-Jay company in 1962. The first single for the new label was the Gaudio-Crewe song "Sherry."

On that record, Crewe created a dense, gimmick-laden feel that had much in common with legendary producer Phil Spector's wall of sound. Gaudio suggested that Valli use falsetto vocals, and the rest was rock history.

"Sherry" reached the top of the charts in four weeks, selling more than two million copies. In November, the group had its second Number One hit with "Big Girls Don't Cry." In March 1963, the single "Walk Like a Man" also topped the charts, and the Four Seasons had become one of the major rock acts of the time.

By the end of the year they had had another hit,

"Candy Girl," which reached number three on the charts. But the British Invasion was fast approaching and with it a new ascendancy in rock.

While many of the American rock acts that predated that revolution would be immediately swept aside, the Four Seasons' career continued unabated. In February 1964, "Dawn (Go Away)" hit number three, denied the top by the Beatles' "I Want to Hold Your Hand."

As the year proceeded, dominated by the Fab Four and their fellow countrymen, the Seasons hit the charts repeatedly. A version of the Maurice Williams and the Zodiacs' hit "Stay" made the top 20, as did "Ronnie." And in September 1964, the Four Seasons hit Number One again with "Rag Doll."

Emblematic of their stature at the time was the release of the album *The Beatles Vs. the Four Seasons,* a packaged product of songs by both groups on the Vee-Jay label (which owned the rights to the Beatles debut album, *Introducing the Beatles*).

The Four Seasons' hits continued. "Save It for Me" and "Big Man in Town" reached the top 20 in 1964, while "Bye Bye Baby" did the same in 1965. At the end of that year, the group and Crewe began to incorporate soul music, particularly that of Motown, into its sound. The result was the hit single "Let's Hang On," which hit number three.

Oddly, at the same time, the quartet covered a series of Bob Dylan songs under the pseudonym the Wonder Who. Released as a single, a version of "Don't Think Twice, It's Alright" became a hit, reaching number 12. When Valli's first solo record, "(You're Gonna) Hurt Yourself," made number 39 in February 1966, the group had three songs on the charts under three different names.

The Four Seasons had another signature hit that year with "I've Got You Under My Skin," which rose to number nine. And in 1967 it would make the top 20 three more times with lesser singles (Valli also had a vastly successful hit, "Can't Take My Eyes Off You," which reached number two that year).

But while the Beatles and the Beach Boys had expanded their musical base and were producing arguably the most creative music of their careers, the

TOP SONGS

SHERRY (Vee-Jay, '62, 1)
BIG GIRLS DON'T CRY (Vee-Jay, '62, 1)
WALK LIKE A MAN (Vee-Jay, '63, 1)
CANDY GIRL (Vee-Jay, '63, 3)
DAWN (GO AWAY) (Philips, '64, 3)
RONNIE (Philips, '64, 6)
RAG DOLL (Philips, '64, 1)
LET'S HANG ON! (Philips, '65, 3)
WHO LOVES YOU (Warner, '75, 3)
DECEMBER, 1963 (OH, WHAT A NIGHT) (Warner, '75, 1)

Additional Top 40 Songs: 20

Four Seasons had continued along their commercial pop path and had begun to seem, as the decade progressed, antiquated.

Reacting to this, after a brief period of chart inactivity, the foursome recorded a pretentious concept album, *Genuine Imitation Life Gazette,* in 1969. It was a commercial and artistic flop, primarily because the group disregarded its primary strength, namely its simple—but smashing—approach to rock and pop. With this failure, they parted with their longtime producer, Crewe.

Over the succeeding years the Four Seasons began to come apart. De Vito retired in 1971 and Gaudio departed in 1972. The remaining members moved to the Motown label's subsidiary, Mowest, in 1973 and released the album *Chameleon,* which was largely ignored. But in 1975, the group made a stunning comeback with its Warner Bros. album *Who Loves You.* It hit number 38, while its title song reached number three as a single. In 1976, the group topped the charts for the first time in 11 years with the single "December, 1963 (Oh What a Night)," capitalizing on the popularity of the disco movement.

Valli's solo career also revived in the mid-1970s, and in 1978 he had one of his biggest hits with the title song from the movie "Grease," which topped the charts.

Other records would follow, including a 1984 collaboration with the Beach Boys, "East Meets West." And with various lineups, Valli continued to tour on the nostalgia circuit.

But none of this later history had much to do with the musical legacy of the group. That legacy—and the Four Seasons' place in rock history—was established in the 1960s, when Frankie Valli's falsetto ruled the day.

PETER GABRIEL

Peter Gabriel stands as one of rock's preeminent pioneers in the truest sense of the word; the musical equivalent of an explorer of the Victorian Age.

He constantly searched out new expressive territories to discover and exploit for his own artistic purposes. In the process, he expanded the frontiers of the music and enriched the wealth of resources on which it could draw.

Defying convention and crossing musical boundaries with a willful abandon, Gabriel created a body of work that was singular in its sound and creative breadth and range.

At the start of the 1970s, Gabriel became one of the founders of the art rock movement through his work as vocalist and songwriter for Genesis. His onstage performances with that group were highly theatrical and idiosyncratic, and his songs were imbued with a complexity and intellectualism that defined much of the art rock ethos.

But while he became one of the leaders of that movement, Gabriel's inquisitive musical instincts forced him in other directions, leading to a solo career that would prove to be as provocative as it was, ultimately, commercially successful.

In a series of eponymous solo albums in the 1970s and early '80s, Gabriel created music that defied categorization. Many of his songs from these albums were imbued with an introspection that approached self-absorption. But others simultaneously reached out to the world, speaking to social and political issues that demanded redress.

Musically, his songs were equally diverse. Gabriel's art rock tendencies were incorporated into music that employed state-of-the-art electronics. At the same time, he began to use rhythmic and thematic material—as well as instrumentation and performers—from a wide range of ethnic sources that literally spanned the globe. On later albums such as 1986's *So* and 1992's *Us,* Gabriel combined high- and low-tech accoutrements in a richly varied but oddly unified sound that seemed to be without definable boundaries.

As an adjunct to his musical explorations, Gabriel founded the WOMAD (World of Music, Art and Dance) festival in 1982. Combining rock artists from the West with musicians from all over the world, WOMAD became, in time, an organization that produced more than 60 related musical events in 12 countries. These "festivals" also came with displays of cutting-edge creative technologies and exhibitions of ethnic handicrafts and artifacts.

With these festivals, Gabriel became a catalyst in the development of the world music scene and, in a broader context, in the multicultural movement that began to make inroads into Western countries, including the U.S. and the U.K., in the 1980s and '90s. He also founded the Real World record label, which released records by a wide range of musicians from various countries. This was an effort by Gabriel to open the music of mostly non-Western cultures to the vast rock and pop marketplace.

Gabriel's inclusion of the world at large into his own artistic vision could also be seen in his participation in various benefit performances and tours for a number of causes and organizations. He was a part of the benefit tours for Amnesty International: 1986's "A Conspiracy of Hope" and 1988's "Human Rights Now." In 1989, he appeared at a concert honoring Nelson Mandela's 70th birthday and at the Prince's Trust rock gala in London. He contributed to the *Greenpeace—Rainbow Warriors* album, also in 1989. And in 1991 he took part in "The Simple Truth" benefit concert for Kurdish refugees.

Gabriel (b. May 13, 1950, Cobham, Surrey, Eng-

land) began his career in 1965 when he formed the group the Garden Wall with fellow Charterhouse Public School classmates guitarist-bassist Mike Rutherford, keyboardist Tony Banks, guitarist Anthony Phillips, and drummer Chris Stewart. In 1967, the group changed its name to Genesis and eventually secured a contract with Decca Records, which yielded the 1969 album *From Genesis to Revelation* (reportedly selling 650 copies).

By 1970, the classic Genesis lineup was completed when Gabriel, Rutherford, and Banks were joined by drummer Phil Collins and guitarist Steve Hackett.

With Gabriel providing most of the group's musical direction and songs, Genesis began to make an impact on the fledgling U.K. art rock scene in the early 1970s. Albums such as 1970's *Trespass,* 1971's *Nursery Crime,* 1972's *Foxtrot,* and 1973's *Selling England by the Pound* included complex instrumentation and lush layers of sound that were augmented by Gabriel's angular melodic sensibilities.

Onstage, Gabriel was a commanding presence. Wearing makeup and masks, dressed in various outlandish costumes, and cavorting about in quasi-choreographed movements, Gabriel provided overtly theatrical performances that supplemented the group's convoluted songs and instrumental forays. This interplay culminated in the 1974 concept album *The Lamb Lies Down on Broadway* and its subsequent tour. On that tour, Gabriel acted out the music's rather involved story line onstage.

But in a surprise move, Gabriel quit the group in 1975—just as it was becoming vastly popular—and began to pursue a solo career.

At the time, Gabriel's decision mystified the group's fans. But over the course of the next decade, the musical differences between him and the rest of the group became increasingly apparent. With Collins assuming much of the musical direction (and Gabriel's vocal role), Genesis began to pursue a more pop-oriented course that proved to be immensely successful. Gabriel's music, conversely, became more experimental and began to include various ethnic sources.

He released his debut solo album in 1977. Eponymously titled, as were its three successors through

---

TOP ALBUMS

PETER GABRIEL (Atco, '77, *38*)
PETER GABRIEL (Mercury, '80, *22*)
PETER GABRIEL (SECURITY)
  (Geffen, '82, *28*)
SO (Geffen, '86, *2*)

TOP SONGS

SHOCK THE MONKEY (Geffen, '82, *29*)
SLEDGEHAMMER (Geffen, '86, *1*)
IN YOUR EYES (Geffen, '86, *26*)
BIG TIME (Geffen, '86, *8*)

Peter Gabriel

1982, the album was a dense combination of his previous art rock sound with a new rhythmic sensibility. The album yielded the U.K. hit single "Salsbury Hill."

Gabriel began a collaboration with King Crimson guitarist Robert Fripp in the later '70s that was imbued with the latter's experimental use of electronic sound. Fripp produced Gabriel's second album, and the two combined their creative forces on Fripp's 1979 album *Exposure*.

Over the course of the next few years, Gabriel's music began to expand and evolve, becoming more personal and, at the same time, activistic. Songs such as 1982's "I Have the Touch" came with a brooding intensity and droning synthesized sound, while "Shock the Monkey," from 1983, was propelled by pounding dance beats and Gabriel's maniacal vocals.

Along the way, Gabriel's social-political instincts began to be expressed in songs like 1980's "Games Without Frontiers," which railed against national and cultural chauvinism, and "Biko," a tribute to the martyred South African activist.

By the mid-1980s, Gabriel was an established and respected figure on the rock scene. But he had yet to emerge as a vast rock star. That changed in 1986 when his album *So* hit number two on the U.S. charts. From that album, the single "Sledgehammer" made Number One. The video for "Sledgehammer," a tour de force of stop-motion animation, was also highly successful, gaining extensive airplay on MTV.

In 1988, Gabriel provided dense, abstract, ethereal music for the soundtrack of the Martin Scorsese film *The Last Temptation of Christ*. That score, subsequently released in 1989 on the album *Passion— Music for the Last Temptation of Christ*, won Gabriel a 1990 Grammy Award for Best New Age Performance.

As he made his way into the '90s, Gabriel built on his popularity and the music he had been pursuing for decades. His 1992 album, *Us*, was a forceful combination of synthesizer-based sound, ethnic influences, charging beats, and, lastly, the lithe, sinewy melodies and vocals that had been a signature of his music from his days with Genesis.

THE GRATEFUL DEAD

Of all the groups that came to prominence during the Summer of Love in San Francisco in 1967, the Grateful Dead was the sole survivor and the one that stayed true to the scene's idealistic philosophy of rock as a musical-social-communal "family" affair.

Over the course of its long and convoluted career, the Dead evolved into a cultural phenomenon, virtually creating a niche of its own in the rock world. Everything about them was without precedent. In a rock business dominated by hit records, the Dead not only survived but flourished for more than a quarter century with just one top 10 album and single (1987's *In the Dark* and its single "Touch of Grey").

It accomplished that by establishing itself, early on, primarily as a live act whose hallmarks were extended improvisations that lasted as long as 25 minutes and more and varied from show to show. The group also eschewed the usual rock practice of performing its hits (since it didn't have any) and "new product," opting instead for a wide range of songs that were seemingly chosen at random from its extensive list of albums and from songs of other artists, along with R&B, folk, rock, and country classics. In an age when most rock shows were minutely staged and choreographed, the Dead's were idiosyncratic affairs, with the musicians taking long breaks between songs and, when performing, interacting in a concertedly musical manner with little regard for non-musical affectations or flourishes.

The Dead also had a unique communal musical philosophy. While the core group was initially made up of guitarists-vocalists Jerry Garcia and Bob Weir, keyboardist Ron "Pigpen" McKernan, bassist Phil Lesh, and drummer Bill Kreutzmann, the group expanded and contracted over the years as new musicians joined and left the fold (the group's long-time second drummer, Mickey Hart, was added in 1968). Offshoot groups were constantly created

from the original—the New Riders of the Purple Sage, the Jerry Garcia Band, Bobby and the Midnights, and countless one-off combinations of group members and their extensive family of part-time collaborators. In a very real sense, the Dead was a musical continuation of the communal days of the Haight-Ashbury period.

This philosophy was extended to the group's audience. The Dead built a devoted base of fans known as Deadheads, many of whom slogged from city to city to see their heroes on tour. Those fans (and their more sedentary counterparts) yielded sell-outs at virtually every Dead show in its later years, consistently making the group one of the top concert draws in the U.S. and abroad. At those shows—and in complete disregard for the music industry's usual abhorrence of such matters—the group encouraged its fans to tape its performances, which yielded countless bootlegs of the Dead's music and, in the process, created a recorded "oral" tradition of its onstage history.

The shows themselves were surrounded by an odd, but supportive, social milieu. The Deadheads were always on hand—having arrived in their psychedelically painted communal buses—hawking homemade wares and trinkets that provided them with money to pay for ticket and travel expenses. The atmosphere was that of a street fair or "love-in" from the 1960s. In fact, going to a Dead show, one was transported, as if by a time warp, to an older rock time.

Musically, the band was equal parts innovation and anachronism. Its songs were a generally rather

The Grateful Dead

nondescript array of derivations that ranged from rock and folk to country and R&B influences. While hardly distinctive, these songs were employed as basic structures from which the Dead could proceed into its improvisations.

The improvisations themselves were all that mattered. An agile guitarist in many genres, Garcia would usually lead the way, with Kreutzmann providing a basic beat while the eclectic Hart would add various ethnic percussion flourishes. In later years, keyboardist Brent Mydland would counter with everything from R&B organ phrases to electronic layers of sound, while Weir and Lesh provided a solid underpinning to it all.

But this is a gross oversimplification of what the Dead's improvisations were about. In fact, the group's vast array of musical interests combined in various ways to give its instrumental interactions a complexity and breadth that were kaleidoscopic. At any given time, and in any given song, the Dead could sound like anything from a garrulous band of bluegrass pickers to an avant-garde electronic ensemble, with traces of blues, soul, R&B, and the musical kitchen sink added along the way. In short, every Dead performance was a unique affair (which made the bootleg tapes a crucial adjunct to the group's career).

The Dead gradually coalesced over a two-year period. In 1963, Garcia (b. Jerome John Garcia, Aug. 1, 1942, San Francisco, California) teamed with Weir (b. Robert Hall, Oct. 6, 1947, San Francisco), Kreutzmann (b. Apr. 7, 1946, Palo Alto, California), and Pigpen (b. Ron McKernan, Sept. 8,

1945, San Bruno, California) in the group Mother McCree's Uptown Jug Champions. Other local blues and bluegrass musicians were involved on an on-again, off-again basis, including the future Dead lyricist, Robert Hunter.

By 1965, the group had developed a more rock-based sound and changed its name to the Warlocks. At that point, Garcia, Weir, McKernan, and Kreutzmann were joined by Lesh (b. Philip Chapman, Mar. 15, 1940, Berkeley, California).

The Warlocks became involved with Ken Kesey's Merry Pranksters and performed as the house band of sorts for the "acid tests" that Kesey staged from time to time. The acid tests were part party, part public experiments with the drug LSD. Performing at these events, the group developed a fledgling version of the extended improvisations that would become the core of its music.

The band's involvement with Kesey immersed it in the burgeoning drug culture that was proliferating in the Bay Area. In 1966, it changed its name to the Grateful Dead and moved into a group house in San Francisco's Haight Ashbury, the focal point of the emerging hippie scene. Over the next year, the Dead played at numerous free shows and participated in two seminal events in that scene. In November 1966, it performed with Jefferson Airplane at the opening night of the soon-to-be-legendary Fillmore Auditorium. In January 1967, it was part of the first Human Be-In in Golden Gate Park.

These performances and others established the Dead as one of the preeminent groups on the scene, along with the Airplane, Big Brother and the Holding Company (which included Janis Joplin), Country Joe and the Fish, and Quicksilver Messenger Service. With the success of the Airplane, that scene came to national attention, and each of these groups and scores of others were quickly signed by major labels.

The Dead was signed by Warner Bros. Records at the start of 1967. Their eponymous debut album was released in May.

But the album was a commercial and musical disappointment. Recorded in three days, it was a mostly dull effort that barely hinted at the power and energy that the group displayed onstage. It would be a recurring problem.

During the recording of its second album in February 1968, Hart was recruited as a second drummer, and keyboardist Tom Constanten also joined. But when that album, *Anthem of the Sun,* was released, it proved to be equally inadequate.

TOP ALBUMS

WORKINGMAN'S DEAD (Warner, '70, 27)
GRATEFUL DEAD (Warner, '71, 25)
EUROPE '72 (Warner, '73, 24)
WAKE OF THE FLOOD (Grateful Dead, '73, 18)
GRATEFUL DEAD FROM THE MARS HOTEL
   (Grateful Dead, '74, 16)
BLUES FOR ALLAH (Grateful Dead, '75, 12)
GO TO HEAVEN (Arista, '80, 23)
IN THE DARK (Arista, '87, 6)
BUILT TO LAST (Arista, '89, 27)

Additional Top 40 Albums: 4

TOP SONG

TOUCH OF GREY (Arista, '87, 9)

Not that it seemed to matter. With its numerous performances across the country, including the Monterey Pop Festival in 1967 and the Woodstock Festival in 1969, the Dead was developing a devoted fan base and an estimable musical reputation.

A third album, *Aoxomoxoa,* also failed in 1969, but 1970's *Live/Dead,* a quasi-"live" album—recorded in a studio with friends as an audience—came closer to capturing their onstage sound. The album included a sprawling 25-minute version of "Dark Star," one of their signature stage songs.

Having gotten its studio "legs," the Dead entered its most creative period as a recording act. Later in 1970, the group released arguably its finest studio album, *Workingman's Dead.* Ironically, they accomplished this by downplaying their "jams," concentrating instead on a set of more compact songs that drew heavily from Garcia's country, folk, and rock derivations. The album yielded another signature song, "Uncle John's Band."

The group pursued a similar course on its next album, *American Beauty,* which was also a musical—if not commercial—success. These albums would be the apex of the group's studio sound.

As the new decade rolled on, the Dead's musical family continued to evolve. Constanten quit in 1970 and McKernan died in 1973. Bay Area keyboardist Merle Saunders joined, temporarily, in 1972 before giving way to Keith Godchaux and his wife, vocalist Donna Godchaux. Along the way, Garcia and Hart formed the New Riders of the Purple Sage with several members of the group's extended circle. Hunter increasingly became active as a lyricist. And Garcia, Hart, Lesh, and Weir began to pursue solo careers as the 1970s progressed.

Over the course of the next two decades, the Grateful Dead became something of a rock institution, creating and functioning virtually in a world of its own. For a time, the group released records on its own self-titled label and an offshoot, Round Records, which was used as a base for its more exotic musical efforts. The Dead also set up its own business organization to oversee their many and varied interests, including a charity foundation and an information hotline for Deadheads. In ways that few other groups could claim, the Dead was in control of its musical career.

New members were added and lost. In 1979, the Godchauxes were sacked because of musical differences; Keith Godchaux died in 1980. He was replaced by keyboardist Brent Mydland, who became a full-fledged member and remained with the Dead until his death in 1990. Grammy-winning keyboardist and vocalist Bruce Hornsby filled in, ultimately giving way to former Tubes keyboardist Vince Welnick.

The Dead's music barely changed during all of this. Onstage, it maintained its time-honored improvisational approach, which remained remarkably constant and consistently intriguing. Its records continued to be mostly disappointing, commercially and musically. The exception was 1987's *In the Dark,* whose satisfying set of songs included the hit single "Touch of Grey," which reached number nine on the charts (the album sold more than one million copies).

But the group continued to be primarily a stage act that—its paucity of hits or, at times, new product of any sort notwithstanding—consistently rated in the top five of touring acts in any given year. High points of the group's touring career included a 1973 performance (with the Band and the Allman Brothers) at the Watkins Glen Festival in New York state, which drew 600,000 fans—the largest crowd in rock history.

The group staged a memorable series of benefit shows at the base of the Great Pyramid near Cairo, Egypt, in 1978. In 1987, the Dead toured the U.S. with Bob Dylan, which yielded—again—a thoroughly dismal live album, *Dylan and the Dead.* The group also frequently participated in concerts for numerous causes and charities, including Greenpeace, the Rainforest Action Network, disaster relief for victims of the 1989 Loma Prieta Earthquake in the Bay Area, and others.

The individual members also became involved in various personal pursuits that were emblematic of the Dead's many and assorted interests. Lesh created a foundation that funded the recording of the compositions of avant-garde classical composers. Hart, an avid fan and student of various ethnic percussive forms, sponsored the recording of music from various parts of the world. In 1991, he published the book *Drumming at the Edge of Magic.*

Garcia's health, exacerbated by drug problems and other excesses, began to decline as the years wore on. He became critically ill in 1992, and the group was forced to cancel its tour schedule for several months. There was even speculation that the Dead would be forced to retire. It didn't happen. By 1993 the group was at it again, touring across the country to the usual delirious response of its Deadheads.

BILL HALEY AND HIS COMETS

E
lvis Presley was bigger.
Chuck Berry was better. But Bill Haley was first.

When Bill Haley and His Comets' "Crazy Man Crazy" was released in 1953, it became the first rock and roll single to make the *Billboard* charts.

That accomplishment in and of itself would have assured Haley a place in the history of rock and roll. But it proved to be merely the musical warmup to the main event. That event was the release of "(We're Gonna) Rock Around the Clock" in 1955.

While musical historians can argue the point, the rock era truly began on July 9, 1955, when "Rock Around the Clock" hit Number One on the singles chart and began a reign of eight weeks. In time, the record would become the biggest single in rock history, selling an estimated 20 million copies worldwide.

But it was much more. "Rock Around the Clock" was a watershed in the history of American popular music. It was the spark that ignited the rock and roll revolution, the song that separated rock from all of its various pop predecessors. It marked the moment at which rock became, in the collective mind of the culture, a definable style and sound and presence.

The success of the record, and its inclusion on the soundtrack of the film *Blackboard Jungle*, immediately propelled Haley and rock and roll into the public consciousness. With its jumping, rockabilly beats and jabbing chords and fleeting guitar solo and Haley's boisterous rockabilly-inflected vocals, "Rock Around the Clock" generated an unprecedented response. During showings of the film, young crowds began to dance in the aisles when the song was played. In the U.K. they rioted in the theatres, creating the first outbreaks of teen "rebellion."

"Rock Around the Clock" also proved to be the inspiration for a new generation of soon-to-be rock-ers. Years later, John Lennon, Keith Richards, and countless others would recall the catalytic impact the record had had on them. It was as if the record had unleashed in teens the power and possibilities of their age, of youth itself, and of the new form of music that they would call their own.

Ironically, at the center of this cultural maelstrom was Haley himself. At 32, Haley was relatively old for his role as rock's first hero, given the younger ages of his fans and the youthful aura of his music. Neither brash nor outwardly outlandish, he was also somewhat chubby, with a round face that was punctuated by a cowlick that curled down over his forehead. In fact, he looked less like what would come to be defined as a rocker than he did a country and western musician from the 1930s and '40s.

Which, in a way, he was.

Haley (b. Willam John Clifton Haley, July 6, 1925, Detroit) began his musical career in the 1930s, playing hillbilly music at local county fairs in Pennsylvania, where he had moved with his family. In 1942 he became a yodeller with a touring show. That work gave way to a stint with various country bands like the Down Homers and the Range Drifters. In 1945, he cut his first solo record, "Candy Kisses." He formed a group, the Four Aces of Western Swing, in 1948 and subsequently recorded the single "Too Many Parties, Too Many Pals." In 1949, he became a radio disc jockey for station WPWA in Chester, Pennsylvania, also performing on-air with the Four Aces.

Over the course of the next few years, Haley began to expand his musical style, increasingly leaning in the direction of the R&B music that was becoming popular. This was a crucial development in his sound, because the combination of country and western, hillbilly, and R&B would soon coalesce—in his music and that of various others—into rock and roll.

In 1951, he recorded a version of Jackie Brenston's R&B hit "Rocket 88" for the Holiday subsidiary of Essex Records. It sold 10,000 copies and

Bill Haley and his Comets

failed to chart. A similar non-charting fate awaited the Haley original "Green Tree Boogie." But in 1952, his version of Jimmy Preston's 1949 R&B record "Rock the Joint" sold 75,000 copies and encouraged Haley to pursue a more rock-oriented course.

He changed the name of his group—whose lineup included guitarist Frannie Beecher, bassist Al Pompilli, saxophonist Rudy Pompilli, and drummer Ralph Jones—to Bill Haley and His Comets to distance himself from the antiquated country and western scene. Making the break complete, he released the single "Crazy Man Crazy," which hit number 15.

While that record was an important milestone for Haley and rock, it barely hinted at what was to come

---

TOP ALBUMS

Rock Around the Clock (Decca, '56, 12)
Rock 'n' Roll Stage Show (Decca, '56, 18)

TOP SONGS

Dim, Dim the Lights (I Want Some Atmosphere) (Decca, '54, 11)
Mambo Rock (Decca, '55, 18)
Birth of the Boogie (Decca, '55, 17)
(We're Gonna) Rock Around the Clock (Decca, '55, 1)
Razzle-Dazzle (Decca, '55, 15)
Burn That Candle (Decca, '55, 9)
See You Later, Alligator (Decca, '56, 6)
R-O-C-K (Decca, '56, 16)

Additional Top 40 Songs: 5

---

for both. In fact, when "Rock Around the Clock" was originally released in 1954, as a B side to "Thirteen Women," it was largely ignored by the public.

But Haley—and rock—were beginning to roll. His next release, a version of Joe Turner's "Shake, Rattle and Roll" reached number 12 in 1954. And subsequent records "Dim, Dim the Lights (I Want Some Atmosphere)" and "Mambo Rock" made the top 20 at the start of 1955. In May of that year, timed to coincide with the film *Blackboard Jungle,* "Rock Around the Clock" was rereleased as an A side.

Immediately, Bill Haley and His Comets, and rock and roll itself, became big news. While the record rode the top of the charts, attention came to be focused on Haley and rock as new forces on the pop music scene. The subsequent outbreaks of violence and dancing at showings of the film increased public awareness of the burgeoning teen culture and its unlikely musical hero.

Haley was at the apex of his popularity. Over the course of the next two years, he and the Comets would become one of the biggest acts in music. Records such as 1955's "Razzle Dazzle" and "Burn the Candle" hit the top 20. And in 1956, "See You Later, Alligator" became an immense hit, making number six and selling more than one million copies. That same year, Haley starred in the first rock exploitation films, *Rock Around the Clock* (with deejay Alan Freed and Little Richard) and its followup, *Don't Knock the Rock.*

Haley and His Comets also became one of the biggest concert draws of the time. Their shows were exuberant affairs, with Beecher dispensing torrid solos and Pompilli wailing away on his sax while slamming himself to the stage. Haley presided over it all with a commanding, paternalistic presence that reflected the family man he was offstage. But it was just that presence that would prove to be his undoing. In 1956, the rock revolution he had begun was hit by an entirely new phenomenon that would remake the music and its image.

That phenomenon was Elvis Presley.

As young as rock's fans and endowed with a sexual energy and style that Haley could never hope to duplicate, Presley created a new epoch in the history of rock and roll. Like Haley, Presley instantly became a rock hero; unlike Haley, he also became a rock idol. In the process, he came to symbolize the essentially youthful nature of rock, with all of its energy and tension and sexual abandon.

Haley and His Comets continued to be a major act. Their 1957 tour of England was greeted with hysteria by the British public; the tumultuous scenes of Haley's arrival by train in London became one of the signature images of fan mania in the history of rock. And during the rest of the decade, Haley and his group scored several top 40 hits in the U.S. and Europe.

Then his career began to falter. By the arrival of the British Invasion of 1964 he was recording primarily for smaller labels (although he continued to be a major concert draw in Europe). And by the end of that decade he had become a nostalgia act. He remained such for the rest of his career. "Rock Around the Clock" would be rereleased at various points, making the charts in Europe again and again.

At the end of 1980, he was forced to cancel an upcoming U.K. tour due to illness. On February, 9, 1981, he died of a heart attack in Harlingen, Texas.

JIMI HENDRIX

W̲hen Jimi Hendrix emerged in 1966 with his group the Jimi Hendrix Experience, he confronted the rock world with an entirely new sound and vision. Hendrix seemed to be all things at once, and others that had never been imagined.

For a start, he was a black man—and an American at that—who affected the frilly, outlandish garb of the '60s British psychedelic scene. At the time, that alone was revolutionary; to that point, black musicians had typically been soul men, with shiny suits and processed hair. But with his high, puffy bouffant and his military coats and scarves and beads, Hendrix knocked down clichés even as he suggested new possibilities.

The look was not deceiving.

Hendrix's music was equally iconoclastic and revolutionary. Over the course of his career, he created a singular sound that was an inspired amalgam of various musical forms, the end result transcending all of them. On his 1967 debut album, *Are You Experienced?* he combined the traditional signatures of blues guitarists like Albert King with the distorted tones and pioneering phrasings of Eric Clapton, the power chords of Pete Townshend, and the feedback and noises of Jeff Beck in a slamming, screeching rock onslaught that had never been heard before.

On his next album, 1968's *Axis: Bold as Love,* his instrumental tirades gave way to a dense, churning sound that came with the whiplash, rhythmic chords of R&B, to which he gave a new thematic role. On that album's successor, the two-record *Electric Ladyland* (also from 1968), he expanded his musical and sonic vocabulary on extended improvisations that had the expressionistic abandon of free jazz.

Onstage, Hendrix was equally contradictory and transcendent. In his performances, he was the epitome of the outlandish showman. He strummed his trademark white Stratocaster guitar behind his back, picked it with his teeth, slammed it into his amplifiers. When he set fire to his guitar during his performance at the Monterey Pop Festival, he created one of the most enduring images of the rock era.

But the histrionics aside, he also performed with a virtuosity that was breathtaking. His improvised rendition of "The Star-Spangled Banner" at the 1969 Woodstock Festival was a tour de force that had few expressive equals in the history of rock. Screaming the song's familiar theme while producing sounds of careening airplanes and exploding bombs, he encapsulated the anger, fear, and anguish of the Vietnam era in a powerful musical assault.

While Hendrix was an epochal rock figure, the same could be said of his group. The Jimi Hendrix Experience was one of the great rock outfits of its time—and of all time—and perfectly complemented Hendrix's vocal and instrumental expressions.

His fiery solos and funky power chords and lithe, rhythm-inflected vocal acrobatics were counterbalanced by Mitch Mitchell's virtuosic drumming and Noel Redding's rolling, articulate bass lines. The Experience didn't play as a group as much as they sparred, musically, as individuals. But there was also an exceptional ensemble cohesiveness to their work.

Hendrix was an immensely influential figure in the evolution of contemporary music. His combination of blues, rock, and R&B was the direct precursor of the music of Sly and the Family Stone and Prince. His guitar innovations set the stage for much of the heavy metal movement and inspired musicians as diverse as Edward Van Halen and Stevie Ray Vaughan. His angular, discordant solos—augmented by the jazz-oriented drumming of Mitchell—were subsequently adopted, and adapted, by the jazz fusion movement of the early 1970s and could be heard in the music of such guitarists as John McLaughlin and Larry Coryell (his funky, expressionistic improvisations had a great impact on Miles Davis, particularly on late-'60s and early '70s albums like *Bitches Brew*). In 1983, the avant-garde classical string ensemble Kronos Quartet recorded a version of "Purple Haze."

Hendrix's career—and life—proved to be tragically brief. But his impact on music spanned generations.

*Jimi
Hendrix*

Hendrix (b. James Marshall Hendrix, Nov. 27, 1942, Seattle, Washington) began his career in 1961. Following a brief stint as a paratrooper in the U.S. Army, he began playing with various R&B groups, touring the South. Along the way, he became a sideman for the likes of Little Richard, Sam Cooke, Ike and Tina Turner, Jackie Wilson, and others.

By 1964, Hendrix had settled in New York City, where he played with the Isley Brothers and King Curtis on the local club scene. In 1965, he struck out on his own, assuming the name Jimmy James and forming his own group, the Blue Flames. With that group, he began to build a reputation as a guitarist and performer.

At the suggestion of Keith Richards's girlfriend, Linda Keith, former Animals bassist Chas Chandler took in one of James's shows at the Café Wha? during the summer of 1966. Impressed with what he saw, Chandler convinced James to return with him to London to form a group.

Reverting to his surname, but changing the spelling of his first name to Jimi, Hendrix made his way to London in September of 1966. With the assistance of Chandler, now Hendrix's manager, he recruited drummer Mitch Mitchell (b. John Mitchell, June 9, 1947, Ealing, London) and bassist Noel Redding (b. David Redding, Dec. 25, 1945, Folkestone, Kent), and the three became the Jimi Hendrix Experience.

The Experience debuted on October 18, 1966, at the Paris Olympia as the opening act for French pop star Johnny Hallyday. Chandler then began to publicize Hendrix and the group with selected showcase performances on the London club scene.

Released at the end of 1966, the group's first single, a cover of the Leaves' hit "Hey Joe," went to number six on the U.K. charts in February 1967. Its second single (and one of Hendrix's signature songs), "Purple Haze," reached number three in May. That same month, the band's debut album, *Are You Experienced?* hit number two. In barely six months, the Jimi Hendrix Experience had become one of the biggest rock acts in the U.K.

In June, it began to do the same in the U.S. That month, Hendrix was invited to perform at the Monterey Pop Festival (at the suggestion of one of the event's directors, Paul McCartney). The group made its debut at the festival on June 16. Amid the event's flower-power imagery, Hendrix performed with a ferocity that stunned the hippie crowd. At the end of his final song, a slashing rendition of the Troggs'

"Wild Thing," Hendrix sank to the stage on his knees and set fire to his guitar.

Over the course of the succeeding months, Hendrix and the Experience established themselves solidly in the U.S. In July, they created a minor furor when they were sacked as the opening act of the Monkees' tour (due to protests from the parents of that group's teen fans). When *Are You Experienced?* was released in the U.S. in October, it went to number five at the start of a chart stay that would last two years.

In February of 1968, the group's second album, *Axis: Bold as Love,* was released and promptly went to number three on the U.S. charts. That same month, the Experience embarked on a major U.S. tour. While much of the country had been listening to the band's records for months, most rock fans had yet to actually see them perform onstage. It was to be an eye-opening experience.

Slashing out his songs with his usual demonic fury and smashing his guitar against mountains of amplifiers, Hendrix produced the same effect on U.S. fans as he had on their English counterparts earlier. He immediately became a new rock idol.

At the end of the tour, he and the group retreated into the studio to begin work on their next album. When the two-record set, *Electric Ladyland,* was released in October 1968, it topped the U.S. charts. One of the finest albums in rock history, *Electric Ladyland* was a tour de force of slamming rock songs and extended cuts on which Hendrix and the group jammed with the likes of such stalwarts as Steve Winwood, Al Kooper, and Jefferson Airplane bassist Jack Casady.

But dissension had begun to emerge, particularly between Hendrix and Redding. In December 1968, the Experience was disbanded. The rift was mended at the start of 1969, and they toured Europe and the U.S. But the differences again emerged, and the Experience played its final performance on June 29, 1969, at the Denver Pop Festival. Redding subsequently formed his own group, Fat Mattress.

Hendrix then began playing with Electric Flag drummer-vocalist Buddy Miles and bassist Billy Cox, a friend from his army days, in a group that would be called Band of Gypsys. But while they were rehearsing, Hendrix formed a separate one-off band, Electric Sky Church (with Mitchell and others), with whom he performed at the Woodstock Festival. That performance yielded Hendrix's tearing, screaming rendition of "The Star-Spangled Banner."

By the end of the year, Band of Gypsys was finally ready to make its debut, which it did on December 31st at the Fillmore East in New York. The performance was captured on tape and released in May 1970 on an eponymous album that hit number five on the charts. But Miles and Cox were mediocre, uninspired musicians whose playing was hardly the equal of the Experience. Within a month of its debut Hendrix disbanded the group.

Cox was, however, invited to join the new version of the Experience, which also included Mitchell on drums. They toured extensively in the U.S. and the U.K. during the first half of 1970, with Hendrix dividing much of his time between performing and setting up his state-of-the-art studio, Electric Ladyland, in New York. He also began recording with a wide range of artists, including Miles Davis and guitar virtuoso John McLaughlin, hinting at a new, more jazz-oriented phase in his career.

But that career soon came to a tragic end. After a performance at the Isle of Fehmarn in Germany on September 6th, Hendrix returned to the U.K. He died in London on September 18, 1970, of barbiturate intoxication.

Scores of albums bearing Hendrix's name were released over the next two decades. With the exception of 1971's *The Cry of Love*—the last album he recorded for release—they were mostly collections of jams and studio discards that varied widely in terms of sound and musical quality. *The Essential Jimi Hendrix, Vols. One and Two* (Reprise) of 1978 was an incisive compilation of his greatest work, while 1989's *Radio One* (Rykodisc) was a remarkable set of live recordings made for the BBC near the start of his career.

TOP ALBUMS

ARE YOU EXPERIENCED? (Reprise, '67, 5)
AXIS: BOLD AS LOVE (Reprise, '68, 3)
ELECTRIC LADYLAND (Reprise '68, 1)
SMASH HITS (Reprise, '69, 6)
BAND OF GYPSYS (Capitol, '70, 5)
THE CRY OF LOVE (Reprise, '71, 3)
RAINBOW BRIDGE (Reprise, '71, 15)
HENDRIX IN THE WEST (Reprise, '72, 12)
CRASH LANDING (Reprise, '75, 5)

Additional Top 40 Albums: 1

TOP SONG

ALL ALONG THE WATCHTOWER
(Reprise, '68, 20)

BUDDY HOLLY

Buddy Holly didn't look like a '50s rock idol. With his horn-rimmed glasses and shy demeanor and his notably un-DA'ed haircut, he was a rock and roll Everyman to wilder counterparts like Elvis Presley, Little Richard, Chuck Berry, and Jerry Lee Lewis.

*Buddy Holly
and the Crickets*

Moreover, when he appeared onstage, he performed in a reserved manner, picking at his Fender Stratocaster guitar and singing his songs with a unassuming presence that was at odds with his hip-thrusting, duck-walking, piano-kicking counterparts.

But Holly was a performer whose music and, ironically, style made him one of the biggest stars of his time and one of the most influential rock artists in history.

Musically, Holly's trademark songs—most of them recorded with his group, the Crickets—were a seamless blend of country and western and rock and roll, to the point that the two became almost indistinguishable. On songs like "That'll Be the Day," "True Love Ways," and others, Holly created music that had a country sweetness and a rock edge but that, unlike rockabilly, wasn't a clear combination of the two. Instead, it was a wholly new and distinctive sound that was unprecedented in 1950s rock.

Vocally, he was equally unique. On "Peggy Sue," his hiccuping phrasings had a rhythmic R&B feel but with little of that genre's earthiness or raw power. In fact, Holly had more in common with the hillbilly vocalists of the 1930s and '40s than with the other rockers of his day. His voice had a smoothness and articulation that were ideally suited to his melodic songs and a power that, like his appearance, was remarkably subtle and affecting compared with that of Presley and the rest.

That appearance was a crucial component of Holly's persona. At a time when rock and roll was establishing itself as a wild, extroverted, exhibitionist form, Holly created an image that was at its polar extreme. He was a rock musician, not a rock star, and with his popularity, he proved that sleek, sexy looks were not essential for rock success.

That point would be well taken by the next generation of rockers. When the Beatles and the rest of the troops of the British Invasion appeared, most would affect Holly's straightforward performance style, as opposed to that of Presley, Lewis, and others, when they appeared onstage (the Shadows' guitarist, Hank B. Marvin, would wear horn-rimmed glasses like Holly's). Years later, the Who's Pete Townshend—no great rock looker in the classic sense—would note that Holly's nondescript appearance had given him hope that he, too, could be a rock idol.

But it was Holly's music that secured his place in the rock pantheon. His songs proved to be a major source of inspiration for the music of the Beatles, the Hollies, the Searchers, and countless others of the '60s British Invasion. The Rolling Stones' first major hit in 1963 was an R&B-inflected cover of Holly's "Not Fade Away." Peter and Gordon had a hit of their own with their rendition of "True Love Ways." The Beatles recorded a version of Holly's "Words of Love," and much of the melodic nature of their own music—particularly the songs of Paul McCartney—came with Holly's musical signature.

Holly's music would continue to be embraced by new generations of rock artists. From the likes of Nick Lowe, Dave Edmunds, and Elvis Costello of the pub rock–punk scene of the late 1970s to the Proclaimers of the '90s, rock was imbued with the sound that Holly articulated in the 1950s. In fact, his influence is so pervasive that it is beside the point listing the artists who have included aspects of his work in theirs. Suffice it to say that as long as music aspires to a country sweetness and a rock bite, Holly's songs will have had some part in the process.

Holly's immense role in the development of rock is all the more remarkable given the tragic brevity of his life and career. From the time of his first hit, "That'll Be the Day," in 1957, to his death in a plane crash in 1959, Holly composed, recorded, and toured almost constantly. In fact, over the decades following his death, albums of his music and sessions continued to appear as new tapes were located, rerecorded, and released. One of the most ambitious of these was a U.K. release, the six-volume set *The Complete Buddy Holly* of 1979.

Holly (b. Charles Hardin Holly, Sept. 7, 1936, Lubbock, Texas) began his career in 1949 when he formed a country duo, Buddy & Bob, with his school mate, Bob Montgomery. Buddy & Bob (joined by bassist Larry Welborn) performed in Lubbock for the next few years, gradually building a modest local following. In 1953, they secured their own radio program, "The Buddy & Bob Show."

With the emergence of Presley, Holly began to add traces of rock to the duo's sound. In 1955 they added drummer Jerry Allison to their lineup and began to play at local rock shows. At one of these, in which they opened for Billy Haley and His Comets, they came to the attention of a Nashville talent scout, Eddie Crandall.

In 1956, Crandall negotiated a contract with Decca Records, and Holly was invited to Nashville to record several demos. In the process, he split with his old friend Montgomery and recruited guitarist Sonny Curtis and bassist Don Guess. As Buddy

Holly and the Two Tunes, the group then began a tour, opening for Hank Thompson. In time, Holly, Allison, Curtis, and Guess would become Buddy Holly and the *Three* Tunes. In April, Holly's first single, "Blue Days, Black Nights," was released but was not successful.

In September of that year, Holly, dissatisfied with the Nashville recording and business scene, split from Decca. He and Allison made their way to producer Norman Petty, who had a studio in Clovis, New Mexico. It would be a crucial development in the evolution of Holly's sound and music.

Petty, who eventually became Holly's manager, had different ideas about the ways Holly's music should be recorded. He gave Holly's songs a crisper and tighter sound that made them more rock-oriented.

At the same time, Holly formed a new group, the Crickets, with Allison on drums, bassist Joe B. Mauldin, and guitarist Niki Sullivan. The group then recorded "That'll Be the Day" at Petty's studio.

In July, Petty booked the group on two national tours, opening for some of the major rock artists of the day; the latter, "The Biggest Show of Stars of 1957," included Berry, Paul Anka, and others. The group's appearances on these tours drew attention to "That'll Be the Day," and by September the single had topped the charts and sold more than a million copies.

That same month, "Peggy Sue" was released; it reached number three by the end of the year and also passed the million sales mark. In the meantime, Holly and the Crickets had appeared on "The Ed Sullivan Show" and had become national rock stars.

In January of 1958, Holly and the Crickets were steamrolling their way up the charts once again with the single "Oh, Boy!" When it hit number 10 it became the third Holly record to make the top 10 in five months. He and the group appeared on the Sullivan show again and then made their way to Australia for a brief tour. In March, they embarked on a tour of the U.K. (during which they would have four top 20 hits in the same week). This was followed by a 61-date tour of the U.S.; Alan Freed's "Big Beat

Show" also included Berry, Lewis, Frankie Lymon, and others.

Holly began recording without the Crickets in June of 1958. While he and the group toured briefly in July, the end of their partnership was in sight, as was that with Petty. In October, Holly severed most connections with his past, dismissing Petty and breaking up the Crickets (who would subsequently record and tour on their own to modest success).

Along the way, Holly met and married Maria Elena Santiago and settled in New York City. By the end of 1958, he began recording songs with a string orchestra.

In January of 1959, Holly and a new group began the "Winter Dance Party Tour" that also included the Big Bopper, Ritchie Valens, Frankie Sardo, and Dion and the Belmonts. On the night of February 3, after a performance in Clear Lake, Iowa, Holly, the Bopper, and Valens decided to hire a plane to take them to the next tour stop in Moorhead, Minnesota. In a driving storm, the plane went down near Mason City, Iowa, and the three rockers and the plane's pilot were killed.

In 1971, Don McLean hit the top of the charts with "American Pie—Parts I & II," a lengthy ballad that was inspired by Holly's death. In the ballad, McLean referred to February 3, 1959, as the day the music died.

But it didn't. Over the succeeding decades, Holly's music would be released again and again on various albums that included not only his hits but also many of the sessions he took part in during his career. Holly's catalog of songs was, fittingly, purchased by Paul McCartney, who began to stage yearly "Buddy Holly Week" shows in London (in 1988, he joined the Crickets onstage for a performance). In 1978, Holly's life and career were depicted in the film *The Buddy Holly Story* with actor Gary Busey in the title role (Busey eventually purchased Holly's guitar and horn-rimmed glasses at an auction of the rocker's memorabilia in New York). And in 1990, the musical *Buddy* was a hit in London's West End.

Holly was inducted into the Rock and Roll Hall of Fame in 1986.

TOP ALBUMS

THE BUDDY HOLLY STORY (Coral, '59, 11)
REMINISCING (Coral, '63, 40)

TOP SONGS

THAT'LL BE THE DAY (Brunswick, '57, 1)
PEGGY SUE (Coral, '57, 3)
OH, BOY! (Brunswick, '57, 10)
MAYBE BABY (Brunswick, '58, 17)
RAVE ON (Coral, '58, 37)
THINK IT OVER (Coral, '58, 27)
EARLY IN THE MORNING (Coral, '58, 32)
IT DOESN'T MATTER ANYMORE (Coral, '59, 13)

THE HUMAN LEAGUE

"**N**o future!"
the Sex Pistols' Johnny Rotten proclaimed in 1977.
But even as he was shouting the punk credo, other groups
of young British musicians were beginning to look ahead to a
new form of music that would soon be called techno-rock.

The techno groups were the polar opposite of the punks. While the latter sought to deconstruct rock, the techno crowd set out to reinvent it with new configurations of electronic instruments that had little to do with the guitars-bass-drums lineups of traditional rock groups. The music they created was similarly new, consisting primarily of droning theme lines, mechanized beats, and dense layers of synthesized sound, all of it set in an overtly futuristic context.

Inspired by the electronic musical experiments of the revolutionary German group Kraftwerk in the early 1970s and by British composer/provocateur Brian Eno later in the decade, the new musicians proceeded to translate those artists' quasi-avant-garde work into a more accessible and pop-oriented form of rock.

In the late 1970s and early '80, their techno version of rock and pop insinuated itself into the scene and provided a new impetus and direction for the music. By the mid-1980s it had become one of the dominant forces in the rock world, and its sound would subsequently be co-opted in varying ways by new generations of rock, pop, dance, and hip-hop artists.

Various groups were involved in the initial development of the techno-rock sound. But the group that first brought that sound to the vast pop world was the Human League. It accomplished that with its worldwide hit of 1982, "Don't You Want Me."

That hit was a watershed not only for techno but for the broader development of rock and pop. With its hook-laden melodies, crisp vocals, and mechanized dance beats, it gave the previously cult-like electronic movement a more pervasive and mainstream presence. Its vast international success—it was a hit in most rock-consuming countries of the world—also proved to the music business that techno was a viable commercial commodity. And it inspired numerous other non-techno artists to include synthesizers in their music until, by the end of the decade, the once-exotic electronic instruments had become standard components of rock's instrumental arsenal.

The initial version of the Human League was formed in 1977 by Martin Ware (b. May 19, 1956, Sheffield) and Ian Craig Marsh (b. Nov. 11, 1956, Sheffield), two former computer operators. Performing as a synthesizer duo (an instrumental configuration that would form the basis of many techno groups), they originally went by the name the Future.

But by the end of the year they had recruited vocalist Philip Oakey (b. Oct. 2, 1955, Sheffield) and Adrian Wright (b. June 30, 1956, Sheffield), the latter enlisted to provide onstage visuals in the form of slides and films.

Ware and Marsh also changed the name of the group to the Human League (the title of a computer game).

In 1978, the group signed with the Edinburgh-based Fast Product label and released its debut single, "Being Boiled." One of the first techno records, it failed to chart. But the single, along with a subsequent EP *The Dignity of Labour,* came to the attention of Virgin Records, which signed the group in 1979. The Human League's debut album, *Reproduction,* was released in October of that year.

TOP ALBUMS

DARE (A&M, '82, 3)
FASCINATION! (A&M, '83, 22)
CRASH (A&M, '86, 24)

TOP SONGS

DON'T YOU WANT ME (A&M, '82, 1)
(KEEP FEELING) FASCINATION (A&M, '83, 8)
MIRROR MAN (A&M, '83, 30)
HUMAN (A&M, '86, 1)
HEART LIKE A WHEEL (Virgin/A&M, '90, 32)

The Human League

But the techno aesthetic had yet to take hold, and the group struggled with public perceptions of its music as being machine made; at the time, the idea of mechanized drum rhythms and preprogrammed synthesized accompaniment and the like seemed too robotic to many rock fans. At the end of 1979, the Human League was sacked from a Talking Heads tour, its music dismissed as remote-controlled.

But as the group toured the U.K. in 1980, it began to gain new converts. In May, the album *Travelogue* was released and reached number 16 on the U.K. charts. Along the way, Wright traded his slides and films for a synthesizer and joined the musical lineup. Other changes were in store.

In October of 1980, Ware and Marsh left the League (to form one of the more intriguing techno acts, Heaven 17). Oakey and Wright maintained control of the group's name and continued on without the founders. By the end of the year, bassist Ian Burden (b. Dec. 24, 1957, Sheffield) had been enlisted along with Joanne Catherall (b. Sept. 18, 1962, Sheffield) and Suzanne Sulley (b. Mar. 22, 1963, Sheffield). Guitarist Jo Callis (b. May 2, 1955, Glasgow, Scotland) joined on synthesizer in May 1981.

Originally hired as onstage dancers, Catherall and Sulley soon teamed with Oakey as the group's vocalists. They added a new, pop-oriented presence to the Human League's sound that was also accentuated by a new producer, Martin Rushent, resulting in a greater degree of accessibility to rock and pop fans. The single "The Sound of the Crowd" was released in May 1981 and hit number 12 on the U.K.

charts. The group then retired to the studio to work on a new album.

When that album, *Dare*, was released in October 1981, it pushed the Human League—and techno-rock—to the upper levels of the pop world. The album charted in the U.K. for 71 weeks and eventually sold more than five million copies worldwide.

The hit single from the album was "Don't You Want Me." At the end of 1981, it topped the U.K. charts for five weeks. Released in the U.S. in July

the doors for legions of techno-rock artists in the early and middle 1980s. Soft Cell hit the top 10 in the U.S. with "Tainted Love" in 1982. Thomas Dolby did the same with "She Blinded Me with Science" in 1983. Depeche Mode became one of the most durable groups of the 1980s with a stark, monochromatic, synthesized sound that was as commercially successful as it was musically provocative. Thompson Twins had numerous pop-tinged hits, including "Hold Me Now," "Doctor! Doctor!" and "Lay Your Hands on Me," and their stage shows were innovative displays of lighting and set design. And Howard Jones created a melodic, pop-based techno sound on such hits as "Things Can Only Get Better."

One of the biggest techno-rock groups was the Pet Shop Boys, who sold millions of records worldwide in the later 1980s with such melodic hits as "West End Girls" and "What Have I Done to Deserve This?" Ironically, given the initial reaction to the Human League's shows, the Pet Shop Boys' onstage performances were almost wholly programmed, with vocalist Neil Tennant singing to the synthesizer-activated sound of keyboardist Chris Lowe.

Other groups that, strictly speaking, weren't techno-rock also emerged with music that was heavily influenced by the movement. Culture Club and its leader, Boy George, gained immense success with a dance-pop sound that came with synthesized chords and drum machines. Tears for Fears and Simple Minds, among others, combined traditional rock instrumentation with liberal doses of synthesizers as part of their basic sound. By the end of the 1980s and into the '90s, the sound of techno-rock that had seemed so revolutionary 10 years

1982, it was Number One for three weeks and sold more than one million copies.

But the Human League did not build on its success. In subsequent years, it had a series of lesser hits that included the mini-album *Fascination* and the single "The Lebanon." In 1986, it staged a brief comeback when its single "Human" topped the U.S. charts. But it faded again. A subsequent single, 1990's "Heart Like a Wheel," reached number 32 in the U.S.

But the success of "Don't You Want Me" opened

before had been thoroughly incorporated into the musical mainstream. Its mechanized beats and synthesizers were routinely used by a large number of rock, pop, and dance acts throughout the pop music spectrum.

While it could be argued that this trend was inevitable given the vast developments in electronic technology, what cannot be denied is that techno-rock groups like the Human League led the way to the future.

TOMMY JAMES

They didn't call it
bubblegum rock for nothing.

While the titans of rock were producing their masterpieces in the mid-1960s, groups of unabashedly brash and frolicsome rockers were making music of their own that defied the artistic aspirations of the time. It was referred to as bubblegum rock and, like the viscous substance that inspired its name, it was sweet and gooey, eminently disposable (made to be chewed, but not digested), and oh so tasty.

The Bazooka of bubblegum rock was Tommy James.

When Tommy James and the Shondells' single "Hanky Panky" hit the top of the charts in June 1966, a clarion call to arms went out to all rockers in the land who had no time—or mind—for politics, social philosophy, or art. With its simple chords, simple words, and James's simply smashing, blatantly teenaged vocals, "Hanky Panky" was rock reduced to its most basic musical and attitudinal level.

"Hanky Panky" was all about teen love and lust. Its playful, strutting refrain was as pure and direct as a teen boy's nod and wink to his mates. It was also, in its way, utterly innocent and cute. But as its basic chords and melody worked their way into the psyche, it also proved to be a forceful display of rock power and energy.

It was a combination whose sound—and success—did not go unnoticed. Producers Jerry Kasenetz and Jeff Katz teamed up with the group the Music Explosion and recorded the single "Little Bit O' Soul." Released in May 1967, it went to number two on the charts on the strength of its jumpy beats, beeping organ notes, and Jamie Lyons's cocky, rollicking teen-inflected vocals (that were a perfect imitation of James's adenoidal outbursts).

At the time, the nascent bubblegum sound had much in common with that of the emerging garage-rock scene. Both movements were of dubious musical quality; the musicians could barely play their instruments, and their songs were generally as dismissable as they were memorable. But while such garage-rock groups as the Music Machine and the Count Five and others tried to be as good as the giants who inspired them, the bubblegum boys positively reveled in their innocuousness. They were trite and cute and sophomoric and they wanted the world to know.

Nothing was musically beneath them. In 1966, the Royal Guardsmen parlayed the popularity of Charles Shultz's "Peanuts" cartoon strip into a big hit with the single "Snoopy vs. the Red Baron." In 1969, the Archies, a group based on a TV cartoon show, topped the charts with "Sugar Sugar," a song that was as sweet as its title.

The apex—if the word can be applied to bubblegum—of the movement was reached in 1968 with the 1910 Fruitgum Co. and the Ohio Express. The former (whose name inspired the "bubblegum" moniker) hit the charts in January with the single "Simon Says." Even more blatantly immature than its predecessors, the New Jersey quintet was almost *pre*-teen in its musical outlook. "Simon Says," a lyrical play on the children's game, came with hopping beats and childlike vocals, but again with an undeniably rocking presence. Serious rock fans of the time derided the song . . . but listened to it anyway.

Producers Kasenetz and Katz were behind this one as well and, quick to capitalize on its number four chart success, churned out another game-related hit later in 1968, "1, 2, 3, Red Light."

They also produced the Ohio Express, who played on the bubblegum name on the songs "Yummy Yummy Yummy" and "Chewy Chewy," which also hit the charts in 1968. The Ohio Express was even more obnoxious than the 1910 Fruitgum Co.—and more devilish. Even Chuck Berry and Little Richard in their naughty prime couldn't approach the double meanings of those songs ("Yummy, yummy, yummy I've got love in my tummy," indeed). "Yummy" and "Chewy" had rock fans smirking to themselves knowingly for the better part of 1968.

But if the 1910 Fruitgum Co. and the Ohio Express were the Beatles and Rolling Stones of bubblegum, James was its Presley.

James (b. Thomas Jackson, Apr. 29, 1947, Dayton, Ohio) not only set the stage for bubblegum, he defined it and expanded it to new levels of pseudo-grandeur and kitsch.

He began his career at age 12 in Niles, Michigan. Forming a group that became the original version of the Shondells, he appeared at local gigs through the early 1960s. In 1962, he recorded the single "Long Pony Tail" for a local label. The song had modest success in the Midwest and came to the attention of deejay Jack Douglas, who signed James and his group to his Snap label.

In 1963, James heard a version of Jeff Barry and Ellie Greenwich's "Hanky Panky" at a nightclub and decided to record it. Released on the Snap label, the single was largely ignored.

But in 1965, it was noticed by a disc jockey in Pittsburgh, who included it in his playlist. James went to the city to perform it on a local TV show. While there, he recruited guitarist Eddie Gray, bassist Mike Vale, drummer Peter Lucia, and keyboardist Ronnie Rosman in a new version of the Shondells.

In July of 1966, "Hanky Panky" was released nationally by Roulette Records and was an immediate hit, selling over one million copies and topping the charts.

James and the Shondells returned to the charts in February 1967, when their single "I Think We're Alone Now" hit number four. With its incessant guitar-and-bass figure and James's lithe vocals, the song had a musicality that tempered and complemented its youthful sound.

TOP ALBUM

CRIMSON & CLOVER (Roulette, '69, 8)

Additional Top 40 Albums: 1

TOP SONGS

HANKY PANKY (Roulette, '66, *1*)
I THINK WE'RE ALONE NOW
  (Roulette, '67, *4*)
MIRAGE (Roulette, '67, *10*)
GETTIN' TOGETHER (Roulette, '67, *18*)
MONY MONY (Roulette, '68, *3*)
CRIMSON AND CLOVER (Roulette, '68, *1*)
SWEET CHERRY WINE (Roulette, '69, *7*)
CRYSTAL BLUE PERSUASION
  (Roulette, '69, *2*)
DRAGGIN' THE LINE (Roulette, '71, *4*)

Additional Top 40 Songs: 8

*Tommy James
and the Shondells*

The combination was repeated on James's 1968 hit "Mony Mony," which reached number three in the U.S. and topped the chart in the U.K. for four weeks. "Mony Mony" was teen rock at its best, with pounding dance beats and a boundless energy that transcended the bubblegum sound.

But James's bubblegum instincts were intact. They could be heard on the single (and album) "Crimson and Clover" in 1968. The song was an inadvertently hilarious take on the Beatles and psychedelia, with its gurgling vocals and droning sound. But it was also notably sincere, and its melodic power was quite affecting. Edited down from the album cut's five minutes, the single was a major hit, topping the charts for two weeks.

The same sincerity and innocence pervaded the follow-up hits "Sweet Cherry Wine" and "Crystal Blue Persuasion," both of which reached the top 10 in 1969. The former came with unique—for bubblegum—time signatures, and the latter was a shimmering pop ballad.

In 1970, James departed from the Shondells to pursue a solo career. He initially withdrew from the scene for a time, but came back in 1971 with the edgy "Draggin' the Line," which sold more than a million copies and eventually charted at number four. It would be his last top 10 hit, although he nonetheless continued to record and perform over the next two decades.

James's basic rock sound and his melodic signatures would influence a vast array of rock and pop artists. In 1982, Joan Jett's version of "Crimson and Clover" reached number seven on the charts. And in 1987, Billy Idol's rendition of "Mony Mony" supplanted teen songstress Tiffany's version of "I Think We're Alone Now" at Number One.

James was bubblegum in the truest and finest sense. While other groups like the 1910 Fruitgum Co. and the Ohio Express traded on the more obvious aspects of the form and exploited them to mostly commercial ends, James was a rock original. His sense of innocence and abandon, not to mention his estimable melodic gifts, provided the '60s rock scene with healthy digressions from the weighty pursuits of the rock artists of the time and, in the process, defined a youthful art of its own.

JEFFERSON AIRPLANE

Perhaps the most arresting and enduring musical image of the Summer of Love of 1967 was that of Jefferson Airplane vocalist Grace Slick intoning the surreal, drug-infused words to the group's hit single, "White Rabbit."

There were others, of course, and some more telling, like Janis Joplin belting her blues at the Monterey Pop Festival, or the Grateful Dead jamming at the intersection of Haight and Ashbury streets. But to the national culture at large, Slick and the Airplane and their music came to symbolize the San Francisco scene that emerged during that momentous year.

Jefferson Airplane was more than a symbol of a scene or an era. It was one of the most musically compelling American groups in the history of rock and roll.

While many of the band's counterparts in the San Francisco rock and roll scene quickly became cultural icons of a sort—the stuff of time capsules and

Jefferson Airplane

media retrospectives —the Airplane created a musical legacy that transcended the very era that it helped to define.

Emblematic of the multifaceted nature of the San Francisco sound, the Airplane's music drew its strength from several sources simultaneously. There were the crystalline vocals of Marty Balin and Slick

and the full-bodied harmonies they made with guitarist Paul Kantner. These were supported—at times, upstaged—by the complex interactions of lead guitarist Jorma Kaukonen, drummer Spencer Dryden, and bassist Jack Casady (the latter one of the true virtuosos of his instrument).

These centrifugal musical forces were directed

and focused in a cohesive creative vision that, among rock groups, has few equals. That vision was a revolutionary amalgam of instrumental daring and pop discipline. On record, the Airplane could reign in its more effusive psychedelic urges to create songs—like "Somebody to Love," "Today," "The Ballad of You, Me and Pooneil," "Martha," and others—that were, at once, compact and powerful expressions. Onstage, the group gave in to those urges in extended improvisations that broadened the boundaries of rock musicianship.

Over the course of its first five albums, the Airplane's music evolved in vast and myriad ways, from

TOP ALBUMS

SURREALISTIC PILLOW (RCA, '67, *3*)
AFTER BATHING AT BAXTER'S (RCA, '67, *17*)
CROWN OF CREATION (RCA, '68, No. 6)
BLESS ITS POINTED LITTLE HEAD (RCA, '69, *17*)
VOLUNTEERS (RCA, '69, *13*)
THE WORST OF JEFFERSON AIRPLANE (RCA, '70, *12*)
BARK (Grunt, '71, *11*)
LONG JOHN SILVER (Grunt, '72, *20*)

TOP SONGS

SOMEBODY TO LOVE (RCA, '67, *5*)
WHITE RABBIT (RCA, '67, *8*)

the folk-rock suppleness found on its debut record to the sophisticated songs, dense experimentation, and complex harmonies that would characterize its later work.

Through it all, the Airplane maintained a distinct identity that was synonymous with the emerging belief that rock was an art form demanding skill and craft as well as inspiration and feeling. There was an integrity to the songs of Slick, Kantner, and Balin and the instrumental displays of Kaukonen, Dryden, and Casady that elevated the Airplane's music above the din of the hippie hoopla that surrounded the San Francisco scene. While Slick became a media celebrity of the time through her aloof sexual image and extroverted lifestyle, she was also the first female rock artist to be viewed as a musician on an equal level with her male counterparts; her prodigious songwriting and vocal talents made her more than merely "the girl singer in the band."

In short, the Airplane bequeathed more than a musical legacy to the rock world. It was one of the

handful of groups that proved that when musicians cared about their work, rock could be an artistic co-equal with its classical and jazz counterparts. In doing this, Jefferson Airplane demonstrated that rock had the potential to be not merely popular but aesthetically vital.

The Airplane was formed in July 1965, when Balin (b. Jan. 30, 1942, Cincinnati, Ohio) recruited Kantner (b. Mar. 12, 1942, San Francisco) from the local folk-rock scene. They were joined by Kaukonen (b. Dec. 23, 1940, Washington, D.C.), bassist Bob Harvey, drummer Jerry Peloquin, and vocalist Signe Toly Anderson. After several weeks of rehearsal, the group made its debut at Balin's nightclub, the Matrix.

By the end of the year, Harvey and Peloquin had been replaced by Casady (b. Apr. 13, 1944, Washington, D.C.) and drummer Skip Spence. Performing at various local gigs, including the seminal concert "A Tribute to Dr. Strange" in October, the Airplane began to assume a leading role in the burgeoning San Francisco rock scene. In November 1965, the group was signed to RCA Records and began to record its debut album. Its first single, "It's No Secret," was released in February 1966 but was largely ignored.

But as the new year began to unfold, the San Francisco groups began to coalesce into the scene that would engulf the rock world in 1967.

During the year, the Airplane's classic lineup was formalized. In October 1966, drummer Spence quit the group to form Moby Grape, and the jazz-trained Dryden was enlisted. And when Anderson became pregnant in November, she also quit, giving way to Slick (b. Grace Wing, Oct. 30, 1939, Chicago), who had previously been a member of the group the Great Society.

That month, *Jefferson Airplane Takes Off* (with the former lineup) was released and eventually charted at number 128.

As the new year dawned, so too did the so-called hippie era. In January 1967, the Airplane and other groups of the scene performed at the first Human Be-In concert in Golden Gate Park. That event and others like it soon came to the attention of the national media, who were drawn to the emerging hippie culture that centered on San Francisco's Haight Ashbury district. As the months progressed and that scene became something of a cultural phenomenon, the Airplane went into the studio—supported by a contract that reportedly allowed the group an unprecedented level of artistic control—to record its next album.

Released in June, *Surrealistic Pillow* was an aesthetic watershed, one of the crucial points at which "rock and roll" began to give way to "rock." Songs such as "3/5 of a Mile in 10 Seconds" displayed an ensemble cohesion and instrumental agility that suggested new directions and possibilities for rock playing. On the folk-based instrumental "Embryonic Journey," Kaukonen finger-picked intricate phrases on his unaccompanied acoustic guitar. Casady and Dryden proved to be more than a traditional rhythm section; the former's rolling, contrapuntal lines and the latter's angular rhythmic accents worked their way through the songs in an almost compositional manner, directing the words and melodies as much as complementing them.

The songs themselves were remarkable musical hybrids that came with the energy and force of rock and roll and the pure melodies and vocal harmonies of folk. Balin's lovely ballad "Today" was countered by the storming rock of the group's signature hit, "Somebody to Love," and the Ravel-influenced cadences of "White Rabbit." The latter two songs (which Slick had brought to the group from the Great Society) were released as singles and went on to sell more than a million copies apiece. In the process they became immortalized as anthems of the Summer of Love.

Partially on the basis of these hits (although singles were becoming less important in such matters), *Surrealistic Pillow* hit number three on the album chart.

By the end of 1967, the Airplane was one of the biggest rock groups in the U.S. It could have easily parlayed its popularity into a series of like-sounding albums. Instead, it went back into the studio and came out with the intimidating *After Bathing at Baxter's*. One of the great albums in rock, Baxter's was basically a set of musical suites divided up into songs. Those songs, like the rampaging "The Ballad of You and Me and Pooneil" and the stark ballad "Martha," were connected by a dizzying series of instrumental sections, some of which were very nearly abstract in their density and complexity. Hardly as accessible as *Surrealistic Pillow,* the album nonetheless charted at number 17.

Through the end of the 1960s, the Airplane was a major concert draw in the U.S. It took part in various festivals of the time, including the Newport Pop Festival in 1968 and Woodstock in 1969 (it had also performed at the Monterey Pop Festival in 1967).

Its music continued to evolve and flourish. The 1968 album *Crown of Creation* was dominated by rich vocal harmonies and a more folk-based sound, while 1969's *Volunteers* came with more rock-oriented songs, including a title cut that became something of an anthem of the radical left political movement of the time. The group also released the live album *Bless Its Pointed Little Head* in 1969, which captured the group's onstage instrumental work.

But even as *Volunteers* reached number 13 at the end of 1969, the group was coming apart. In February 1970, Dryden departed after an argument with Balin. Slick, pregnant with a child by Kantner, retreated from performing for a time. And Kaukonen and Casady formed an offshoot group of their own, Hot Tuna, later in the year; in 1972 they left the Airplane to pursue their new group on a full-time basis. And in 1971, Balin departed to pursue a solo career.

With an almost constantly changing array of musicians, Kantner being the one constant member, the group made its way through the 1970s. These various versions of the Airplane (which officially became Jefferson Starship in 1974) were dismal contraptions compared with the classic group of the '60s. The music of the Airplane/Starship became increasingly diffuse. An exception was the generally fine album *Red Octopus,* which topped the charts in 1975, and Balin's eloquent ballad, "Miracles," which hit number three and sold more than one million copies that year.

But by the end of the 1970s, the Starship had evolved into a quasi-metal, pop hit machine that was far removed from its origins. Kantner, after departing, seemed to think as much. In 1985, he filed a lawsuit that ultimately forced the band to drop the "Jefferson" from its name. Henceforth it was Starship.

In 1990, Balin, Kantner, Slick, Kaukonen, and Casady reunited as Jefferson Airplane for an eponymous album and tour. The album was mediocre, but the tour proved to be surprisingly forceful. Nonetheless, the group was voted the Most Unwelcome Comeback in *Rolling Stone* magazine's 1989 critics poll.

It was a regrettable but probably warranted slap at a remarkable group that had done so much for rock its first time around.

JETHRO TULL

O

ne of the more controversial moments in recent rock history occurred in February 1989, when Jethro Tull's album *Crest of a Knave* won a Grammy Award in the newly minted Heavy Metal category.

The Grammy voters were immediately set upon by critics and fans, the latter jeering the announcement at the ceremony itself. To many minds, the award couldn't have been more inappropriate. After all, for nearly two decades Jethro Tull had made its artistic fame and name with a sound that was firmly rooted in the English folk tradition.

But the Grammy voters didn't have it all wrong. While Tull had indeed been key in popularizing the musical hallmarks of that ancient tradition, it had done it, for the most part, not with the dulcet tones of recorders and dulcimers but with the jackhammer sound and beats of metal.

In fact, that seeming contradiction, along with several others, were central to the history of this eccentric group.

Named for an 18th-century English agriculturalist, Jethro Tull emerged on the British scene in 1968 with a sound and look that had few, if any, antecedents. At a time when dandyish British lads in post-psychedelic gear were parading about, playing their version of the blues, the members of Tull dressed down in tights and ragged smoking jackets, with their tousled hair and wizened expressions giving them the air of aging forest imps.

To make matters more confusing, they too played the blues—of a sort. Guitarist Mick Abrahams (b. Apr. 7, 1943, Luton, Bedfordshire, England) was a blues-based revisionist in the Clapton mold. And bassist Glenn Cornick (b. Apr. 24, 1947, Barrow-in-Furness, Cumbria, England) and drummer Clive Bunker (b. Dec. 12, 1946) stormed through the songs with a force and agility that resembled that of Jack Bruce and Ginger Baker of Cream.

But the focal point of Tull, musically and visually, was Ian Anderson (b. Aug. 10, 1947, Edinburgh, Scotland). With his spindly arms and legs crossing and crisscrossing wildly, Tull's irrepressible leader sang with a rasp and roar that seemed to come from the mists of centuries past. Like a highwayman or pirate, he leapt about and thrust his flute to and fro like a saber, then brought it up to his lips and chugged into it with the rhythmic fury of jazz titan Roland Kirk, all the while summoning from it melodies as sweet and simple and pure as those played by ancient minstrels.

Whatever it was, it was a sound and look that immediately established itself with fans and critics, who hailed the group's 1968 debut album, *This Was*. That disc, which reached number 10 on the U.K. charts, was an idiosyncratic blend of riff-based rock (soon to be known as heavy metal), British blues, and traditional folk music, with Anderson's flute work making its own jazz insinuations.

But just as the group was beginning to establish itself, another trademark of its long history—frequent personnel changes—began to emerge with the departure of Abrahams in December of that year, due to musical differences with Anderson. Tommy Iommi (later of ultra-metal group Black Sabbath) filled in for a brief time until a new guitarist was added in the person of Martin Barre, who would stay with Tull through the rest of its career. In the 11 subsequent lineups of the group, he and Anderson would be the only constants.

With this revised version, the group expanded its base on 1969's *Stand Up* and 1970's *Benefit*, with the refrains of English traditional music growing

Jethro Tull

more dominant even as the volume and force of the group's proto-metal sound increased in tandem.

Given their diversity, Jethro Tull's songs, written by Anderson, displayed a remarkably coherent artistic vision even as they ran the gamut from the jazz-baroque interplay of "Bourrée" (an Anderson adaptation of a Bach composition) to the folk of "Fat Man" and the rock of "A New Day Yesterday."

The group's popularity began to expand from the underground base it had initially established. While singles like "Sweet Dream" and "Teacher" made the top five in the U.K., Tull was also becoming increasingly popular as an album act in the U.S., with *Stand Up* hitting number 20 and *Benefit* number 11 on the *Billboard* album chart. The range of the group's fans was as expansive as its sound; in 1969, Tull performed at the Newport Jazz Festival and followed it up in 1970 with an appearance at the Atlanta Pop Festival.

That same year, Cornick departed and was replaced by bassist Jeffrey Hammond-Hammond. The latter had been a founding member of the Blades, a group formed in 1963 in Blackpool that had included Anderson and then-drummer John Evan. This group, later to be called the John Evan Band, had been the basis of the nascent Tull; Cornick had also been a bassist in the group for a time, and Evan would join Tull in 1970 as a keyboardist and would stay with the group for the next 10 years.

TOP ALBUMS

BENEFIT (Reprise, '70, *11*)
AQUALUNG (Reprise, '71, *7*)
THICK AS A BRICK (Reprise, '72, *1*)
LIVING IN THE PAST (Chrysalis, '72, *3*)
A PASSION PLAY (Chrysalis, '73, *1*)
WAR CHILD (Chrysalis, '74, *2*)
MINSTREL IN THE GALLERY (Chrysalis, '75, *7*)
SONGS FROM THE WOOD (Chrysalis, '77, *8*)

Additional Top 40 Albums: 9

TOP SONGS

LIVING IN THE PAST (Chrysalis, '72, *11*)
BUNGLE IN THE JUNGLE (Chrysalis, '74, *12*)

By 1971, the group—particularly Anderson—was gazing beyond songs to loftier creative efforts. The result of this was the rock opera *Aqualung*, released as an album that vaulted to number seven on the U.S. charts and catapulted Tull to a new level of rock stardom. The title song, and others such as "Locomotive Breath," became staples of FM radio in the U.S. and created a new form of folk-rock—English folk-rock—in the public mind. While the album's tirades against religion and social injustice would become dated over the years, its folk-based sound would become a standard of the genre soon populated by the likes of the Strawbs and, to a lesser extent, of the art rock of groups like Yes and King Crimson. And while other groups like Steeleye Span, Fairport Convention, and Pentangle would pursue a purer folk path and would make English folk-rock with elegance and style, it was *Aqualung* that established it with the rock masses.

Tull was now a major touring act, filling arenas across the U.S. In 1972, its album *Thick as a Brick* topped the charts for two weeks, and later in the year, the compilation album *Living in the Past* hit number three.

But when the group unveiled its next project, *A Passion Play*, in 1973, it was greeted with disdain by many critics, and Anderson announced that the group would disband (although the album hit Number One in the U.S.).

He changed his mind abruptly, and in 1974, the album *War Child*, which had originally been planned as part of a film project, was released. The largely orchestral album reached Number One in the U.S., and the group toured with a string quartet to perform its songs.

As the 1970s progressed, Tull continued to release albums and tour with various musicians joining and departing the band behind Anderson and the ever-present Barre. *Songs from the Wood*, from 1977, was more folk-oriented than its predecessors, while 1979's *Stormwatch* was a full-blown return to a folk-rock sound.

These albums, and others that followed in the next decade, were attended by a modest diminution in the group's chart success. *Broadsword and the Beast* made number 19 in the U.S., while 1984's *Under Wraps* hit number 76. The Grammy-winning *Crest of a Knave* peaked at number 32.

But another trademark—and contradiction—of Tull's history was that its popularity as a live act continued to be immense even as it declined on the charts. This was due primarily to the fact that while the group had become almost a distraction for Anderson (who had established a successful salmon fishery on his estate on the Isle of Skye), it consistently maintained a level of virtuosity and creativity that was provocative and entertaining. The group's 1992 concert album, *A Little Live Music*, with a new lineup that included former Fairport bassist Dave Pegg and drummer Dave Mattocks, was a formidable display of the inspired mix of English folk and rock with which the group had made its name more than 25 years earlier. With its energetic revampings of its old hits, the album proved that Tull wasn't simply living in the past but drawing inspiration from it. And it should continue to do so—as long as Anderson has a leg to stand on.

ELTON JOHN

As much a pop as a rock artist, Elton John dominated both forms, commercially, in the middle 1970s to an extent unequalled by any other act since the Beatles.

From 1970 through 1976, he scored an astonishing 17 top 20 hits. During that same period, his albums hit the top 20 14 times. At the height of his popularity during this period, John reportedly accounted for a staggering 6 percent of record revenues in the world.

By the very nature of the music business, such an overpowering success made John a decisive figure in the rock of his time. For better and worse, he had a pervasive impact not only on the music itself but on its role in the culture at large.

A fastidious songwriter, John displayed a melodic gift that approached those of the pop masters of the 1930s and '40s and, later, of Paul McCartney. On such signature hits as "Your Song," "Daniel," "Candle in the Wind, " and "Don't Let the Sun Go Down on Me," John (with longtime lyricist Bernie Taupin) created remarkable tunes that proved to be instant classics. Some of his compositions had stunning durability and power: "Burn Down the Mission," "Take Me to the Pilot," and others were among the most sturdy and affecting of their time.

That said, it must be added that John also squandered his talents on songs that were, by turns, cute and exploitive and annoyingly cloying. "Bennie and the Jets," "Philadelphia Freedom," "Crocodile Rock," and others were lowest-common-denominator efforts that contributed to the generally dismal state of '70s rock (admittedly, even these were undeniably catchy).

Similarly, John had his points, good and bad, as a musician. His abilities as a vocalist and pianist were relatively limited. Vocally, he had a modest range; technically, his piano work was competent at best. But in both cases he made up for his deficiencies with idiosyncratic flourishes that made him one of the more distinctive rock performers. His vocals and piano playing were endowed with tremendous rhythmic force and fervor. Hardly a soul belter in any sense, he could, nonetheless, slur a note or phrase, then draw it out and twist it about in ways that transformed his inspired melodies into R&B-tinged shout-outs. His talents as a performer were displayed on the exceptional live album (actually a recording of a live radio broadcast) *11-17-70*, in which he, bassist Dee Murray, and drummer Nigel Olsson cavorted about exuberantly on extended versions of songs like "Burn Down the Mission," with John churning out his vocals and piano chords with an almost demonic passion. Moreover, John never lost that feeling. Even on his later albums and tours in the 1980s and '90s, he displayed a remarkable enthusiasm, his rhythmic power and intensity undiminished despite years of personal and professional turmoil.

In fact, it was in his live performances that John had his most decisive impact on the development of rock. Again, these came with their good and bad sides. As his popularity rose to unprecedented proportions in the early and middle 1970s, John's enthusiastic stage shows went from the sublime to the ridiculous. In the pre-Elton-mania days of 1970–72, those shows were primarily music oriented, John hinting at things to come with the odd kick of the piano stool and his glittery attire. But later, his onstage garishness mushroomed in direct proportion to the height of his increasingly stacked heels. One of his shows was dominated by five primary-colored grand pianos whose tops were opened up to reveal large letters spelling E-L-T-O-N. His glasses—which had hitherto been unobtrusive horn-rimmed affairs—suddenly blossomed into huge contraptions that came with sparkles and stars and bangles and such. At one show, he might appear dressed as a cosmic cowboy; at another, a banana republic dictator, replete with gold braid and officer's cap. By the mid-1970s, he was being referred to as the Liberace of Rock.

While it was all done with an undeniable wit and charm, John's shows transformed traditional rock

Elton John

concerts into rock spectacles. They created a new stage aesthetic that suggested that rock was no longer an expressive pursuit but a new form of mass entertainment. In time, rock fans came to expect such diversions not merely from John but from all of their rock heroes. And the business, noting John's success and popularity, began to expect the same.

But good or bad, John was, for a time, unstoppable. The proverbial 800-pound gorilla of rock, he created some of the greatest musical high points of the post-Beatles era.

John (b. Reginald Kenneth Dwight, Mar. 25, 1947, London) had studied piano from the age of four. In 1958, he was awarded a part-time scholarship at the Royal Academy of Music. But by the early 1960s, his classical studies had given way to a love of rock and roll, and in 1961, he became a member of a fledgling R&B group, Bluesology.

By 1965, the group had graduated from its amateur status and begun to perform as a support act for various U.S. R&B acts who were touring the U.K., including Major Lance, Patti LaBelle, the Ink Spots, and others. In 1966, Bluesology hooked up with British R&B vocalist Long John Baldry. But Dwight became disenchanted with Baldry's music and quit the group to pursue a career of his own.

He changed his name in 1967 to Elton John (taken from the forenames of saxophonist Elton Dean and John Baldry). The same year, he answered a songwriter ad in a British music trade publication placed by Liberty Records, where, in time, he was paired with an equally unknown lyricist, Bernie Taupin (b. May 22, 1950, Lincolnshire). Eventually dropped by Liberty, the two teamed up with music publisher Dick James (who had worked with the Beatles) and began collaborating on songs. By 1968, they were signed to Phillips Records, which released John's debut single, "I've Been Loving You Too Long." The record failed to chart, as did its follow-up, "Lady Samantha," in 1969. That year also saw the release of John's debut album, *Empty Sky*.

In 1970, John's career began a slow but inexorable ascent into the charts. Signed to UNI Records in the U.S., he released a single, "Border Song," that eventually reached number four and brought attention to his music in the rock press. When his eponymous album was released in October of 1970, it also rose to number four. The album was an almost stately affair, with an orchestra backing many of the songs. That same month, the first version of the Elton John Band was formed, the core lineup based on Murray (b. David Murray Oates, Apr. 3, 1946, London) and Ollson (b. Feb. 10, 1949, Wallasey, Merseyside).

With this group—augmented by other musicians at various points—John recorded the exceptional album *Tumbleweed Connection*. Its songs based on an Old West motif, the album proved to be vastly popular, charting at number five. Touring in support of the album, John, Murray, and Ollson began to display the wild antics and boisterous musicality that would become signatures of John's onstage performances during the 1970s. The typical finale of these performances was a sprawling version of "Burn Down the Mission," with John leading the group into side versions of the Beatles' "Get Back" and other rock classics while standing on top of his piano, dancing about maniacally.

By 1972, John's records and shows were generating ecstatic responses from fans. The album *Madman Across the Water* reached number eight, while its successor, *Honky Chateau,* topped the charts for five weeks. John was quickly becoming a musical phenomenon.

Over the course of the next four years, John became the biggest rock act in the world. During that time, seven of his albums, including *Don't Shoot Me I'm Only the Piano Player, Goodbye Yellow Brick Road,* and *Captain Fantastic and the Brown Dirt Cowboy,* topped the charts, many for several weeks running. His Number One singles included "Crocodile Rock," "Bennie and the Jets," "Philadelphia Freedom," and others.

Onstage, his wild performances were greeted with a similar response. When his shows were announced, they sold out immediately. In 1975, John became the first rock artist to play Los Angeles' Dodger Stadium since the Beatles; he arrived onstage in a sequined Dodger uniform. In 1976, he broke the attendance record set by the Rolling Stones at New York's Madison Square Garden, selling out seven nights and taking in over $1 million.

There were other high points. In 1974, John sang on John Lennon's Number One hit "Whatever Gets You Through the Night." Lennon returned the favor by singing on John's version of the Beatles' 1967 classic, "Lucy in the Sky with Diamonds," which topped the charts at the end of the year. Lennon also joined John onstage at Madison Square Garden in a rendition of "I Saw Her Standing There"; it would be Lennon's final stage performance.

John also participated in the 1975 film version of the Who's rock opera *Tommy.* And in 1976, he performed on television's "The Muppet Show" with Miss Piggy.

TOP ALBUMS

Honky Chateau (Uni, '72, *1*)
Don't Shoot Me I'm Only the
    Piano Player (MCA, '73, *1*)
Goodbye Yellow Brick Road
    (MCA, '73, *1*)
Caribou (MCA, '74, *1*)
Captain Fantastic and the Brown
    Dirt Cowboy (MCA, '75, *1*)

Additional Top 40 Albums: 21

TOP SONGS

Crocodile Rock (MCA, '72, *1*)
Bennie and the Jets (MCA, '74, *1*)
Lucy in the Sky with Diamonds
    (MCA, '74, *1*)
Philadelphia Freedom (MCA, '75, *1*)
Island Girl (MCA, '75, *1*)

Additional Top 40 Songs: 42

John's lifestyle was as garish as his public image. He began to collect fine art and resided in palatial houses. He reportedly purchased seven luxurious Bentley automobiles—one for each day of the week. He spent hundreds of thousands of dollars on outlandish clothes, for use onstage and off. John wasn't merely a rock idol; he became a full-blown media star.

But the success and excess began to take their toll. His 1975 ballad "Someone Saved My Life Tonight" was reportedly based on an attempted suicide. At various points, he collapsed onstage from exhaustion.

In 1977, John announced his retirement from the stage. In 1978, he ended his collaboration with Taupin (although they would resume their work together in 1983 on the album *Too Low for Zero*).

By the end of the decade, John's career began to settle into a comfortable, if much less commercially successful, routine. He began touring again in 1979, but his first outing was an uncharacteristically low-keyed affair, with John at his piano accompanied only by percussionist Ray Cooper.

As the new decade unfolded, John continued to tour and record. In 1983, his single "I Guess That's Why They Call It the Blues" hit number four, and in 1984, "Sad Songs Say So Much" made number five. Other hits followed: "Nikita" (1986, number seven), "Candle in the Wind" (1987, number six), and "I Don't Want to Go On with You Like That" (1988, number two). These records and others, such as the strutting 1983 rocker "I'm Still Standing," were among the finest songs of John's career.

That career continued unabated into the 1990s. In 1992, John sold out shows across the U.S. during his world tour, and his records—new and old— became fixtures on "classic" radio. John's continuing popularity with fans of several pop generations proved that he was more than a '70s phenomenon, that he would be treasured for the enduring quality of his songs rather than the tremendous success that, at one point, attended them.

JANIS JOPLIN

Janis Joplin was no hippie.
She burst on to the national rock scene during 1967's
Summer of Love with her galvanizing performance
at the Monterey Pop Festival.

Before that, Joplin and her group Big Brother and the Holding Company had been one of the leading forces in the emerging San Francisco "hippie" scene.

But other than those matters of place and time, Joplin had little in common musically (or temperamentally) with the San Francisco rock scene. While many of her Bay Area counterparts were fusing folk and rock into a new, so-called psychedelic sound, Joplin was belting out the blues with an astonishing emotion and ferocity. With her gravelly voice, soaring screams and wails, and almost animalistic abandon, she had more in common with blues performers than with any of her rock contemporaries. Her idol, in fact, was blues great Bessie Smith.

Joplin's presence was also something of an anomaly in an age of peace, love, and understanding. She lived fast and hard, or at least projected that image. And at a time when mind-expanding substances were being used by hippies and others to explore sensory frontiers, Joplin generally opted for the harder stuff. She single-handedly made Southern Comfort the liquor of choice in the rock world. And as the years and her notoriety wore on, she developed a dependence on heroin that ultimately killed her.

But while her fall was as precipitous as her rise to fame, during the brief span of her career she cut a wide and enduring swath across the rock of the time.

Joplin (b. Jan. 19, 1943, Port Arthur, Texas) spent the early 1960s singing in the blues and folk scenes of Houston and Austin. In 1963, she made her way to San Francisco, where she performed at local clubs (at times, with guitarist Jorma Kaukonen, who would later be a founding member of Jefferson Airplane).

Tiring of that scene, she returned to Texas in the mid-'60s and gave up her musical career. But her passion for the blues was undimmed, and by 1966 she was back in San Francisco. Getting involved in the burgeoning rock movement, she formed Big Brother and the Holding Company with guitarists James Gurley and Sam Andrew, bassist Peter Albin, and drummer David Getz. The group immediately became a hit on the local scene and secured the house band position at one of the seminal meeting places of hippiedom, the Avalon Ballroom.

Joplin's most inspired performances, on record and onstage, came during her days with Big Brother and the Holding Company. The group was rough, ragged, and barely competent. But its exuberant, slashing, and jagged sound was the perfect complement to Joplin's raw vocals.

Joplin and Big Brother came to the attention of the national rock media and music business with their appearance at the Monterey Pop Festival in 1967 (their rendition of the blues classic "Ball and Chain" would be immortalized in the 1969 documentary *Monterey Pop*). Based on that performance, Big Brother and the Holding Company was immediately signed by Bob Dylan's manager, Albert Grossman, who began to pursue a record deal.

The group's eponymous debut album was released in August 1967 on the Mainstream label. An abysmally recorded affair, the record nonetheless captured Joplin's blues-saturated vocals and the group's raw sound. The album hit number 60 on the charts.

Big Brother began to make a name for itself on the East Coast in 1968 with its performances at New

York's Anderson Theatre and the opening of the Fillmore East. Grossman, meanwhile, had negotiated a new record contract with Columbia. In August, the album *Cheap Thrills* was released and topped the charts two months later, in the process yielding the blues-infused hit single, "Piece of My Heart."

Ironically, the album proved to be Big Brother's undoing. While the group actually sounded much more refined on *Cheap Thrills,* Joplin's vocals dominated the record. By the end of the year, Joplin had decided to pursue a solo career, and Big Brother disbanded.

It would prove to be a vast miscalculation on Joplin's part. In 1969, she debuted her new group, the Kozmic Blues Band. Comprising musicians who were more musically adept than the fiery amateurs of Big Brother, the new group had little feel for Joplin's undisciplined expressions (despite the thrashings of Andrew, who was added to the lineup in February).

She toured with the group during the year and, in October, released *I Got Dem Ol' Kozmic Blues Again Mama!* The album was a hit, reaching number five, but musically it had little of the raucous excitement and fervor of Joplin's work with Big Brother. She disbanded the group at the end of the year.

But she fared no better with her next outfit. Formed in 1970, the Full-Tilt Boogie Band was another assemblage of competent but uninspired rockers whose playing was pale in comparison with Joplin's exuberant and full-tilt style. She toured with the group during 1970 and began to record a new album in September.

Joplin's excessive lifestyle was catching up with her. Bouts with drugs and alcohol were gradually destroying her vocals and health, and she increasingly seemed to be going over the edge. On the night of October 4, 1970, she was found dead in her room at a hotel in Hollywood, the victim of a heroin overdose.

But her music lived on. In fact, for a time, it thrived. In February 1971, the album *Pearl*—drawn from her final sessions—was issued. It topped the charts, as did its single, Joplin's rasping rendition of Kris Kristofferson's "Me and Bobby McGee." Joplin's music was brought to life again in 1975 in the documentary *Janis.* And in 1979, Bette Midler starred in the film *The Rose,* purportedly based on Joplin's life.

Several biographies of Janis Joplin have been published, including *Buried Alive* by Myra Friedman and *Going Down with Janis* by Peggy Caserta.

Janis Joplin

TOP ALBUMS

BIG BROTHER AND THE HOLDING COMPANY
(Mainstream, '68)
CHEAP THRILLS (Columbia, '68, 1)
I GOT DEM OL' KOZMIC BLUES AGAIN MAMA!
(Columbia, '69, 5)
PEARL (Columbia, '71, 1)
JOPLIN IN CONCERT (Columbia '72, 4)
JANIS JOPLIN'S GREATEST HITS (Columbia, '73, 37)

TOP SONGS

PIECE OF MY HEART (Columbia, '68, 12)
ME AND BOBBY MCGEE (Columbia, '71, 1)

THE KINGSMEN

If the song "Louie Louie" had been the Kingsmen's only significant musical contribution, it would have been enough to ensure them a cherished place in the annals of rock and roll. As a matter of fact, it was.

When "Louie Louie" was released in 1963 on a minor Seattle-based label, Jerden, it made local noise but not much more. But when the record began to receive airplay and attention in the Boston area, the record and the Kingsmen were signed to the national label Wand, and a rock phenomenon began to unfold. By the end of the year, "Louie Louie" had hit number two on the charts, sold over a million copies, and entered the realm of pop cultural myth.

At the core of this myth were the garbled vocals of the Kingsmen's Jack Ely. With the group pounding out the prototypical three-chord progression that is basic to almost all of rock and roll, Ely rasped out words that launched a thousand raunchy lyrical offshoots in the minds of a generation of hormone-crazed teenaged boys.

In fact, the song, written in 1958 by an obscure R&B artist named Richard Berry, was fairly simple and apparently about a sailor singing of his love. But in Ely's strangled vocals, an entire nation of teens seemed to hear lyrics about something much more interesting: sex. That interpretation seemed to be confirmed when several radio stations in various parts of the U.S. banned the song (it was also banned by the BBC in Britain) and the governor of Indiana declared that it was "pornographic." The controversy was such that the Federal Communications Commission was called in to make a ruling, but the FCC's members could only conclude that "Louie Louie" was "unintelligible at any speed we played it."

Whatever. "Louie Louie" entered the culture not merely as a rock and roll hit but as a perennial theme song for teenagedom. In London, it became a favorite of the Mods and was recorded by the Kinks

and others. In the U.S., it was recorded by everyone from the Beach Boys to Paul Revere and the Raiders. As the years and decades went by, "Louie Louie" was passed down from one generation of teens to the next, becoming a musical addendum to the rite of puberty. In 1983, a radio station in northern California staged an all-day "Louie Louie" fest, playing as many recorded versions of the song as it could find. In South Carolina in 1989, 432 guitarists performed "Louie Louie" for 30 minutes, breaking the Guinness world record for most guitarists playing in unison for the longest period of time.

While "Louie Louie" became a cultural phenomenon, the Kingsmen went about their business as a sturdy if unexceptional band. Over the next three years, the group had a steady stream of dismissable hits, including versions of Barrett Strong's "Money," the Righteous Brothers' "Little Latin Lupe Lu," and "Death of an Angel," all of which charted in 1964. In 1965, the Kingsmen recorded a novelty song, "The Jolly Green Giant," based on a popular TV commercial for canned goods. That same year, it charted with a version of the U.S. Rocky Fellers' 1963 hit, "Killer Joe." Ironically, all of these were recorded without Ely, who had left the group just as "Louie Louie" was becoming a hit; onstage, saxophonist Lynn Easton took over on vocals.

The group was formed in Portland, Oregon, in 1958 by Easton and Ely. By 1963 they had been joined by lead guitarist Mike Mitchell, bassist Bob Nordby (who would leave with Ely that year), keyboardist Don Gallucci, and drummer Gary Abbott. The Kingsmen became a part of the burgeoning rock scene of the Pacific Northwest that included Paul

The Kingsmen

Revere and the Raiders (who also recorded on the Jerden label before moving on to national attention and hits with Columbia Records).

While "Louie Louie" was the Kingsmen's primary contribution to rock history, the group was also important because it was one of the first of a line of groups whose single, signature hits littered the charts during the rest of the 1960s. In subsequent decades, these groups would come to be known as garage bands (for the place where they usually rehearsed, and because most of their records sounded as if they'd been recorded in one).

These groups were, for the most part, barely competent musically, and they tended to latch onto various rock movements—psychedelia, folk-rock, and so forth—made famous by the really important rock innovators. But what distinguished each, briefly, was the ability to create one monolithic, wonderful record that forced its way into the collective rock consciousness for a few weeks and enlivened the top 40 radio airwaves with its sophomoric bravura.

High points of this decidedly low art included the Shadows of Knight spelling out "G-l-o-r-i-a" with guitars cranking away in the background, the shattering echo-box explosion of the Electric Prunes' "I Had Too Much to Dream (Last Night)," and the Music Machine chop-chopping the title of "Talk Talk."

Several of these one-hit wonders actually had two or more hits. Thus the Seeds followed their slashing version of "Hey Joe" with "Pushin' Too Hard." The Standells hit with "Dirty Water" then came back with "Sometimes Good Guys Don't Wear White."

TOP ALBUMS

THE KINGSMEN IN PERSON (Wand, '64, *20*)
THE KINGSMEN, VOLUME II (Wand, '64, *15*)
THE KINGSMEN, VOLUME 3 (Wand, '65, *22*)

TOP SONGS

LOUIE LOUIE (Wand, '63, *2*)
MONEY (Wand, '64, *16*)
THE JOLLY GREEN GIANT (Wand, '65, *4*)

The Left Banke sustained its pop-classical sound on "Walk Away Renée," "Pretty Ballerina," and "Desirée." And the folk-rock meisters the Grass Roots—as garage as it got—actually had a series of hits that began with "Where Were You When I Needed You" and continued on through "Let's Live for Today," "Midnight Confessions," and others. But in each case, the first time was the best.

The Syndicate of Sound had to be content with "Little Girl," the Count Five with "Psychotic Reaction," the Castaways with "Liar, Liar," the Strawberry Alarm Clock with "Incense and Peppermints," and the Blues Magoos with "We Ain't Got Nothin' Yet."

Some of these bands had members who would eventually open the garage door and drive out into a bigger pop world. Screeching his way through the Amboy Dukes' "Journey to the Center of the Mind"—as he would through his blaring, rocking solo career in the 1970s—was the young Ted Nugent. And long before he sold out country music to become a crossover goliath, the First Edition's Kenny Rogers did the same to psychedelia on the 1968 hit "Just Dropped In (To See What Condition My Condition Was In)."

But for every opportunistic Rogers, there were scores of diligent rockers busting their chops just to get by and have one hit they could look back on in their old age (their 30s). It was this diligence, this sheer unabashed dedication that made their hit songs such a sound to behold. Ignoring their own banality, derivativeness, and overarching musical incompetence, they made rock as best they could. And rock—as it did with the Kingsmen—occasionally repaid them with a hit and a small place in rock history.

THE KINKS

Of all the groups that emerged during the British Invasion of 1964, the most British of all was the Kinks.

In the songs of its leader, Ray Davies, the group created a body of work that was as steady and stolid as the Empire, yet as contemporary and iconoclastic as the Swinging London scene from which it came. One of the finest composers of his generation—arguably, on a level with Lennon and McCartney and Pete Townshend—Davies cast knowing eyes at the social landscape, which he commented upon in songs that were a remarkable amalgam of poetic lyricism, dry wit, and affectionate tolerance.

Davies had a genius for expressing the ordinary in the most extraordinary musical manner. On 1965's "A Well Respected Man," his frail but somewhat edgy vocals subtly spoke of the desperation of the common man going about his daily duties, the timeless portrait set to a strumming, folk-based sound. On 1966's "Dedicated Follower of Fashion," he set his sights on the foibles of Carnaby Street culture, supporting his spry sarcasm with deft flourishes drawn from the British music hall tradition. That same year, "Sunny Afternoon" was another music hall jaunt, this time through the travails of love. "Waterloo Sunset" of 1967 was an evocative depiction of English life, while 1970's "Lola" was an eye-rolling romp through that most traditional of English national pastimes, transvestism.

But Davies was more than an insightful social commentator and the Kinks more than his backing group.

In fact, the Kinks were, initially, one of the most

forceful rock outfits on the British scene. Their debut hit, 1964's "You Really Got Me," was a charging rock tirade that came with saw-toothed chords and a distorted, cranking solo from Ray's brother, Dave, the group's lead guitarist. And bassist Peter Quaife and drummer Mick Avory were one of the most energetic rhythm sections in the rock of the time.

"You Really Got Me" was a maniacal blast that countered the more pop-oriented sound of the Liverpool rock and roll contingent. It was one of the first examples—along with the music of the Rolling Stones and the Who—of the harder, more R&B-inflected sound that dominated London in the early 1960s. Along with the group's soundalike follow-up single, "All Day and All of the Night," it also provided one of the first hints of the clanking, crashing rock sound that would develop into heavy metal later in the decade.

The Kinks came together in 1963, when Ray (b. Raymond Douglas Davies, June 21, 1944, Muswell Hill, London) joined Dave Davies (b. Feb. 3, 1947, Muswell Hill) in the latter's band, the Ravens. That band also included Quaife (b. Dec. 31, 1943, Tavistock, Devon, England). By the end of the year, Avory (b. Feb. 15, 1944, Hampton Court, London) had joined on drums.

The group secured a contract with Pye Records in 1964 and began recording with pop producer Shel Talmy. The Kinks' debut single, a rendition of Little Richard's "Long Tall Sally," failed to chart, as did the second, "You Do Something to Me." But the third single, "You Really Got Me," reached the summit of the British charts and went to number seven in America.

Every so-called beat group of the time had to have a "look." And the Kinks', oddly enough, was

The Kinks

that of a group of rocking Edwardian dandies. Geared up in sleek velvet huntsman's jackets, the Kinks lolled about on album covers and publicity pictures, all the while turning out their raw, R&B sound.

The group's debut album and its successor, whose titles came from the first two hit singles, were loaded with R&B covers and a few Davies originals. But by 1965, Davies had begun to explore new songwriting avenues. The single "Tired of Waiting for You" came with a new melodic sensibility, as did its successor, "Set Me Free." But beneath the melodies of these songs the Kinks still provided a hard, if now

---

TOP ALBUMS

KINKS-SIZE (Reprise, '65, *13*)
THE KINKS GREATEST HITS! (Reprise, '66, *9*)
LOW BUDGET (Arista, '79, *11*)
STATE OF CONFUSION (Arista, '83, *12*)

Additional Top 40 Albums: 6

TOP SONGS

YOU REALLY GOT ME (Reprise, '64, *7*)
ALL DAY AND ALL OF THE NIGHT (Reprise, '64, *7*)
TIRED OF WAITING FOR YOU (Reprise, '65, *6*)
A WELL RESPECTED MAN (Reprise, '65, *13*)
LOLA (Reprise, '70, *9*)
COME DANCING (Arista, '83, *6*)

Additional Top 40 Songs: 6

---

understated, rock sound. That sound continued to be heard on such flat-out rockers as "Everybody's Gonna Be Happy" and "Till the End of the Day," with Quaife and Avory slapping out steady rhythms to Dave Davies' churning guitar.

During this period, the Kinks became a top concert draw in the U.K. and appeared on such American television programs as "Shindig." But when the group pulled out of a performance on its debut U.S. tour in 1965, it was blacklisted in that country for the next four years. The result of this disaster was that the group, while scoring hits on the charts, would have a minor presence in the U.S. through the end of the decade.

Similar problems attended the group's tours of the U.K. and the continent, the Kinks cancelling shows on a steady basis due to exhaustion and various illnesses, injuries, visa difficulties, and such. The

group also seemed to be constantly on the verge of breaking up. Quaife was the first to leave, in 1966, but returned off and on until the split was final in 1968, at which time he was formally replaced by John Dalton. Ray Davies also threatened to leave the group at several points but was always persuaded to change his mind.

But amid the turmoil, the hits continued. Along with the earlier "You Really Got Me" and "All Day and All of the Night," others like "Sunny Afternoon" became signature songs of 1960s Britain. In 1967, Ray Davies struck out on his own, scoring the soundtrack for the film *The Virgin Soldiers*. He also composed the debut hit of Dave's solo career, "Death of a Clown," which hit number three on the U.K. charts in 1967.

Near the end of the decade, Ray Davies began to compose conceptual pieces. This shift in songwriting approach yielded the albums *The Kinks Are the Village Green Preservation Society* (1968) and *Arthur (Or "The Decline and Fall of the British Empire")* (1969). But his talent for the brief, telling pop song was undiminished. "Lola" hit number nine on the U.S. singles chart in 1970.

With its touring blacklist issue resolved that year, the Kinks began the second phase in its career, which saw the group become a successful concert draw in the U.S. during the 1970s. During that time, the Kinks often used a horn section to augment their sound in live shows. They also issued the album *Sleepwalker* in 1977, and it rose to number 21 on the American charts.

While Ray Davies' songwriting talents were hardly as prodigious as they had been in the 1960s, he still knocked out the odd gem from time to time. In 1981, the rocking "Destroyer," with its rather liberal borrowings from "All Day and All of the Night," hit number 15. And the lilting, romantic ballad "Come Dancing," which charted at number six in 1983, was an ebullient and welcome reminder of his old melodic gifts.

The Kinks ultimately proved to be one of the most durable groups of the '60s British Invasion, continuing to tour and record into the '90s, with the Davies brothers fronting a frequently shifting cast of new Kinks lineups.

In 1990, the Kinks were inducted into the Rock and Roll Hall of Fame. And that same year, they were honored with the Special Contribution to British Music award at the annual Ivor Novello Awards ceremony in London.

ALEXIS KORNER

Ascertaining the specific source of any musical movement would seem to be an almost impossible task. Such movements are usually the end result of months or years of musical evolution, a confluence of like-minded musicians, and fortuitous circumstances.

That is not the case with the British R&B movement of the early 1960s that, in time, yielded such groups as the Rolling Stones, Cream, Manfred Mann, the Graham Bond Organization, and Led Zeppelin. Each of those groups and scores of others—indeed, the British R&B scene itself—could all trace their roots in some manner back to one man. That man, who came to be known as "the father of white blues," was Alexis Korner.

When Korner formed his legendary group Blues Incorporated in 1961, he single-handedly set the stage for the development of R&B and the blues in Britain. From 1961 through 1967, Blues Incorporated, perhaps the first white blues band in the world, became the meeting ground for some of the most illustrious musicians in rock history.

With Korner as its leader and catalyst, Blues Incorporated's constantly changing lineups included a staggering list of future rock legends. One of the first versions of the group included Mick Jagger on vocals, Charlie Watts on drums, and Jack Bruce on bass. At one point or another, the group also introduced the likes of Brian Jones, Keith Richards, Manfred Mann's Paul Jones, Ginger Baker, Free's Paul Rodgers, guitarist John McLaughlin, and future members of such diverse groups as Soft Machine, Pentangle, John Mayall's Bluesbreakers, Blodwyn Pig, and countless others.

But Korner, a guitarist and sometime vocalist, was more than a bandleader. He was a patriarchal figure in British blues and R&B who created the scene from his own vision and guided the paths of its mostly young participants. He opened his home to

musicians, offering it as a crash pad and meeting place where he would hold forth on his passion for American blues and R&B.

His Ealing Rhythm and Blues Club in London became the focal point for a new generation of blues musicians and fans and provided a stage for Korner and Blues Incorporated to perform. It was there that Jagger and Richards first heard a young slide guitarist from Cheltenham, Brian Jones, with whom they would subsequently form the nucleus of the Rolling Stones. There, too, Baker, Bond, and Bruce were introduced, a meeting that would lead to their collaboration in the Graham Bond Organization, from which Baker and Bruce ultimately graduated to Cream.

Korner was at the center of it all, with Blues Incorporated providing an ongoing platform and sounding board for the development of the emerging blues scene. When he closed the Ealing club and moved the action to London's legendary rock club the Marquee, he continued to be a focal point and a catalyst for the careers of other musicians.

The most auspicious moment in this regard came in 1962 when he deputized several of his collaborators to fill in for Blues Incorporated at its usual gig at the Marquee while that group went off to perform on a radio program. That Marquee gig proved to be the first performance by the Rolling Stones.

Ironically, in spite of his seminal influence on the scene, Korner was not a part of the British blues boom of the mid and late '60s that saw many of his musical offspring achieve vast commercial and artistic success. As a musician, Korner was passable but

Alexis Korner

hardly distinctive; his raspy vocals and rather subdued guitar work were mostly derivations of the
American originals, quite unlike the revolutionary
reinterpretations of his young protégés. He also
steadfastly refused to make any concessions to com-
mercialism, pursuing an eccentric course that ranged
from blues to R&B, jazz, and even music for children's television programs. Nearing 40 by the mid-

'60s, Korner was also too old to pass for a rock idol.

But Korner was a revered figure in Britain. Association with his name and various groups validated
the reputations of young musicians on their way to
other musical destinations. Simply put, Korner was
the "guv'nor."

Korner (b. 1928, Paris) was the son of an Austrian father and Greek-Turkish mother. His family

traveled through Europe during the 1930s and eventually settled in England in the '40s. Trained as a musician since the age of five, Korner began his career with British jazz pioneer Chris Barber and his band in the late 1940s.

By the mid-'50s, Korner, an avid fan of American blues, met up with harmonica player Cyril Davies, and the two began to pursue their passion for that neglected form. At the end of the 1950s, they opened their own club, the London Blues and Barrelhouse Club, as a one-off affair at the Roundhouse Pub in Soho. But the prevailing "trad" movement of the time, which stressed a more purist, acoustic form of blues and jazz, wasn't ready for their new electric music. They returned to Barber's band, performing as an R&B adjunct to that group with vocalist Ottilie Paterson.

By the start of the 1960s, young audiences of students and bohemian sorts were becoming interested in R&B and proved receptive to the music that Korner and Davies had in mind. When they founded Blues Incorporated and opened their Ealing Club on March 17, 1962, young musicians and fans began to flock to their performances.

With Blues Incorporated, Korner was less a front man than a musical magnet, drawing to the group scores of young musicians who were eager to learn about the blues and perfect their individual styles. Onstage, Korner would frequently sit on a chair at the side, playing guitar while such vocalists as Jagger, Paul Jones, or Long John Baldry would perform in the spotlight.

Korner and Davies (who left the group in 1962 to form the Cyril Davies All Stars) were joined by a constantly changing array of sidemen, including drummers Watts and Baker, horn men Bond and Dick Heckstall-Smith (later of John Mayall's Bluesbreakers and Blodwyn Pig), and such future fusion jazz stars as guitarist John McLaughlin (who founded the Mahavishnu Orchestra in the '70s) and bassist Dave Holland (who went on to play with Miles Davis).

The music of Blues Incorporated—and Korner—evolved during the 1960s, embracing a wide range of black American idioms. Early versions of the group specialized in R&B classics like Willie Dixon's "I'm a Hoochie Coochie Man" and Billy Boy Arnold's "She Fooled Me" along with Korner originals such as "I Wonder Who" that sounded like those classics.

While Blues Inc.'s sound wasn't innovative, it was revolutionary in the sense that white musicians, particularly from Britain, had rarely played such music until that point.

As it developed and new musicians came and went, Korner became increasingly interested in a more jazz-oriented sound. Later versions of the group included such jazz-based musicians as saxman John Surman and string bassist Danny Thompson.

With Thompson and drummer Terry Cox, Korner retreated from the scene in the later 1960s to compose music for children's television programs. He then formed the group Free at Last for a brief time and, in 1968, worked in a duo with Led Zeppelin vocalist Robert Plant. At the end of the decade, another new group, New Church, was formed, and Korner performed with it at the fabled Rolling Stones concert in Hyde Park in 1969.

CCS (Collective Consciousness Society) followed in 1970. With CCS, Korner finally made the charts in the U.K. with a version of the Led Zeppelin hit "Whole Lotta Love." The subsequent singles "Walking" and "Tap Turns on the Water" made the charts in 1971.

In June of that year, Korner's role in the blues was acknowledged by one of the idiom's masters when he was invited by B.B. King to perform on the latter's album *B.B. King in London*. The album included the Korner original "Alexis' Blues," with King and Korner playing acoustic guitars. The album marked Korner's recorded debut on a U.S. release (an American record deal negotiated by Beatles manager Brian Epstein had previously failed to materialize in 1967).

While Korner never made much of an inroad into the country that had inspired him musically, he did tour the U.S. briefly in 1972 with the group Snape. Included was Danish blues vocalist Peter Thorup, with whom Korner enjoyed considerable success in Europe in the 1970s.

His gravelly voice, oddly enough, brought him a certain fame and fortune via British television commercials, for which he provided voiceovers. And he became a television personality in that country in the 1970s hosting the series "The Blues" on the BBC.

But Korner's true claim to fame came in the early '60s when he set in motion the blues and R&B scene in Britain that ultimately conquered the rock world.

Korner died on January 1, 1984.

TOP ALBUM

BOOTLEG HIM! (Warner Bros., '72)

KRAFTWERK

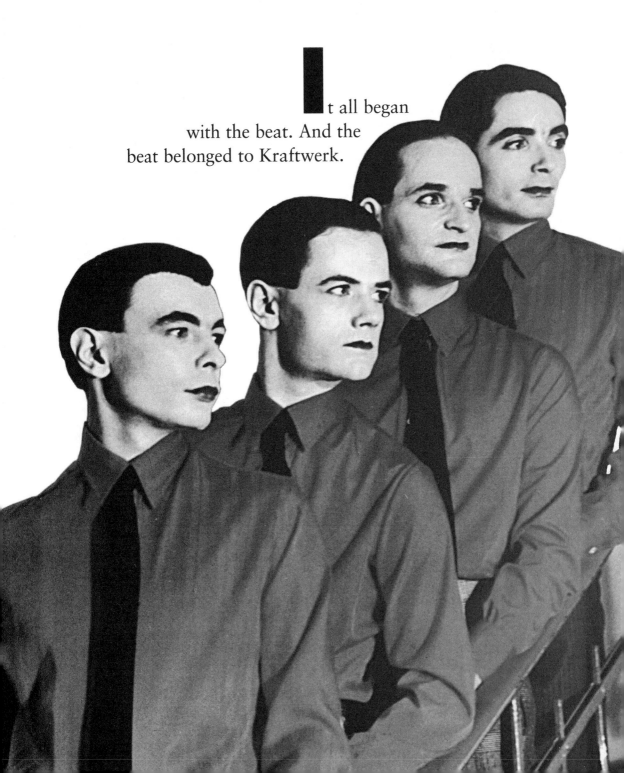

It all began with the beat. And the beat belonged to Kraftwerk.

Thumping beneath the surface of most dance-pop genres of the past 20 years has been a monolithic, repetitive, metronomic beat. That beat has been at the core of everything from Euro-pop and disco to techno-pop, rap, and the dance-based pop that permeates the 1990s.

Oddly, what acts as diverse as Gary Numan, Donna Summer, Madonna, Depeche Mode, Paula Abdul, and scores of rappers have in common is a musical motif originally suggested by two German electronic music nerds named Ralf and Florian.

Ralf Hutter (b. 1946, Krefeld, Germany) and Florian Schneider-Esleben (b. 1947, Dusseldorf, Germany) formed Kraftwerk in Dusseldorf in 1970 and, in collaboration with Klaus Dinger and Thomas Homann, began experimenting with synthesized sound. Recording their first album, *Highrail,* in a studio inside a local oil refinery, the group decided to name itself after the German word for power plant. When Dinger and Homann left to form Neu in 1971, Hutter and Schneider-Esleben continued their experiments on the 1972 album *Var* and 1973's *Ralf and Florian.* For the most part, those records were minimalistic electronic affairs (*Ralf and Florian* also included sections that were scored for string and woodwind parts) that blended a vague pop sensibility with allusions to the work of the German classical avant-gardist Karlheinz Stockhausen.

Hutter and Schneider-Esleben augmented that sound with a look that conspicuously diverted from the '70s norm. At a time when the rest of the pop world was either glittered out or strutting about in long locks, T-shirts, and bell-bottoms, Ralf and Florian posed in short hair and drab business suits like refugees from a John Cage symposium.

It was all very eccentric in a nondescript way. But hardly earthshaking.

And then there was "Autobahn."

In 1974 Hutter and Schneider-Esleben, along with new partners Wolfgang Flur and Klaus Roeder, released the album *Autobahn.* The title cut was a 22 1/2-minute masterpiece that changed the course of contemporary pop.

A depiction of a car journey, the song was propelled by an electronic beat that hurtled along with all the cold efficiency of a BMW cruising the German highway system. As Kraftwerk made its way through

the song, they inserted sleek layers of synthesized chords, pointilistic theme lines, and vocals that were cool and machine-like.

But it was the beat that was the focal point. It was, at once, hypnotic and oddly energizing, part mantra and part invitation to dance. It was also a revolution in pop songwriting. With this song, the focus of pop music was shifted from the melody to the beat. On "Autobahn," the beat was the hook.

An edited version of the song went to number 25 on the U.S. charts, and the album reached number five in 1975. But the artistic fallout far exceeded Kraftwerk's impact on the charts. The electronic beat that Kraftwerk had created began to insinuate itself into the nonstop rhythms—played variously by human drummers or drum machines—of the emerging disco phenomenon.

While the music of Donna Summer, the Bee Gees, and Abba had little in common, from a melodic standpoint, with that of Kraftwerk, they and other disco-based performers relied on a metronomic beat on many of their dance hits. When those hits were played side by side at discos, their beats created a continuous pulse to which dancers could move nonstop for hours on end. It was the energy created by the rhythm that was at the core of the disco phenomenon, with its subordination of thought to movement (which was why disco was often described as mindless by its detractors).

In a thoroughly contrary sense, that had been the purpose of *Autobahn.* But while the disco artists pursued this for primarily commercial ends, Kraftwerk had intended the mechanistic beats as a creative expression of the human mind giving way to the monotonous efficiency of the machine.

While disco was adopting and subverting its music, Kraftwerk pursued its highly idiosyncratic ways. Its 1977 album *Trans-Europe Express* and 1978's *The Man Machine* were accented with stark, electronic textures and darker musical motifs. At the same time, the group appeared onstage dressed as mannequins and performing like human robots.

By 1981, the group had perfected its sound and look. The album *Computer World* was a striking combination of pop and synthesized music, with songs like "Pocket Calculator" mixing winning melodies with tense and edgy electronic beats. The group's world tour of that year was an astonishing

TOP ALBUM

AUTOBAHN (Vertigo, '75, 5)

TOP SONG

AUTOBAHN (Vertigo, '75, 25)

visual display, with a stage set that looked like a garish mockup of a missile control room on which the musicians manipulated their automated instruments.

But as the decade unfolded, Kraftwerk retreated from the scene. In 1983, the group recorded the album *Techno Pop* but subsequently withdrew it from release and cancelled an upcoming tour. That same year, the group was commissioned to write the official theme for the Tour de France in 1983, which subsequently became a part of the soundtrack for the film *Breakdance*. In 1986, the album *Electric Café* was released but charted only modestly in the U.K. and the U.S.; the title cut, however, did yield a computer-generated video that received a modicum of attention. The group continued to record for the rest of the decade, although they released no new records; they also toured sporadically in Europe.

In 1991, the group released *Mixes,* which included reworked versions of "Trans-Europe Express" and "Autobahn."

But its relative inactivity notwithstanding, Kraftwerk had a tremendous effect on rock and pop. Techno-rockers like Numan and the Austrian Falco based much of their sound and look on Kraftwerk, as did Soft Cell. In 1983, Neil Young, of all people, paid tribute to the group with his album *Trans.* That same year, Africa Bambaataa's *Planet Rock* borrowed heavily from *Trans-Europe Express* and indirectly set the stage for the boom-box beats that would become central to the rap movement. Many others based their sound and songs on the sleek, steady beats that Kraftwerk had pioneered nearly 20 years before, beats that launched a thousand hips and changed rock along the way.

LED ZEPPELIN

Ironically, the group that spawned heavy metal had little in common with most of the form's subsequent practitioners. That group was Led Zeppelin.

By the beginning of the 1990s, heavy metal had long since become a mutant form of music, loaded with guitar heros in outrageous costumes and hairdos performing loud and simplistic songs about death, sex, drugs, and excess in general. It outraged parents and critics even as it proved to be an almost magnetic musical force, drawing in legions of mostly male fans who saw in its wildness a release from the tensions and frustrations of adolescence.

Heavy metal, at its most banal, was a case of musical acne that had refused to clear up with age. It had become less a form of musical expression than a rite of passage, the sound not of a generation but of seemingly every generation as it entered teendom.

Led Zeppelin was the first heavy metal group. It defined the form's musical signatures and sound, guided its evolution, and in the process became one of the most popular and successful groups of the 1970s.

The group's eponymous debut album, released in 1968, was a culmination of the music of groups like the Who, the Kinks, the Yardbirds, and others. On songs such as "Communication Breakdown," "Good Times, Bad Times," and "Dazed and Confused," guitarist Jimmy Page, vocalist Robert Plant, bassist-keyboardist John Paul Jones, and drummer John Bonham created a sublime reduction and expansion of the riff-based songs, power chords,

Led Zeppelin

blues-tinged vocals, and storming bass-and-drum onslaughts that each of those groups had pioneered in their individual ways.

While that album looked back to the 1960s for its inspiration, its successor, 1969's *Led Zeppelin II,* distilled the various aspects of '60s British blues into the form that metal would subsequently assume. On "Whole Lotta Love," Page's guitar lines rode the slamming beats of Bonham while Plant's wailing vocals cut across the song like a scythe. The guitar break on "Heartbreaker" was a fleeting, distorted tour de force, while the strummed acoustic chords on "Ramble On" provided a lithe, folk-tinged contrast to the pounding rhythm that ensued. On these songs and others, Led Zeppelin transcended the blues-rock

---

TOP ALBUMS

Led Zeppelin II (Atlantic, '69, *1*)
Led Zeppelin III (Atlantic, '70, *1*)
Led Zeppelin IV (untitled) (Atlantic, '71, *2*)
Houses of the Holy (Atlantic, '73, *1*)
Physical Graffiti (Swan Song, '75, *1*)
Presence (Swan Song, '76, *1*)
The Soundtrack from the Film *The Song Remains the Same* (Swan Song, '76, *2*)
In Through the Out Door (Swan Song, '79, *1*)
Coda (Swan Song, '82, *6*)

Additional Top 40 Albums: 1

TOP SONG

Whole Lotta Love (Atlantic, '69, *4*)

Additional Top 40 Songs: 5

---

of the past and created a sound that, in its mixture of familiar elements, was entirely new.

Led Zeppelin II was the first true metal album. Its musical signatures formed the basis of all the metal that would come. Its songs proved a point of departure for groups like Black Sabbath, Judas Priest, and countless others, who employed Zeppelin's new rock sound to their own creative ends.

But with those groups and most of the ensuing metallurgists, that new sound became codified into set of musical clichés that seemed cast in steel.

Led Zeppelin, on the other hand, refused to be confined by the form it had created. Over the course of the rest of its career, the group displayed a remarkable propensity for changing its sound, plac-

ing it in new contexts that expanded its expressive range. On the album *Led Zeppelin III,* for example, the group added melodic, folk-infused sounds on "Immigrant Song" and other tracks.

Subsequent albums yielded a vast array of musical idioms and approaches. There were the reggae-based beats and clicking chords of "D'yer Mak'er" and the traditional folk harmonies and themes of "The Battle of Evermore." On "The Rain Song," Page's sinuous guitar phrases were augmented by the droning sound of Jones's mellotron. "Kashmir" came with incessant cello-based figures and a vast, orchestrated backdrop that was offset by Plant's supple, expressive vocals. On the funky "Trampled Underfoot," the group created a blend of rock and the soul of Stevie Wonder. And on "Achilles' Last Stand," Page, Bonham, and Jones unleashed a careening attack that would subsequently inspire legions of speed-metal groups in the 1990s.

The apex of the group's sound, at least in a cultural sense, came on its 1971 ballad "Stairway to Heaven." The song began with folk-based arpeggios provided by Page's guitar. But these soon gave way to a majestic full-metal sound, with Bonham and Jones playing in tandem and Plant's vocals riding over the top. It was an epochal song that became one of the defining anthems of the decade.

Onstage, the group was equally famous—or infamous—for its grandiose musical performances. On songs like "Dazed and Confused," the musicians dueled in extended improvisations, Page bowing the strings of his guitar like a violin while Plant stood and emoted in his legendary pose, his back arched and his chest bared. Jones switched regularly from bass to keyboards to mandolin, providing tonal color and nuance to the exploding sound. And Bonham pounded out drum solos that lasted 20 minutes and more.

It was this combination of brashness, invention, and excess that made Led Zeppelin a larger-than-life rock group. Everything about it, from the vast proportions of its sound and success to the over-the-top personalities of its members, contrived to create an image that scores of metal groups in future rock generations would try their best to duplicate. None of them succeeded.

Led Zeppelin's origins date back to the Yardbirds. When that group disbanded in March 1968, Page (b. Jan. 9, 1944, Heston, London) recruited Plant (b. Aug. 20, 1948, West Bromwich, Midlands, England), Jones (b. John Baldwin, June 3, 1946, Sid-cup, Kent, England), and Bonham (b. May 31, 1948, Bromwich, Staffordshire, England) as the New Yard-birds. The group toured Scandinavia in September, having previously recorded its debut album in a two-week span. In October, Page changed the name to Led Zeppelin at the suggestion of the Who's drummer, Keith Moon (it was the latter's slang term for a bad gig).

In February 1969, Led Zeppelin's eponymous debut album was released and reached number 10 on the U.S. charts. While the group never sanctioned singles releases during its career, the song "Good Times, Bad Times" was issued by Atlantic Records and charted at number 80.

During the succeeding year and a half, Led Zeppelin toured constantly in Europe and the U.S. to increasing acclaim and adulation. In October 1969 it became the first group to play at New York's Carnegie Hall since the Rolling Stones.

In November, *Led Zeppelin II* was released and immediately topped the U.S. charts in a stay that lasted 138 weeks. The album established the group as one of the biggest rock acts in the world, with "Whole Lotta Love" becoming a signature of the group's sound. Released as a single—again, without the group's approval—it climbed the charts to number four.

The group took time off during the middle of 1970, but when it toured the U.S. again in September it set a new record for concert grosses when it earned more than $100,000 per performance for a 10-night stand at New York's Madison Square Garden. That same month it was voted the top group in a *Melody Maker* poll, unseating the Beatles.

They released the slightly more melodic *Led Zeppelin III* in October, and it topped the charts in both the U.S. and the U.K.

The touring continued into 1971 to the usual ravenous response from fans—and the somewhat ambivalent reaction of various critics. But the latter's comments went unheeded by the vast rock marketplace, especially when "Stairway to Heaven" hit the record racks in November via the *Led Zeppelin IV* album.

The group settled into an unvarying, and unvaryingly lucrative routine during the next several years. There were vastly successful tours augmented by vastly successful albums. *Houses of the Holy* (1973), *Physical Graffiti* (1975), and *Presence* (1976) all hit the top of the charts.

In October 1976, the group released its concert film, *The Song Remains the Same,* which documented its performances at Madison Square Garden.

But the success and acclaim gave way to problems and tragedy in 1977. On July 23 of that year, Bonham and manager Peter Grant were arrested and charged with assault on a security guard during a show at the Oakland Coliseum. Four days later, Plant's son Karac died in Britain from a stomach infection. Devastated, Plant returned home, and the tour was cancelled. He retreated from the scene for a year.

In July 1978, Led Zeppelin regrouped and journeyed to Sweden to record a new album at studios owned by Abba. Those sessions yielded 1979's *In Through the Out Door,* a Number One album in the U.S.

On July 7, 1980, Led Zeppelin gave its final performance at the Eissporthalle, West Berlin. In September, they convened at Page's home in Windsor to rehearse for an upcoming tour. After a night of heavy alcohol consumption at Page's home, Bonham was found dead in his room, on September 25th. In December, Led Zeppelin formally announced that it was disbanding.

Led Zeppelin subsequently re-formed on a one-off basis for several performances. The group participated in 1985's Live Aid benefit for victims of the Ethiopian famine. In 1988, with Jason Bonham filling in on drums for his late father, the group performed at a Madison Square Garden show commemorating the 40th anniversary of Atlantic Records. In 1990, they played at Bonham's wedding reception at the Heath Hotel in Bewdley, England.

Page pursued a career in the 1980s with the Firm, which included Paul Rodgers, the former vocalist of Bad Company. In 1992, he formed Coverdale/Page with Whitesnake vocalist David Coverdale, and the group released an eponymous album.

Plant pursued a successful solo career that began with his 1982 debut album *Pictures at Eleven* and continued through 1993's *Fate of Nations,* all of which came with a new wave–oriented sound that was notably, and probably intentionally, different from that of his former group. Jones became a record producer.

Zeppelin's music assumed a new guise in the late 1980s and early '90s when several rap groups sampled its old records for use in their own. Those records also served as the repertoire of the group Dread Zeppelin, which performed various reggae versions of Led Zeppelin classics.

JERRY LEE LEWIS

J erry Lee Lewis was
the proverbial loose cannon waiting to explode. Onstage
and off, he pursued his music and life with a fury
and intensity that bordered on the irrational.

As rock and roll made its way through the 1980s and into the '90s, it appeared to become the province of middle-aged musicians masquerading as leather-clad heavy metallists and young punks (not necessarily in the musical sense of the word), banging heads and flailing about while trying to look good for the video cameras. Their calculatedly wild images and antics—career moves in a literal sense—amounted to a caricature of the real crazies and craziness that defined the ethos of rock from its fledgling days in the 1950s. The craziest of those crazies was Jerry Lee Lewis.

His life was littered with scandals, stormy scenes, lawsuits, and tragedies. In 1973 alone, he shot his bass player (purely by accident), ran his Rolls Royce into a ditch and was arrested for drunk driving, and was arrested again for brandishing a derringer in front of Elvis Presley's Memphis mansion demanding that he be allowed to see the King.

If that was all there was to Lewis, however, he would have merely been one more southern hell-raiser in a region full of them. But Lewis was more: he was a fire-breathing rock and roll hell-raiser.

He burst onto the scene in 1957 with a sound and style that upped the ante on everyone. Not content to shake a hip like Presley or duckwalk like Berry, he slammed himself all over the place, kicking over piano stools, playing the keys with his heels, and dancing on the instrument, all while churning out some of the most inspired and demonic music of his time.

His version of rock and roll was like an evangelical tent revival set to music. But in his case, hellfire, and brimstone weren't the punishments; they were the rewards.

The titles of his three big rock hits told the tale:

"Whole Lotta Shakin' Goin' On," "Great Balls of Fire," and "Breathless." On these songs, and on literally everything else he came into musical contact with, Lewis crashed along with a force unsurpassed by anyone in rock. His voice defied the term "range," going from warbling lows to fevered shrieks with a crooner's slipperiness, a rocker's ferocity, and a madman's hysteria. Lewis didn't sing his songs as much as he ravaged them.

And while he was ravaging them, he pounded out chunky chords and lithe, tinkling country-sweet high notes on his piano—when he wasn't doing all sorts of other unspeakable things to the instrument. Like his vocals, Lewis's piano playing defied technical analysis. He wasn't a virtuoso by any means; instead, he got by, and then some, on sheer rock and roll bravura.

But his three big rock hits told another tale, and it was a short one. While he became a perennial hit-maker on the country and western scene, Lewis was a rock and roll force only briefly. The time clocked in at roughly one year, during which he had the good sense to release the singles "Whole Lotta Shakin' Going On" and "Great Balls of Fire" and the incredibly bad sense to marry his 13-year-old second cousin, Myra Gale Brown (while still married to second wife Jane Mitcham), thus sparking a controversy that basically ended his commercial rock career.

But that was all a part of the legend that Lewis became, a legend that, like his life, proved to be remarkably hard to snuff out. Lewis's story reads like a sprawling novel, one by Tolstoy perhaps, if that writer had grown up eating chitlins.

Lewis (b. Sept. 29, 1935, Ferriday, Louisiana) came into contact with the South's rich musical stew as a child. His parents mortgaged their house to buy

Jerry Lee Lewis

him a piano when he was in his teens and encouraged him to pursue a musical career, his father driving him to gigs with the piano strapped to the back of the family's truck.

He studied music formally for a time at the fundamentalist Assembly of God Institute in Waxahachie, Texas, but was soon kicked out. In 1952, at age 16, he married a preacher's daughter and then, in 1953, got married again, bigamously. It would become a habit he couldn't shake.

Amid the personal soap operas, he continued his musical career, performing wherever he could in the South. By 1956, inspired by the success of Presley, he decided to take his case to the legendary Sun record label in Memphis. He and his father sold 33 dozen eggs to finance the trip, and he camped out on the door of the studio until he was allowed to cut several demos. Label head Sam Phillips liked what he heard, and Lewis recorded "Whole Lotta Shakin' Going On" and "Crazy Arms" for his debut single. Released at the end of the year, it was banned across the country because of its alleged vulgarity.

In December of that year, Lewis was invited to record with Presley, Carl Perkins, and Johnny Cash at the Sun studio. Cash bowed out at the last moment, but the resulting session became legendary, the participants often referred to as the Million Dollar Quartet.

Lewis hit the national spotlight in July 1957, when he appeared on "The Steve Allen Show." With the attention generated by that appearance, the single "Whole Lotta Shakin' Going On" shot up the charts, hitting number three and selling more than six million copies.

Lewis was immediately catapulted into the top ranks of rock heroes. He toured the rest of the year to tremendous acclaim and adulation. But then there was the issue of a new marriage—to the 13-year-old Myra.

It didn't cause an uproar at first, and Lewis's popularity continued to soar. When "Great Balls of Fire" was released in January 1958, it went to number two on the charts and sold more than five million copies. In April, the next single, "Breathless," reached number seven.

But during a U.K. tour in May, all hell broke loose. When he introduced Myra to the British press, a storm of controversy engulfed the couple. The fans railed against him when he appeared onstage, and he was forced to cancel the rest of his tour. Making his way back to the U.S., he was confronted with bans on his music by various radio stations and Sun's refusal to promote his records.

Over the course of the next two years, the waning of radio and record label support gradually brought Lewis's rock career to a close. The single "High School Confidential" (from the film in which Lewis appeared) was a modest hit, reaching number 21. And in 1961, he hit the rock charts again with "What'd I Say," which made number 30.

Lewis maintained a relatively low profile through most of the 1960s, his music and image overshadowed by the next generation of rockers.

In 1968, he switched musical course and began a career in the country and western scene that yielded a bigger and more durable (if less epochal) success than anything he had enjoyed in rock. From the end of the 1960s through the '70s, he had more than 30 hits on the C&W chart with songs such as "Another Place, Another Time," "To Make Love Sweeter for You," and the fittingly titled "Middle Age Crazy."

The latter record could have been a soundtrack for Lewis's later years. During the 1970s and '80s he went through several new wives (two of whom subsequently died) and numerous skirmishes with the law, and his excessive alcohol- and drug-fueled lifestyle began to take its toll. In 1981, he was hospitalized in critical condition for a hemorrhaging ulcer. He nearly died, but he rebounded and was back on tour four months later. The next year, Myra (whom he had divorced in 1971) got her revenge with her book *Great Balls of Fire,* whose account of their wild marriage ironically heightened his legend.

In 1983, his fifth wife died under suspicious circumstances; a scandal ensued, but Lewis rocked on. That same year he was charged with tax evasion and then acquitted. And in 1985, he was hospitalized again for his ulcers, but he survived. In 1986, he was inducted into the Rock and Roll Hall of Fame.

TOP ALBUM

The Session (Mercury, '73, 37)

TOP SONGS

Whole Lot of Shakin' Going On (Sun, '57, 3)
Great Balls of Fire (Sun, '57, 2)
Breathless (Sun, '58, 7)
High School Confidential (Sun, '58, 21)
What'd I Say (Sun, '61, 30)
Me and Bobby McGee (Mercury, '71, 40)

LITTLE RICHARD

No one in rock
could hit a high, trilling "oooooo" like Little Richard.

That thrilling vocal quirk, which became his musical signature, was but one of the many things Richard gave to rock and roll of the 1950s, the others being an infectious gospel fervor, driving piano chords, and his own outlandish personality.

There were songs as well, of course, astonishing, exuberant songs like "Tutti-Frutti," "Long Tall Sally," "Lucille," and "Good Golly, Miss Molly," all of which Richard endowed with his singular, charismatic presence.

On record, that presence came across with an almost evangelical enthusiasm (that nonetheless seemed to be at the service of more primal urges). Songs like "The Girl Can't Help It," "Rip It Up," "Jenny, Jenny," and the others were flat-out romps on which Richard sang and played with a maniacal abandon. Onstage, his presence assumed an even flashier form. Slamming away at his piano, rolling out those "ooooo's," and decked out in baggy suits, processed 'do, and facial makeup, Little Richard was a sight to behold.

Little Richard did more than play a major role in defining the sound and image of rock and roll in the 1950s; he was also a primary inspiration for the next generation of rockers who would emerge in Britain in the '60s. Most of his big hits, and many of his minor ones, turned up in the repertoires of the British Invasion groups that stormed ashore in the U.S. in 1964. Chief among these was the Beatles, who borrowed Richard's "ooo's" and tacked them onto several of their own songs, most notably "She Loves You." Paul McCartney, in particular, drew much of his vocal sound from Richard; his cover of "Long Tall Sally" was one of the high points of the Fab Four's work on record and onstage in the initial phase of their career.

Over the decades, it seemed that just about every-

one who ever aspired to being a rocker performed a cover of a Little Richard song; his influence was that pervasive, his music that irresistible.

His vast importance in the world of rock and roll was all the more remarkable given the brevity of his time as a history maker. That came during the years 1956–57, when he recorded all of his major hits and sold a reported 18 million records. The rest of his career, which continued into the 1990s, would be marked by the constant pull between God and rock, each side winning out at various points.

Which was probably as it should have been given his background.

Richard (b. Richard Wayne Penniman, Dec. 5, 1935, Macon, Georgia) came from a religious family, both his father and grandfather being preachers. With the Penniman Singers, he often performed in church, gaining an affection and feel for gospel that would later become a crucial component of his rock sound. In his teens, he ran away and joined Dr. Hudson's Medicine Show, hawking snake oil at county fairs. He also joined Sugarfoot Sam's Minstrel Show for a time.

In 1950, he was adopted by a white family, Ann and Johnny Johnson of Macon. He began performing R&B songs in their Tick Tock Club, learning piano along the way.

At the suggestion of his mentor, gospel blues singer Billy Wright (whose vocal sound and penchant for makeup he would adopt), Penniman entered a talent contest in Atlanta in 1951. Using the name Little Richard for the first time, he won. The prize was a contract with RCA Records.

Richard cut several songs for the label, among them "Get Rich Quick" and "Every Hour," which were released in 1952 and failed to chart. But in 1954, he had better luck when he sent several demos to Art Rupe of Los Angeles–based Specialty Records. In 1955, Specialty signed Richard, and Rupe sent him to New Orleans to record with producer Robert "Bumps" Blackwell. With Blackwell, Richard cut several songs, including "Tutti-Frutti." Released in February 1956, it hit number 17 on the charts and sold three million copies; a white-bread version of the song by pop star Pat Boone subsequently passed it at number 12.

Encouraged by that success, Rupe sent Richard back to New Orleans in March of that year. In May, "Long Tall Sally" was released and hit number 13. Again, Boone covered the song and took it to number eight.

The rest of the year was a whirlwind of recording and touring. Richard appeared in the Bill Haley movie *Don't Knock the Rock*. In August, his new single "Rip It Up" charted at number 17.

As the new year dawned, Richard was still at it. At the start of 1957, he appeared in the films *Mr. Rock 'n' Roll* and *The Girl Can't Help It*, the latter yielding the number 49 hit of the same title. In April, "Lucille" made number 27, and in July, "Jenny, Jenny" hit number 14.

But at the height of his popularity, Richard called it quits, formally renouncing rock and roll during a tour of Australia in October. When he returned to the U.S., Richard went back into the studio for a final time, recording "Keep a Knockin'," "Good Golly, Miss Molly," and others. In January 1958, he entered the Oakwood Theological College in Huntsville, Alabama, from which he emerged an ordained minister in the Seventh Day Adventist church.

TOP ALBUM

HERE'S LITTLE RICHARD (Specialty, '57, *13*)

TOP SONGS

TUTTI-FRUTTI (Specialty, '56, *17*)
LONG TALL SALLY (Specialty, '56, *6*)
SLIPPIN' AND SLIDIN' (PEEPIN' AND HIDIN')
   (Specialty, '56, *33*)
RIP IT UP (Specialty, '56, *17*)
LUCILLE (Specialty, '57, *21*)
JENNY, JENNY (Specialty, '57, *10*)
KEEP A KNOCKIN' (Specialty, '57, *8*)
GOOD GOLLY, MISS MOLLY (Specialty, '58, *10*)
OOH! MY SOUL (Specialty, '58, *31*)

Little Richard's days as a major rock hitmaker were over. Over the next three decades he bounced back and forth between the church and his musical career, the latter including forays into gospel as well as rock. At the start of the 1960s, he recorded a number of gospel records on various labels including Coral and Guest Star, with several cuts produced by Quincy Jones. He also worked for a time with legendary soul and blues producer Jerry Wexler at Atlantic Records.

In 1962, he made a formal comeback in rock with a tour of the U.K. The next year, he toured again in the U.K. with the Beatles, striking up a friendship with the group in the process (one story has it that McCartney asked Richard to give him singing lessons). In 1964, Richard released the storming rock single "Bama Lama Bama Loo," which eventually charted at number 82.

In the later 1960s and into the '70s, Richard recorded a series of negligible records on various labels, none of which had the fire or the feel of his masterpieces. He also became something of a self-parody in the process, performing in pink outfits and going over the top on the makeup. It was not a pretty sight or sound.

He became an evangelist in 1979, preaching about his redemption through God and recording new gospel albums. In 1985, British writer Charles White published the biography *The Life and Times of Little Richard,* which strengthened his legend and generated renewed interest in his career.

In the later 1980s, Richard enjoyed his highest visibility in rock since his days in the '50s. In 1986, he reached the charts with the single "Great Gosh A' Mighty (It's a Matter of Time)," which peaked at number 42 (it was drawn from the film *Down and Out in Beverly Hills*). That same year, he released the album *Lifetime Friend* and recorded the song "Happy Endings" with the Beach Boys. And he was inducted into the Rock and Roll Hall of Fame.

He recorded with New Edition in 1987 on the song "Tears on My Pillow" and in 1990 rapped on the song "Elvis Is Dead" on the quasi-metal album *Time's Up* by Living Colour.

While none of these efforts were in any way relevant to Richard's role in rock history, they nonetheless pointed up the enduring nature of that role. Nearly 40 years after he had first galvanized the rock world, Little Richard was still at it, his fevered vocals and outlandish presence making themselves felt by a new generation of rockers and rock fans.

Little Richard

THE LOVIN' SPOONFUL

One of the minor jewels in the rock and roll crown, the Lovin' Spoonful persists in memory with its lithe and winsome sound, its penchant for bearskin coats and striped shirts, leader John Sebastian's wire-framed glasses, and its generally eccentric, irascible image.

In fact, the New York–based foursome was much more. In the mid-1960s the Spoonful was one of the first American rock groups to embrace the eclecticism that was being pioneered by its British counterparts.

While the Spoonful's experiments were never as grandiose or exotic as those of the Beatles, it did create a remarkable amalgam of various American musical idioms. "Do You Believe in Magic" and "You Didn't Have to Be So Nice" were rolling, pop-inflected songs that came with Sebastian's warm, folkish vocals and signature electric autoharp, guitarist Zal Yanovsky's country-flavored lines, and the steady rhythmic accompaniment of bassist Steve Boone and drummer Joe Butler. Both songs established the Spoonful as one of the premiere groups in American rock.

The Spoonful displayed one of the most incisive, expansive musical visions of their day. Its signature hit, "Daydream," had a skipping, honky-tonk feel, while "Summer in the City" came with odd time changes and the cacophonous sounds of honking cars and rattling jackhammers. And the group's "Nashville Cats" was one of the first fusions of country and rock.

Along the way, the Spoonful delved into the country's musical heritage like a group of Smithsonian scholars on sabbatical in the rock world. What they came up with was a seamless combination of country and western, folk, jug band music, R&B, and rock, with traces of jazz and 1940s pop added to the brew. They called it good-time music, and it was.

There was also an edge to their sound, the wiseass charm of New Yorkers out slumming in the sticks for a musical good time. On "Jug Band Music," Sebastian sang the words "and the doctor said give him jug band music/it seems to make him feel just fine" with his tongue firmly ensconced in his cheek. On "Nashville Cats," he trotted out every cliché in the Buck Owens songbook.

But the Spoonful could also turn out songs that were as affecting as anything in rock. On "Coconut Grove," from their 1966 masterpiece *Hums of the Lovin' Spoonful,* the group conjured haunting images of '40s pop, all in softly shifting waltz time. And on its 1967 hit "Darling Be Home Soon," the group created a ballad of Beatles-like elegance.

Through it all, the Spoonful displayed a musical innocence and ingenuity that would evoke a timeless charm. Miraculously, their music was witty without being parodistic, and exciting without being earnest. In the process, they created a sound that was utterly new for its time and that remained distinctive over the course of decades.

The group came out of the multidimensional rock scene of mid-'60s New York that also included the likes of the Young Rascals and the Blues Project. Sebastian (b. John Benson Sebastian, Mar. 17, 1944, New York) and Yanovsky (b. Zalman Yanovsky, Dec. 19, 1944, Toronto, Canada) had been members of the Mugwumps, a folk-based group that also included future Mamas and Papas Cass Elliot and Denny Doherty. When the latter members split from the group at the end of 1964, Sebastian and Yanovsky decided to team up on their own. In January 1965, they recruited Boone (b. Sept. 23, 1943,

North Carolina) and Butler (b. Sept. 16, 1943, Glen Cove, Long Island) and began rehearsing in the basement of New York's Hotel Albert.

They performed during the year at the Night Owl Café and came to the attention of producer Erik Jacobsen, who secured a record deal with the new Kama Sutra label. Impressed with Sebastian's songs, the producer encouraged the group to pursue his whimsical path.

The Lovin' Spoonful

The first result of their efforts, "Do You Believe in Magic," hit number nine on the charts in October 1965 while the group's album of the same title reached number 32.

The group's prominence on the scene was confirmed at the start of 1966, when its second single, "You Didn't Have to Be So Nice," hit number nine. In April, "Daydream" reached number two, its ambling sound becoming the symbol of the Spoonful's good-time music.

That sound, redolent of an older pop era, coincided with moves by the Beatles, the Rolling Stones, the Kinks, and others in the direction of the British music hall tradition. When the Spoonful went to England in

---

TOP ALBUMS

DAYDREAM (Kama Sutra, '66, 10)
HUMS OF THE LOVIN' SPOONFUL (Kama Sutra, '67, 14)
THE BEST OF THE LOVIN' SPOONFUL
 (Kama Sutra, '67, 3)

Additional Top 40 Albums: 1

TOP SONGS

DO YOU BELIEVE IN MAGIC (Kama Sutra, '65, 9)
YOU DIDN'T HAVE TO BE SO NICE
 (Kama Sutra, '65, 10)
DAYDREAM (Kama Sutra, '66, 2)
DID YOU EVER HAVE TO MAKE UP YOUR MIND?
 (Kama Sutra, '66, 2)
SUMMER IN THE CITY (Kama Sutra, '66, 1)
RAIN ON THE ROOF (Kama Sutra, '66, 10)
NASHVILLE CATS (Kama Sutra, '66, 8)

Additional Top 40 Songs: 3

April of 1966, it proved to be vastly popular—one of the first American acts to stage an "invasion" of its own. The connection between the Spoonful and its British counterparts was emphasized when the group appeared on the Elektra album *What's Shakin'*, a compilation of songs by various British and American groups that included Powerhouse (with Eric Clapton) and the Butterfield Blues Band.

The rest of 1966 saw the Spoonful moving from hit to hit. In July, the pleasantly pop-flavored "Did You Ever Have to Make Up Your Mind?" reached number two. And in August, the group topped the charts with "Summer in the City." Later in the year, Sebastian's songs were featured in the Woody Allen film farce *What's Up, Tiger Lily?* And in December,

the group released the album *Hums of the Lovin' Spoonful.*

Hums contained a wide-ranging amalgam of musical idioms, from the folk feel of "Lovin' You" and the rock of "Voodoo in the Basement" to the eloquent melodicism of "Rain on the Roof," and it established the Spoonful as a potent creative force in rock.

From that album, which charted at number 14, the single "Nashville Cats" made number eight in January 1967, becoming the group's sixth straight top 10 hit. They also recorded a second soundtrack album, this one for Francis Ford Coppola's film *You're a Big Boy Now.*

But in the next few months, disaster struck when Yanovsky was arrested on a marijuana charge. The problems this created for the Spoonful were compounded when he allegedly implicated others in return for a suppression of the charges against him. Amid the ensuing uproar, he quit the group in June and was replaced by Jerry Yester.

The Spoonful continued to record and tour, but the end was in sight. The pop sound that was the group's specialty began to give way to the progressive rock emerging from the San Francisco scene. Its good-time music was also overtaken by the energy and musical virtuosity of Britain's second wave—the heavy blues and rock mixture of groups like Cream and the Jimi Hendrix Experience. The rock world had had its moment of inspired calm with the Spoonful; now it was waiting for the storm.

In October of 1968, Sebastian quit the group and it quickly folded.

Individually, the members failed to equal the success of their days with the Spoonful. Sebastian pursued a solo career that included a fine performance at the Woodstock festival in 1969. He released a number of solo albums, none of which were particularly successful, musically or commercially. He did hit the top of the charts in 1976 with the single "Welcome Back," the theme song from the television series "Welcome Back Kotter," starring John Travolta.

Yanovsky also pursued a solo career that failed to ignite. He retired to Ontario and opened a restaurant, Chez Piggy. Yester joined his brother Jim in the Association and subsequently produced Tom Waits's remarkable debut album, *Closing Time.* Butler appeared on Broadway in the rock musical *Hair.* And Boone faded into obscurity.

The Lovin' Spoonful re-formed in 1980 for a cameo appearance in Paul Simon's film, *One Trick Pony.*

THE MAMAS
AND THE PAPAS

In the middle 1960s,
the Mamas and the Papas bridged the gap between the
emerging countercultural scene and the broad pop marketplace.
With their ebullient vocal harmonies and melodic songs
they made the folk-rock scene, along with its attendant look
and lifestyle, accessible and acceptable to vast numbers
of more mainstream musical fans.

With their flowing, outlandish pseudo-psychedelic clothes and fur hats and such, the Mamas and the Papas offered a sanitized and unthreatening image of the "hip" subculture that was beginning to make itself felt in the rock world. Michelle Phillips's long, blonde locks and dreamy presence summed up "California" to all those who had never been there (and even to those who had). Cass Elliot was big and brassy, with a stupendous voice to match. And Denny Doherty and the group's leader and songwriter, John Phillips, had . . . facial hair.

While the group's look was enough to make hip fans snicker, its sound was really quite another matter. That sound was as sleek as Hollywood studios of the time could deliver, but the songs that came with it were sublime by any standard.

"California Dreamin'," "Monday, Monday," "I Saw Her Again," and others were sumptuous combinations of folk, rock, and straightahead pop that came with simple, direct melodies and intricate layers of vocal harmony. Those harmonies—some of the finest in all of rock—were fastidiously sculpted and directed, the voices of the four folding in and arching over each other in waves of almost transparent sound. The loveliness of those vocals was contrasted with the R&B-tinged accents of John Phillips

and Doherty and the lugubrious pop flourishes of Elliot.

The Mamas and the Papas' sound was irresistible to rock and pop fans alike, and it helped open up the boundaries between the two forms and the two vastly different cultural milieux they represented. The Mamas and the Papas were the musical calm before the deluge that would eventually engulf rock in the later 1960s.

The group was formed in 1964 when the individual members met in the Virgin Islands. Phillips (b. Aug. 30, 1935, Parris Island, South Carolina) and his wife Michelle (b. Holly Michelle Gilliam, June 4, 1945, Long Beach, California) originally teamed up with Doherty (b. Nov. 29, 1941, Halifax, Canada) as the folk trio the New Journeymen. They were soon joined by Elliot (b. Ellen Naomi Cohen, Sept. 19, 1941, Baltimore, Maryland), who had been a member with Doherty in the New York folk-rock group the Mugwumps (which had also included the Lovin' Spoonful's John Sebastian and Zal Yanovsky).

In 1965, John Phillips relocated the quartet to Los Angeles, where they came to the attention of Dunhill Records head Lou Adler. Adler hired them to sing background vocals for Barry ("Eve of Destruction")

McGuire's new album. Impressed with the group's work and Phillips's songwriting talents—his song "California Dreamin' " was included on McGuire's album *Precious Time*—Adler signed them to his label.

The group then changed its name to the Mamas and the Papas, and its first single was its own version of "California Dreamin'." Released in March 1966, it went to number four on the charts and sold more than a million copies.

"Dreamin' " introduced the group's harmonious sound and its distillation of the folk-rock of the time and more traditional pop values. It was a winning combination that the Mamas and the Papas would pursue for the rest of their career to vast commercial success.

"Monday, Monday," "I Saw Her Again," and "Words of Love" all hit the top five in 1966. The following year, the group charted again with the more straightforward, pop-based songs "Dedicated to the One I Love" and "Creeque Alley," the latter a history of the group's early days set to music.

On these songs and others, the Mamas and the Papas walked a fine line between accessibility and the more serious musical values being propounded by the groups of the countercultural West Coast scene. The dual nature of this role was most apparent in 1967. In March of that year, the group won a Grammy Award—that symbol of the musical establishment—for "Monday Monday" in the Best Group Performance category. And in June, the group performed at the seminal event of the emerging West Coast scene, the Monterey Pop Festival. Phillips and Adler, in fact, were two of the principal organizers of the event.

Emblematic of John Phillips's pan-musical influence at the time was the song "San Francisco (Be Sure to Wear Flowers in Your Hair)," which he composed for Scott McKenzie, a member of the original Journeymen in the early 1960s. With its jangling folk-rock sound and Mamas and Papas–like sleekness, the song was a superficial paean to the San Francisco scene, but one that struck a chord in the broad pop consciousness, symbolizing to the country at large the idyllic spirit of the hippie ethos. Released as a single during the Summer of Love, it charted at number four.

But amid the success surrounding the Mamas and the Papas, dissension was growing. The Phillipses marriage was coming apart during 1967 and in June of 1968 Michelle found herself sacked from the group. The next month, the Mamas and the Papas disbanded.

Each of the members pursued solo careers, none of which approached the success of the group. Of the four, Elliot, subsequently billed as Mama Cass, proved to be the most commercially visible. In 1968 she had a hit with "Dream a Little Dream of Me," which peaked at number 12. She made the lower reaches of the charts on subsequent singles and, in 1971, recorded a splendid album with Traffic's Dave Mason that made number 49. In 1974, she had a heart attack while choking on food and died in her London hotel.

Divorced from Michelle in 1970, John Phillips had a minor hit with "Mississippi," which made number 32 that year. He subsequently retreated from the scene. In 1980, he was arrested on a drugs charge in Los Angeles and was subsequently incarcerated briefly. In 1982, he and Doherty reformed the Mamas and the Papas, with Phillips's daughter MacKenzie and former Spanky and Our Gang vocalist Spanky McFarlane both joiming the new lineup.

Michelle Phillips became an actress and appeared in such films as *Valentino* and *Dillinger*.

In 1988, John Phillips and Scott McKenzie cowrote the song "Kokomo," which became a Number One hit for the Beach Boys. In 1989, the two formed a new lineup of the Mamas and Papas—with MacKenzie Phillips and McFarlane back on board—that dutifully made the rounds of the ever-present oldies scene.

TOP ALBUMS

IF YOU CAN BELIEVE YOUR EYES AND EARS
(Dunhill, '66, *1*)
THE MAMAS & THE PAPAS (Dunhill, '66, *4*)
THE MAMAS & THE PAPAS DELIVER
(Dunhill, '67, *2*)
FAREWELL TO THE FIRST GOLDEN ERA
(Dunhill, '67, *5*)

Additional Top 40 Albums: 1

TOP SONGS

CALIFORNIA DREAMIN' (Dunhill, '66, *4*)
MONDAY, MONDAY (Dunhill, '66, *1*)
I SAW HER AGAIN (Dunhill, '66, *5*)
WORDS OF LOVE (Dunhill, '66, *5*)
DEDICATED TO THE ONE I LOVE
(Dunhill, '67, *2*)
CREEQUE ALLEY (Dunhill, '67, *5*)

Additional Top 40 Songs: 3

The Mamas and the Papas

BOB MARLEY

At the end of the 1960s and the start of the '70s, a new sound began to insinuate itself into the ranks of rock. That sound was reggae. And its acknowledged master was Bob Marley.

At its base were simple 4/4 rhythms that were propelled by asymmetrical accents, strutting vocals, and chunky guitars. It was an odd if inviting sound, made more odd by the fact that it came from Jamaica, a country known primarily for the metallic, rhythmic melodies of its steel bands.

To the rock world at large, Marley's name came to prominence when Eric Clapton's cover of his song "I Shot the Sheriff" hit Number One in 1974.

But by then, Marley had already made his presence felt among rock cognescenti with the classic albums *Catch a Fire* and *Burnin'* in 1972. On those records and others that would follow over the next eight years, Marley pioneered a new form of rock with his equally legendary group, the Wailers (which included future reggae/rock star Peter Tosh).

There was about Marley a spiritual and expressive power that set him apart not only from his reggae counterparts but also from most of the other rockers of his time. Listening to him perform, there was the inexpressible feeling that he was, like one of the blues masters, a true musical original—the Real Thing.

His hoarse vocals, with their distinctive Jamaican inflections, were unbridled and raw but also expressive of an inner vision that was, at once, profound and earthy. On songs like "Exodus" and "No Woman No Cry" he immersed himself in his music, not performing it as much as living it. In that sense, Marley transcended the more obvious rhythmic aspects of reggae. For him, it wasn't simply a sound or a beat; it was almost a way of life.

In a way, it was. Marley's music was an extension of his religion and his socio-political beliefs. A devout Rastafarian, Marley was also something of a Jamaican leader, who toiled for political change and stability in his country. His stature was such that, in 1978, he was able to persuade Jamaican political rivals Prime Minister Michael Manley and the opposition leader Edward Seaga to join him onstage in a show of national unity. To Jamaicans, Marley wasn't merely a rock star; he was a national hero.

To the rest of the rock world, Marley was a respected figure whose music and attitudes and look were much imitated. While reggae itself never conquered the rock world, as many predicted it would in the mid-'70s, it did become a pervasive style. Through Marley, it came to influence new generations of rockers, most notably the punks of London in the later 1970s. The Police, the biggest group of the early '80s, based much of their sound on reggae. And groups like the English Beat, the Specials, and scores of others adapted rock and pop to reggae beats and musical accents. In fact, by the 1990s the sound had become so prevalent that musicians of almost every idiom felt the desire to include at least one reggae song—or reggae versions of their own songs—in their performances onstage or on records.

Marley had a look that became almost as popular as

TOP ALBUMS

CATCH A FIRE (Wailers, Island, '72)
NATTY DREAD (Wailers, Island, '75)
RASTAMAN VIBRATION (Island, '76, 8)
EXODUS (Island, '77, 20)
UPRISING (Island, '80)
LEGEND (Island, '84)

TOP SONG

ROOTS, ROCK, REGGAE (Island, '76)

Bob Marley

his music. His tangled, tousled Rastafarian dreadlocks and his penchant for the red-yellow-green color scheme of African nationalism were adopted not merely by adherents of his religion and politics but by a segment of the culture at large.

In that way, Marley changed not only the musical but also the visual face of rock.

Marley (b. Feb. 6, 1945, Nine Miles, Rhoden Hall, St. Anne's, Jamaica) was the son of an English army captain and a Jamaican mother. While a student at Jamaica's Stepney School he became friends with future Wailers Tosh (b. Winston Hubert McIntosh, Oct. 19, 1944, Church Lincoln, Westmoreland, Jamaica) and Bunny Wailer (b. Neville O'Riley, b. Apr. 10, 1947, Kingston, Jamaica).

Marley began his career in 1961 when he recorded the pop single "Judge Not (Unless You Judge Yourself)" for the Kingston-based Beverley label. In 1962, he followed that with a version of Brook Benton's "One Cup of Coffee." Neither was particularly successful.

Undeterred, Marley formed the Wailin' Wailers with Tosh and Wailer and Junior Braithwaite and Beverley Kelso in 1964. Switching to the Studio One label, he recorded the single "Simmer Down," which sold 80,000 copies in Jamaica. Between 1964 and 1966, Marley and the Wailin' Wailers recorded a vast range of songs. During that period, Marley also married Alpharita Anderson, who would later gain a musical career of her own as Rita Marley and would subsequently be involved in protracted legal disputes over the trusteeship of Marley's estate.

In 1966, Marley left Jamaica and went to live with his mother in the United States. Over the course of the next year he worked in various non-musical situations, including a job in a Chrysler auto factory.

With the money he had saved, he returned to Jamaica in 1967 and formed his own record label, Wailin' Soul (for which he signed and recorded vocalist Johnny Nash). He also teamed up with Tosh and Wailer, using the name the Wailers.

By 1969, the group had begun work with producer Lee Perry, forming their own label, Tuff Gong. With Perry, they began to develop their nascent reggae sound on songs such as "Soul Rebel" and "Small Axe."

The group's big break came in 1972 when they were signed to Island Records by the label's Jamaican-born head, Chris Blackwell. Promoting Marley and the Wailers—and reggae—as the next big thing in rock, Blackwell released the albums *Catch a*

Fire and *Burnin'* that year. Those records were an immediate critical and artistic success and propelled Marley and the group (whose classic lineup also included drummer Carlton Barrett and bassist Aston "Family Man" Barrett) into the broad rock world. In 1973, they toured the U.K. and the U.S., opening for Sly and the Family Stone on the latter.

But Wailer and Tosh were disenchanted with Island and left the group in 1974. Marley enlisted his wife, Judy Mowatt, and Marcia Griffiths as the I-Three's; formed a new version of the Wailers; and, in 1975, released what was arguably his finest album: *Natty Dread.* In the meantime, Clapton scored his Number One with Marley's "I Shot the Sheriff."

Marley's career was on the rise. In 1976, he had his biggest U.S. hit single when "Roots, Rock, Reggae" reached number 51. But in that same year, he was wounded in an attack that he believed was motivated by a Jamaican faction opposed to his political activities. He left Jamaica and settled in Miami for the next two years.

While in Miami, Marley was hospitalized for a cancerous growth on his toe, which was removed. But he continued to record, releasing the album *Exodus,* a top 20 hit in 1977. When he returned to Jamaica later in 1978 he was hailed as a national hero.

Marley toured the world over the next two years, performing to vast crowds in Europe and the U.K. But while preparing for a U.S. tour with Stevie Wonder in 1980, Marley collapsed onstage. His cancer had come back and spread and was diagnosed incurable.

After a number of hospitalizations in New York and Bavaria, Marley was on his way back to Jamaica when he was hospitalized in Miami. He died at Miami's Cedars of Lebanon Hospital on May 11, 1981.

Previously awarded Jamaica's Order of Merit, Marley was flown back to his native land, where his body was given a state funeral.

Records of Marley's music continued to be released over the years, including a compilation set, *Legend,* in 1984.

Tosh and Wailer, having pursued careers of their own, both died in 1987; in separate cases, they were murdered. Rita Marley began a solo career, as did Marley's son Ziggy, the latter achieving a modicum of commercial and critical success.

In 1990, Marley's birthay was declared a national holiday in Jamaica.

JOHN MAYALL

If Alexis Korner was the father of British blues, John Mayall was its godfather.

While his counterpart founded the scene and nurtured it with a passive paternalism, Mayall was out front, running the action. In the process, he created some of the most inventive and innovative blues and rock in history.

As a bandleader, Mayall was without peer. Over the course of the 1960s, various versions of his group, the Bluesbreakers, proved to be sounding boards and staging areas for some of the finest blues musicians of the time. Guitarists Eric Clapton, Peter Green, and Mick Taylor spent time in the group, honing their skills and defining their sounds. Sidemen included the likes of drummers Mick Fleetwood, Aynsley Dunbar, and Jon Hiseman; bassists Jack Bruce and John McVie; and various horn men who would go on to populate the better part of the British blues and jazz scene.

Mayall did not squander their talents. With them, he created a series of albums during the '60s that stand as some of the finest of all time. *Bluesbreakers—John Mayall with Eric Clapton,* in particular, is on a creative level with B.B. King's *Live at the Regal* and

Muddy Waters' initial electric work and is, arguably, the finest record of white electric blues in history.

Mayall was also a tireless innovator, who expanded the artistic boundaries of the blues. He was one of the first to form a white blues-rock group with a horn section. On one album, *Bare Wires,* he created, in effect, a blues suite. And ultimately breaking from the blues-band-with-guitar-genius format he himself had pioneered, Mayall reinvented the blues group in 1969 with a semi-acoustic, drummerless quartet.

Particularly on his later '60s albums, Mayall proved to be a fine composer. Many of the songs were innovative fusions of blues, rock, and jazz that transcended those individual idioms and became an entirely new amalgam that defied categorization.

While Mayall was not a virtuoso in any sense, he did have distinctive vocal and instrumental talents that complemented those of his illustrious collaborators. His voice had a kind of warbling frailty that nonetheless was endowed with emotional force and power. A multi-instrumentalist, Mayall played guitar, organ, and harmonica with a flair—if not technical brilliance—that perfectly framed the astonishing work of Clapton, Green, and the rest.

John Mayall

In all of this, Mayall was something of a renaissance man. From the various musicians he introduced and guided, to the records he made with them and the innovations he propagated, Mayall changed the course of rock music.

Mayall (b. Nov. 29, 1933, Macclesfield, Cheshire, England) began his musical career in the 1950s in Manchester. Returning from a stint in the British Army (during which he had served in Korea), Mayall entered Manchester Art College and subsequently worked with a local advertising agency. In his spare time, he began playing R&B and blues with various local groups.

Inspired, like virtually everyone else, by Alexis Korner's revolutionary group, Blues Incorporated, Mayall formed his own outfit, called the Blues Syndicate, in 1962. At the suggestion of Korner, he moved to London to get involved in the growing blues and R&B scene that Korner had established.

In 1963, Mayall formed the first version of the Bluesbreakers with bassist John McVie, drummer Peter Ward, and guitarist Bernie Watson. By 1964, Mayall had signed a deal with Decca Records, which released his debut single, "Crawling Up a Hill." In the following year he released his debut album, *John Mayall Plays John Mayall,* along with a second single, "Crocodile Walk."

While these records generated a certain amount of attention, they failed to chart. But in April 1965, Mayall's fortunes changed. That month, he extended an invitation to Eric Clapton—who had left the Yardbirds because of their pop direction—to join the Bluesbreakers. The result proved to be inspired. With McVie and new drummer Hughie Flint, Mayall and Clapton began to create a storming new version of the British blues that would come to define the sound of that movement.

In July of 1966, the album *Bluesbreakers—John Mayall with Eric Clapton* was released and subsequently hit number six on the British charts. Literally every cut was a major or minor classic, including Mayall's reinterpretations of such warhorses as "All Your Love" and "Parchman Farm" and the charging, horn-driven "Key to Love." But the focal point of the album was Clapton. On songs like "Double Crossing Time," "Little Girl," and, most notably, the instrumentals "Hideaway" and "Steppin' Out," Clapton revolutionized blues and rock guitar with a new, distorted tone and angular phrasings that were unprecedented. The album also included Clapton's vocal debut on the Robert Johnson classic "Ramblin' on My Mind." Thirty years later, the album was still astounding.

That's what it was at the time, and it immediately elevated Clapton, Mayall, and the Bluesbreakers to the top of the British blues scene. But the collaboration with Clapton proved short-lived. In July of 1966, he departed the group to form Cream with Ginger Baker and Jack Bruce (the latter also having played in the Bluesbreakers for a brief time in 1965).

Confronted with the almost impossible task of replacing Clapton, Mayall promptly did the impossible. Recruiting guitarist Peter Green, Mayall resumed his course, undiminished by Clapton's absence. While influenced by Clapton's sound, Green had a dense, brooding style that was almost as distinctive. On the classic 1967 album *A Hard Road,* Green played breathtaking minor-keyed solos that seemed to mesh magically with Mayall's high, passionate, bittersweet vocals.

But Green soon quit as well. And Mayall came through again. This time it was in the person of 17-year-old guitar prodigy Mick Taylor, whom Mayall had recruited from the Gods. Taylor's work was clean and clearly stated—the ideal match for the new, horn-augmented version of the Bluesbreakers that Mayall had pieced together in 1967. This lineup yielded the remarkable album *Crusade* and the subsequent live sets *Diary of a Band, Volumes 1 and 2.*

Members of this lineup would also contribute to the 1968 album *Bare Wires*. Basically a blues suite, with recurring themes and an overall sound that was an incisive blend of everything from rural and urban blues to rock and jazz, *Bare Wires* had a compositional complexity that had never been heard before in the genre.

Amid all this, Mayall took time out at the end of 1967 to record the solo album *Blues Alone*. Playing all the instruments, Mayall paid homage to the rural blues of the "guv'nors"—including J. B. Lenoir—who had inspired him. An often neglected album, *Blues Alone* was nonetheless one of his more affecting high points.

After the release of *Bare Wires* in 1968, Mayall broke up the Bluesbreakers and relocated to Los Angeles, where he would subsequently reside. He formed a new group and released the album *Blues from Laurel Canyon*. In 1969, Taylor departed the group to join the Rolling Stones, replacing the late Brian Jones.

This time, Mayall decided not to search for a new guitar hero. Instead, he enlisted acoustic guitarist Jon Mark, bassist Steve Thompson, and saxophonist-flutist Johnny Almond. With this new, drummerless lineup, he began to tour in 1969, in the process recording one of the group's performances at the Fillmore East.

The resulting album, *The Turning Point,* was one of the most original and musically intriguing records in rock. Without the steady but attention-grabbing beats of a drummer, the group played with a sublime subtlety and fluidity that virtually redefined the expressive parameters of rock and blues. Intense, driving songs like "The Laws Must Change" were contrasted with the long, rolling "California," the latter unfolding like a musical map, with Mayall and Almond gliding above the repeated figures of Mark and Thompson, creating languorous lines that interacted with a jazz-like intricacy. There were rhythms as well, but they were provided by vocal sounds and by the clicks of picks and hands on instruments and microphones. The result was infectious, and it amounted to an utterly new and distinctive musical blend.

But *The Turning Point* marked the apex of Mayall's creative career. A subsequent album with the same personnel, 1970's *Empty Rooms,* was a disappointment. And as the 1970s and '80s unfolded, little of his new music was as inspired, or inspiring, as that of his days in the '60s. Numerous compilations of those days appeared over the decades, including 1971's *Thru the Years,* 1973's *Down the Line,* and 1988's *Archives to the Eighties: Featuring Eric Clapton and Mick Taylor.*

As was his habit, Mayall organized new groups on a steady basis. He also continued to record albums of new material, including 1975's *New Band, New Year, New Company,* 1988's *Chicago Line,* and 1990's *A Sense of Place.* Invariably, these and other records were sturdy and competent and proved that Mayall's feel for the blues was intact. They simply didn't have the sense of innovation and excitement of their counterparts of the 1960s, on which Mayall had changed the course of rock and blues.

TOP ALBUMS

BLUES BREAKERS—JOHN MAYALL
    WITH ERIC CLAPTON (London, '66)
A HARD ROAD (London, '67)
CRUSADE (London, '67)
THE BLUES ALONE (London, '67)
BARE WIRES (London, '68)
BLUES FROM LAUREL CANYON
    (London, '68)
THE TURNING POINT (Polydor, '69)

JONI MITCHELL

Joni Mitchell emerged at the end of the 1960s as part of the singer-songwriter movement. But over a period of years, she distanced herself from that sometimes cloying, slavishly sensitive form to become a formidable creative and commercial force whose eclectic vision had few equals in the '70s.

The similarities between Mitchell and her counterparts were purely superficial. Yes, she was a singer who accompanied herself on acoustic guitar. And yes, she was a songwriter. But while most of her contemporaries seemed content to leave it at that, Mitchell struck out in various musical directions, creating a seamless synthesis of rock, folk, pop, and, ultimately, jazz.

Unlike many rock artists of a somewhat similar eclectic mind, Mitchell didn't change her songs to conform to the derivation of the moment but instead used those derivations to give shape and color to a creative vision that remained remarkably consistent.

At the core of that vision was a sound that was overtly melodic, but that also came with angular harmonies and convoluted theme lines that gave her songs an unexpected edge and urgency. Whether it was expressed in a fairly straightforward folk manner, as on such early songs as "Both Sides Now," or in the more complex constructions of later efforts like 1976's "In France They Kiss on Main Street," that melodic sensibility remained intact; it simply evolved along with, and was sculpted by, Mitchell's musical interests.

Her lyrics were similarly idiosyncratic, often to the point of eccentricity. While she was as captivated by the vicissitudes of romance as the rest of her contemporaries, Mitchell rarely gave in to sensitivity (in the flaccid singer-songwriter sense). Instead, she met love head on, knocked it about a bit, gave it a kiss and pushed it away, and then studied its aftermath with an incisive, analytical aloofness. Sometimes witty, at other times utterly scathing,

Mitchell's lyrics were sophisticated, almost literary, in their romantic wordplay.

And the way she sang them was equally intriguing. On songs like "Help Me" she didn't merely recite the words in strict meter or rhyme but toyed with them constantly, snapping off ends of lines, drawing them out, and then muttering wise (or wiseacre) remarks delivered as rhythmic asides, all of which amounted to the expressive equivalent of a jazz scat singer holding forth from an analyst's couch.

But there was a traditionalism to Mitchell that tempered her idiosyncrasies. On songs like "Woodstock," her paean to the tumultuous 1969 rock festival, she played down her more eccentric inclinations and created a moving depiction of the event with a narrative grandeur that was as old and evocative as the musical tales sung by ancient troubadours.

When all of this was given expression through her liquid, vaguely adenoidal vocals whose sound was as instantly recognizable as her songs, it made for a particularly provocative and entrancing whole. Like Elvis Costello and other musical eccentrics, she didn't change the course of the music as much as show the many and varied ways in which it could be expressed.

In 1962, Mitchell (b. Roberta Joan Anderson, Nov. 7, 1943, Fort McLeod, Alberta, Canada) began playing the ukulele while studying painting at the Alberta College of Art. Over the next two years, her interest in music increased and she began to perform at various local folk clubs like the Depression coffee house.

Joni Mitchell

By 1964 she had become part of the Yorktown folk scene in Toronto. During this time she met folk singer Chuck Mitchell, with whom she formed a personal and professional partnership. Married in June 1965, the duo based themselves in Detroit and began performing in the local folk scene. When they divorced in 1966, Mitchell moved to New York and began appearing as a solo act at clubs like the Café Au Go Go.

She soon came to the attention of manager Elliot Roberts, who negotiated a deal with the Reprise label in 1967. Before her debut album was released, Mitchell began to gain a reputation as a songwriter, with several of her songs being covered by the likes of Gordon Lightfoot, Johnny Cash, and Tom Rush. Judy Collins had a hit with her cover of Mitchell's "Both Sides Now" in 1967.

The eponymous debut album (also referred to as

Song for a Seagull) was released in June 1968. Produced by David Crosby, it was a mostly folk-oriented effort that gained much attention for Mitchell outside the usual folk scene.

Mitchell began to make her name in the broad rock and pop world in 1970 with her second album, *Clouds,* and with appearances in the U.S. and the U.K.

But it was in 1970 that she achieved a broad-based success. In March of that year, *Clouds* won a Grammy Award for Best Folk Performance; her new album, *Ladies of the Canyon,* went gold; and the single "Big Yellow Taxi" made the charts, reaching number 67. Crosby, Stills, Nash & Young charted at number 11 with their cover of "Woodstock," and Matthew's Southern Comfort topped the U.K. charts in October with their version of the song.

Mitchell's career began to rise steadily over the next few years, and her music began to evolve and mature. Her 1971 album *Blue* came with a new and increasingly electric sound that was embraced by growing legions of fans: it charted at number 15. In 1972, the album *For the Roses* was similarly well received.

But it was 1974's *Court and Spark* that proved to be the musical watershed in Mitchell's career. Primarily an electric effort backed by the fusion band L. A. Express, the album was the point at which Mitchell departed from an essentially folk sound. Here she began to display a more expansive musical vision, incorporating rock and jazz and setting up intriguing interplay between her voice and various instruments. With this album, Mitchell's songs became more complex and eclectic, a trend that would increasingly come to mark her work over the rest of the decade. In 1975, Mitchell and her collaborator, horn man Tom Scott, won a Grammy award for Best Arrangement Accompanying Vocalists for *Court and Spark.*

Subsequent albums such as the following year's *The Hissing of Summer Lawns* and *Hejira*—arguably her finest records—were musically dense and lyrically introspective. The hints of jazz that had accented her music to that point were now full-

fledged components of her sound, and her songs began to evolve into mini-suites with complex constructions, intricate instrumental flourishes, and ancillary themes. While many of her folk fans were disturbed, the records generated increased attention from a wide range of rock and pop listeners. The former disc charted at number four, and the latter, number 13.

The trend toward jazz continued in 1978 on *Don Juan's Reckless Daughter,* in which Mitchell's languid vocals interacted with the lithe bass lines of Jaco Pastorius. The album came to the attention of legendary jazz bassist-composer Charles Mingus, who invited Mitchell to collaborate with him on a musical interpretation of T. S. Eliot's *Four Quartets.* When that project failed to materialize, Mitchell began work on a set of songs based on several melodies Mingus had previously composed.

In July of 1979, six months after Mingus's death, those songs appeared on Mitchell's album *Mingus.* It would prove to be the apex of Mitchell's jazz period and was a remarkable amalgam of her musical signatures and the playing of Gerry Mulligan, John McLaughlin, and others.

After a decade of almost ceaseless musical creativity, Mitchell began to retreat from the scene to pursue her other great artistic love, painting (her album covers usually came with reproductions of her art work). She continued to release albums, like 1982's *Wild Things Run Fast.* And her eclectic interests continued apace: in 1985 she pursued a new, synthesizer-inflected sound on the album *Dog Eat Dog,* which was co-produced by techno-wizard Thomas Dolby. (He had also worked with her on 1988's *Chalk Mark in a Rainstorm.*)

While she refrained from touring during most of the 1980s, she did participate in Roger Waters' gigantic performance of *The Wall* that was staged in Berlin in 1990 and telecast around the world.

In 1991, she released *Night Ride Home,* a fine if not particularly noteworthy record that came with her by-then signature combination of folk, rock, and jazz.

TOP ALBUMS

BLUE (Reprise, '71, *15*)
FOR THE ROSES (Asylum, '72, *11*)
COURT AND SPARK (Asylum, '74, *2*)
MILES OF AISLES (Asylum, '74, *2*)
THE HISSING OF SUMMER LAWNS (Asylum, '75, *4*)
HEJIRA (Asylum, '76, *13*)
MINGUS (Asylum, '79, *17*)

Additional Top 40 Albums: 5

TOP SONGS

HELP ME (Asylum, '74, *7*)
FREE MAN IN PARIS (Asylum, '74, *22*)
BIG YELLOW TAXI (Asylum, '74, *24*)

Additional Top 40 Songs: 1

THE MONKEES

Long before groups like Duran Duran and the Stray Cats had their careers made for them via MTV at the start of the 1980s, the Monkees did the same by riding the airwaves to fame and fortune in the '60s.

They did it on a television series that bore their group's name. Or rather—and tellingly—it was the group that bore the TV show's name.

The Monkees began not as a musical act but as "The Monkees," a television program about a rock group. Davy Jones, Mickey Dolenz, Michael Nesmith, and Peter Tork came together as actors hired to replicate the irreverent, madcap imagery of the Beatles in their hit films *A Hard Day's Night* and *Help!* But the Monkees quickly became a recording entity, and one that exceeded just about everyone's wildest expectations.

The weekly television program catapulted the group to dizzying heights of commercial success and hysterical adulation. During its two-year run, the Monkees became one of the biggest rock acts in the world, selling millions of records, selling out tours, and becoming idols to hordes of teen fans. Their eponymous debut album sold over three million copies; the second and third sold over a million each.

Along the way, the Monkees's conquered the singles charts with a series of crisp, hook-laden songs like "Last Train to Clarksville," "I'm a Believer," "A Little Bit Me, A Little Bit You," and others. They performed to capacity crowds from London to Los Angeles. And in 1967, their program won an Emmy Award for Outstanding Comedy Series.

Also along the way, they became something of a joke. At a time when rock was moving in a more serious, artistic, "noncommercial" direction, the Monkees seemed to symbolize everything that was trivial, artificial, and mercenary. The group was, after all, a product, manufactured by show-biz types who had little feel, or feelings, for rock as music. At the time, the Monkees came to be referred to as the Prefab Four.

The group itself didn't help matters. To a man—or Monkee—they were mostly blatant, vapid caricatures. Davy was the cute short one, with a British accent that sounded fake (even if it wasn't). Mickey was the cutup, the one with the big smile and the one-liners. Tork and Nesmith (the two who rated use of their last names) were actually musicians, but they were reduced to playing roles, as well. The former was cast as a quasi-George Harrison type, shy but devilish; the latter, the strong, quiet, Lennon-esque leader figure.

In fact, the Monkees had the makings of a vast cultural self-parody. Given the contrived nature of their origins, their vast commercial success, and the fact that it had all come about via television, the group could have—and should have—symbolized the ultimate degradation of rock.

But this was the 1960s, a time when miracles happened. And the Monkees proved to be one of them.

For a start, they were funny. While the story lines to their shows were invariably silly and contrived, with plenty of spots left open for the group to perform its latest hits, the Monkees rose above the occasion with a comedic abandon that was affecting. As actors, they had a remarkable rapport. Jones and Dolenz—the real actors—used their professional timing and skills to help Nesmith and Tork along. This created a sense of camaraderie that gave the Monkees the feel of a real all-for-one-and-one-for-all rock group.

There was also their music. While the Monkees—like other groups of the time, even including the sainted Byrds—didn't play their own instruments on their initial recordings, they did have a vocal sound that was more than adequate. And the quality of

The Monkees

their records could not be denied. "Last Train to Clarksville" had a propulsive rock sound while "I'm a Believer" and "A Little Bit Me, A Little Bit You" bubbled with an effervescence that was pure pop. And the group's later hits, on which the Monkees did play most of the music, proved to be equally energetic and ebullient: "Pleasant Valley Sunday," "Valleri," and others were remarkable rock songs.

The quality of the Monkees, more than their commercial success, gave the group a sense of musical integrity that transcended the television program and the ersatz manner in which the group had been formed. It also validated their success and adulation. Monkee-mania might have been a secondhand version of Beatlemania, but at least it was directed at a

group that, in some ways, warranted the acclaim.

The Monkees—the program and the group—came into being in 1965, when writer-director Bob Rafelson and Bert Schneider teamed up to create a pilot. To do that, they had to form a group, so they proceeded to advertise for actors and musicians in *Daily Variety*. Hundreds applied, and in the end, Nesmith, Jones, Dolenz, and Tork made the cut.

Jones (b. Dec. 30, 1945, Manchester, England) was a former jockey and had been a child star in various TV shows, musicals, and plays in Britain. Dolenz (b. George Michael Dolenz, Jr., Mar. 8, 1945, Los Angeles) had pursued a similar course: as a child he had starred in the series "Circus Boy" and had appeared on other TV shows in the 1950s and

'60s. Nesmith (b. Robert Michael Nesmith, Dec. 30, 1942, Dallas, Texas) and Tork (b. Peter Halsten Thorkelson, Feb, 13, 1944, Washington, D.C.) had been a part of the L.A. folk and rock scene that emerged in the mid-'60s.

When the pilot program was shown to a test audience of teens at the end of 1965, the response was such that NBC agreed to add the series as part of its fall 1966 lineup.

Over the course of the next several months, the program and the group began to take shape. Rock

---

TOP ALBUMS

THE MONKEES (Colgems, '66, *1*)
MORE OF THE MONKEES (Colgems, '67, *1*)
HEADQUARTERS (Colgems, '67, *1*)
PISCES, AQUARIUS, CAPRICORN & JONES LTD.
   (Colgems, '67, *1*)
THE BIRDS, THE BEES & THE MONKEES
   (Colgems, '68, *3*)

Additional Top 40 Albums: 2

TOP SONGS

LAST TRAIN TO CLARKSVILLE (Colgems, '66, *1*)
I'M A BELIEVER (Colgems, '66, *1*)
A LITTLE BIT ME, A LITTLE BIT YOU (Colgems, '67, *2*)
PLEASANT VALLEY SUNDAY (Colgems, '67, *3*)
DAYDREAM BELIEVER (Colgems, '67, *1*)
VALLERI (Colgems, '68, *3*)

Additional Top 40 Songs: 6

---

mogul Don Kirshner was brought in as musical producer, and he enlisted the illustrious stable of songwriters of his Aldon Music company to provide the group's material. Neil Diamond contributed "I'm a Believer" and "A Little Bit Me, A Little Bit You." The duo of Tommy Boyce and Bobby Hart wrote "Clarksville" and "The Monkees Theme." Legendary rock songwriters like Barry Mann and Cynthia Weil and Neil Sedaka also wrote songs for the series.

The Monkees themselves were mostly ignored in this process, a move that would later cause difficulties between them and Kirshner.

When the program debuted, on September 12, 1966, it wasn't an immediate hit. The same was not true of the group.

By November, the Monkees had topped the charts with their debut album and the single "I'm a

Believer." The success of the records increased the popularity of the program, which in turn plugged the records even more. It was a dazzling display of cross-marketing that would not go unnoticed in the rock business.

The Monkees also began to assert themselves as musicians. In February 1967, they embarked on a brief tour that was greeted with a hysteria that had not been seen since the early days of Beatlemania. This encouraged the members, particularly Nesmith, to confront the program's musical status quo. Nesmith demanded that the group be allowed to perform on its own records and that Kirshner be sacked from the series.

The group's success continued apace. In March 1967, "A Little Bit Me, A Little Bit You" topped the charts, and in June, *Headquarters* did the same. Ironically, it was knocked from the Number One slot by the originals'—the Beatles'—*Sgt. Pepper's Lonely Hearts Club Band.* The Monkees then made their way across the U.S. in July, on a tour that included Hendrix as the opening act (he was released from the tour after two weeks due to protests from parents of the Monkees' teen fans).

The Monkees were, by then, a full-fledged rock phenomenon. And for a time, they continued to roll. The series' second season began to assume more of a countercultural edge, with guests like Frank Zappa and Tim Buckley making cameo appearances. The Monkees' records also dominated the charts, the album *Pisces, Aquarius, Capricorn & Jones Ltd.* hitting Number One in November and the single "Daydream Believer" doing the same in December.

The Monkees also began to expand their creative horizons. Tork had performed at various shows as a solo act during 1967. At the end of the year, Nesmith began recording a solo record, *The Wichita Train Whistle Sings.* And on the group's next album, *The Birds, the Bees & the Monkees* (which was released in May 1968) each of the members contributed songs of their own.

But the Monkees' demise would come as quickly as its rise to fame and fortune. In May 1968, the program was cancelled by NBC after the broadcast of the 58th episode. In November, the group's movie, *Head,* was a flop; it was a sprawling, almost incoherent effort directed by Rafelson and co-written by Jack Nicholson, the movie had none of the charm of the series. And in December, Tork defected.

The Monkees continued as a trio for another year, but subsequent singles and albums failed to equal the chart success of the early hits. Jones decided to leave the group in January 1970, and Nesmith did the same in March.

The members pursued solo careers of various sorts. Nesmith continued to record, doing mostly country-tinged rock songs with the group the First National Band. He later formed Pacific Arts Corporation and was one of the pioneers of the rock video movement. Dolenz moved to England and became a director of TV commercials. Jones went back to the stage and appeared in the musical *Godspell.* Tork, by all accounts, went broke. Jones and Dolenz reformed the Monkees with Boyce and Hart in 1975, but the new version of the group was a failure.

Jones, Dolenz, and Tork—with Nesmith abstaining—had better luck when they re-formed in 1986. Coinciding with the reemergence of the group, MTV rebroadcast all the episodes of the TV series. Rhino Records also reissued the group's albums from the 1960s. And a new album, *Then and Now . . . The Best of the Monkees,* with the old hits and three new songs by Jones, Dolenz, and Tork, reached number 21 on the charts. The group then set out on "The Monkees' 20th Anniversary World Tour," which was greeted by the screams of a new—and old—generation of Monkees fans.

During an appearance by the Monkees in Los Angeles in 1989, Jones, Dolenz, and Tork were joined onstage by Nesmith. It was the first time the Prefab Four had performed together in 20 years.

VAN MORRISON

Like an early minstrel wandering the lanes of Ireland, or perhaps an aging bluesman toiling his way through the American South, Van Morrison pursued his music with a spirituality and passion that were singularly personal.

One of the most elusive and enigmatic figures in rock, Morrison was also one of the music's true originals. Born in Ireland and bred on the blues of Leadbelly, he took the musical traditions of his own land and those of America and transformed them into songs that were, by turns, lilting and melodic, bluesy and potboiling. All of them, at all times, bore his distinctive musical stamp.

Over the course of a career that spanned three decades, Morrison assumed numerous and diverse musical guises. As a member of Them in mid-'60s London, he was a British Invader, rasping out R&B-tinged rock songs with a fervor matched only by the Animals' Eric Burdon. Later in the decade, he released an album, *Astral Weeks,* that would be universally hailed as one of the finest rock records of all time.

On subsequent albums, spanning the 1970s and '80s (and into the '90s), Morrison created a vast body of music that, at various points—and sometimes simultaneously—encompassed jazz, R&B, traditional folk, rock, pop, and soul.

Along the way, Morrison composed songs that became both hits (for himself and others) and classics. Recorded during his days with Them, "Gloria" became a rock standard and, covered by the Shadows of Knight, a top 10 hit. Scores of other songs, mostly notably his signature "Into the Mystic," while neither hits nor standards, were simply sublime.

Moreover, unlike that of many rockers, Morrison's music did not decline over the decades. His albums continued to be passionate and powerful, while into the '90s, he still displayed an overwhelming energy and expressiveness onstage.

Through it all, Morrison—again, unlike other rockers—maintained a reclusive presence. Intensely cynical regarding the rock business and the press, he kept his personal affairs, and even his musical beliefs, to himself. He rarely gave interviews, preferring to let his music speak for itself. Before performances he was known to go for long, solitary walks, as if to prepare himself for laying his soul bare onstage. He also moved about peripatetically, from Belfast to London, the San Francisco Bay Area, Dublin, and points in between. Never one to attach himself to any particular scene, Morrison lived his life the way he made his music: in a world of his own choosing.

Morrison (b. George Ivan, Aug. 31, 1945, Belfast, Northern Ireland) was encouraged in his musical career by his parents, who raised him on a steady diet of jazz and blues. He began that career in 1960, playing guitar and sax with a local country group, Deanie Sands and the Javelins.

In 1961, he joined an R&B group, the Monarchs, with whom he toured Europe for a time. Returning to Belfast, he left that group and with two of its members formed Them. By 1964, that group had become the house band at Belfast's Maritime Hotel, where they gained a substantial base of local fans. The group's popularity was such that it was offered a contract with Decca Records that year. Touring the U.K., Them came to the attention of American producer Bert Berns, who had written such classics as "Twist and Shout" and "Hang on Sloopy." They moved to London and recorded one of Berns's songs, "Here Comes the Night," which made number two on the U.K. charts and number 24 in the U.S. in 1965. They also released an eponymous debut album, whose various session musicians included Jimmy Page.

The use of those musicians (a common practice at the time) infuriated Morrison. He was also disillusioned by the beat-group persona created for Them by the record company.

Them recorded a second album, *Them Again*, in 1966, again with session musicians. A subsequent U.S. tour was disappointing. In 1967, Morrison quit the group; it continued without him until 1968.

TOP ALBUMS

MOONDANCE (Warner, '70, 29)
HIS BAND AND THE STREET CHOIR (Warner, '70, 32)
TUPELO HONEY (Warner, '71, 27)
SAINT DOMINIC'S PREVIEW (Warner, '72, 15)
HARD NOSE THE HIGHWAY (Warner, '73, 27)
WAVELENGTH (Warner, '78, 28)

TOP SONGS

BROWN EYED GIRL (Bang, '67, 10)
DOMINO (Warner, '70, 9)
BLUE MONEY (Warner, '71, 23)
WILD NIGHT (Warner, '71, 28)

Additional Top 40 Songs: 1

At the suggestion of Berns, Morrison flew to New York in 1967 to sign a deal and record with the former's new Bang label. One of the first songs recorded as part of the deal was "Brown Eyed Girl," which hit number 10 on the U.S. charts in June. But problems arose when Berns subsequently released an album, *Blowin' Your Mind*, without bothering to consult Morrison. The episode bolstered Morrison's growing distrust of the rock business.

But at the end of the year, Berns died of a heart attack, and Morrison was on his own. He performed in various jazz and blues groups, briefly, before signing a new contract with Warner Bros. that allowed him a considerable amount of artistic freedom.

The result of that deal was the album *Astral Weeks*. Recorded in 48 hours, the album was Morrison's masterpiece. *Astral Weeks* was a smashing set of folk-based songs colored by traces of everything from jazz and rock to R&B and soul. These songs were also imbued with Morrison's introspective and evocative romanticism that unified the disparate musical aspects into a seamless whole. It was an approach to music making that would become a Morrison hallmark over the years.

As Morrison made his way into the '70s, he continued to expand his musical vision, and his fan base, on albums such as 1970's *Moondance* and *His Band and the Street Choir*. The former, with its horn-driven songs, became for many the quintessential Van Morrison album. The latter yielded the top 10 single "Domino."

In 1973, he formed the 11-piece Caledonia Soul Orchestra, with which he toured and recorded for a time. The following year, he released the concert album *It's Too Late to Stop Now*, one of the best live records in rock history. Morrison's sense of musical integrity was such that he refused to rerecord any of the rougher moments in the studio, allowing his live sound to stand on its own. It did.

Other albums of the period included 1974's *Veedon Fleece*, a breathtaking album that had much the same grandiose feel as *Astral Weeks;* 1977's boisterous *Period of Transition* (recorded with Dr. John); and 1978's *Into the Music*.

In all of these, Morrison displayed a spiritualism

Van Morrison

that seemed to come from his Irish soul. His lyrical musings and introspective forays became increasingly prevalent on early '80s albums such as *Common Ground*, *Beautiful Vision*, and *Inarticulate Speech of the Heart*. The 1986 collection *No Guru, No Method, No Teacher* was Morrison's response to media and public analyses of his spiritual and religious beliefs.

In the later years of the decade, Morrison began to stretch himself musically in more fanciful ways. In 1988, he sang a series of ancient Irish folk songs with the Chieftains fiddling behind him on the ebullient, eloquent album *Irish Heartbeat*. In 1989, he teamed up with British blues and jazz master Georgie Fame on *Avalon Sunset*, which also included the U.K. hit

single "Whenever God Shines His Light," a duet with Cliff Richard.

In 1992, Morrison released the two-disc set *Hymns to the Silence*, which demonstrated that his inspired musical sensibilities were as affecting and vibrant as they had always been. This was confirmed by a series of remarkable one-off shows he performed that year.

Not that any confirmation was necessary. To Morrison, music seemed to be more an avocation than a career, a means of expression unencumbered by the dictates of the business or the expectations of the public. He pursued his vision in a remarkably solitary manner and, in the process, created music that was universal.

RICKY NELSON

By the time rock
and roll had entered the 1990s, it had become an accepted
component of the culture and society at large.

A "good citizen" in a collective sense, it was a big business, generating billions in annual revenues and employing tens of thousands. It paid its taxes. It entertained the masses quite like TV or baseball or any other national pastime. Its heroes were often flashy and at times obnoxious, but they also contributed time and money to worthy causes. In short, rock was safe.

That wasn't the case when rock and roll began in the 1950s. To the broad consciousness of the sleepy, secure Eisenhower era, rock and roll was downright scary. Presley shook his hips, and the TV cameras of "The Ed Sullivan Show" turned away lest a nation of viewers should be exposed to wild, untamed sex. Jerry Lee Lewis jumped on his piano, and parents across the country hid their daughters in panic.

Add to these the sneer of Brando and the lost soul of James Dean—rock and roll's silver screen counterparts—and the music assumed the menacing air of juvenile delinquency, teens run amok, civilization as we know it going to ruin in ducktails.

And then there was Ricky Nelson.

Ricky was a good kid. Everyone in the country knew it, because they knew him. He had grown up before the nation's eyes, literally, as the fine, young son of the fine, young Nelson family on the hit television series "The Adventures of Ozzie and Harriet."

When Ricky decided to become a rock and roller, the first fissure in rock's bad boy image appeared. That occurred on April 10, 1957, when Nelson performed a version of Fats Domino's "I'm Walking" on that week's installment of the family's TV show.

Within a month, his father, Ozzie, had secured a deal with Verve Records, which promptly released his debut single "A Teenager's Romance" (with "I'm Walking" as its B side). In its first three days in the stores, it sold 60,000 copies. A month later, that fig-

ure had reached a million. Ricky Nelson had become a rock star.

But he had also become something vastly more important, for rock and for the culture as a whole. With his clean, wholesome good looks and familiar and likable public image, Nelson had become the bridge between rock and roll and civilized society. To young teen girls of the time, he was pretty and aw-shucks charming and unthreatening. To parents of the time, he was the kind of rocker they could accept without an undue amount of fear and loathing. Miraculously, to fans of the harder stuff, he also turned out to be surprisingly affecting and exciting.

Over the course of the rest of the decade and into the next, Nelson churned out a series of hits that came with his distinctively smooth vocals and established him as one of the finer rock and roll stars of his day. Many of them also highlighted the talents of some illustrious musicians, including guitarist James Burton (who provided some of the classic solos of the era) and bassist Joe Osborn, who were members of Nelson's band during the early years of his career.

Moreover, Nelson's records were perfectly valid as real rock and roll records. While playing a crucial role in opening up rock to the vast, previously non-rock public, he did so without pandering to that public. Unlike other clean, young, white performers—most notably Pat Boone—who had diluted rock to make it accessible and acceptable to the public for their own commercial ends, Nelson played rock simple and straight and with few compromises. In the process, he and his music made vast and enduring contributions to the repertoire.

The start of Nelson's career reads very much like a television script. By the time he was 16, Nelson (b. Eric Hilliard Nelson, May 8, 1940, Teaneck, New Jersey) was already a star. Along with his brother

Ricky Nelson

David, he had been a regular member of his parents' highly successful radio program in the 1940s (which had moved to television in 1952). His rock career began as a defensive reaction to his girlfriend's adulation of Elvis Presley. Nelson had decided that he, too, would record a rock and roll single.

Nelson made good on his boast when that single became a major hit in 1957, with "I'm Walking" eventually rising to number four. His partnership with Verve Records came to an end in September that year and he signed with Imperial (ironically, the label that had produced Domino's original version of "I'm Walking").

That new deal yielded immediate results when his rockabilly-inflected single "Be-Bop Baby" was released in October 1957 and hit number three on the charts, selling more than one million copies.

Over the course of the next six years, Nelson charted regularly with a long string of records. From 1957 through 1963, his singles made the top 10 an astonishing 18 times, with numerous others reaching the top 20.

While much of this success was due to the quality of those records, Nelson's popularity was also boosted by the "Ozzie" connection. During that time, he and his band were seen on a weekly basis performing their newest records on his family's television show. But Nelson's success was more than a product of television exposure. Songs such as "Poor Little Fool" and "Hello Mary Lou" had a rolling feel that was augmented by Nelson's understated but rocking vocals. Others, such as "Travelin' Man," were quasi-ballads whose sleek, seamless sound and supple phrasings were new slants on traditional, straightahead rock and roll. Nelson's music was also strikingly varied at a time when most rockers laid down their "sound" and stuck to it. "My Bucket's Got a Hole in It," of 1958, was one of his first forays into the country music he would pursue later in his career. In 1961, he recorded an R&B-tinged version of the classic "Milk Cow Blues." There were smooth ballads like 1958's "Lonesome Town" and jumping rockers like 1959's "It's Late." In 1963, Nelson tried his hand at the

Latin rhythms that were becoming popular at the time with an ebullient version of Glenn Miller's "Fools Rush In."

As he grew older, Nelson also began to distance himself from his teen idol persona. In 1961, he changed his stage name from Ricky to Rick. He also made a move into the movies, taking on non-musical roles in the 1959 film *Rio Bravo* and 1960's *The Wackiest Ship in the Army*.

His music also began to evolve. As with most of his '50s counterparts, his career as a hitmaker was cut short by the Beatles and the British Invaders of 1964. But unlike many of his contemporaries, he didn't settle into a comfortable musical middle age as a nostalgia act. During the 1960s, he began to pursue an interest in country music that yielded such acclaimed albums as 1966's *Bright Lights and Country Music* and the energetic *Country Fever* of 1967. While these albums were hardly hits, they did enhance his musical reputation.

In the later 1960s, he became increasingly influenced by folk music, recording songs by Bob Dylan and Tim Hardin, among others. This interest was combined with his previous country work in a country-rock sound he began to pursue in the '70s with the Stone Canyon Band (which included future Eagles founder Randy Meisner).

In 1972, Nelson had one more major hit with the single "Garden Party." The record was a country-rock ballad that he released as a protest to fans who had booed him at a rock revival show at New York's Madison Square Garden in which he had tried to play new material along with his old '50s hits. "Garden Party" reached number six on the charts.

In the later years of his career—from the later 1970s into the '80s—Nelson began to settle into the oldies role the fans expected of him. But he continued to release new material along the way, as on the 1981 album *Playing to Win*. His shows were a mix of his '50s classics and the country-rock sound he had come to embrace.

On December 31, 1985, Nelson was killed in a plane crash on his way to a show in Dallas, Texas.

TOP ALBUM

RICKY (Imperial, '57, 1)

Additional Top 40 Albums: 9

TOP SONGS

I'M WALKING (Verve, '57, 4)
A TEENAGER'S ROMANCE (Verve, '57, 2)
BE-BOP BABY (Imperial, '57, 3)
STOOD UP (Imperial, '57, 2)
BELIEVE WHAT YOU SAY (Imperial, '58, 4)
POOR LITTLE FOOL (Imperial, '58, 1)
TRAVELIN' MAN (Imperial, '61, 1)
YOUNG WORLD (Imperial, '62, 5)
TEEN AGE IDOL (Imperial, '62, 5)

Additional Top 40 Songs: 26

THE NEW YORK DOLLS

The New York Dolls came along in the early 1970s, at a time when the Rolling Stones were entering their "greatest rock and roll band in the world" phase. The Dolls tried to look and sound like them but failed miserably. That's why they were so important.

The secret to the Dolls' failure—and importance—was that, unlike the Stones, they weren't the greatest. Nor were they even close to it. They were a group of rank, raw, ragged amateurs who were playing rock simply because they loved it. While rock's "greatest" were refining their sound and look and becoming exceedingly processed, the Dolls, lacking any kind of expertise, were inadvertently pushing rock in the opposite direction. The Dolls weren't stars, or professionals, or musicians worth speaking of. They were punks.

But that's getting ahead of the game—which was where the Dolls were all along.

Not that they or anyone else realized it at the time. In 1972, the group's sound and look was a sort of Stones-redux. Vocalist David Johansen, full of lips and brash of style, flounced about on the stages of New York's glam-rock scene in Jagger drag. Guitarists Sylvain Sylvain and Johnny Thunders (the latter a Keith Richards look-alike, with his dark, spiked hair and staring countenance) churned out distorted, jagged chords and solos. Bassist Arthur Kane and drummer Jerry Nolan propelled it all with an energetic roughness that turned the group's music into a brawl. (The group's original drummer, Billy Murcia, died of a heroin overdose before it recorded its first album.)

Given their penchant for androgyny, the Dolls were dismissed by many of their contemporaries as simply another addition to the glam-rock scene that was flourishing in New York and London. But others saw in the group a new way of making rock, or rather, deconstructing it. One of the latter was Todd Rundgren, who teamed up with the group after it had signed a contract with Mercury Records in 1973 and became its producer. The New York Dolls' eponymous debut album appeared that year.

With its strutting, crashing, almost impenetrable sound, the album was a commercial flop. While the group had gained a local following in New York with that sound, it proved to be too harsh and demanding for the rest of the rock world.

Switching producers, the Dolls recorded their next album, *Too Much Too Soon*, with George "Shadow" Morton at the helm. But the results, musically and commercially, were the same. Disillusioned and disappointed by the failure of its records, the band began to come apart, and they quickly faded from the scene.

But the scene went on. Inspired by the raucous, musical raggedness of the New York Dolls, a new generation of New York rockers began to emerge. Rock poetess Patti Smith, who had opened for the Dolls at various shows in 1972, used a Dolls-like sound as a musical foil for her dense, iconoclastic lyrical tirades, particularly on her 1975 album *Horses*. Rock visionary Tom Verlaine pursued a similar musical course with his group Television, which added an overt intellectualism to the musical thrashings.

But the principal musical beneficiaries of the New York Dolls were the Ramones. Inspired by the Dolls' ineptness, the Ramones purposely set about to create a new form of rock that was stripped down to its musical basics. In the Ramones' songs, slamming beats, slashing chords, and shouted vocals were all performed with a savage simpleness and directness.

The New York Dolls

While the Dolls had done the same—simply because that was the best they could do—the Ramones did it that way to make an artistic point. At a time in the middle '70s when much of rock was wallowing in pretension and excess, the Ramones were out to prove that rock could be an expression of unrefined feeling and abandon. That belief would be at the core of the punk movement that would take hold in Britain in 1976 and emerge in the form of the epochal Sex Pistols.

In fact, the New York Dolls had their own, direct connection with the British punk scene and, specifically, the Sex Pistols. In 1975, Malcolm McLaren, the future manager of the Pistols, journeyed to New York in an attempt to revive the Dolls' flagging career. He worked with the group for more than six months, his efforts failing to achieve any success. But when he returned to Britain, later in the year, he put the lessons he had learned from the Dolls to use when he began to sculpt the Sex Pistols. A master image maker and provocateur,

McLaren translated the Dolls' slovenly sound and look into a new, almost formalized anarchy that the Pistols would employ in creating the punk ethos.

The Dolls themselves, as inept at pushing their career as they were at playing music, did not benefit from any of this. Johansen and Sylvain kept the group going in one form or another until 1977, when it finally folded. Johansen would achieve fleeting success in the guise of the decadent lounge lizard Buster Poindexter in the 1980s. Thunders and Nolan formed the group the Heartbreakers and moved to London, but were as unsuccessful there as they had been in New York. Not that any of this had any bearing on the New York Dolls' role in the development of rock. That role was both pivotal and symmetrical.

The New York Dolls were one of a number of amateurs whose musical "shortcomings" were crucial to the evolution of rock and roll. In the 1950s, Elvis Presley had tried to sound like his country and R&B heroes but in his

---

TOP ALBUMS

NEW YORK DOLLS (Mercury, '73)
TOO MUCH TOO SOON (Mercury, '74)

inability to do so had created a sound that was all his own. In the '60s, Paul McCartney had done the same with his idol, Little Richard. Bob Dylan had done so with Woody Guthrie, with the same results.

In fact, a direct if superficially improbable line can be drawn between the blues and the punks. In their ineffectual attempts to sound like the blues masters, the Rolling Stones had, instead, become the Rolling Stones. And in the Dolls' failed efforts to sound like the Stones, they had become the New York Dolls, a group that would be punks before their time.

The New York Dolls were also the godfathers of the new wave scene that emerged in New York in the later 1970s. Their brash, bashing sound, as distilled through the Ramones, would be the basis of the musical rebellion that would be carried out by groups like Talking Heads, Blondie, and various others against the rock status quo of the time. Ironically, several of groups of that status quo would subsequently co-opt the basic rock sound and look of the rebelling groups. One of them was the Rolling Stones, who reinvigorated their career with hard-biting songs like the rocking "Shattered," from their 1978 album *Some Girls*. In the roundabout way in which rock usually reinvents itself, the Stones were, in a sense, remaking their sound in a form that had been pioneered by the New York Dolls.

ROY ORBISON

Standing above the teen crooners and novelty acts of the early 1960s was one shining figure whose music was a beacon during the Dark Ages of rock and roll. Dressed in black, his head topped with a Brylcremed pompadour and his face framed by everpresent shades, Roy Orbison made rock and roll the way it had never been made before.

Orbison elevated the romantic rock ballad to a new level of expression and emotion. Lifting his high tenor voice to soaring crescendos, he endowed songs like "Only the Lonely (Know How I Feel)," "Crying," and "In Dreams" with an almost operatic elegance and eloquence. Orbison was the Caruso of rock and roll.

But he was also a rock and roller, period. On "Mean Woman Blues," he cut and scratched his way across the song with a biting intensity that deftly belied the beauty of the record's B side, "Blue Bayou." And on "Oh, Pretty Woman," he purred the words, added a tiger's growl, and finished it off with a tremulous "mercy."

With these records and others, Orbison became one of the most successful rock artists in the world during the years 1960 through 1964. And not only in the commercial sense: he was also a bridge of musical quality and integrity between rock's first Golden Age, which ended with the 1950s, and its second, which began with the Beatles and the British Invasion.

It was a role he would act out in various ways during a long and illustrious career. With his background in rockabilly and country music he tied the rock of the 1960s to its roots in the '50s. His rock credentials made him a hero to three generations of rockers, from the Beatles and Bruce Springsteen to k.d. lang and others. And near the end of his career, he anchored the multi-generational supergroup the Traveling Wilburys.

While his vocal delivery and range were unsurpassed in rock, his records were more than mere showcases for his voice. With their sweeping strings, vast harmonies, and panoramic sound, records like "Crying," "In Dreams," and others pointed to a new musical approach that transcended the energy and abandon of rock's earlier wild men. And when he performed them onstage, standing stock still (in a stance that would be copied almost directly by John Lennon), Orbison brought to rock a simple, understated grandeur that it had never had to that point.

All of this came to him over a period of years.

Orbison (b. Apr. 23, 1936, Vernon, Texas) began his career in his teens as a member of the the hillbilly group the Wink Westerners (named for their town, Wink, Texas). In 1955, while studying at North Texas State University (where Pat Boone was a classmate), he began performing with the group the Teen Kings. They recorded the single "Trying to Get to You" at the Clovis, New Mexico, studio of producer and future Buddy Holly manager Norman Petty.

The record didn't sell, but Orbison soon set his sights on Sun Records and its founder, Sam Phillips, for whom he auditioned in 1956. Signed to the label, he released the single "Ooby Dooby," which reached number 59 on the charts that year. But the overtly rockabilly style he affected on that and subsequent discs didn't prove to be suitable to his vocals.

In 1958, he moved to Nashville and immediately scored as a writer when his song "Claudette" was recorded by the Everly Brothers and released as the B side to their million-selling hit "All I Have to Do Is Dream." But the country sound he pursued on several records cut for RCA at the time proved to be as disappointing as the singles he had made at Sun.

In 1959, he left RCA and moved to the smaller Monument label, where he began his initial collaboration with longtime producer Fred Foster. With Foster he found the sound he had been striving for, and after two modestly successful singles, he released "Only the Lonely" in 1960. The record was an immediate hit, reaching number two and selling

more than one million copies.

"Blue Angel" followed, reaching number nine. In January of 1961, "I'm Hurtin' " made number 21. And in June of that year, "Running Scared" topped the charts and broke the million sales mark. "Crying," which would become one of Orbison's signature songs, hit number two in October.

He tried a new direction in 1962 with the jumpier single "Dream Baby"; it also proved vastly popular, reaching number four. But after several more releases, he returned to his musical strength in 1963 with the luscious ballad "In Dreams," which hit number seven.

A major rock star in the U.S., Orbison was also immensely popular in Britain. He toured the U.K. in 1963, headlining a series of shows that also included the Beatles and Gerry and the Pacemakers. He would tour that country to great acclaim through the rest of the decade.

While the emergence of the Beatles and the British Invasion would effectively end the careers of many older rockers, Orbison continued to hit the charts for a time. In September 1963, "Mean Woman Blues" hit number five. And in 1964, "Oh, Pretty Woman" simultaneously topped the charts in the U.S. and the U.K., becoming one of his most popular records (in 1982 it would chart at number 20 in a version by Van Halen).

But as rock tastes began to change in the mid-1960s, Orbison's career finally started to fade. His life would also be ravaged by tragedy during the later years of the decade. In 1966, his wife, Claudette (for whom he had written the song), died in a motorcycle crash. In 1968, while he was on tour in the U.K., two of his three sons died in a fire at his home in Nashville.

Orbison gradually receded from the rock scene during the 1970s. But at the end of the decade he made something of a comeback when he duetted with Emmylou Harris on the single "That Lovin' You Feelin' Again," for which the two won a Grammy Award in the Best Country Performance category in 1981.

TOP ALBUM

MYSTERY GIRL (Virgin, '89, 5)

Additional Top 40 Albums: 4

TOP SONGS

ONLY THE LONELY (KNOW HOW I FEEL) (Monument, '60, 2)

BLUE ANGEL (Monument, '60, 9)

RUNNING SCARED (Monument, '61, *1*)

CRYING (Monument, '61, 2)

DREAM BABY (HOW LONG MUST I DREAM) (Monument, '62, 4)

IN DREAMS (Monument, '63, 7)

MEAN WOMAN BLUES (Monument, '63, 5)

OH, PRETTY WOMAN (Monument, '64, *1*)

YOU GOT IT (Virgin, '89, 9)

Additional Top 40 Songs: 14

A true comeback commenced in 1986, when "In Dreams" was included in the soundtrack of the hit film *Blue Velvet*. The film created a new interest in Orbison's music, and he rerecorded several of his older hits for the album *In Dreams: The Greatest Hits,* released in 1987.

That same year, Orbison was inducted into the Rock and Roll Hall of Fame.

In 1988, he was invited by George Harrison to join the Traveling Wilburys along with Tom Petty, Bob Dylan, and Jeff Lynne. Performing as Lefty Wilbury (the others had their own pseudonyms), Orbison contributed his timeless vocals to the hit album and its single "Handle with Care," which charted at number 45.

Amid this new success, Orbison died from a heart attack on November 6, 1988.

An album of new Orbison material, *Mystery Girl*—recorded with Petty and Lynne—was released posthumously in 1989. Imbued with the good-natured Wilbury sound, the record proved that Orbison's vocal powers had not been dimmed by the years. In fact, the album was one of the finest of his career, earning it a peak chart position of number five.

Numerous compilation albums and tributes followed Orbison's death. In 1989, *In Dreams: Greatest Hits* was released in the U.S. along with Rhino Records' compilation *For the Lonely: An Anthology, 1956–1965.* It was followed by *A Black and White Night,* a recording of a live tribute taped in 1987 by Bruce Springsteen, k.d. lang, Elvis Costello, and others. In May 1987, Orbison was inducted into the Songwriters Hall of Fame. And in 1991, he was honored posthumously with a Grammy Award for Best Pop Vocal Performance, Male, for his work on *A Black and White Night.*

Roy Orbison

CARL PERKINS

With the success of
Elvis Presley in 1956, record companies across the U.S. began
to jump on the rock and roll bandwagon. In their eagerness to
capitalize on the popular new form, industry executives attempted to
recreate the Presley phenomenon by signing new Elvises of their own.

The result, over the course of the rest of the decade, was a series of new rock stars, all of them young white men, whose music and images were similar to that of the king of rock and roll.

While that could have been a musical debacle, it wasn't. In fact, several of these secondhand Presleys turned out to be inspired and distinctive performers in their own right, who made crucial contributions to the golden age of rock and roll.

One of the first of them was Carl Perkins.

Ironically, Perkins's career was instigated by Sam Phillips, the Sun Records founder who had discovered Presley and first recorded his music. When Presley's contract with Sun was purchased by RCA at the end of 1955, Phillips began to build Perkins into the "next Elvis."

Perkins (b. Apr. 9, 1932, Lake City, Tennessee) was an unknown performer who had been signed by Phillips to the Sun subsidiary Flip Records in 1955. That year, he had released the singles "Movie Magg" and the rockabilly "Gone Gone Gone" (the latter on the Sun label), neither of which had charted. But Phillips was convinced that Perkins could be a potential rock star of Presley's magnitude.

His instincts proved to be as prescient as they had been about Presley. When Perkins's next single, "Blue Suede Shoes," was released in March 1956, it climbed to number two on the *Billboard* "Best Seller" chart and passed the one million sales mark. The first major rockabilly record to score on the charts, "Blue Suede Shoes" became one of the signature songs of the rock era. With Perkins's boisterous

vocals and its jumping beats, the record captured the feel and energy of the emerging rock movement like few others of its time.

But just as Perkins's career—and "Blue Suede Shoes"—was getting started, it came to a sudden halt when he was injured in a car crash enroute to an appearance on "The Perry Como Show," his first major television date. Hospitalized for several weeks, Perkins was unable to capitalize on the attention generated by his hit.

At the end of 1956, Perkins took part in the "Million Dollar Quartet" session with Presley, Jerry Lee Lewis, and Johnny Cash at Sun studios. But his career never approached the potential suggested by "Blue Suede Shoes." Instead, Phillips turned his attentions to Lewis, and Perkins left the Sun label in 1958 to record on Columbia (where he was soon to be overshadowed by Cash). He had a minor hit with "Pointed Toe Shoes" in June 1959, but his career soon faded, and he became a sideman to Cash for a number of years.

But Perkins was one of the seminal figures in '50s rock. Several of his songs, including "Matchbox," "Everybody's Trying to Be My Baby," and "Honey Don't" were revived by the Beatles in the 1960s. He contributed to Paul McCartney's 1982 album, *Tug of War*. And in 1985, George Harrison and Ringo Starr and an all-star lineup of rockers came together to commemorate the 30th anniversary of the release of "Blue Suede Shoes" for British television. In 1987, Perkins was inducted into the Rock and Roll Hall of Fame.

Carl Perkins

Other rock artists emerged during the 1950s as pretenders to Presley's throne. Two of them, Gene Vincent and Eddie Cochran, had careers that proved to be remarkably—and tragically—similar to that of Perkins. Vincent (b. Eugene Craddock, Feb. 11, 1935, Norfolk, Virginia) was a performer on a country music radio station in the mid-'50s when he recorded a demo that came to the attention of Capitol Records. The company signed him to a contract as part of its attempt to create its own version of Presley. Like Perkins, Vincent was an immediate hit when his debut single, "Be-Bop-A-Lula," reached number seven on the charts in 1956.

Like "Blue Suede Shoes," that record became a rock classic and one of the staples of the repertoire over the decades. Vincent also became a timeless symbol of rock's wildness, performing exuberant shows with his group, the Blue Caps, and generally wreaking havoc during his tours: he was one of the first rock stars to trash hotel rooms (a somewhat minor, if telling, claim to rock fame).

But Vincent's career also proved to be fleeting. While he scored a second hit single with "Lotta Love" in 1957, his popularity soon waned. During a tour of the U.K. in April 1960, he was injured in a car crash near London that took the life of Cochran. In later years, Vincent's health declined, exacerbated by a drinking problem, and he died in Hollywood on October 12, 1971.

Cochran (b. Oct. 3, 1938, Oklahoma City, Oklahoma) came along slightly later than Perkins and Vincent. But the arc of his brief, illustrious career

TOP ALBUMS

ORIGINAL SUN GREATEST HITS (Rhino, '86)
BORN TO ROCK (MCA, '89)
HONKY TONK GAL (Rounder, '89)
JIVE AFTER FIVE: THE BEST OF CARL PERKINS
    (Rhino, '90)

TOP SONGS

MOVIE MAGG (Flip, '55)
GONE GONE GONE (Sun, '55)
BLUE SUEDE SHOES (Sun, '56, 2)
YOUR TRUE LOVE (Sun, '57)
PINK PEDAL PUSHERS (Columbia, '58)
POINTED TOE SHOES (Columbia, '59)

was much the same. A former hillbilly performer, Cochran began to assume a rock sound and image in 1957 when he signed with Mercury Records. His debut hit was the negligible single "Sittin' in the Balcony," which reached number 18 on the charts. His next single, however, was a rock classic, "Summertime Blues." One of the most ebullient and evocative teen songs of all time, the single was a major hit, charting at number eight in 1958.

That record came with Cochran's clicking, twanging guitar chords, which would have an immense influence on future generations of rock musicians. And his ultra-hip look and presence, onstage and off, made Cochran one of the preemi-

nent rock idols of his time. But at the height of his fame, Cochran was killed in the same car crash that injured Vincent, on April 17, 1960.

Perkins, Vincent, and Cochran were meteoric figures at a crucial, formative moment in rock history. Each had a quick rise to fame and produced a rock classic that defined themselves and rock and roll. Their music and their rock image would inspire subsequent generations of musicians, from the British Invaders of the 1960s to the punks of late '70s London and the rockabilly revivalists of the early '80s. If the Beatles, the Clash, the Stray Cats, and many others had anything in common, it was the music of these rock pioneers.

PINK FLOYD

Pink Floyd unfolded across nearly 30 years of rock history like a vast surrealistic tapestry of sound and imagery.

Over the course of those years, Pink Floyd was one of the most innovative groups—creatively and technologically—in rock, constantly confronting and confounding the scene with musical and visual stimuli that pushed forward the boundaries of expression. In the process it evolved from a proto-psychedelic group operating on the fringe of the mid-'60s London scene into one of the biggest rock acts in the world.

From the start, the group revelled in strangeness. In its initial phase, it was the platform for leader Syd Barrett's odd, whimsical musical noodlings and brief, spry songs. When he began to fade from the scene—and from reality—in the later 1960s, the group moved into more sweeping and sprawling musical forays. Succeeding albums had mostly dense, slow-moving songs that came with the ethereal vocals of bassist Roger Waters and guitarist David Gilmour, the sweeping keyboards of Richard

Wright, and the inexorable drumming of Nick Mason.

They also included odd, surrealistic sound effects: huge heartbeats, gigantic footsteps, and others that created an evocative aural/visual counterpoint to the group's songs. Over the years, the music evolved into vast, image-laden soundscapes.

Such imagery was gradually brought into the group's onstage performances during its tours of the 1970s. At the start of the decade, Pink Floyd's shows included such visual effects as flashing police car lights and man-made fog. The group also pioneered the use of stage technology that was developing at the time. Pink Floyd was one of the first rock groups to employ a quadraphonic sound system that could place various sounds in different hall locations and then move them around. During the shows, thundering footsteps would begin behind the stage and "walk" about the audience, opening doors and slam-

Pink Floyd

ming them shut as other noises intruded on the music. These effects and others helped expand the parameters of rock performance.

The props got more spectacular and garish as time went on. During Floyd's 1977 tour for the album *Animals,* the group shared the stage with 40-foot-high, inflatable barnyard denizens that floated above the musicians. On the 1980 tour in support of *The Wall,* the stage was dominated by a brick wall 160 feet long and 30 feet high, which the group demolished during its performance.

While Pink Floyd was variously praised and derided by critics for its onstage excesses, its popularity with the rock masses grew to proportions that were as immense as its props. Pink Floyd shows sold out consistently during the 1970s, and several of its albums reached high into the charts. The most successful of these was 1973's *Dark Side of the Moon,* which eventually sold more than 13 million copies worldwide and remained on the U.S. charts for an astounding 736 weeks—longer than any other album.

But its vast success and popularity aside, Pink Floyd consistently created rock music that was provocative and intriguing. At times, the band could be overbearing and pretentious (*The Wall*), and at others, its music failed to equal its vision (*Wish You Were Here*). But at all times, Pink Floyd provoked the rock world and suggested new ways in which the music could be created and performed.

The group began in 1965 when Waters (b. Sept. 9, 1944, Great Bookham, England), Wright (b. July 28, 1945, London), and Mason (b. Jan. 27, 1945, Birmingham) formed the rock trio Sigma 6 while attending school in London. By the end of the year, Barrett (b. Roger Barrett, Jan. 6, 1946, Cambridge, England), formerly of the Hollering Blues, had also joined. He suggested the name Pink Floyd, based on those of two Georgia rural bluesmen, Pink Anderson and Floyd Council.

Pink Floyd began to make a name for itself on the underground scene in London with a series of performances at clubs like the Marquee, the London Free School's Sound/Light Workshop, and the Roundhouse. By 1967 the group had become one of mainstays of the leading psychedelic club of the time, the UFO. There, the group established the basics of its future sound and style, performing long, complex sets of music that also came with projected slides, films, and other visual effects.

In March of 1967, the group was signed by EMI and released its debut single, Barrett's whimsical account of the tranvestite "Arnold Layne." The record reached number 20 on the U.K. charts and propelled Pink Floyd into the leading ranks of the underground scene. Its subsequent single, "See Emily Play," hit number six in July; in August, its debut album, *Piper at the Gates of Dawn,* did the same.

But during a tour of the U.S. at the end of 1967, Barrett began to display erratic behavior (probably related to the use of LSD) that created problems for the group. When these worsened, Gilmour (b. Mar.

TOP ALBUMS

THE DARK SIDE OF THE MOON (Harvest, '73, *1*)
WISH YOU WERE HERE (Columbia, '75, *1*)
ANIMALS (Columbia, '77, *3*)
THE WALL (Columbia, '79, *1*)
A COLLECTION OF GREAT DANCE SONGS
   (Columbia, '81, *31*)
THE FINAL CUT (Columbia, '83, *6*)
A MOMENTARY LAPSE OF REASON (Columbia, '87, *3*)
DELICATE SOUND OF THUNDER (Columbia, '88, *11*)

Additional Top 40 Albums: 1

TOP SONGS

MONEY (Harvest, '73, *13*)
ANOTHER BRICK IN THE WALL (PART II)
   (Columbia, '80, *1*)

6, 1947, Cambridge, England) was recruited in January 1968 to fill in for Barrett onstage. By April, Barrett had decided to leave the group. (He subsequently pursued a brief solo career that included an eponymous debut album and the aptly titled *The Madcap Laughs;* he later became a recluse.) Gilmour then assumed a full-time role in Pink Floyd.

In June of 1968, the group released the album *A Saucerful of Secrets,* a tentative record with songs like "Set Controls for the Heart of the Sun" that hinted at musical directions to come.

These hints became stronger on its third album, 1969's *Ummagumma.* A two-record set divided into live and studio sections, *Ummagumma* came with long and complex songs that highlighted Waters' and Gilmour's evocative vocals and Wright's droning, melodic keyboard work.

The group's new sound came to fruition on 1970's *Atom Heart Mother* and was reinforced on 1971's *Meddle.* These albums, two of the group's finest, were vast, densely produced efforts that included the extra-musical sound sources and stark musical and lyrical imagery that would become the hallmarks of Pink Floyd's classic sound.

The culmination of that sound came on 1973's *Dark Side of the Moon.* The group's defining masterpiece, the album was a brooding lyrical assessment of the human condition, conjuring images of madness, fear, and spiritual and intellectual debasement. Musically, the album came with the same, dense, minor-keyed songs, stark melodicism, and sound effects of its predecessors. On the album's sole single, "Money," a rhythmic bass line gave way to clanging chords and crashing cash registers as the words etched out images of greed and immorality. The song made number 13 on the charts,

Dark Side of the Moon immediately elevated Pink Floyd into the top ranks of the rock world. But it was also the group's musical apex. Subsequently albums such as 1975's *Wish You Were Here* and 1977's *Animals* were mostly static, if intriguing, affairs, with the group offering a sound that was virtually unchanged from its work from the start of the 1970s. Increasingly, Waters was becoming the guiding force within the group, a trend that would ultimately generate dissension in the ranks and lead to the group's demise in the early '80s.

But in the meantime, Pink Floyd made its way through the rest of the decade as one of rock's leading groups. *Wish You Were Here* topped the charts, and *Animals* hit number two.

By the end of the 1970s all of this contrived to make *The Wall* an immense worldwide hit. Dominated by Waters' cynical views of the betrayal and abandonment of innocence, *The Wall* topped the U.S. charts for 15 weeks in 1979, with its single "Another Brick in the Wall" also hitting Number One. *The Wall* was subsequently made into a 1982 movie starring the Boomtown Rats' Bob Geldof.

The success of *The Wall* notwithstanding, Pink Floyd began to come apart, starting with Wright's departure in 1980 because of disagreements with Waters.

On the next album, 1983's *The Final Cut,* Waters' dominance was almost absolute. A bleak tirade against war, the album contained mostly his songs and vocals. And the group's sound was becoming somewhat stale and hackneyed.

In May of 1983, the group dissolved amid much rancor between Waters and his bandmates, Gilmour and Mason.

Each of the members pursued solo careers. Gilmour's 1984 solo album *About Face* was a smashing record that was highlighted by his lithe, R&B-inflected guitar work. That same year, Waters released the Pink Floyd–like album *The Pros and Cons of Hitch Hiking,* the first of several concept records that would also come with elaborately staged tours: on a 1987 outing for his subsequent album *Radio K.A.O.S.,* phone booths were set up in the crowd so that fans could call him onstage to request old hits.

That same year, Waters' former mates reunited for a new Pink Floyd album and tour. With Waters threatening legal action over their use of the group's name, they went ahead anyway. The album *A Momentary Lapse of Reason* was a major hit, reaching number three in the U.S. In 1988, the group recorded *The Delicate Sound of Thunder,* which proved to be similarly popular, hitting number 11. Like Waters, the group still displayed its penchant for the grand gesture. In 1989, they staged a world-telecast concert set on a gigantic barge moored in the Grand Canal in Venice.

Not to be outdone, Waters created a new version of *The Wall* in 1990 that was performed before a crowd of 200,000 and a television audience that spanned the globe. Staged in Berlin's Potzdamer Place (the former site of the Berlin Wall), the performance came with an all-star cast that included Sinead O'Connor, Joni Mitchell, Van Morrison, and others.

Together and or apart, Pink Floyd had a style all its own.

THE POLICE

The Police emerged from the punk maelstrom of the late 1970s as a full-fledged rock force. Over the course of its six-year career, the group evolved into one of the biggest rock acts of its time and one of the finest rock bands of all time.

It also served as the springboard for the subsequent solo career of its leader, Sting, who went on to create a vast body of sophisticated, eloquent music in the 1980s and '90s.

While the Police were initially associated with the punk movement, the group employed that rebellious musical form more as a means to an end than as a specific expressive statement. With their purposely slapdash clothes and trademark blonde, spiky locks, the Police moved for a time in the punk circles of London in the later 1970s, using the notoriety of that milieu to gain attention for themselves.

But from the start, the Police had other things on their mind than the simplistic and ragged musical bashings of their counterparts. Early albums such as 1978's *Outlandos d'Amour* and 1979's *Reggatta de Blanc* were remarkable amalgams of punk-infused energy and Sting's melodic songwriting sensibilities. And on songs like "Roxanne" and "Message in a Bottle," the Police displayed a musical mastery and instrumental agility whose resulting sound was at once groundbreaking and accessible.

The focal point of that sound was Sting's vocals. Endowed with an elastic range and a remarkably

The Police

natural expressivity, Sting sang with an edgy intensity and an alluring sleekness that were stunning. Through his work in the Police, it was clear that Sting was a rock vocalist for the ages.

But the group was more than a platform for Sting's expressive vocals. Instrumentally, the Police created a sound that, in its initial phase, combined a punkish simplicity with more complex musical aspects.

With Sting providing straightforward if rhythmically complex lines on his bass, guitarist Andy Sum-

mers delivered colorful, rolling chords and intricate pointillistic figures that gave the Police's music a vast, expansive feel. To these, Stewart Copeland—arguably the finest rock drummer since Ginger Baker and Mitch Mitchell of the 1960s—added angular, technical flourishes that were strongly derived from the slanted beats and asymmetrical rhythms of reggae.

Over a period of years, the group's music evolved into a dense blend of thematic and harmonic textures that were far removed not merely from the punks but also from mainstream rock. Ranging from propulsive, electronically layered songs and moody, ethereal pieces to the classic 1983 ballad "Every Breath You Take," their sound was unique.

The Police performed a pivotal role in the development of rock. In its initial phase, it acted as a musical bridge of sorts, moving the punk sound into the rock and pop mainstream. In time, it expanded the bounds of that mainstream, becoming, along with Talking Heads, the most innovative group of the early 1980s.

The Police began in January 1977, when former Curved Air drummer Copeland (b. July 16, 1952, Alexandria, Egypt) teamed with Sting (b. Gordon Sumner, Oct. 2, 1951, Wallsend, Tyne and Wear, England) and guitarist Henri Padovani. The trio released its debut single, "Fall Out," in May on the independent Illegal label founded by Copeland and his brother Miles (who would subsequently become the group's manager).

The group made its initial connection with the punk scene when it toured with acts such as Cherry Vanilla, Johnny Thunders, and Wayne County and the Electric Chairs during the spring of 1977.

But it also began to move in the more esoteric circles of the '70s rock scene. In May, it performed on a show with Gong in Paris, where that group's Mike Howlett invited Copeland and Sting to join him in a one-off lineup with guitarist Andy Summers. Summers (b. Andrew Somers, Dec. 31, 1942, Poulton Le Fylde, Lancashire, England) had been a longtime participant in the rock scene, having performed with the New Animals, Soft Machine, Kevin Ayers, and others. By August, he had joined the Police, and Padovani had departed.

The group's career developed relatively slowly. Over the course of the rest of 1977 and into 1978, the Police divided its time between touring in the U.K., recording its first album, and performing with avant-gardist Eberhard Schoener in Germany. During this period, it also appeared in an ad for Wrigley's Chewing Gum; for the ad, the members dyed their hair blonde. Their blonde locks would subsequently become one of the group's visual signatures.

When their debut album, *Outlandos d'Amour*, was released in November of 1978, it generated much attention and eventually hit number six on the U.K. charts. The album included the song "Roxanne," a reggae-tinged affair about a boy's innocent affections for a prostitute. Released as a single, it made number 12 on the U.K. charts in May 1979 and eventually became one of the band's musical signatures.

The Police embarked on several modest tours of the U.S. in 1978 and 1979, stirring up interest in the group in the vast U.S. rock marketplace. The result was that by May 1979, *Outlandos d'Amour* had hit number 23 on the U.S. charts, an encouraging showing for a group perceived as punk-oriented.

Sting also began to emerge as a rock star. In 1979, he appeared in the film version of the Who's rock opera *Quadrophenia* (starting a side career in acting that he would pursue throughout the 1980s). At the end of the year, the Police's second album,

TOP ALBUMS

ZENYATTA MONDATTA (A&M, '80, 5)
GHOST IN THE MACHINE (A&M, '81, 2)
SYNCHRONICITY (A&M, '83, 1)
EVERY BREATH YOU TAKE—THE SINGLES
  (A&M, '86, 7)

Additional Top 40 Albums: 2

TOP SONGS

DE DO DO DO, DE DA DA DA (A&M, '80, 10)
DON'T STAND SO CLOSE TO ME (A&M, '81, 10)
EVERY LITTLE THING SHE DOES IS MAGIC
  (A&M, '81, 3)
EVERY BREATH YOU TAKE (A&M, '83, 1)
KING OF PAIN (A&M, '83, 3)
WRAPPED AROUND YOUR FINGER (A&M, '84, 8)

Additional Top 40 Songs: 3

Regatta de Blanc, hit number 25 in the U.S. One of its songs, "Message in a Bottle," demonstrated the band's developing sophistication in its intriguing chordal movement and melodic phrasing. With Summers' rolling arpeggios, Copeland's slamming beats, and Sting's ebullient vocals, the single was one of the high points of '70s rock (although it performed modestly on the charts, reaching number 74 in the U.S.).

But while the album and single were minor successes in the States, the Police were becoming a major act everywhere else. In 1980, the group embarked on a world tour, solidifying their international base of popularity (and during which they became the first Western rock group to appear in Bombay, India).

In 1981, the Police finally established itself in the U.S. when its third album, *Zenyatta Mondatta*, hit number five. From the album, the playful pop single "De Do Do Do, De Da Da Da" charted at number 10, and later in the year, "Every Little Thing She Does Is Magic" reached number three. In February 1981, the group won its first Grammy Award, in the category of Best Rock Instrumental Performance for the song "Regatta de Blanc."

The successes of 1981 set the stage for the Police's rise to the top of the rock world. In 1982, its brooding album *Ghost in the Machine* occupied the second position on the U.S. charts for six weeks. In June, the band performed before a crowd of 400,000 at the US Festival in San Bernardino, California.

The apex of the group's career came in 1983. In June, the Police released its masterpiece, *Synchronicity,* which topped the U.S. charts for seven weeks. The album, one of the finest in rock history, came with elegant songs, like "Wrapped Around Your Finger" and "Tea in the Sahara," that pushed rock to new expressive and creative levels. Perhaps the most affecting of these was the simple ballad "Every Breath You Take," whose melodic beauty and disturbing lyrical imagery immediately established it as a classic. The single topped the U.S. charts for eight weeks. With their music dominating the charts and radio, the Police embarked on a tour that filled stadiums and arenas across the U.S.

But at the height of its popularity, the Police disbanded at the end of 1983 when Sting decided to pursue a solo career. (They subsequently reunited for a one-off performance in Atlanta, Georgia, in 1985 for Amnesty International.)

While Sting had been the focal point of the Police, the group was actually an amalgam of the various, eclectic interests of all three members. Those interests were highlighted in the subsequent careers they pursued as individuals.

Copeland released the album *The Rhythmatist,* a study of African-based rhythms and music, in 1985. He also teamed with jazz bassist Stanley Clarke and vocalist Deborah Holland in the fusion group Animal Logic, releasing an eponymous album in 1989. But his most interesting work came in the scores he composed in various forms during the 1980s. These included the 1985 ballet *King Lear,* the 1988 opera *Holy Blood and Crescent Moon* (written for the Cleveland Opera), and soundtracks for the films *Rumblefish, Wall Street,* and *First Power* and the TV series "The Equalizer" (the latter of which formed the basis for his 1987 album *The Equalizer and Other Cliff Hangers*).

Resuming the more experimental interests he had pursued before he joined the Police, Summers began a collaboration with former King Crimson guitarist Robert Fripp, which yielded the jazz- and avant-garde–oriented albums *I Advanced Masked* (1982) and *Bewitched* (1984). He also recorded the more rock-based albums *XYZ* (1987) and *World Gone Strange* (1991).

While his counterparts' careers proved moderately successful, Sting's proceeded to go through the ceiling, creatively and commercially.

Having begun his career in the Newcastle jazz scene of the early 1970s, Sting began to pursue his interest in that form as soon as he left the Police. Recruiting a new band of young jazz virtuosos, including saxophonist Branford Marsalis, bassist Darryl Jones, keyboardist Kenny Kirkland, and drummer Omar Hakim, he released *The Dream of the Blue Turtles* in 1985. A remarkable effort that blended his eloquent vocals and richly textured songs with the group's smashing improvisational forays, the album also proved to be a hit with fans, charting at number two. With that group, Sting also released the 1986 live album *Bring on the Night* and the film documentary of the same title, directed by Michael Apted.

Disbanding the group in 1987, Sting proceeded to release a series of albums that came with a stunning array of sounds and songs that displayed one of the most expansive and eclectic musical visions in rock. On those albums—1987's *Nothing Like the Sun,* 1991's *Soul Cages,* and 1993's *Ten Summoner's Tales*—Sting combined jazz, rock, and pop in a sound that proved to be as accessible as it was musically provocative.

Sting pursued a vast range of additional projects that were intriguing departures from his rock career. In 1988, he formed the Pangea label, for which he recorded a version of Igor Stravinsky's 1917 masterpiece, *L'Histoire du Soldat.* In 1989, he performed in the Broadway production of Kurt Weill and Bertold Brecht's *The Threepenny Opera.*

His acting career included roles in the films *Dune, Brimstone and Treacle, The Bride, Plenty, Stormy Monday,* and *Julia, Julia.*

Over the years, Sting also became involved in an assortment of political causes, mostly notably those related to saving the Brazilian rainforest and the human rights organization Amnesty International, for which he performed a number of benefit tours and concerts.

ELVIS PRESLEY

Elvis Presley *was* the king of rock and roll.

While there were other pretenders to the throne, from Chuck Berry to the Beatles, Bob Dylan, the Rolling Stones, and others, Presley stood above them all as the timeless symbol of the music and the ethos it espoused and expressed.

When he made his way into the national spotlight in 1956 with his single "Heartbreak Hotel," Presley set in stone the image and sound of rock and roll that would endure as long as the music persisted in fact or in memory.

With the swivel of his hips, the slur of his voice, the curl of his lip, Presley evoked the force and feeling of youth and sex and rebellion that would be at the core of rock's image. At the same time, he stamped rock as both the sound of the emerging teen culture that became a dominant social force of his time and as an original American musical form.

In the process, be became the biggest-selling recording artist in the history of popular music. During his 21-year career, he had an astounding 67 top 20 hits on the singles charts, with scores of others charting in the top 100. He also had 38 top 20 albums, again with numerous others making the charts. He sold hundreds of millions of records in the process.

Presley's music was a sublime amalgam of quintessentially American musical idioms. On such early hits as "Hound Dog," "Don't Be Cruel," and "All Shook Up," he combined the melodic signatures of country and western music and the rhythmic and emotional thrust of R&B and gospel in an entirely new way.

With his low, vocal growls, hiccuped syllables, and exuberant histrionics, Presley was a quantum leap in the evolution of pop singing. As a vocalist he leapfrogged and sidestepped genres and styles with an ease and assurance and distinction that were unprecedented. On ballads like "Love Me Tender," he affected the luxurious tones of '40s crooners; then he contrasted it with roughhouse, gut-busting tirades on storming numbers like "Jailhouse Rock." But Presley never simply tried out vocal stylings; instead, he endowed each with his own singular sound.

Presley embodied the sense of reckless abandon that would underlie the performances of most rock-ers who followed. Using an acoustic guitar more as a prop than an instrument, he swung his hips violently, shouted his vocals, and shook his head from side to side as if his music was as much release as strictly musical expression. It was a spectacle that had never been seen before and one that, in the quiescent Eisenhower era, created some controversy. When Presley appeared on Ed Sullivan's TV program in 1956, the show's host ordered his cameramen to focus on Presley's face to avoid displaying his gyrations to the national television audience. In time, Presley's movements would inspire a nickname: Elvis the Pelvis.

When Presley became the first phenomenon of the rock and roll era, he immediately spawned a generation of rock stars who traded, in their individual ways, on the sound and image he had created. In its haste to capitalize on the Elvis craze, the record industry began to recruit a legion of potential new Elvises. They included Carl Perkins, Gene Vincent, Del Shannon, Ricky Nelson, Eddie Cochran, and others, many of whom would make their own seminal contributions to the rock scene and repertoire. The legend spread to England, where artists such as Tommy Steele and Cliff Richard affected Presley's look—the slicked-back hair and sideburns and sleek suits and two-toned shoes—as well as his sound. Presley also had an impact on that country's next generation of rockers, including the Beatles, who would fashion their own groundbreaking version of rock and roll in the 1960s.

The power of Presley's celebrity was such that it fueled one of this century's more bizarre social phenomena. Following his death, Presley became the focus of an almost fanatical adulation. Ardent rock fans, along with their more hysterical, mindless counterparts, made pilgrimages to his Memphis mansion, Graceland. Armies of imitators—not musicians as much as look-alikes—took to stages around the world, dressing and performing like their hero. Into the 1990s, Presley's name and questions about his existence became the stuff of tabloids and jokes. Frequent "sightings" of the supposedly still-living rock idol made the rounds, to general derision.

TOP ALBUMS

ELVIS (RCA, '56, *1*)
LOVING YOU (RCA, '57, *1*)
ELVIS' CHRISTMAS ALBUM
  (RCA, '57, *1*)
G.I. BLUES (RCA, '60, *1*)
BLUE HAWAII (RCA, '61, *1*)

Additional Top 40 Albums: 44

TOP SONGS

HEARTBREAK HOTEL (RCA, '56, *1*)
ALL SHOOK UP (RCA, '57, *1*)
JAILHOUSE ROCK (RCA, '57, *1*)
ARE YOU LONESOME TO-NIGHT?
  (RCA, '60, *1*)
SUSPICIOUS MINDS (RCA, '69, *1*)

Additional Top 40 Songs: 102

Yet this near-religious fixation, as odd as it was, in no way diminished the singer's epochal role or the power of his early music.

Given the all-encompassing nature of Presley's fame and influence, the revolutionary, history-making initial phase of his career was remarkably brief. Presley (b. Jan. 8, 1935, Tupelo, Mississippi) began that career in the most inadvertent of ways. On July, 18, 1953, he took time off from his truck-driving job to record a private record at Memphis Recording Service, owned by Sun Studio's Sam Phillips. That record, and subsequent sessions in 1954, eventually gained the attention of Phillips, who invited Presley to record a single for the Sun label.

Teaming Presley with guitarist Scotty Moore and bassist Bill Black, Phillips recorded a version of Arthur "Big Boy" Crudup's blues song "That's All Right Mama" on July 5, 1954. Presley's debut single was released later that month and generated much attention on the local scene.

Other singles on Sun were released in 1954, and Presley began to make his name on the southern country scene, appearing at state fairs and on radio programs like "Louisiana Hayride" in Shreveport. Along the way, Presley's performances began to elicit tumultuous audience response—a taste of the adulation that was to come. In July 1955, Presley had his first chart hit when the single "Baby Let's Play House" made number 10 on the *Billboard* country charts.

But the Sun label was too small to adequately distribute Presley's records, and in November 1955, his manager, "Colonel" Tom Parker, negotiated a new deal with RCA, which purchased Phillips's contract for the then-astounding fee of $35,000.

In 1956, Presley became a rock star of unprecedented fame. With his group, which included Moore, Black, and new drummer D.J. Fontana, Presley began to reach a national audience via his appearances on such major TV programs as Tommy and Jimmy Dorsey's "Stage Show" and "The Milton Berle Show."

When his debut RCA single, "Heartbreak Hotel," was released, it hit the top of the charts in April and stayed there for eight weeks. That same month, Presley signed a three-movie deal for $450,000.

The hits, most of them to become rock and roll classics, began to climb the charts in rapid succession. "I Want You, I Need You, I Love You," "Don't Be Cruel," "Hound Dog," and "Love Me Tender" all topped the charts in 1956, with seven other singles hitting the top 40. The albums *Elvis* and *Elvis Presley* did the same that year. And Presley's film debut, *Love Me Tender,* proved to be a box-office smash.

The success continued to grow in 1957. That year, Presley hit Number One with the singles "Too Much," "All Shook Up," "(Let Me Be Your) Teddy Bear," and "Jailhouse Rock." The album *Loving You* also topped the charts that year, as did the seasonal *Elvis' Christmas Album.*

In September, the movie *Jailhouse Rock* opened to a ravenous response from the public. The title song sequence, in which Presley strutted and danced with his fellow "cons," became a classic image of the rock era.

At the height of his success, Presley was forced to put his career on hold when he was drafted into the U.S. Army, in March 1958. But RCA continued to release singles during his 18-month stint, scoring chart-toppers in 1958 with "Don't" and "Hard Headed Woman."

But that same year, Presley took a devastating blow when his mother, Gladys, died. It would have a sobering impact on his life and music.

When he was discharged from the army in 1960, Presley resumed his career. The single "Stuck on You" topped the charts, and its successor, "It's Now or Never," did the same, selling over 20 million copies worldwide.

While his success continued—"Are You Lonesome Tonight," "Surrender," and "Good Luck Charm" were Number One hits in 1960 and 1961—Presley began to devote most of his time to making movies. Scores of them were commercial successes, as were the inevitable soundtrack albums. Many were also dreary, blatantly commercial "products."

With the emergence of the Beatles, the Rolling Stones, Bob Dylan, and others in the middle 1960s, Presley began to fade as a major force. But he rebounded in 1968 with the TV special "Elvis," on which he jammed with several of his backing musicians (including Moore, Fontana, and Charlie Hodge) in a segment that recalled the vitality and emotion of his halcyon days. In 1969, he topped the charts for the final time with the single "Suspicious Minds."

But just as Presley was reigniting his music and career, he moved into a new phase that—again, while successful—cast him as something of a cultural cliché. Dressed in outlandish jump suits, with scarves and bangles and sequins, he took to the stage in flashy shows that reduced him to the level of self-parody. His tours of the early 1970s, in which he played in vast arenas and Las Vegas showrooms, were hyperbolic affairs carefully crafted to pander to the adulation of his aging fans.

Ironically, the man who had virtually created the image of the rock and roll star also became the sym-bol of the flabby, out-of-control rock star burnout. In his private life, he increasingly retreated into seclusion with his family and a cadre of bodyguards at his Memphis mansion. Giving in to an excessive lifestyle, he became bloated, and his health began to wane. He died on August 16, 1977, of heart failure. Elvis had left the auditorium.

PRINCE

Prince might not have been all things to all people, but he was certainly all things to himself. He made his way through the world of rock with a remarkable sense of independence and individuality.

Constantly inventing and reinventing himself, his music, and his career, he pursued a creative course that was entirely of his own concoction—and that often seemed to be pointing in several directions simultaneously. In the process, he became one of the most charismatic, creative, and commercially successful rock artists of the 1980s.

A prodigious composer and multifaceted musician, Prince produced his own records—14 over a 15-year period—providing all the vocal and instrumental tracks on six of them. During that period he also appeared in, and virtually created, four films. In 1985 he formed his own record label, Paisley Park, which became the focal point of his work and that of various groups and artists whose careers he directed and guided. He also composed songs for a number of acts ranging from the pop siren Sheena Easton to post-punk maven Sinead O'Connor.

Along the way, Prince became a media icon of immense proportions, largely due to a persona he carefully crafted and manipulated over the years. Reclusive in his private life, he was a splashy public figure whose exploits were often eccentric and purposely garish. With the vast success of his 1984 film and soundtrack album *Purple Rain,* he expropriated the color as part of his image, using it in his clothes, houses, and cars. A self-styled philosopher of sorts, he increasingly focused his artistic statements on sex as a redemptive force and the idea of gender as a shifting presence as opposed to a physiological reality.

Prince's all-encompassing interests and image were reflected in his music. On his first three albums, he combined the funk of James Brown, the rock hyperbole of Jimi Hendrix, and the rock-inflected soul of Sly and the Family Stone in a dense and sexually charged musical brew. Subsequently, on *1999,* he incorporated the electronic sounds and flourishes of the techno-pop movement into his funk-rock sound to create a sprawling, expressive, apocalyptic musical onslaught. On *Purple Rain,* he began to include traces of mainstream rock, particularly on the album's anthemic title cut. Later in the decade and into the 1990s, he ventured into musical psychedelia and took side trips into pop, the hardcore funk of George Clinton, and the dance music of the time. In the process, he created a new synthesis of rock, pop, funk, R&B, and soul, forging them into an all-inclusive and personal musical form.

Prince's live performances were the embodiment of his music and image. Onstage, he exuded an aggressive sexuality and exhibitionism that were both provocative and self-parodistic. At the start of his career, he performed rather like a latter-day Hendrix, slashing away at his guitar and singing with undiluted fervor while remaining in near-constant motion. But these performances soon evolved into highly staged choreographed displays of showmanship and theatrical excess. During his tour of 1982, the shows culminated with Prince on a bed, high above the stage, simulating various sexual acts. His 1985 tour was a phantasmagoric display of swirling sounds and images, one of which included Prince bathing in a shower of neon light. To depict the basic story line of his 1993 album, titled after a symbol for male/female, Prince created a show that included gangs of roving sheiks, an Arab princess whom Prince romanced, and various vignettes that were a cross between a rock opera and a Vegas stage act.

Prince's films were highly uneven affairs. His first, 1984's semi-autobiographical *Purple Rain,* was a vast commercial success that also produced a number of glowing reviews in which Prince's young, misunderstood, and alienated character was compared with that of James Dean. But his follow-up movies were less successful, both at the box office and in creative terms.

While Prince's varied output did not always hit its aesthetic mark, it displayed, as a whole, a remarkably agile and fertile creative sensibility. At a time when most rock artists were content to turn out predictable hits and settle into whatever images they or others had devised, Prince constantly tried new ideas and ways of expressing himself. In doing that, he reaffirmed the power of the individual artist in rock and proved that it was still possible for rock musicians to direct and dictate their own musical destinies.

Prince (b. Prince Rogers Nelson, June 7, 1958, Minneapolis, Minnesota) got his name from the Prince Roger Trio that was fronted by his father, John Nelson. By the time he was 10, Prince had begun to teach himself the basics of the piano and guitar and to perform at various local talent contests.

One of decisive and earliest musical moments of his life occurred when his stepfather took him to see a James Brown show in 1968. The funk of the Godfather of Soul would prove to be one of the seminal influences in his subsequent career.

Beset by problems at home, Prince ran away at age 12 and was eventually adopted by the Anderson family. Their son, André (who later assumed the surname Cymone), became a close friend and would play with Prince in one of his future groups.

Over the course of the early 1970s, Prince—who by then had taught himself to play bass, drums, and saxophone as well as piano and guitar—began to perform with the group Grand Central. That outfit, subsequently renamed Champagne, also included Mark Brown, Terry Lewis, and Morris Day (later, the vocalist of the Time), all of whom would become integral components of the "Minneapolis sound" that Prince would establish in the later 1970s.

In 1976, Prince journeyed to New York in an attempt to gain a recording contract. When that failed, he returned to Minneapolis to refine his sound and songs and produce a demo tape. That tape eventually came to the attention of Warner Bros. Records and yielded a long-term deal with the label in 1977.

Released in November 1978, his debut album, *For You,* was a self-produced record that came with a boiling R&B sound and overtly sexual subject matter in songs like "Soft & Wet." The sound and lyrics of the album proved untenable in the broad rock marketplace, and it was a commercial disappointment, charting only at number 163.

Undeterred, Prince pursued a similar course on his next three albums to increasing notoriety and success. His 1979 eponymous album reached number 21 and yielded the number 11 single "I Wanna Be Your Lover." 1980's *Dirty Mind* hit number 45, and its 1981 successor, *Controversy,* peaked at number 21.

But it was his 1982 album, *1999,* that pushed Prince to the upper ranks of the rock world. One of the masterpieces of the 1980s, *1999* was a two-record set that came with churning synthesizers and guitars and funky, dance-inflected beats that were combined in a dizzying vision of decadence and excess. Buttressed by constant MTV airplay of the video for its first single, "Little Red Corvette," the album hit number nine and eventually sold more than one million copies.

While that album proved to be a watershed in Prince's career, it was merely the warm-up for the phenomenal success he would achieve in 1984. With the release that year of the film and album *Purple Rain,* Prince became one of the leading rock stars of the time. *Purple Rain* was an immediate box-office smash: filmed at a cost of $7 million, the film grossed $60 million in the first two months of its release. The album was greeted with equal adulation and acclaim.

Propelled by its first single, the starkly eloquent "When Doves Cry," the album topped the charts for 24 weeks and eventually sold an astonishing nine million copies, with the single selling more than two

TOP ALBUMS

PURPLE RAIN (Warner, '84, *1*)
AROUND THE WORLD IN A DAY (Paisley, '85, *1*)
BATMAN (Warner, '89, *1*)

Additional Top 40 Albums: 6

TOP SONGS

WHEN DOVES CRY (Warner, '84, *1*)
LET'S GO CRAZY (Warner, '84, *1*)
PURPLE RAIN (Warner, '84, *2*)
RASPBERRY BERET (Paisley, '85, *2*)
KISS (Paisley, '86, *1*)
U GOT THE LOOK (Paisley, '87, *2*)
BATDANCE (Warner, 89, *1*)

Additional Top 40 Songs: 14

million copies and topping the charts for five weeks. Other singles from the album reached into the top 10, and the *Purple Rain* soundtrack subsequently won a Grammy in 1985 for Best Group Rock Vocal Performance. The "Purple Rain" tour of 1984–85 sold out across the U.S., drawing nearly two million fans.

While *Purple Rain* elevated Prince to the same level of pop stardom as Michael Jackson, Bruce Springsteen, and Madonna, he refused to rest on either his newfound success or the sound that had made it possible. Over the course of the rest of the '80s, Prince used the independence afforded by his stature to expand the range of his music and other creative projects.

His first new move came in 1985, when he released the album *Around the World in a Day*. A showcase for his new psychedelic sound, the album topped the charts and yielded the winsome single "Raspberry Beret." That same year, he began work on his next film, to less satisfactory creative and commercial results. Directed by Prince (who was also its star) and released in 1986, *Under the Cherry Moon* was a dismal, directionless effort that was universally slammed by critics and ignored by fans. But Prince's musical fortunes were hardly waning. From the film, the album *Parade* charted at number three.

On that album and its successors, Prince's music became highly eclectic, while he continued his lyrical explorations of sex. 1987's *Sign o' the Times* (which had a corresponding film: a documentation of his live shows of the time) came with Prince's female alter ego, Camille, singing a duet with him on the single "If I Was Your Girlfriend." 1988's *Lovesexy* created something of a controversy when it was released as a substitute for another record—the so-called Black Album—which Warner Bros. executives reportedly believed was too sexually oriented for the marketplace.

Subsequent Prince albums were similarly wide-ranging, within the rhythmically charged parameters he had set for himself. His 1989 soundtrack, *Batman,* came with dense, brooding dance cuts and became one of his biggest hits, topping the charts for six weeks. The soundtrack for his 1990 film *Graffiti Bridge* and the 1991 *Diamonds and Pearls* both veered from the usual funk-based sound on various songs, while the 1993 symbol-titled album included everything from rock and funk workouts to dance-floor vamps.

That same year, Prince announced that he was claiming the symbol as his name. It was yet another idiosyncratic development in a singularly odd and idiosyncratic career.

THE RAMONES

O ne, two, three, four . . .
With their classic count-off, the Ramones roared
away through their songs.

It didn't matter which one—"Sheena Is a Punk Rocker," "Blitzkrieg Bop," or "Teenage Lobotomy"—they all sounded roughly the same, which was very rough indeed. Dee Dee Ramone's bass throbbed. Tommy Ramone's drums bashed. Johnny Ramone's guitar churned out distorted chords. And Joey Ramone gargled his vocals. In about two minutes, the song would be finished and another would begin.

Long before "punk" entered the rock lexicon as anything other than a generic put-down, the Ramones personified everything that was implicit in the word. They were brash, loud, noisy, and obnoxious—and that was *before* they started playing.

Musically, they were all that and less. Eschewing such nonessentials as instrumental ability, melodic form, harmony, dynamics, and such, they made rock that was reduced to raw power and feeling and volume. On records such as "Blitzkrieg Bop," "Don't Come Close," and others, the Ramones didn't play rock and roll as much as pound it out with a wild, anarchic abandon. Their songs were mostly two-minute exercises in energy, with chords, vocals, and beats being the means to that end.

Similarly, their onstage performances were less musical displays than brawls. Slamming about in their trademark leather jackets, shredded jeans, and ragged T-shirts, the Ramones obliterated all previous definitions of a show. They weren't there to chat with fans or pose or push their "product." They had come to play their music flat-out.

But in fact, their music and look were as much poses and postures as those of the most garish rock superstar; Joey Ramone's jeans and shades were no less a uniform or costume than the stacked heels and glitter suits of Elton John.

The difference was in the aesthetic aim.

While the Ramones' minimalism was the logical extension of the stark music of the Velvet Underground in the 1960s and the forceful ineptness of the New York Dolls of the early '70s, they made it into a thoroughly new and oddly formalized rock aes-

thetic. It was an idea based on the utter deconstruction of rock, which was divested by the Ramones of any musical values, visual adornment, or other professional virtues and aspects.

But while that aesthetic was as contrived as any other, it was also genuine. The Ramones might have sounded and looked the way they did to make a point about the way they thought rock should be, but they were also out to make rock, period.

That they did. In the middle 1970s, the Ramones' extreme reductions of rock to its basic building blocks were a slap in the face to a rock scene that had grown increasingly superficial and commercially obsessed. The Ramones reminded the rock world of the simple force the music had once had, and suggested a way in which it could regain that force in the future.

Theirs was a call to arms that would subsequently be taken up by the punks of the London scene of the later '70s. Basing much of their music and attitude on that of the Ramones, groups like the Sex Pistols, the Clash, and others would create the punk ethos and era, a new sound and look and cultural phenomenon that would be the next great revolution in the history of rock and roll.

The roots of that revolution were in Forest Hills, New York.

The Ramones were formed there in August 1974. From the start, the musicians purposely set out to create an image that was their own, each assuming the Ramone surname. Johnny Ramone (b. John Cummings, Oct. 8, 1948, Long Island), Dee Dee Ramone (b. Douglas Colvin, Sept. 18, 1952, Fort Lee, Virginia), Joey Ramone (b. Jeffrey Hyman, May 19, 1952, Forest Hills), and Tommy Ramone (b. Thomas Erdelyi, Jan. 29, 1949, Budapest, Hungary) made their performing debut at New York's Performance Studio. Gaining the house band slot at the proto-punk club CBGB, they began to develop a local fan following over the next year.

In June of 1975, they auditioned for Blue Sky Records by opening for Texas blues-rocker Johnny Winter at an arena show in Connecticut. But the rock fans booed them off the stage, and the label refused to sign them.

That same year, they came under the wing of manager Danny Fields, who had previously been associated with the MC5, Lou Reed, and the Stooges. Fields negotiated a deal with Sire Records (one of the most innovative labels of the time), which yielded the group's eponymous debut album in 1976. Neither that album nor the single "Blitzkrieg Bop" did well on the charts, but both would be watershed events in the development of the new wave scene that would emerge in New York later in the decade.

The Ramones had a similar effect on the punks when they toured Britain later in the year. At the time, the punk scene had just begun to flourish in London, and the Ramones inspired and validated the new movement with their ragged, high-energy performances. While there, they also participated in the punk film *Blank Generation*.

Their influence on the New York and London scenes notwithstanding, the Ramones continued to have problems with the broad rock public. In 1977 their second album, *Leave Home*, charted only at number 148, while the single "Sheena Is a Punk Rocker" peaked at 81. But as the punk scene began to gain ascendancy during the year, attention was drawn to the Ramones. In December 1977, the album *Rocket to Russia* charted at number 49 and gave the group a presence—however modest—on the national rock scene.

TOP ALBUMS

LEAVE HOME (Sire, '77)
ROCKET TO RUSSIA (Sire, '77)
ROAD TO RUIN (Sire, '78)
END OF THE CENTURY (Sire, '80)
ANIMAL BOY (Sire, '86)
RAMONES MANIA (Sire, '88)
BRAIN DRAIN (Chrysalis, '89)

TOP SONGS

BLITZKRIEG BOP (Sire, '76)
SHEENA IS A PUNK ROCKER (Sire, '77)
ROCKAWAY BEACH (Sire, '78)

Tommy Ramone left the group in 1978 to become its producer, and Marky Ramone joined on drums. That year, the group began to expand its sound, literally, on the album *Road to Ruin*, which came with songs that were longer than two minutes—unheard-of for the group in earlier outings.

Attention was also focused on the Ramones in 1979 when they appeared in the Roger Corman film *Rock 'N' Roll High School*, performing the title cut. But the soundtrack album proved to be a commercial disappointment.

It did lead, however, to a collaboration with legendary producer Phil Spector, who had remixed the album. In 1980, Spector and the Ramones collaborated on *End of the Century*, on which the group toned down its sound somewhat. (They would later call it their worst record.) With Spector, they also recorded a string-based version of the 1964 Ronettes hit "Baby I Love You," reaching the top 10 in the U.K.

The Ramones soon parted ways with Spector and resumed their brash and blaring musical course. The group went on to release 1981's *Pleasant Dreams*, 1983's *Subterranean Jungle*, and 1986's *Animal Boy*, each of which was as energetic and rocking—and uncommercial—as their predecessors. In 1991, they issued the concert album *Loco Live*, recorded during a show in Barcelona, Spain.

Along the way, new Ramones joined and left, the core group of Joey, Johnny, and Dee Dee remaining constant (until the latter's departure in 1989).

Ironically, the Ramones were overshadowed by the very groups they had originally inspired. The Sex Pistols created an all-encompassing rock sound and presence leaps beyond what the Ramones had achieved (or intended to achieve, for that matter). And subsequent New York new wave groups like Talking Heads gained vast musical and commercial success with music that was more substantive and, in its way, accessible than anything the Ramones ever offered.

Ultimately, the Ramones' uncompromising approach limited the breadth of their cultural impact. But that did not negate the seminal influence the group had on the course of rock and roll.

R.E.M.

....

Rock and roll had
always revelled in the new—new sounds, new looks,
new attitudes. But by the early 1980s, it had
seemingly run out of fresh ideas.

The punk and new wave revolutions had subsided. Heavy metal (with the exception of Van Halen and a few others) had descended into self-parody. The techno-rock groups, for all their allusions to modernity, were proving to be a creative cul-de-sac. And as the older rock fans began to move into middle age, their heroes—the Rolling Stones, the Who, and others—came to dominate mainstream radio in what was called the "classic rock" format.

As a reaction to all this, a new generation of rock fans and musicians began to create an alternative scene of their own. They turned to groups such as X or the Replacements or scores of others who were thriving in clubs across the U.S. Shut out, for the most part, by mainstream radio, these groups and fans began to tune in to college radio, which became the primary disseminator of alternative music. In time, over the course of the 1980s, this scene would expand and flourish, becoming a major force in rock.

The group that came to symbolize it more than any other was R.E.M.

Formed at the end of the 1970s, R.E.M. was one of the first representatives of rock's fourth generation. Musical offspring of the punk movement and, specifically, the new wave scene of Athens, Georgia, that had generated the B-52's, the group had cut its creative teeth on songs like the Sex Pistols' "God Save the Queen" and rock classics like "Needles and Pins."

It was an idiosyncratic blend of old and new—a trademark of the Athens scene—that provided R.E.M. with a way out of rock's aesthetic dilemma of the time.

Confronted with the near impossibility of creating a new sound in a rock world that had, by the 1980s, seemingly sampled everything, R.E.M. pursued a course of retrenchment and reevaluation that, ironically, yielded a fresh slant.

Combining the raw simplicity of the punks with a purposely minimalistic revamping of classic rock, R.E.M. took an approach that would come to serve as a model for much of the alternative music of the '80s.

Guitarist Peter Buck provided wiry, trebly, needle-nosed phrases and jangly chords that recalled the music of the Byrds, but without any overt references to folk-rock. Bassist Mike Mills and drummer Bill Berry played with a solid if basic sturdiness that had much in common with the garage-rock groups of the 1960s. And vocalist Michael Stipe whined, droned, and slurred his way through dense, obscure lyrics whose very indecipherability gave the group's songs an aura of mystery.

R.E.M.'s visual presence complemented its music. Dressed down in calculatedly casual clothes, the musicians were neither punk slobs nor mainstream rock star types. Like their music, they affected a persona that was an inspired reduction of rock's most intrinsic virtues. Simply speaking, they were a rock group, nothing more, nothing less.

While there was a certain contrivance to this approach, it worked remarkably well, on record and onstage. On its 1983 debut album, *Murmur,* R.E.M. displayed a dense, almost abstract simplicity that had an ethereal presence and grandeur. The follow-up, 1984's *Reckoning,* displayed a notably harder sound. Touring constantly to support these records,

R.E.M.

R.E.M. proved to be an energetic and mesmerizing stage act, with Stipe leading the way with intense, brooding performances that were countered by his mates' no-frills demeanor.

The group's approach also allowed it a certain freedom to expand and evolve musically without losing its identity. Thus, 1987's *Document* came with songs like "It's the End of the World as We Know It" that had a drive and melodic expansiveness that were far more sophisticated than the more simplistic music of the band's earlier years. In time, their sound would evolve into the string-based songs of a 1992 album, *Automatic for the People,* that proved to be R.E.M.'s most creatively ambitious work to date.

Along the way, R.E.M. became the prototypical "alternative" group, surviving and flourishing on the fringes of the mainstream rock world. R.E.M. consistently ranked high on the lists of critics and fans polled by publications such as the *Village Voice,* the U.K.'s *Q* magazine, and *Rolling Stone* (the latter devoting a cover to the group in 1988, proclaiming it "America's Best Rock 'n' Roll Band"). Ironically,

this groundswell of attention ultimately propelled the group so far into the rock mainstream that by the start of the 1990s, it was one of the most successful acts in the U.S.

While that success validated R.E.M.'s status in the broad rock world, it also catapulted the so-called alternative scene into the forefront of the rock consciousness. The slow, steady course that R.E.M. had pursued via the rock press and college radio during the 1980s would come to be pursued by the newer rock acts.

In the early '90s, a number of these groups—most notably Nirvana and Pearl Jam of Seattle's "grunge" scene—would make the leap from the rock fringe to vast mainstream commercial success. Those groups and scores of others would also affect their versions of the basic rock sound and look that R.E.M. had crafted a decade before.

R.E.M. began to come together in 1978, when Stipe and Buck met at a record store in Athens, Georgia. In 1980, they teamed with Mills and Berry, who had formed a group in high school in Macon and then journeyed to Athens to attend college. They based the group's name on the acronym for rapid eye movement, a physiological sleep state linked with the dream process.

The rest of 1980 was devoted to performing on the active local scene in Athens, during which time R.E.M. began to develop a devoted fan base. In 1981, they recorded their first single, "Radio Free Europe," on the Athens-based Hib-Tone label.

While the record didn't chart nationally, it became a favorite on college radio. Over the course of the decade, R.E.M.'s increasing popularity in the broad rock marketplace—gained initially through the support of college radio—would underscore the importance of that new rock outlet and the scene it represented.

"Radio Free Europe" came to the attention of Police manager Miles Copeland's I.R.S. label, which signed the group in 1982. That year, the label released the group's five-song EP *Chronic Town*, which came with R.E.M.'s signature guitar-based sound and Stipe's edgy, mumbled vocals. The album quickly became a staple of college radio, and the group developed a major following at the alternative level.

The group's debut full-length album, *Murmur*, was released in 1983, and based on the strength of its constant college radio airplay, reached number 36 on the charts. It was the first hint of the broad success the group would achieve later in its career.

Their popularity increased substantially during the middle 1980s, when their albums made steady progress in the charts and gradually extended the group's name to a vast number of rock fans. The hits included *Reckoning* (number 27, 1984), *Fables of the Reconstruction* (number 28, 1985), and *Lifes Rich Pageant* (number 21, 1986).

Along the way, R.E.M. toured constantly. As it did on its records, R.E.M. pursued a notably basic, unadorned approach, focusing on the music rather than the flashy displays of lighting and staging that were common in rock shows of the time. Stipe emerged as a charismatic figure—his fans began to call themselves "distiples"—and the group as a whole became heroes to a new, younger generation of rock listeners.

The group's record success continued apace. Its 1987 album *Document* hit number 10, while *Dead Letter Office*—a compilation of B sides and the songs from *Chronic Town*—hit number 52 that same year. Switching labels from I.R.S. to Warner Bros. in 1988, the group scored again with the album *Green,* which made number 12. A single from that album, "Stand," charted at number six in 1989. Emblematic of R.E.M.'s transformation from alternative to mainstream status was its first arena tour, which the group commenced in 1989 to promote *Green.* It was a watershed not merely for the group but also for the alternative scene as a whole. Times were changing in the rock world, and R.E.M. and its alternative counterparts were assuming an increasingly important musical and commercial role.

As the group became more and more successful, the members began to indulge in a series of extracurricular projects. In 1987, Buck, Mills, and Berry performed on Warren Zevon's album *Sentimental Hygiene.* They subsequently collaborated on Zevon's next two albums and, in 1990, teamed with him in the one-off group Hindu Love Gods, releasing an eponymous album of blues and R&B-tinged songs.

Stipe moved into studio work, producing the Chickasaw Mudpuppies' 1989 debut album *White Dirt* and performing with Syd Straw on "Future '40s" on the album *Surprise.* He also founded his own video company, C-OO, and scripted a series of public service commercials about AIDS, the environment, and other issues.

In 1991, R.E.M. solidified its success when *Out of Time* topped the album chart. The single "Losing My Religion," an archetypal R.E.M. song, became one of the biggest hits of the year.

By 1992, R.E.M. was firmly established as one of the most important groups in rock. Its album reached the upper levels of the charts, and its varied songs suggested that R.E.M. was set to move on and redefine its sound in a more expansive configuration.

TOP ALBUMS

MURMUR (I.R.S., '83, *36*)
RECKONING (I.R.S., '84, *27*)
FABLES OF THE RECONSTRUCTION (I.R.S., '85, *28*)
LIFES RICH PAGEANT (I.R.S., '86, *21*)
R.E.M. NO. 5: DOCUMENT (I.R.S., '87, *10*)
GREEN (Warner, '88, *12*)
OUT OF TIME (Warner, '91, *1*)
AUTOMATIC FOR THE PEOPLE (Warner, '92, *2*)

TOP SONGS

THE ONE I LOVE (I.R.S., '87, *9*)
STAND (Warner, '89, *6*)
LOSING MY RELIGION (Warner, '91, *4*)

THE RIGHTEOUS BROTHERS

Long before the term "crossover" made its way into the pop lexicon, Bobby Hatfield and Bill Medley—the Righteous Brothers—crossed the boundaries between rock and soul music.

They did so with their epochal 1964 hit, "You've Lost That Lovin' Feelin'," in which Hatfield's high tenor and Medley's baritone were fused with producer Phil Spector's massive wall of sound.

It was more than a hit: it was a revolution in musical perceptions.

At the time, the music scene, particularly in the U.S., was as segregated as the culture at large. As preposterous as it might seem decades later, the general perception was that whites could not sing soul, that idiom being the exclusive realm of black artists.

The Righteous Brothers proved otherwise. "You've Lost That Lovin' Feelin' " transcended musical or racial categorization. Hatfield and Medley sang with a power and emotional intensity that were soulful by any estimation, while the overall sound of Spector's production was essentially rock-based.

The record's success proved to have a liberating affect on musicians and the music business. Over the course of the rest of the 1960s, young white rock groups increasingly tried their hands at soul music, and record companies were receptive to what they were offering. In 1966, the Young Rascals topped the charts with their rock-soul song, "Good Lovin'." That same year, Mitch Ryder and the Detroit Wheels charted at number four with their signature hit "Devil with a Blue Dress On & Good Golly Miss Molly."

Similarly, soul artists began to delve into rock. In 1966, Otis Redding hit the charts with his version of the Rolling Stones' "(I Can't Get No) Satisfaction." And in 1969, Wilson Pickett released a soulful rendition of the Beatles' "Hey Jude." That same year, Dionne Warwick hit the top 20 with her version of "You've Lost That Lovin' Feelin'."

In subsequent decades, the "blue-eyed soul" pioneered by the Righteous Brothers would become a major facet of the rock scene. In the 1970s, Hall and Oates created their own fusion of rock and soul in a vast series of hits. In the '80s, groups like Culture Club and Spandau Ballet would add the electronic flourishes of techno-rock to their soul-inflected

music. And vocalists like Paul Young and Simply Red's Mick Hucknall were soul vocalists of the first order, blue-eyed or otherwise. The Righteous Brothers continued to make the point themselves on a series of hits during the mid-'60s, proving that soul music wasn't a matter of skin color but a state of mind and feeling.

Ironically, and fittingly, the Righteous Brothers got their professional name from black audiences. When Hatfield (b. Aug. 10, 1940, Beaver Dam, Wisconsin) and Medley (b. Sept. 19, 1940, Santa Ana, California) began performing as a duo at the Black Derby club in Santa Ana in 1962, their singing was dubbed "righteous" by the black Marines who came by to hear them. They adopted the word as their stage name. Signed to the Moonglow label, the Righteous Brothers made their record debut with the Medley-written single "Little Latin Lupe Lu," which hit number 49 in 1963.

In 1964, they came to the attention of Spector, who saw them perform as part of a package tour at San Francisco's Cow Palace. Negotiating a deal with Moonglow, Spector signed the duo to his Phillies label, making them the label's first white act. He also commissioned the songwriting team of Barry Mann and Cynthia Weil to provide them with new material.

The Righteous Brothers came to the attention of the rock public in 1964 through their appearances on the Beatles' U.S. tour and their performance on the weekly ABC rock television program "Shindig!"

With the release of "You've Lost That Lovin' Feelin' " in December, the Righteous Brothers became a major rock act. Topping the charts in the U.S. and the U.K., the record was hailed as a classic by many at the time. It would subsequently be rereleased and make the charts at various points during the next two decades.

Over the course of 1965 and 1966, the Righteous Brothers charted with numerous songs based on the soul-rock fusion they had created with the visionary Spector.

TOP ALBUMS

YOU'VE LOST THAT LOVIN' FEELIN'
(Philles, '65, 4)
RIGHT NOW! (Moonglow, '65, 11)
JUST ONCE IN MY LIFE (Philles, '65, 9)
SOUL & INSPIRATION (Verve, '66, 7)

Additional Top 40 Albums: 6

TOP SONGS

YOU'VE LOST THAT LOVIN' FEELIN'
(Philles, '64, 1)
JUST ONCE IN MY LIFE (Philles, '65, 9)
UNCHAINED MELODY (Philles, '65, 4)
EBB TIDE (Philles, '65, 5)
(YOU'RE MY) SOUL AND INSPIRATION
(Verve, '66, 1)
ROCK AND ROLL HEAVEN (Haven, '74, 3)

Additional Top 40 Songs: 6

"Just Once in My Life," "Unchained Melody," and "Ebb Tide" all made the top 10 in 1965. At the end of the year, Spector ended his work with the duo to devote time to his next act, Ike and Tina Turner. But the Righteous Brothers carried on, with Medley producing what would be their next hit. With its big, brash sound and the Brothers' soulful vocals, 1966's "(You're My) Soul and Inspiration" topped the charts and became as much a signature song as "You've Lost That Lovin' Feelin'."

Subsequent singles made the charts in 1967. But in 1968, Medley left the duo to pursue a solo career. Hatfield formed a new version of the Righteous Brothers with Jimmy Walker, formerly of the Knickerbockers.

But neither the new duo nor Medley's solo career managed to equal the success and popularity of the original Righteous Brothers.

In 1974, Hatfield and Medley reunited and returned to form with their number three rock novelty hit "Rock 'n' Roll Heaven." That same year, the title cut from their album *Give It to the People* made number 20. But the duo soon went their separate ways.

The Righteous Brothers didn't fade entirely from the rock world. They reunited briefly in 1982 for an appearance on Dick Clark's television show commemorating the 39th anniversary of "American Bandstand." And in the 1990s, they made cameo appearances, separately, on the television series "Cheers." Medley also continued his solo career and in 1987 hit the top of the charts with "(I've Had) The Time of My Life," a duet with Jennifer Warnes that was included in the soundtrack of the film *Dirty Dancing*. In 1988, the duo won a Grammy Award for Best Pop Performance.

The group's old hits also refused to go away. In 1986, "You've Lost That Lovin' Feelin' " was included in the soundtrack of the film *Top Gun* and was released as the B side to Berlin's "Take My Breath Away" (the film's theme song). And in 1990, "Unchained Melody" created vast new popular interest in the group when it was given a musical role in the film *Ghost*.

With the visibility provided by these films, the music of the Righteous Brothers proved to be as popular with new generations of rock fans as it had been in the group's halcyon days in the 1960s.

THE ROLLING STONES

The Rolling Stones were almost universally referred to as "the world's greatest rock and roll band." It was a cliché, to be certain; but it was also true.

While the Beatles and Elvis Presley were otherworldly creatures who transcended rock and roll and were thus divorced from much of its reality, the Stones basked in that reality, relished it, and ultimately transformed it.

At the core of all rock and roll was the notion that people could do what they wanted, when they wanted, and how they wanted, and the rest of the world be damned. More than any other rock artist or group, the Rolling Stones epitomized that idea in their music, look, attitude, and behavior. They continuously followed their rebellious course and got away with it. In the process, they became the most important rock group of the 1960s next to the Beatles and one of the most artistically and commercially successful rock groups of all time.

It began with their sound. When the Rolling Stones first made their way into the fledgling R&B

The Rolling Stones

scene of London with their engagement at the Craw-daddy Club in 1963, their music changed the course of that scene and of rock and roll.

At the time, the general opinion was that white men couldn't play the blues. But the Rolling Stones wanted to—and they did.

Mick Jagger didn't sing quite like Muddy Waters. Keith Richards' two-note chords weren't exactly like those of Chuck Berry. Brian Jones barely approximated the slide guitar of Elmore James. And bassist Bill Wyman and drummer Charlie Watts, while steady, added little new to the role of the rhythm section.

The Stones didn't attempt to replicate the blues faithfully; they simply played it the way they felt it. But the result was a reinvention of the form, injected with their own national and cultural sensibilities.

The Stones popularized R&B and the blues even as they changed the nature of rock. Their music and success inspired a new generation of British rockers—from Steve Winwood to Eric Clapton, Pete Townshend, and the rest—to try their hand at this new amalgam of sounds. It was music that would vastly influence future rock generations.

When Jagger and Richards began to write original songs, they produced many of the classics of the rock repertoire. "The Last Time," "Get Off of My Cloud," "19th Nervous Breakdown," and "(I Can't Get No) Satisfaction"—arguably the finest rock single in history—all animated the mid-'60s and defined the era.

Along the way, the Stones' music evolved and matured. On the 1967 hit "Ruby Tuesday," Brian Jones augmented the group's sound with keyboards, cellos, and a recorder. The 1967 album *Their Satanic Majesties Request* presented a harder-edged version of the psychedelic music pioneered by the Beatles. On the 1968 single "Jumpin' Jack Flash,"

Richards created jagged guitar lines that would define much of the rock of the '70s. Throughout, Wyman and Watts displayed a solid, distinctive sound that made them one of the finest rhythm sections in all of rock.

But the Stones were, significantly, far more than a strictly musical force. Their look and attitude added to their impact.

The Rolling Stones were the first rock group to appear onstage dressed in street clothes. At the time, such a sight was revolutionary. Rock groups wore uniforms on stage; that was that. But the Stones didn't. Never before or since in the history of music has the sight of a rubber-lipped London boy in a T-shirt cavorting about a stage so shocked or galvanized the world.

Abetted by the active contrivance of their manager, Andrew Loog Oldham, the Stones also created a "bad boy" image that was the polar opposite of the wholesome personas of the Beatles and their imitators. The Beatles had long hair; the Stones' was longer. The Beatles were cuddly; the Stones were "the ugliest group in pop." The Beatles were knighted by the Queen; the Rolling Stones were arrested for urinating on the walls of a gas station. The Beatles had wives and girlfriends; the Stones had women—decadent, sexy women like Marianne Faithfull and Anita Pallenberg—who became adjuncts to their legend.

In later years, rock revisionists would claim that rock fans of the 1960s sided either with the Beatles or the Stones. It was nonsense. In fact, fans of the time loved both groups simultaneously. It was the opposing forces of both group's images and sounds that generated much of the era's excitement.

But there was a dark side to the Stones' excessive and rebellious lives. And in those, as well, they came to symbolize certain aspects of rock and roll. In 1967, Jagger and Richards (and Jones, in a separate case) became the first major rockers of their time to be arrested for possession of drugs. Their cases made international headlines that at once shocked the establishment and titillated the rock world.

But the Stones always pressed on. While the Beatles, the Who, and other '60s groups eventually disbanded, the Stones—in what could be seen as their ultimate act of rebellion—kept going and going. More than 30 years into their career, they were still active. And though their revolutionary days were apparently over and their music was once again only rock and roll, everyone continued to like it.

The origins of the Rolling Stones' career began when boyhood friends Jagger (b. Michael Philip Jagger, July 26, 1943, Dartford, Kent, England) and Richards (b. Dec. 18, 1943, Dartford) met up again on a train in 1960. Renewing their friendship, they discovered that they shared an interest in American blues and R&B.

Over the succeeding two years, they began to move in the fledgling R&B scene of London, playing in various groups that were coalescing around the "guv'nor" of the scene, Alexis Korner. In 1962, through Korner's group, Blues Incorporated, they came into contact with Jones (b. Lewis Brian Hopkin-Jones, Feb. 28, 1942, Cheltenham, Gloucester, England), who played slide guitar with the group on an occasional basis. He in turn introduced them to pianist Ian Stewart.

Jagger, Richards, and Jones played in Blues Incorporated at various points along with drummer Charlie Watts (b. Charles Robert Watts, June 2, 1941, Islington, London). By 1963, the group, calling itself the Rollin' Stones (based on Muddy Waters' "The Rollin' Stone Blues"), had recruited bassist Wyman (b. William Perks, Oct. 24, 1936, Lewisham, London). They began to perform as a sextet with Stewart on piano.

In April of that year, they began their legendary engagement at the Crawdaddy Club in London, where they established themselves as key participants in the R&B scene. It was there that they were seen by Andrew Loog Oldham and his partner Eric Easton, who became their managers. Oldham and

TOP ALBUMS

OUT OF OUR HEADS (London, '65, 1)
STICKY FINGERS (Rolling Stones, '71, 1)
EXILE ON MAIN ST. (Rolling Stones, '72, 1)
GOATS HEAD SOUP (Rolling Stones, '73, 1)
IT'S ONLY ROCK 'N ROLL (Rolling Stones, '74, 1)

Additional Top 40 Albums: 28

TOP SONGS

(I CAN'T GET NO) SATISFACTION (London, '65, 1)
PAINT IT, BLACK (London, '66, 1)
RUBY TUESDAY (London, '67, 1)
HONKY TONK WOMEN (Rolling Stones, '69, 1)
ANGIE (Rolling Stones, '73, 1)

Additional Top 40 Songs: 36

Easton negotiated a contract with Impact Records, which leased the group's music to Decca. At that point, Oldham suggested that the group change its name, slightly, to the Rolling Stones. He also began to nurture the rebellious image that would distinguish the group from the Beatles. At his suggestion, Stewart was dropped from the group because of his "straight" appearance. (He subsequently played on the group's records and became its road manager. Stewart died in 1985.)

The Stones' debut single, a version of the obscure Chuck Berry song "Come On," was released on June 7, 1963. It eventually reached number 21 on the U.K. charts and generated much attention in the British rock scene. Its follow-up was a churning, R&B-inflected version of "I Wanna Be Your Man," written by John Lennon and Paul McCartney. That single peaked at number 12 in the U.K..

The group toured constantly and saw their popularity begin to mushroom. When the Stones' eponymous debut album was released in May 1964, it topped the British charts (and later in the year, under the title *England's Newest Hitmakers—The Rolling Stones*, hit number 11 in the U.S.). From that album, a version of Buddy Holly's "Not Fade Away" charted in the U.K. at number three.

With its success in the U.K. established, the group staged its debut tour of the U.S. in June 1964. Largely a fiasco, it nonetheless created a growing body of stateside fans.

The Stones recorded mostly cover versions of songs during 1964, including renditions of Bobby Womack's "It's All Over Now" and Willie Dixon's "Little Red Rooster." But Jagger and Richards, at Oldham's insistence, began to write their own songs.

In 1965, the Stones released two originals, which became musical signatures and rock classics. "The Last Time" charted at number nine in the U.S. while its follow-up, the epochal "(I Can't Get No) Satisfaction," hit Number One.

Those records the made the Stones international stars. They responded with "Get Off of My Cloud" in 1965 and "19th Nervous Breakdown," "Paint It Black," "Mother's Little Helper," and "Have You Seen Your Mother, Baby, Standing in the Shadow?" in 1966.

"Ruby Tuesday" topped the U.S. charts in 1967. But the group spent months of that year defending itself in court after a drug bust, which nearly demolished its career.

When the next album, *Their Satanic Majesties Request,* proved to be a musical disappointment, Oldham was dismissed, and dissension began to develop between Jones and the rest of the group over the Stones' musical direction.

The group rebounded in 1968 with one of its greatest singles, "Jumpin' Jack Flash," and one of its finest albums, *Beggars Banquet.* But Jones, beset by drug problems and concerned about his diminishing role in the group, left the Stones in June 1969. On July 3, 1969, he drowned in the pool at his country house.

Jones was then replaced by blues virtuoso Mick Taylor (b. Michael Taylor, Jan. 17, 1948, Welwyn Garden City, Hertfordshire, England), who was recruited from John Mayall's Bluesbreakers. Taylor made his debut with the Stones at a concert at London's Hyde Park on July 5th before a crowd of 250,000. But the success of that concert was countered by an incident at Altamont, California, on December 6th, in which one of the fans in attendance was murdered in front of the stage while the Stones performed. (It would subsequently serve as a focal point of *Gimme Shelter,* the 1970 documentary of the Stones' tour.)

With Taylor, the Stones began to pursue a more rock-oriented sound that was soon heard on the group's outstanding 1969 album, *Let It Bleed.* That new sound would form the basis of much of the Stones' output during the early 1970s.

In fact, Taylor never seemed entirely compatible with the Stones, and his tenure with the group during the early '70s proved to be a creative nadir (with the possible exception of 1972's *Exile on Main St.*). In 1974, Taylor quit the group.

Ron Wood (b. June 1, 1947, Hillington, London) was recruited from the Faces to fill the vacancy.

Just as the Stones were being surpassed by the burgeoning punk scene, they rebounded with the 1978 album *Some Girls,* which reestablished them as one of the finest groups in rock. 1980's *Emotional Rescue* and 1981's *Tattoo You* were nearly as satisfying; all three albums topped the U.S. charts.

As the '80s progressed, the Stones settled into their personal lives and released a series of mediocre albums, including 1983's *Undercover* and 1986's *Dirty Work.* But in 1989 they came back with *Steel Wheels* and its spectacular tour, proving that they could still make rock of substance. In that same year, they were inducted into the Rock and Roll Hall of Fame. And in 1991, they signed a contract with Virgin Records reportedly worth $20 million.

ROXY MUSIC

When Roxy Music was formed in 1970, the rock world was in a befuddled state due, in large part, to the breakup of the Beatles.

At opposite ends of the decibel and sensitivity scale, the heavy metallists and the singer-songwriters were vying for dominance while, in the middle, the roots-rock movement exemplified by Creedence Clearwater Revival was trying to reassert rock's timeless virtues.

Roxy Music was none of the above. In fact, the group reflected rock's ambivalence in a way that made it one of the more distinctive and eccentric bands of its time.

Roxy Music didn't have a "sound" in any readily definable sense. Nor was it a part of any specific movement. Instead, it operated within the rather amorphous and uncategorized confines of its own curious vision.

That vision was translated into an arch, highly mannered version of rock that included everything from '50s accents to avant-garde washes of sound and traces of '40s pop. Vocalist Bryan Ferry had a melodic pop sensibility that was countered by a cynical, parodistic edge. Guitarist Phil Manzanera and saxophonist Andy Mackay worked convoluted lines into a dense wall of sound that was distorted and refracted by the electronic keyboards and musical "treatments" of Brian Eno.

When their various and sundry musical predilections—backed by drummer Paul Thompson and an assortment of bassists over the years—were injected into a single song or album, the result was a carefully controlled musical anarchy of a sort: nihilistic music for a directionless rock period.

Emblematic of that approach was one of the group's early signature songs, "Do the Strand." A savage slap at the dance records of the 1950s and '60s, the song came with Ferry spitting out oddly literate lyrics with a vocal sneer while the group unleashed a blaring, almost atonal barrage of sound. There were also hints of mangled fandango rhythms and crooner-like vocal inflections that gave the song an unmistakable feeling of artificiality and decadence.

That feeling was extended to the group's image. Onstage, Ferry slithered and preened like a lounge lizard. Dressed in a tuxedo and with his hair deftly slicked back, he looked like James Bond on assignment in the rock world. Behind his myriad electronic gadgets, Eno affected a glam-rock glitz and flash.

The group's album covers displayed a similar decadence. Most of them came with garish photos of scantily clad women in pinup poses or nature girls cavorting in bras and panties amid fake foliage. None of these had the slightest connection with the music, which was probably the point. It was all part of the group's eccentric, iconoclastic attitude.

That music did evolve over the years. The mannered if alluring rock of the group's debut single, "Virginia Plain," was expanded to include the electronic experiments of Eno, which were strongly influenced by the music of classical avant-gardists John Cage and Terry Riley. They were particularly prevalent on the group's second album, *For Your Pleasure,* in 1973. When Eno left the group that year, he was replaced by keyboardist-violinist Eddie Jobson, whose more melodic contrivances complemented Ferry's own pop sensibilities. This newer approach was maintained on album such as 1973's *Stranded,* 1974's *Siren,* and 1975's *Country Life.*

Over the years, Roxy Music developed a sleek, shimmering rock sound that was an inspired blend of the stark imagery of its early days and a seamless instrumental elegance. That sound—which Ferry would subsequently pursue in his successful solo career on the albums *Boys and Girls, Bette Noir,* and *Taxi* in the 1980s and '90s—emerged on 1982's "More than This" and its remarkable album, *Avalon,* from the same year.

Roxy Music's vision was so distinctive and singular that it did not spawn legions of imitators. However, aspects of its later sound were adopted by such quasi-techno groups as Tears for Fears, Simple Minds, and others.

But Roxy Music's significance mostly resided in its musical state of mind. At a time when rock was becoming increasingly fragmented and simplistic, Roxy Music was an oasis of intellectual élan and creative ferment. Its complex and contradictory music proved that rock could still be a forum for disparate and expressive ideas, that it could still engage the mind as well as the ears.

Roxy Music was formed by Ferry (b. Sept. 26, 1945, Washington, Tyne and Wear, England) and bassist Graham Simpson at the end of 1970. In 1971, Mackay (b. July 23, 1946, London) and Eno (b. May 15, 1948, Woodbridge, Suffolk, England) were added to the lineup along with drummer Dexter Lloyd. Guitarist David O'List, formerly of the Nice, also joined the group for a brief time.

By February 1973, Simpson, Lloyd, and O'List had departed and Manzanera (b. Philip Targett-Adams Manzanera, Jan. 31, 1951, London) and Thompson (b. May 13, 1951, Jarrow, Tyne and Wear, England) had been added, and Roxy Music's classic lineup was in place.

Roxy Music was an almost immediate success in the U.K. Following a number of acclaimed appearances during the first part of 1972, the group released its eponymous debut album in August. Hailed by critics, the album made number 10 on the charts, and the debut single, "Virginia Plain" (not

included on the album), reached number four.

The hits continued apace into 1973 when the single "Pyjamarama" and the album *For Your Pleasure* both reached number 10. But dissension began to emerge between Ferry and Eno over the direction of the group, the former favoring a more pop-oriented approach and the latter preferring an avant-garde course. Eno departed the group in July 1973 to pursue a solo career that would yield a vast and influential body of provocative work.

Ferry then assumed command of the group and, with Jobson on board in a more traditional keyboard role (augmented by his violin), Roxy Music rolled on. In December 1973, its album *Stranded* (with *Playboy* magazine's Playmate of the Year on its cover) topped the U.K. charts.

The rest of the initial phase of the group's career—which ended when it disbanded in 1976—was marked by remarkable success in the U.K. and Europe, its albums and singles consistently reaching the upper levels of the charts. The U.S., however, proved to be somewhat ambivalent about the group's charms: Roxy Music's cerebral approach was mostly too subtle to make itself heard amid the disco beats that were mesmerizing the U.S. at the time.

Along the way, Roxy's central members began to pursue solo careers that were maintained in tandem with that of the group. In 1973, Ferry released his solo debut album *These Foolish Things*. Mackay did the same in 1974 with the largely instrumental *In Search of Eddie Riff*. Later in the decade, Manzanera released *Diamond Head*, performed with his former group Quiet Sun, and collaborated with Eno in 801, which released the remarkable concert album *801 Live*.

At the end of 1978, Ferry, Mackay, Manzanera, and Thompson reunited (with numerous other musicians joining on an interim basis). They subsequently released the more accessible if no less musically intriguing albums *Manifesto, Flesh + Blood,* and *Avalon* (the latter recorded without Thompson, who had quit by that time).

Avalon proved to be the group's last studio record. It was also its masterpiece. The album's sleek, melodic sound and incisive lyrics displayed the sophistication that had distinguished Roxy Music's work over the years. Songs such as "More than This," "Take a Chance on Me," and others had an elegance and an intellectual edge that separated Roxy Music from many of its rock contemporaries.

Roxy Music

TOP ALBUMS

COUNTRY LIFE
(Atco, '75, 37)
MANIFESTO
(Atco, '79, 23)
FLESH + BLOOD
(Atco, '80, 35)

TOP SONG

LOVE IS THE DRUG
(Atco, '75, 30)

SANTANA

· · · · · · · · · · · · · · · · · · ·

Santana—the group
and its guitarist, Carlos Santana—brought the fire and
fervor of Latin music to the world of rock and roll.

Before the group emerged on the rock scene in 1969, rock and roll had flirted with Latin music but never fully embraced it. In 1958, Ritchie Valens had enjoyed a major hit with "La Bamba," his rocking version of a traditional Mexican wedding song. Rick Nelson had included Latin-inflected rhythms in his 1963 version of Glenn Miller's "Fools Rush In." Traffic provided a pastiche of the genre on the song "The Dealer" from its 1967 debut album. And Peter Green, the British guitar virtuoso, employed Latin-flavored, minor-keyed phrasings in his blues-based work with John Mayall and, most notably, on the ballad "Black Magic Woman," which he recorded with Fleetwood Mac.

But none of these, or any of the various other Latin-tinged songs in the rock repertoire, even hinted at the power and rhythmic complexity that were at the core of Latin music.

When Santana appeared at the Woodstock festival in 1969, its new Latin-based rock sound was something of a revelation. The group's performance (particularly on the song "Soul Sacrifice," which was captured in the 1970 album and film of the event) galvanized the rock crowd. Drummer Michael Shrieve and percussionists Mike Carabello and Jose Chepito Areas pounded out furious rhythms that boiled under Carlos Santana's lithe, soaring guitar solos.

That performance, one of the most electrifying in the history of rock, immediately propelled Santana to the forefront of the rock scene. Over the next few years, their success was reflected in the *Billboard* charts. By November of 1969, the group's eponymous debut album had hit number four and sold more than one million copies. In 1970, the single "Evil Ways" (from the debut album) reached number nine; the second album, *Abraxas,* topped the

charts for six weeks and sold more than a million copies. In 1971, their version of "Black Magic Woman" made number four, and the album *Santana III* hit Number One.

Like the British musicians of the 1960s who had created a new amalgam of rock and blues (and popularized the older idiom in the process), Santana took the rhythms and melodic textures of Latin music and set them in an energized rock context. Its sound, to rock listeners at any rate, was new and surprising but also accessible and familiar.

The slamming, rolling congas, timbales, and other percussive instruments formed the core of the sound, with drummer Shrieve providing a rock beat that anchored the more complex rhythmic flourishes. But the group's focal point was Carlos Santana.

One of the true virtuosos of rock guitar, the Mexican-born Santana was the bridge between the rock and Latin sounds. His solos were imbued with the minor-keyed melodicism of Latin music and the more raucous, earthier expressions of rock and blues. Much of his phrasing and intonation were drawn from the work of Eric Clapton and Peter Green, but he used their musical signatures as points of departure for his own singular expressions. He wailed and screamed his solos like a blues-rocker, then at times resolved them with eloquent, Latin-based counter themes that were articulate reminders of his musical and cultural background.

Over the course of 25 years, Santana the musician came to personify Santana the group. During that time, 17 musicians moved in and out of Santana's lineup (with scores of others participating on a one-off basis for recordings or tours). But Carlos Santana was the constant, the leader whose vision guided and directed the evolution of its sound.

Santana

That vision was not limited to Latin music. Santana displayed a voracious musical appetite over the years, constantly seeking out new influences. In the early 1970s he became increasingly interested in the improvisational aspects of jazz, which he infused into the group's 1972 album, *Caravanserai*.

The next year, Santana became a devotee of religious mystic Sri Chinmoy and assumed the name Devadip, which translated into "the light of the lamp of the Supreme."

Along with fellow Chinmoy follower John McLaughlin, the jazz-rock fusion master, Santana recorded the album *Love Devotion Surrender,* in which he displayed new guitar lines modeled on the modal motifs of legendary jazz saxophonist John Coltrane. That album gave way to 1974's *Illuminations,* a more complex, jazz-inflected set in which he collaborated with Alice Coltrane. That same year, he combined his interest in rock, jazz, and Latin music on *Borboletta*.

Recording and performing with the group and as a solo artist, Santana pursued his musical interests with an idealistic eclecticism and abandon that never waned over the years. In the later 1970s, he temporarily resumed a more rock-oriented course and, with the group, recorded versions of Buddy Holly's "Well All Right" and the Zombies' "She's Not There." In the 1980s, he got back into jazz on the album *The Swing of Delight*. In 1983, his solo album *Havana Moon* included collaborations with Willie Nelson, Booker T. Jones, and the Fabulous Thunderbirds. And in 1989, he contributed to the album *The Healer* by the venerated blues master John Lee Hooker.

While Santana's music and guitar work never strayed entirely from their Latin roots, both evolved over the decades as he expanded his musical vision and tastes.

Santana began not as a Latin-rock group but as the Santana Blues Band when it was originally formed in San Francisco in 1966. Santana (b. July 20, 1947, Autlan de Navarro, Mexico) teamed with keyboardist Gregg Rolie, guitarist Tom Frazer, drummer Rod Harper, and bassist David Brown in a group that began to play around the Bay Area. During 1967, they began to develop the Latin sound that would become their signature.

Frazer and Harper soon quit the lineup. Drummer Shrieve and percussionists Carabello and Areas joined, and the group shortened its name to Santana.

With its new sound and personnel, the group debuted in 1968 at the legendary Fillmore Auditorium in San Francisco. It began to make a name for itself at various rock festivals in the U.S. and was signed by Columbia Records in 1969.

Amid a number of successes, including the 1969 Woodstock performance, Santana's lineup began to fluctuate, a trend that would mark the group's entire career. By 1971, Brown, Areas, and Carabello had departed and guitarist Neal Schon had joined. That group soon disbanded, but various members continued to work with Carlos Santana while other musicians entered and departed the group on a steady basis. (Schon and Rolie would subsequently form the arena-rock group Journey, which became one of the most commercially successful rock acts of the 1970s.)

Carlos Santana began to pursue a solo career in parallel with his involvement in the group. In 1972, he recorded the album *Carlos Santana and Buddy Miles Live!* with the rock drummer-vocalist, hitting number eight on the charts. In 1976, he participated in Bob Dylan's "Rolling Thunder Revue."

The jazz-oriented direction of his albums with McLaughlin and Coltrane carried over into his work with new Santana incarnations. Albums such as 1973's *Welcome* and 1975's *Lotus* were imbued with jazz-fusion accents applied to a Latin-rock sound.

Festival (1977) and *Inner Secrets* (1978) both offered a return to rock. But in 1979, he released the jazz-inflected instrumental solo album *Oneness/Silver Dreams*. And the following year's *The Swing of Delight* was a full-fledged jazz work that came with performances by keyboardist Herbie Hancock, bassist Ron Carter, and saxophonist Wayne Shorter.

During this period, Santana's popularity proved remarkably durable. Most of the group's albums and Santana's solo projects consistently ranked in the upper levels of the charts, and their tours in the U.S. and various countries (particularly Western Europe) were greeted with acclaim by critics and fans.

Over the course of the 1980s and into the '90's, Santana remained one of the major acts in rock. In 1982, the group appeared before 400,000 rock fans at the US Festival in San Bernardino, California. On July 4, 1987, they took part in one of the first big rock festivals to be staged in the Soviet Union, performing in Moscow with the Doobie Brothers, James Taylor, Bonnie Raitt, and various Soviet groups.

In 1989, Santana's solo album *Blues for Salvador* won a Grammy Award for Best Rock Instrumental Performance.

Over the course of their long and distinguished career, Santana maintained a sense of musical integrity that transcended trends and tastes. Carlos Santana was a musician's musician, and his group was a musician's band. It was that legacy that proved to be as enduring as the Latin-rock sound he and his group had initially pioneered in rock and roll.

TOP ALBUMS

SANTANA (Columbia, '69, 4)
ABRAXAS (Columbia, '70, 1)
SANTANA III (Columbia, '71, 1)
CARAVANSERAI (Columbia, '72, 8)
AMIGOS (Columbia, '76, 10)
MOONFLOWER (Columbia, '77, 10)
ZEBOP! (Columbia, '81, 9)

Additional Top 40 Albums: 7

TOP SONGS

EVIL WAYS (Columbia, '70, 9)
BLACK MAGIC WOMAN
   (Columbia, '70, 4)
EVERYBODY'S EVERYTHING
   (Columbia, '71, 12)

Additional Top 40 Songs: 7

NEIL SEDAKA

Neil Sedaka symbolized an era in rock history that was often unjustly dismissed as a dark age, a time of trivial music purveyed by innocuous teen stars, "girl groups," and other pop-oriented artists.

In fact, that era—roughly the years between the decline of the original rock pioneers in the late 1950s and the advent of the Beatles and the rest of the British Invasion in 1964—was a time of remarkable musical activity. It was a relatively benign period in which rock and roll retreated from rebellion and instead became an expression of the joys and cares of teen life and love. While the era and its artists had none of the raucous excitement of rock's founders or the musical grandeur and expansiveness of the later '60s, it did produce a stunning series of records that became rock classics.

Sedaka's career was emblematic of the music and musical attitude that pervaded his rock era. On record and onstage, he exuded a winsome, carefree exuberance and youthful charm that were the antithesis of the wild, sexually charged music and images of Elvis Presley, Chuck Berry, Little Richard, and the rest.

Clean-cut and cleaner sounding, Sedaka wasn't a rock and roll rebel; he was a pop artist who substituted sincerity for passion and a pimply romanticism for burning love. Little Richard sang "Rip It Up"; Sedaka warbled "I Go Ape." Presley checked into "Heartbreak Hotel"; Sedaka climbed a "Stairway to Heaven."

In his onstage performances, he was similarly "clean." He didn't shake, rattle, and roll, swivel his hips, or kick over a piano stool. Instead, he simply sang his songs in much the same way as generations of pop performers before him, straight and unadorned of poses save for a winning and charming smile and, perhaps, the odd dance move to prove that he was "with it."

But if Sedaka was hardly the greatest vocalist or performer in the history of rock, it was hardly important. It was his songs that mattered. With his longtime partner, lyricist Howard Greenfield, Sedaka created a body of work that reaffirmed and cemented rock's role as the music of the young. On such hits as "Calendar Girl," "Happy Birthday, Sweet Sixteen," "Breaking Up Is Hard to Do," and scores of others, Sedaka and Greenfield expressed the excitement and innocence of love the first time around with an ebullience that was timeless.

On these songs and others, Sedaka's melodies were instantly memorable, just as Greenfield's lyrics had a sophistication that belied their overtly teen-based topics. While their songs were set in a rock and roll context, Sedaka and Greenfield were actually traditionalists whose music was endowed with the same craftmanship and professionalism that had characterized the songwriting greats of the 1930s and '40s.

Which was as it should have been, given the fact that Sedaka and Greenfield were, in the truest sense, professionals. They were one of several songwriting teams that were part of the Brill Building scene that flourished in New York in the late 1950s and early '60s.

The Brill Building was as much a musical movement as a specific address (1619 Broadway, to be exact). Its songwriters came to symbolize a new form of rock, one that was based on professionally crafted songs as opposed to wild, rebellious rock heroes whose images and actions were often as important as their music. The songwriters of the Brill Building attempted to fit rock into the pop mainstream, or at the very least, to rein in rock's excesses and make it a durable commercial and creative form.

At the core of the Brill Building "movement" was the stable of songwriters who were employed—literally—by Al Nevins and Don Kirshner as part of their company, Aldon Music. During the aforementioned transitional years in rock (Aldon was formed in 1958), the company's songwriters created a vast series of hits that virtually defined the rock of the time and spanned the yawning stylistic gap between the sleek, sophisticated Tin Pan Alley era and the rock epoch.

The list of hits by these songwriting teams is astonishing, both in its quantity and quality. Gerry Goffin and Carole King composed "Will You Love

---

TOP SONGS

OH! CAROL (RCA, '59, 9)
STAIRWAY TO HEAVEN (RCA, '60, 9)
CALENDAR GIRL (RCA, '60, 4)
LITTLE DEVIL (RCA, '61, 11)
HAPPY BIRTHDAY, SWEET SIXTEEN (RCA, '61, 6)
BREAKING UP IS HARD TO DO (RCA, '62, 1)
NEXT DOOR TO AN ANGEL (RCA, '62, 5)
LAUGHTER IN THE RAIN (Rocket, '74, 1)
BAD BLOOD (Rocket, '75, 1)
BREAKING UP IS HARD TO DO (Rocket, '75, 8)

Additional Top 40 Songs: 11

Me Tomorrow" (recorded by the Shirelles), "Take Good Care of My Baby" (Bobby Vee), "The Loco-Motion" (Little Eva), and "Up on the Roof" (the Drifters), among many others. Barry Mann and Cynthia Weil contributed "Uptown" (the Crystals), "Walking in the Rain" (the Ronettes), and "You've Lost That Lovin' Feeling" (the Righteous Brothers), again, among many others.

The Brill Building "sound" also inspired, and came to be associated with, songwriting teams that were not employed by Aldon. Among them were Jeff Barry and Ellie Greenwich, who composed such hits as "Da Doo Ron Ron" (the Crystals), "Be My Baby" (the Ronettes), and the girl-group masterpiece "Leader of the Pack" (the Shangri-Las). Doc Pomus and Mort Shuman wrote a number of classics, including "Teenager in Love" (Dion and the Belmonts) and "Hushabye" (the Mystics).

These Brill Building songwriting teams were musical journeymen—and women—who went to work in their offices and churned out a constant sup-

ply of songs for other artists (although writer Carole King would gain recognition as a soloist in the 1970s, starting with her album *Tapestry*).

Sedaka and Greenfield differed from the rest in that regard. They wrote most of their songs not for other artists but for Sedaka. It proved to be a notably fortuitous decision. In the initial phase of Sedaka's career, from 1958 to 1963, his records hit the top 40 13 times. In the process, Sedaka came to symbolize the sound and songs that made the Brill Building scene a key part of rock and roll history.

Sedaka (b. Mar. 13, 1939, Brooklyn, New York) had been classically trained as a pianist since age nine. At 16, he teamed up with his Lincoln High School friend Greenfield, and the two began writing songs. At the same time, Sedaka became romantically involved with another student, Carole Klein (King), for whom he and Greenfield would later write the song "Oh! Carol."

Sedaka was awarded a scholarship to the Juilliard School of Music in New York in 1957, but he and Greenfield continued their songwriting efforts. In the following year, they came to the attention of Kirshner, who signed them to a songwriting contract with Aldon.

The team scored one of the Brill Building's first hits when "Stupid Cupid," recorded by Connie Francis, hit number 14 in 1958. But the duo's career took a new course when Nevins played a demo of their song "The Diary" for RCA executive Steve Scholes at the end of the year. RCA signed Sedaka to a recording contract.

His career got off to an encouraging start with "The Diary," a number 14 hit in February 1959. In May, the rocking "I Go Ape" went to number 42, and in December, "Oh! Carol" hit number nine.

Over the course of the next four years, Sedaka became a major star, scoring hits, penning classics, and establishing himself as a songwriter and performer of the first order.

But like most of the other rock artists of the 1950s and early '60s, Sedaka was eclipsed by the Beatles and the new generation of rock that emerged in 1964. He retreated from the scene for the rest of the decade and into the '70s. His popularity remained strong in the U.K., however, and in 1972, he and his family moved to London. That move also marked the end of his partnership with Greenfield. Sedaka found a new lyricist in Phil Cody.

Recording with a backup group that would subsequently become 10cc, Sedaka released the albums

Neil Sedaka

Solitaire and *The Tra-La Days Are Over*. While these albums failed to chart (they weren't released in the U.S.) they yielded several minor singles hits in the U.K. in 1972–73.

But Sedaka soon staged a major comeback. Signing with Elton John's Rocket label in 1975, he hit the top of the U.S. charts in February with the single "Laughter in the Rain," a million-plus seller. In September, his single "Bad Blood" (with John joining in on backing vocals) duplicated that chart success. And in December, a new version of "Breaking Up Is Hard to Do" hit number eight, becoming the only Number One U.S. hit to make a second appearance in the top 10 in a different version by the same artist.

He continued his career, with less success, through the rest of the decade and made his final appearance on the charts in 1980 with the single "Should've Never Let You Go," a duet with his daughter Dara. Sedaka subsequently became a performer on the oldies circuit, particularly in Las Vegas and Lake Tahoe. In 1987, he published his autobiography, *Laughter in the Rain*.

THE SEX PISTOLS

Just as rock was reaching its lowest creative ebb in the mid-1970s—with the Beatles a distant memory, others wallowing in ennui and excess, and the spandexed disco crowd slithering up the charts— out of the seething underclass of London came a brash young man with green teeth to rescue the day.

His name was Johnny Rotten, and his band was the Sex Pistols.

Spitting and swearing, dressed down in slashed shirts and swastikas, and spewing out the raunchiest rock this side of a garage, the Sex Pistols slapped the flabby, increasingly airbrushed rock world with a sound and an image that were seemingly anti-everything. In the process, they spawned the punk movement and triggered one of the three great revolutions—Presley and the Beatles accounting for the other two—in the history of rock and roll.

The Sex Pistols were an attitude as much as a musical style. Abetted by their iconoclastic manager, Malcolm McLaren, they set out to ravage the prevailing rock clichés of their day while inadvertently restoring some of the time-honored traditions of rockers past.

With violent, expletive-laced onstage performances that were as calculatedly incendiary as the hip swings of Elvis, and with ragged street clothes and spiked, tousled haircuts that were the equivalents, if polar opposites, of the Beatles' mop tops and collarless coats, the Sex Pistols created a new rock aesthetic.

The Sex Pistols couldn't be said to have founded their particular form of music. Like Presley and the Beatles, they emerged from a loose conglomeration of musicians who were pursuing a roughly similar artistic course. But what separated all three from their contemporaries was that they came to symbolize their movements to such an overwhelming extent that they virtually defined its image and sound.

The Sex Pistols' history—again like that of Presley and the Beatles—was shaped and guided by a dominant manager. In the Pistols' case, that role was filled by McLaren, a London boutique proprietor and self-styled social provocateur who developed their image and created much of the media-related frenzy that attended their career.

It was McLaren who was at the center of the group's ethos and formation. His clothing shop, Sex, was the Pistols' meeting ground, where original bassist Glen Matlock worked as an assistant and where Rotten auditioned for the band (as the story goes, by mimicking the words to Alice Cooper's "School's Out" on the store's jukebox). It was McLaren who gave John Lydon the name "Rotten" and helped originate the punk look and attitude via the outrageous clothes he sold in his store.

But the Sex Pistols were more than just a by-product of McLaren's social provocations. Formed in 1975, the group stormed onto the London scene in 1976 with a series of performances and incidents that immediately made them a seminal rock force. Onstage, Rotten (b. John Lydon, Jan. 31, 1956) shouted his vocals like a frenzied zealot, driving the crowds to fits of pogo dancing and random violence. Behind him, guitarist Steve Jones (b. Sept. 3, 1955, London), drummer Paul Cook (b. July 20, 1956, London), and Matlock (b. Aug. 27, 1956) cranked out a ragged, distorted, quasi-metal sound that was as much noise as music.

It wasn't a pretty sight or sound. In fact, it was all quite ugly. And that was the point.

Signed to music-biz monolith EMI, the Sex Pistols prepared to release their first single, "Anarchy in the UK," in late 1976. But almost immediately they became embroiled in a major controversy when members of the band began yelling obscenities on a British TV program. The ensuing uproar made them heroes to a new generation of English rock fans—and got them banned throughout the country.

The Sex Pistols

After being released by EMI, the Pistols were signed and dumped by A&M before they finally settled in at Virgin. In May 1977, they unleashed the single "God Save the Queen" (whose cover photo of Queen Elizabeth II with a safety pin sticking through her mouth created almost as much controversy as the song itself). The record was immediately banned by the BBC, and many record stores in the U.K. refused to stock it. But the single sold 150,000 copies in its first five days of release and hit number two on the U.K. charts.

The importance of "God Save the Queen" had less to do with chart success than with its impact on the burgeoning punk scene. The song's "No future!" refrain became a rallying cry for a new generation of British rock acts. While acts like the Clash, the Slits, and Siouxsie and the Banshees had distinctive sounds and images and would make their own contributions to the punk movement, each was an offspring of the Sex Pistols.

As the year progressed and the punk movement gained momentum, the Pistols released two subsequent singles, "Pretty Vacant" and "Holidays in the Sun," both of which made the U.K. top 10. In a rock atmosphere increasingly polluted by the clichés of Rod Stewart, Pink Floyd, and the like, the Sex Pistols' rantings were a revitalizing breath of foul air.

Much of that foulness was provided by the group's new bassist, the unlovely and talentless Sid Vicious (b. John Simon Ritchie, May 10, 1957, London), who had replaced Matlock in February 1977. If Rotten was as rotten as his name, Vicious was, well, vicious. Abusing himself chemically, physically, emotionally, and otherwise, both onstage and off, Vicious became the icon of punk nihilism.

Never had safety pins assumed such ominous implications.

All of that negative energy had to go somewhere. Thus, like legions of English rock bands before them, the Pistols pointed their barrels at the biggest rock target of them all: America. At the end of 1977, Warner Bros. released the group's debut album, *Never Mind the Bollocks, Here's the Sex Pistols,* and as the new year rolled in, the group embarked on a U.S. tour.

It was an unmitigated disaster.

Set adrift from the insular and supportive punk scene of London, the Pistols literally fought their way across the U.S., besieged not only by hordes of new punk fans but also by detractors who saw in the Sex Pistols the end of rock and roll.

Instead, the tour was the end of the Sex Pistols.

After a performance at the fabled Winterland in San Francisco, the Pistols flew to New York, where Rotten announced the group's breakup. The Sex Pistols had proved to be as self-destructive as their image. But matters got worse. Vicious was later arrested for the murder of his equally punkish girlfriend, Nancy Spungen, in New York. And before he could go to trial, he was found dead from a drug overdose.

Albums by the Sex Pistols would continue to be issued, but they were mostly drawn from tapes of live performances, interviews, and studio odds and ends. The disc and quasi-documentary film *The Great Rock 'n' Roll Swindle* were released in 1979, the former hitting number seven on the U.K. charts (it would be reissued on CD in the U.S. in 1992). That same year, the interview album *Some Product—Carry on Sex Pistols* reached number six in the U.K. The group's final set, *Flogging a Dead Horse,* charted at number 23 in the U.K. in 1980. *Bollocks,* as it turned out, was the only Sex Pistols album released while the group was in existence.

After the breakup, the members went their separate ways. Rotten proceeded to form Public Image Ltd., which would become a platform for his increasingly self-parodic iconoclasm. Cook faded into obscurity. And Jones emerged in the 1990s as a bombastic, long-haired metallist—just the sort of fatuous rocker that the Pistols had rebelled against in the first place.

In 1986, the three surviving members and Vicious's mother got together in a £1 million suit against McLaren that was eventually settled out of court. That same year, the Alex Cox film *Sid and Nancy* provided an intriguing—if revolting—look at the Sex Pistols in their prime.

Not that any of the later history was particularly important.

In their garish, brief career, the Sex Pistols changed the course of rock and roll and much of pop

---

TOP ALBUMS

NEVER MIND THE BOLLOCKS, HERE'S THE SEX PISTOLS (Warner, '77)
THE GREAT ROCK 'N' ROLL SWINDLE (Virgin, '79)

TOP SONGS

ANARCHY IN THE UK (EMI, '76)
GOD SAVE THE QUEEN (Virgin, '77)
PRETTY VACANT (Virgin, '77)
HOLIDAYS IN THE SUN (Virgin, '77)

---

culture. They reasserted rock's rebellious self-image by forcing it to rebel against itself. Their rough and ragged music reminded rock that it was usually best served by the heartfelt musical amateur, not the slick professional. And with the help of McLaren's provocative publicity schemes, they reestablished rock's crucial connection with its surrounding culture. To them and him, rock wasn't simply entertainment for the rock masses; it was a dramatic expression and reflection of those masses in the form of fashion, hairstyles, behavior, and sound.

Musically, the group not only spawned the punks but set the stage for the emergence of the new wave of the late 1970s, and its ragged, back-to-basics sound paved the way for the alternative, rebellious rock of groups like R.E.M. and Nirvana.

Astonishingly, a decade and more after the group's breakup, its leather-clad, slobbed-out, hair-askewed look and noisy, inept sound still defined what was "new" to many rock fans and musicians. Ironically, the Sex Pistols created a new set of conventions that have long outlasted the group itself.

THE SHIRELLES

When the Shirelles' single "Will You Love Me Tomorrow" reached Number One in 1960, they became the first all-girl group in history to top the U.S. charts.

While that fact was significant in and of itself, it also signalled the emergence of a new movement in rock that would produce some of the most inspired musical moments of the early 1960s.

The movement came to be called the girl-group sound.

The Shirelles weren't the first girl group, and they may not have been the best. But the group and its Number One hit proved to be a watershed.

With its youthful exuberance and passion and its ebullient mix of rock and pop, "Will You Love Me Tomorrow" set many of the stylistic precedents for the girl-group era. The seamless vocals and harmonies of Shirley Owens, Addi "Micki" Harris, Doris Coley, and Beverly Lee were elegant, but in a rocking way, and romantic in a thoroughly teenaged way. The lyrics expressed an undeniably feminine point of view; indeed, the song's title and refrain echoed what was widely perceived to be a timeless question on every girl's lips when it came to matters of love (and sex). And all of it—the vocals, the point

of view, and the song itself—were wrapped in a musical package masterminded by a producer, Luther Dixon, who shaped and directed the group and its sound. All of these aspects would form the core of the girl-group style.

The movement itself began in the mid-1950s when producer George Goldner worked musical wonders with the Chantels. On such songs as "Maybe," "I Love You So," and others, Goldner created a production sound that was at once panoramic and entirely alluring. In time, producer Phil Spector took that approach—and the role of the producer—to a new level. With his legendary wall of sound, Spector created such timeless records as the Crystals' "He's a Rebel" (1962) and "Da Doo Ron Ron" (1963) and the Ronettes' "Be My Baby" (1963) and "Walking in the Rain" (1964).

Along the way, other girl groups produced a vast number of hits, all of which were emblematic of a period in rock when innocence and the joys and cares of teen life were the focal points of the music

The Shirelles

and its fans. Songs like the Chiffons' 1963 classics "He's So Fine" and "One Fine Day" were paeans to teen romance, while the Marvelettes' 1961 hit "Please Mr. Postman" and others came with an earthier R&B-tinged sound that was, nonetheless, infused with the same youthful yearnings of young teen hearts.

Teen rebellion and angst also put in an appearance, most notably in the wonderfully hokey, tragic-romantic teen operas of the Shangri-Las. On songs like 1964's "Remember (Walkin' in the Sand)" and "Leader of the Pack," the Shangri-Las sang of love and loss with an almost Wagnerian sense of drama (Wagnerian, that is, if that composer had grown up in New Jersey).

Like the Chantels, the Shirelles came along in the late 1950s, when the girl-group sound had yet to be defined as such. In 1958, their debut single "I Met Him on a Sunday" presaged the style and sound that they and their counterparts would subsequently pursue at the beginning of the '60s. During the girl-group era, the Shirelles maintained the middle ground in the movement, opting neither for the overblown drama of the Shangri-Las nor the pop silliness of Lesley Gore (while the latter was a solo artist, she was a leading exponent of the girl-group sound and sensibility).

Instead, the Shirelles' records were impeccably produced wonders that encapsulated various aspects of the movement in a remarkably coherent and expressive manner. Thus, 1960's "Tonight's the Night" and 1961's "Baby It's You" had the R&B

fervor of the Marvelettes, while their 1962 Number One hit, "Soldier Boy," had the pop inflections of the Chiffons and the Ronettes.

It was an expansive sound that would influence the songs and vocal harmonies of the next generation of rockers to a great extent. Many of Lennon and McCartney's early compositions came with the melodic and vocal signatures of the girl groups in general and the Shirelles in particular. On their debut album, the Beatles recorded covers of "Baby It's You" and "Boys," the B side of "Will You Love Me Tomorrow."

Ironically, the emergence of the Beatles and the British Invasion of 1964 eventually rendered the girl groups obsolete, as they would other artists of the 1950s and early '60s. But for a time, at the start of the decade, the Shirelles and the rest of the girl groups made music that would endure as a timeless reminder of an innocent age.

The Shirelles were initially called the Poquellos when Owens (b. June 10, 1941, Passaic, New Jersey), Harris (b. Jan. 22, 1940, Passaic), Coley (b. Aug. 2, 1941, Passaic), and Lee (b. Aug. 3, 1941) teamed up in 1957. That year, the group wrote the song "I Met Him on a Sunday" and auditioned for the local Tiara label, which subsequently released it as a single in 1958. The single was credited to the Shirelles, the name the group had chosen when label head Florence Greenberg had suggested that the Poquellos was uncommercial. Realizing that Tiara wasn't big enough to handle the record, Greenberg leased it to Decca. In a new release in May 1958, the single eventually hit number 50 on the charts.

Greenberg formed Scepter Records in 1959 and teamed the Shirelles with producer Luther Dixon. The group recorded and released several singles that year with negligible results. But in 1960, they had their first top 40 hit when "Tonight's the Night," written by Owens and Dixon, hit number 39.

That set the stage for "Will You Love Me Tomorrow," which topped the charts in November 1960 and broke the million sales mark.

With Dixon guiding the Shirelles' sound and fortunes, 1961 proved to be the biggest year of their career. In January, a reissued version of one of its older singles, "Dedicated to the One I Love," hit number three. In April, "Mama Said" rose to number four. Other singles were less successful, but in December, "Baby It's You" reached number eight.

The group's chart activity continued into 1962. During a session at the beginning of the year, Dixon and Greenberg wrote a new song that the Shirelles recorded at the end of the day. The song, "Soldier Boy," was released in May, topping the charts and selling over a million copies. In December of that year, "Everybody Loves a Lover" reached number 19, and in January of 1963, "Foolish Little Girl" became the group's sixth top 10 hit, peaking at number four.

But that record proved to be the Shirelles' final major chart entry. By 1963, the girl-group sound had become a dominating force on the charts—largely due to the Shirelles' success—and new acts like the Chiffons, the Ronettes, and the Shangri-Las were scoring their own hits.

The Shirelles faced a number of problems and defections. Dixon ended his association with the group in 1963 when he moved from Scepter to Capitol Records. In 1964, the Shirelles themselves left the label and were subsequently involved in legal disputes that prevented them, for a time, from signing elsewhere. Then various members of the group began to depart and rejoin. In 1963, Dionne Warwick was a frequent part-time member, filling in for missing voices.

The Shirelles continued to release records—their last chart entry came in 1967 with "Last Minute Miracle"—but by the end of the 1960s, the group had become primarily an oldies act. As such, they persevered into the '80s, performing with various lineups. In October 1983, the Shirelles were invited by Dionne Warwick to record "Will You Love Me Tomorrow" on her album *How Many Times Can We Say Goodbye*.

TOP ALBUM

THE SHIRELLES' GREATEST HITS (Scepter, '63, 19)

TOP SONGS

WILL YOU LOVE ME TOMORROW (Scepter, '60, 1)
DEDICATED TO THE ONE I LOVE (Scepter, '61, 3)
MAMA SAID (Scepter, '61, 4)
BABY IT'S YOU (Scepter, '61, 8)
SOLDIER BOY (Scepter, '62, 1)
WELCOME HOME BABY (Scepter, '62, 22)
EVERYBODY LOVES A LOVER (Scepter, '62, 19)
FOOLISH LITTLE GIRL (Scepter, '63, 4)
DON'T SAY GOODNIGHT AND MEAN GOODBYE (Scepter, '63, 26)

Additional Top 40 Songs: 3

SIMON AND GARFUNKEL

Simon and Garfunkel
were the calm in the storm that was '60s rock.

While the Beatles were pursuing their expansive vision and groups such as Cream were defining rock as a virtuositic form, Paul Simon and Art Garfunkel made their mark with sublime vocal harmonies and timeless songs that blurred the boundaries between rock, folk, and pop.

Records such as "The Sounds of Silence," "Homeward Bound," "Mrs. Robinson," and their masterpiece, "Bridge over Troubled Water," weren't a part of any rock movement or trend; they simply existed as eloquent pieces of music to be taken on their own distinctive merits.

Those merits were many and manifold. Simon's songs were highly literate and sophisticated affairs whose lyrics dealt with loneliness, isolation, and personal estrangement with an introspection that often bordered on the obsessive. At times, his ruminations were angry and aggressive, as on the rocking ballad "I Am a Rock." At others, they were imbued with a delicacy and an almost poetic fragility.

Musically, Simon's songwriting moods were equally varied. At the core of his sound was the melodicism of folk, particularly on ballads like "The Sounds of Silence." But he also blended into this the urgency of rock and the hook-based sensibility of a pop tunesmith. The combination yielded a diverse range of songs, from the jangly, folk-rock sound of "Homeward Bound" to the winsome "59th Street Bridge Song (Feelin' Groovy)" and the edgy, earthy "Mrs. Robinson."

While each of these, and scores of others, had their own moods and sounds, they all came with his unique musical signature.

But Simon and Garfunkel were more than a platform for those songs. One of the most effective and affecting musical partnerships in rock, the duo used those songs to display their unique sound. Garfunkel provided rich, vocal textures that complemented and counterbalanced Simon's more down-to-earth singing approach. On songs like "Bridge over Troubled Water," Garfunkel displayed a vocal majesty that had few equals in rock; in fact, his voice defined Simon's songs and endowed them with a shape and substance that would not be surpassed by the countless artists who would record their own versions over the decades.

The result of Simon's songwriting virtuosity and Garfunkel's vocal interpretations was a sound that vaulted over the various aesthetic boundaries of '60s rock. Simon and Garfunkel's immense popularity wasn't confined or segmented to a particular rock listenership: they were simultaneously acclaimed and adored by casual pop fans in the broad marketplace and more ardent "underground" types for whom rock wasn't as much a pastime as an avocation.

Simon (b. Oct. 13, 1941, Newark, New Jersey) and Garfunkel (b. Nov. 5, 1941, Queens, New York) became friends while both were students at Forest Hills High School in New York. In 1957, they formed the musical duo Tom and Jerry (Garfunkel was Tom Graph and Simon was Jerry Landis) and recorded the single "Hey Schoolgirl" on the Big label. In November of that year, they performed on Dick Clark's "American Bandstand" TV program, and the single subsequently made number 49 on the charts.

But it was clear that their imitation of the Everly Brothers look and sound would hardly compare with the original. And when two new singles on Big were unsuccessful in 1958, the duo split to attend college.

Over the course of the next several years, while pursuing their studies, they continued to release singles on independent labels, Simon recording as Jerry Landis and Tico and the Triumphs and Garfunkel releasing singles of his own as Artie Garr. None of their records proved to be hits.

Simon and Garfunkel

In 1964, Simon moved to England and began performing in London's folk scene, where he was joined from time to time by Garfunkel. That year, they were signed—as Simon and Garfunkel—by Columbia Records, which released their debut album, *Wednesday Morning, 3 AM*. The album came with several Simon originals as well as various folk covers, including a version of Bob Dylan's "The Times They Are A-Changin'."

But when the album failed to chart, Simon returned to England, where he recorded the solo album *The Paul Simon Songbook* for the U.K. division of Columbia in 1965. In October of that year, producer Tom Wilson decided to record a new version of a folk ballad from the duo's debut album with a rock backing track. The ballad was "The Sounds of Silence."

Released as a single at the end of the year without Simon or Garfunkel's knowledge, it quickly became

a hit, topping the charts in the U.S. for two weeks in January of 1966. Simon and Garfunkel reunited and began to promote the single along with their debut album, which had been rereleased. By March, *Wednesday Morning, 3 AM* had hit number 30 on the charts, and a new album, *Sounds of Silence* (including the hit folk-rock version of the song) soon shot to number 21.

Over the course of 1966, Simon and Garfunkel remained on the charts with "Homeward Bound," "I Am a Rock," and "The Dangling Conversation." At the end of the year, their album *Parsley, Sage, Rosemary and Thyme* reached number four and firmly established the duo as one of the major acts in rock.

In 1967, Simon and Garfunkel continued to tour and record to increasing acclaim. That year, the single "At the Zoo" hit number 16, and its follow-up, "Fakin' It," made number 23. Emblematic of the duo's wide-ranging popularity was its invitation to perform at the Monterey Pop Festival in June of that year—Simon and Garfunkel were one of the few mainstream acts to perform at the "underground" event. Then, at the end of the year, they were commissioned to provide songs for the upcoming film *The Graduate.*

Upon its release in 1968, the accompanying soundtrack album—which included the theme song, "Mrs. Robinson"—topped the U.S. charts for nine weeks. Later that year, the duo's new album, *Bookends,* replaced the *Graduate* soundtrack album at Number One, where it resided for seven weeks. The duo then scored another chart-topper with the "Mrs. Robinson" single, released in June. It subsequently won Grammy Awards in 1969 as Record of the Year and Best Contemporary Pop Performance—Vocal, Duo or Group.

The apex of Simon and Garfunkel's career came in 1970 with the release of *Bridge over Troubled Water* and the single of the same title. In February of that year, the album and single topped their respective charts in the U.S. and the U.K. simultaneously—one of the rare times that had ever been accomplished. In 1971, the album and single dominated the Grammys to the tune of six awards, including those for Song, Record, and Album of the year.

But dissension between Simon and Garfunkel had begun to emerge during the recording of the album. There were musical disagreements as well as problems that had been aggravated by Garfunkel's decision to pursue a film acting career. By the time *Bridge over Troubled Water* had been released, the duo had decided to call it quits.

They subsequently reunited for a one-off performance at Central Park in New York in 1981 that drew over 400,000 fans. The performance yielded the 1982 album *The Concert in Central Park,* which charted at number six. In June, they toured Europe, and in 1983, they did the same in the U.S. But a planned new album was called off due to musical differences.

Over the course of the 1970s, Garfunkel appeared in such films as *Carnal Knowledge* and *Catch 22.* He also recorded several solo records that were modestly successful. Simon's career and songwriting, meanwhile, continued to flourish. During the '70s he released a series of remarkable albums and singles that reached the upper levels of the charts. On 1972's *Paul Simon,* 1973's *There Goes Rhymin' Simon,* and 1975's *Still Crazy After All These Years,* he proved to be a songwriter of exceptional range, depth, and intellect. He also began to broaden his creative output, varying his usual mix of folk, rock, and pop with songs that embraced gospel and Latin influences.

At the end of the decade and into the 1980s, Simon's career faltered for a time. His film, *One Trick Pony,* which he directed and starred in, was a resounding commercial and critical flop. And his 1983 album *Hearts and Bones* was somewhat disappointing, musically and commercially.

But he came back in 1986 with the album *Graceland.* A set of songs based on the rhythms and melodies of African pop music, the album was as successful as it was controversial. Critics and fans hailed the album for its musical daring, while others saw in its ethnic derivation a form of "cultural imperialism." In 1988, the album won a Grammy Award as Record of the Year.

Simon became involved in a similar controversy in 1990 upon the release of *The Rhythm of the Saints*—an album based on the music of Brazil. In fact, as with *Graceland,* Simon had not co-opted an indigenous musical form as much as he had popularized it and employed it to enrich his own art and vision. The album ultimately peaked at number four on the charts.

The controversies and charges aside, Simon's music endured because of its unsurpassed quality. With his musical partner and as a soloist, Simon created a vast body of songs that has few creative equals in rock or pop.

TOP ALBUMS

PARSLEY, SAGE, ROSEMARY AND THYME (Columbia, '66, 4)
THE GRADUATE (Columbia, '68, 1)
BOOKENDS (Columbia, '68, 1)
BRIDGE OVER TROUBLED WATER (Columbia, '70, 1)

Additional Top 40 Albums: 4

TOP SONGS

THE SOUNDS OF SILENCE (Columbia, '65, 1)
HOMEWARD BOUND (Columbia, '66, 5)
I AM A ROCK (Columbia, '66, 3)
MRS. ROBINSON (Columbia, '68, 1)
BRIDGE OVER TROUBLED WATER (Columbia, '70, 1)
CECILIA (Columbia, '70, 4)

Additional Top 40 Songs: 9

SLY AND THE FAMILY STONE

Sly and the Family Stone burst upon the scene of the late 1960s with a furious new amalgam of funk and rock.

Sly Stone

Arrayed in the flashy psychedelic finery of the time, his hair rounded and tousled into an enormous Afro, Stone was an extroverted performer, equal parts James Brown and Jimi Hendrix, with traces of Wilson Pickett and Otis Redding added to the bargain.

Similarly, the group's music was a fiery blend of Brown's churning funky rhythms, Hendrix's slashing psychedelic rock, and the emotional, gospel-tinged music of the soul masters. On songs such as 1968's "Dance to the Music," 1969's "Everyday People," and 1970's "Thank You (Falettinme Be Mice Elf Agin)," Sly and the Family Stone combined Stone's brawling baritone vocals with piercing vocal harmonies, Larry Graham's popping bass lines, and R&B-inflected horns and slammed it all home with charging, distorted guitar chords. The result was an eclectic onslaught that encompassed many of the major musical movements of the 1960s and transformed them into a single—and singularly expressive—creative end product.

The Family Stone was also something of a metaphor for the social sensibilities of the time. Its seven-member lineup included blacks and whites, males and females, a true "family" of races and genders that reflected rock's social and cultural openness. Long before catchwords like "diversity" and "multicultural" invaded the social lexicon, Sly and the Family Stone personified the ideals those words represented. And they extended to the lyrics of Sly Stone's songs, many of which were soulful paeans to tolerance and inclusion; as he sang on "Everyday People," "different strokes for different folks."

But Sly was never much of an activist. His stinging wit was often as sly as his name. And his energetic, earthy music was aimed more at releasing emotional and sexual tensions than those of a more political nature.

For a time, in the late 1960s and early '70s, Sly and the Family Stone were one of the most successful rock acts in the U.S. From 1968 to 1971, the group had five top 10 singles and three top 10

albums. Their performance at the Woodstock festival in 1969 was a high point of the three-day rock spectacle. The group was also invited to perform at that year's Newport Jazz Festival on a bill that included other rock acts; it was a first in the history of the prestigious event.

But the group was also beset by drug problems, and it became notorious for not appearing at scheduled shows. By the mid-'70s its popularity had waned. The group ultimately disbanded, with the members pursuing individual projects.

Its music, however, endured. Sly and the Family Stone's ebullient blend of rock and soul and funk inspired new artists over the course of the next 20 years, including War, George Clinton, Prince, and Earth, Wind and Fire.

Sly Stone (b. Sylvester Stewart, Mar. 15, 1944, Dallas, Texas) had been active in the Bay Area music scene during the early and middle 1960s. With the group the Viscanes, he had recorded the single "Yellow Moon," which had become a modest local hit. He had also produced records by the Beau Brummels, the Mojo Men, and Bobby Freeman; had worked for a time as a disc jockey; and had formed the group the Stoners.

In 1966, he recruited his brother Freddie on guitar and sister Rosemary on keyboards, along with trumpeter Cynthia Robinson, saxophonist Jerry Martini, bassist Larry Graham, and drummer Greg Errico and formed Sly and the Family Stone.

Performing on the local R&B circuit in Oakland and later in the emerging psychedelic scene in San Francisco, the group began to gain a local fan base. In 1967, it signed a contract with Epic Records and released the album *A Whole New Thing*.

The group gained national attention in 1968 when the single "Dance to the Music" charted at number eight. A subsequent album and single were released in 1969 with modest results.

But in 1969, the group shot to the top of the charts with "Everyday People" and the album *Stand!*, the latter reaching number 13. That album

---

TOP ALBUMS

STAND! (Epic, '69, *13*)
GREATEST HITS (Epic, '70, *2*)
THERE'S A RIOT GOIN' ON (Epic, '71, *1*)
FRESH (Epic, '73, *7*)

Additional Top 40 Albums: 1

TOP SONGS

DANCE TO THE MUSIC (Epic, '68, *8*)
EVERYDAY PEOPLE (Epic, '68, *1*)
HOT FUN IN THE SUMMERTIME (Epic, '69, *2*)
THANK YOU (FALETTINME BE MICE
  ELF AGIN) (Epic, '70, *1*)
FAMILY AFFAIR (Epic, '71, *1*)
IF YOU WANT ME TO STAY (Epic, '73, *12*)

Additional Top 40 Songs: 5

---

and the group's subsequent performance at Woodstock (including a memorable rendition of "I Want to Take You Higher") propelled Sly and the Family Stone into the leading ranks of the rock scene of the time.

Over the course of the next three years the group could do no wrong—on record at any rate. "Hot Fun in the Summertime" hit number two in 1969; "Thank You (Falettinme Be Mice Elf Agin)" topped the charts in 1970, as did "Family Affair" in 1971. The group's *Greatest Hits* album reached number two in 1970, and *There's a Riot Goin' On* topped the album chart in 1971.

But by 1972, it all began to fall apart. Graham quit the group that year to form his own rock-funk outfit, Graham Central Station. Sly Stone's financial and drug problems increased. And while the group's records continued to sell—the album *Fresh* reached number seven in 1973—the singles began to fade on the charts. The group's final charting record, "Loose Booty," peaked at number 84 in 1974.

Stone subsequently recorded with Clinton and the Funkadelics on the 1981 album *The Electric Spanking of War Babies*. He participated in a tour with Bobby Womack in 1984 and recorded with Jesse Johnson in 1986. But his drug problems resurfaced later in the decade when he was incarcerated in 1989 for cocaine possession.

THE SOFT MACHINE

When Jimi Hendrix embarked, in 1968, on his first major tour of the U.S., he brought with him, as an opening act, a group from London that mesmerized and entirely baffled his growing legions of rock fans. That group was the Soft Machine.

The group was unusual in many ways. For a start, it was a trio, but one that—a true heresy for the time—did not include a guitarist. Keyboardist Mike Ratledge, drummer Robert Wyatt, and bassist Kevin Ayers were the very antithesis of Hendrix's rocking, guitar-driven Experience, and of most of the rest of rock, for that matter.

Their music was ethereal and complex, punctuated with dissonant chords, abstract washes of sound, and the off-key—almost anti-key—vocals of Wyatt. The group didn't perform songs as such; instead, they spun out suites of songs with dense, interconnecting improvisational forays that went on for half an hour and longer. While the musicians played, a light show was projected in the background. But it wasn't like the psychedelic light shows of the time as much as a series of abstract shapes and forms, globules of color that expanded and contracted as the music swelled and gurgled about it.

No one knew quite what to think of the Soft Machine. And over the course of the next seven years, they continued to not know. During that time, the Soft Machine—or rather, the 14 subsequent versions of the group that went by the name—confounded the rock world with a sound, or a series of sounds, that had never been heard before.

In the process, the group expanded the definition of rock and virtually redefined it, introducing ideas that had hitherto been relegated to jazz and the classical avant-garde.

Simply stated, the Soft Machine was one of the most innovative and creative groups in rock history.

The first version of the group—the one that toured with Hendrix and released the album *Volume One* at the end of 1968—was a rock-based trio. But what sort of rock? Ratledge unleashed barrages of jagged chords and phrases on an organ souped up with distortion boosters and wah-wah pedals, producing a sound that resembled the free jazz of saxophonist John Coltrane. Bassist Ayers—his instrument similarly arrayed—provided incessant, repeated figures in a Terry Riley/minimalist vein along with counter themes that had more in common with those normally played on a guitar or other lead instruments.

And then there was Wyatt. A virtuoso drummer in a rock age full of them, he rolled and slammed his way through the songs with a dexterity and finesse that were all the more remarkable for the fact that many of the group's songs came in difficult time signatures, including the 7/4 that became a Soft Machine hallmark. In addition, he didn't play the drums as much as compose on them, using beats and individual tom and snare parts as thematic devices; on the group's second album, *Volume Two,* Wyatt performed a drum solo, most of it on cymbals, that was more soundscape than show piece.

And when he sang, the traditional approach to rock vocals went out the window. Without the slightest range to speak of, Wyatt's voice was a tuneless instrument, its hoarse phrasings skipping and stuttering their way through the songs like a cross between the improvisational acrobatics of scat jazz and the *sprechstimme* vocalise innovations of the early 20th century classical composer Arnold Schoenberg.

Wyatt was also something of a songwriting terrorist. His lyrics avoided rhymes whenever possible. Instead, they unfolded like discussions set to musical meter, full of parched wit, biting insights, and an irrepressible irascibility. On "Moon in June," he sang, "Music making still/Performs a normal function/Background noise for people/Eating and talking and drinking and smoking/That's all right by us/Don't think that we're complaining/After all, it's only leisure time/Isn't it?"

It wasn't and he knew it. In fact, Wyatt and the Soft Machine pursued their iconoclastic music with an uncompromising fervor and purpose that made them all but noncommercial. Their records never charted substantially in the U.S., and their popularity was confined to the outer fringes of the rock avant-garde in the U.K. and Europe.

But the group had a vast impact on musicians. Many of their innovations—including the use of extended song formats, improvisation, dissonance, and electronically altered keyboards—were subsequently co-opted by the art rock groups of the early 1970s. In its later lineups (after Wyatt had quit the group in 1971), the Soft Machine increasingly employed horns and synthesizers, evolving into a more jazz-oriented ensemble that provided the basis and inspiration for many of the jazz-rock fusion groups that emerged during the decade.

The original version of the Soft Machine—the one that appeared on the group's debut record of 1968—was formed in 1966 by Ratledge, Wyatt, and Ayers. But its background was somewhat more convoluted.

The group was an outgrowth of the active avant-garde rock scene that emerged in Canterbury, England, in the early 1960s. That scene revolved around the loosely knit Wilde Flowers, which included Ratledge and Wyatt and other experimental musicians like bassist Hugh Hopper and keyboardist David Sinclair (the latter two of whom would subsequently have a major role in the progressive rock movement in England during the 1970s).

Wyatt quit the group in 1962 to wander around Europe. During his travels he eventually came in contact with Daevid Allen, a young Australian who was interested in avant-garde and electronic music.

When Wyatt finally returned to England, he rejoined the Wilde Flowers, which by that time included Ayers, Hopper, and various others. Allen was invited to join the group, and he provided a new direction that embraced rock and jazz mixings and the use of tape loops in performance.

When Hopper and the others quit the Wilde Flowers to form their own groups, Ratledge, Ayers, Allen, and Wyatt pressed on, changing the group's name to the Soft Machine, from a novel by William Burroughs.

The group relocated to London in 1966 and

TOP ALBUMS

THE SOFT MACHINE (Probe, '68)
VOLUME TWO (Probe, '69)
THIRD (Columbia, '70)
FOURTH (Columbia, 71)
FIFTH (Columbia, '72)
SIXTH (Columbia, '73)
SEVENTH (Columbia, '74)
BUNDLES (Harvest, '74)
SOFTS (Harvest, '75)

began performing at clubs like the UFO amid a growing psychedelic scene that included such as the fledgling Pink Floyd. In 1967, the Soft Machine recorded a single, "Feelin', Reelin', Squeelin" b/w "Love Makes Sweet Music," a rock-based effort (including Jimi Hendrix on guitar) that did not make the charts.

That same year, the group went to St. Tropez, France, to participate in experimental director Alan Zion's production of Pablo Picasso's play *Desire Attappe Par Le Queue,* a multimedia performance that created something of a sensation when it was broken up by the French police. When the group made its way back to England, Allen was refused entry into the country due to visa problems. He bowed out of the Soft Machine and subsequently formed Gong, a seminal progressive group of the 1970s.

Wyatt, Ratledge, and Ayers continued as a trio. They soon came to the attention of Chas Chandler, Hendrix's manager, who invited them to open for the Jimi Hendrix Experience on its upcoming U.S. tour.

The tour was a vast success for Hendrix and generated a certain interest in the Soft Machine, who were encouraged to record an album. That album, *Volume One,* was released in November 1968. While the record had its intriguing moments—including the extended

songs and improvisations that were the group's trademark—its sound barely hinted at the expressive power the Soft Machine could generate onstage. It was largely ignored by the rock public.

Disenchanted with the entire process, the group disbanded for a time in 1969. But it soon re-formed, with Hopper replacing Ayers on bass. The new trio released the album *Volume Two* at the end of the year. While its recorded sound was abysmal, the album was one of the most daring musical experiments in rock history. Wyatt's unique vocals and lyrical contrivances were displayed in all their eccentricity, as were the atonal, abstract musical barrages of Ratledge and Hopper. The overall effect was that of reducing rock to expressionistic noise.

While the album was far too avant-garde to be embraced by the broad rock public, it did gain the interest of a devoted cult of fans in the U.S., the U.K., and Europe.

In 1970, the Soft Machine released the album *Third,* a two-record set that came with revolutionary layers of keyboards, electronic bass, and horns set in a free-jazz context.

The group then reduced itself to a quartet, with Wyatt, Ratledge, and Hopper joined by saxophonist Elton Dean. This

The Soft Machine

version of the group released the album *Fourth* in 1971. The first record that did not include the vocals of Wyatt, it was an instrumental effort based on modal jazz.

The direction did not please Wyatt, who quit that year to form the progressive rock group Matching Mole. Wyatt's career as a drummer was cut short in 1973 when he broke his back and was paralyzed from the waist down. Despite this setback, he subsequently released a series of provocative vocal and keyboard-based albums, including the remarkable *Rock Bottom* of 1974.

From 1971 to the group's demise in 1975, the Soft Machine evolved into a jazz-rock fusion group of sorts, but one that had an overtly avant-garde,

electronic edge. During that period, the group changed lineups constantly, with Hopper, Dean, and Ratledge (the last original member to finally leave) giving way to new musicians who increasingly came under the direction of keyboardist-oboist Karl Jenkins. Guitar virtuoso Allan Holdsworth worked with the group for a time, appearing on the 1974 album *Bundles*.

These later versions of the group, while interesting and technically exceptional, had almost nothing in common with the Soft Machine's classic lineup of the album *Volume Two*. On that album, Soft Machine set the stage for the progressive scene that would create some of the most intriguing rock music of the 1970s.

PHIL SPECTOR

Of all the producers who made contributions to rock over the years, one stood apart, not merely as a guide or creative partner, but as a creator. That producer was Phil Spector.

Record producers have long played a crucial role in the evolution and development of rock and roll. From George Martin's inspired collaborations with the Beatles in the 1960s to the dance and hip-hop studio masterminds of the '90s, producers have guided the sound of their musical partners and often had decisive effects on the end products: the records.

Spector didn't simply produce records; in a strictly musical sense, he made them. He hand-picked the musicians for the recording sessions. He chose the members of some of the girl groups with whom he would create a series of classic records in the early 1960s. In several cases, like the Crystals' "There's No Other (Like My Baby)," he co-wrote the songs they recorded. In fact, many of the records he made during his meteoric career came to be associated

more with Spector than with the artists who performed them.

Which was perfectly fitting. On all the records Spector "produced," his presence was of such an all-encompassing nature that everyone else involved in the process, including the groups themselves, became expressive conduits for his creative vision.

At the core of these records was the Sound, or, to be exact, the "wall of sound." The wall of sound was Spector's musical signature, a vast, imposing onslaught that was Wagnerian in scale and aural impact. Not a sound in the usual generic sense, nor a set of technical flourishes or studio gimmicks, Spector's "wall" was truly a sound in and of itself, as much a distinct musical entity as any song.

And it was a wall almost literally. Spector

arranged musicians in a phalanx of musical shock troops—regiments of them. He used multiple sets of drummers and basses along with masses of horns and vocals; on the Checkmates' 1969 recording of "Proud Mary," Spector reportedly used more than 300 musicians.

The results were spectacular. On records like the Righteous Brothers' 1964 hit "You've Lost That Lovin' Feelin' "—considered by many to be Spector's masterpiece—he created a sound that was almost physical in presence, with a depth and grandeur that were unparalleled.

It was a sound that had a profound impact on the way that rock records were subsequently made. Before Spector, the recording of rock music had primarily been a matter of capturing an artist's songs and personality on record. Spector proved that the recording itself could be an equal part of the creative process.

Specifically, Spector's work influenced a wide range of producers, most notably Brian Wilson, who employed Spector's methods and recording philosophy in the records he made with the Beach Boys.

But aesthetically, Spector's impact was far greater. It would be the basis of the Beatles' revolutionary use of the studio as an "instrument" on their later records in the 1960s. This, in turn, gave rise to new generations of producers who would use the recording process to sculpt the sounds of the artists with whom they worked. The very idea of the record as a work of art can be directly traced back to Spector.

And if the record was art, it followed that the producer was an artist. Spector pioneered that idea as well. At a time when most producers were adjuncts to the music business—middlemen of a sort, who produced the product—Spector was the epitome of the eccentric creator.

He cut a swath across the rock scene of his time, dressed in capes, Cuban-heeled boots, and shades, his hair cut long. Attended by sycophants and bodyguards, Spector wasn't a businessman in the typical mold; he was a rock star.

But he was also a businessman. Dubbed "The First Tycoon of Teen" by writer Tom Wolfe, and a millionaire by the time he was 21, Spector revolutionized the way rock conducted its business as much as the way it made its music. Refusing to subordinate himself to the big record companies of his time, he formed his own label, Philles, at the beginning of the 1960s. This allowed him a level of creative control that was virtually unprecedented. Using that control, he formed and signed the groups that he knew he could work with to achieve the records and sound he had in mind. He manipulated those groups and their careers, writing their material or commissioning songs he believed would become hits and using the groups to record them.

One result was the girl-group sound that yielded some of the most enduring musical moments of the early '60s. While Spector didn't initiate the form—the Chantels had done that in the '50s—he co-opted it and made it his own with such hits as the Crystals' "He's a Rebel" and the Ronettes' "Be My Baby."

The epoch-making phase of Spector's career was fairly brief. It began to wane in the mid-'60s after a roughly five-year run of immense success. But Spector's impact on rock and roll would endure for decades.

Spector (b. Phillip Harvey Spector, Dec. 26, 1940, Bronx, New York) began his career in Los Angeles in 1958 when he formed the group the Teddy

Phil Spector

Bears with Carol Connors and Marshall Lieb. Recording his song "To Know Him Is to Love Him," the group scored an immediate Number One hit in September of 1958.

When the Teddy Bears disbanded shortly thereafter, Spector moved to New York and became a protégé of producers Jerry Leiber and Mike Stoller at Atlantic Records. With Leiber, he co-wrote the classic "Spanish Harlem," which became a big hit for Ben E. King. During that period, he also played guitar on various records, including the Drifters' "On Broadway."

He soon began to pursue his career as a producer, issuing Ray Peterson's "Corinna, Corinna," Curtis Lee's "Pretty Little Angel," and Gene Pitney's

---

TOP ALBUM

To Know Him Is to Love Him
(Teddy Bears, Dore, '58, 1)

TOP SONGS

He's a Rebel (Crystals, Philles, '61, 1)
Da Doo Ron Ron (When He Walked Me Home)
(Crystals, Philles, '63, 3)
Then He Kissed Me (Crystals, Philles, '63, 6)
Be My Baby (Ronettes, Philles, '63, 2)
You've Lost That Lovin' Feelin'
(Righteous Brothers, Philles, '64, 1)
Unchained Melody (Righteous Brothers,
Philles , '65, 4)
Ebb Tide (Righteous Brothers, Philles, '65, 5)
My Sweet Lord (George Harrison, Apple, '70, 1)
Instant Karma (John Lennon, Apple, '70, 3)

"Every Breath I Take." But the New York music business scene proved too confining, and he moved to Los Angeles at the end of the '50s and set up his Philles label with producer Lester Sill.

Over the next four years, Spector began to develop his wall of sound on a series of girl-group hits. The initial entry was the Crystals' "There's No Other (Like My Baby)," which reached number 20 in 1961. It was followed by the teen anthem "He's a Rebel," whose romantic lyrics and dense production yielded million-plus sales.

In 1963, Spector assembled the Ronettes and along with the songwriting team of Ellie Greenwich and Jeff Barry co-wrote "Be My Baby," an eventual number two hit and a million-seller.

With his stable of groups growing and his "wall"

firmly established, Spector became a commercial and creative phenomenon of vast proportions. There were the Crystals' hits "Da Doo Ron Ron" and "Then He Kissed Me," the Ronettes' "Baby I Love You," Bob B. Soxx and the Blue Jeans' "Zip-A-Dee-Doo-Dah," and Darlene Love's "(Today I Met) The Boy I'm Gonna Marry," all of which were musical high points during the early and middle 1960s.

Spector's sound and career reached their apex with the release of the Righteous Brothers' "You've Lost That Lovin' Feelin'," which topped the charts at the end of 1964. He went on to produce a number of hits with the duo, including "Unchained Melody" and "Ebb Tide."

But when he ended that collaboration in 1965 and subsequently turned his attention to Ike and Tina Turner, his fortunes began to wane. He produced their magnificent "River Deep, Mountain High," but despite its tremendous sound and Tina Turner's ebullient performance, the single proved to be only modestly successful.

Disappointed at its failure, Spector began to retreat from the rock scene of the later '60s, moving into a sprawling mansion in Beverly Hills and becoming something of a recluse.

He made a comeback at the end of the decade when he was invited by John Lennon to produce the song "Instant Karma," which subsequently became a major hit in 1970. Lennon also asked Spector to remix the Beatles' final album release, the soundtrack to the film Let It Be. The results were controversial: Paul McCartney was furious at the grandiloquent sound Spector created, particularly on the song "The Long and Winding Road."

But Lennon and George Harrison subsequently recruited Spector to produce the initial albums of their post-Beatles solo careers. Spector's sound was heard to full effect on Harrison's album All Things Must Pass, a chart-topper in 1970.

Spector's partnership with the former Beatles was fleeting, and over the course of the remaining '70s, the producer became increasingly reclusive. He subsequently worked on a one-off basis with Cher and Darlene Love, among other artists, but it was clear that his tenure as the most important producer in rock was over.

Not that that diminished in any way his importance in the grand scheme. With his classic hits of the early '60s and his wall of sound, Spector left a rock legacy that has few equals. In 1989, he was inducted into the Rock and Roll Hall of Fame.

BRUCE SPRINGSTEEN

Springsteen was the great populist, the rock and roll Everyman who virtually remade the music in his own image—and his image of it. In the process, he transformed rock of the 1980s, for better and worse, into an almost monolithic cultural force while becoming one of its biggest stars.

With Springsteen, rock was elevated and reduced to a timeless expression of contemporary life. He endowed it with an iconographic presence that encapsulated the spirit of its time.

Springsteen's music evolved and matured over the course of his life and career. But at its core, his vision remained remarkably intact. His songs were stories about growing up and growing older, populated by characters for whom he seemed to have a marked affinity.

From the almost mythological depictions of urban life and culture on his first two albums, *Greetings from Asbury Park, New Jersey* and *The Wild, the Innocent and the E Street Shuffle,* to the grittier and far more realistic songs on *The River* and other later albums, Springsteen painted images that had an almost universal substance and grandeur, that defied trends and fads and changing tastes and attitudes.

From a strictly musical standpoint, he did the same. Springsteen's version of rock transcended stylistic eras, or rather blended them into a transcendent whole. While his early music was as much folk as rock—earning him the impossible appellation "the new Dylan" at the time—it soon evolved into an imposing amalgam of energetic music with allusions to '50s rock, Motown soul, '60s folk-rock, and Phil Spector's wall of sound. Over the course of his career, he rarely strayed from that mixture, with the exception of the intense folk of his 1982 album, *Nebraska.*

On all of his records, Springsteen's vocals spanned musical boundaries and epochs. His voice was imbued with the chiseled expressivity of Woody Guthrie, the almost operatic passion of Roy Orbison, the energy of Elvis Presley, and the bluesy lyricism of Van Morrison.

The universality of Springsteen's music was reflected in a public image that was tied inextricably to his art. If his songs seemed to come straight from the people, so did he as a person. On album covers, he was invariably depicted as "one of the guys," dressed down in jeans and a T-shirt, joking with a sideman, staring sullenly back at the camera. There was little rock star posing or posturing, no attempt to place him on a level above the masses. He and his music were one with them.

That image was extended to his performances. Onstage, Springsteen worked like a stevedore. His shows were long, involved affairs that were loaded with sweat and honest toil. His group, the E Street Band, didn't stand in the background, but was pushed up front alongside him. In fact, in true populist fashion, his relationship with the group—an integral part of his image—was imbued with the camaraderie of the workplace. He and his band weren't an act; they were more like a back-slapping, high-fiving bunch of friends out to make meat-and-potatoes rock and roll.

In time, that image exceeded Springsteen's control, to the detriment of his music. When *Born in the U.S.A.* became a major hit in the mid-1980s, Springsteen immediately became a media icon, a symbol of

Bruce Springsteen

nationalistic pride and fervor, due primarily to a mass misreading of the record's anthemic title cut. Springsteen's all-encompassing fame diluted his musical message, and his common-man image was co-opted by the culture at large. The man of the people became "the Boss." And his universal rock became the stuff of car commercials.

But, to his enduring artistic credit, Springsteen eluded his new status just as he once had with the "new Dylan" hyperbole. While his legions of new fans screamed for more of the same, he increasingly created music that explored the questions and doubts of love, life, and encroaching middle age, suggesting that Springsteen was more concerned with his musical vision than with his role as a hero of rock and roll.

Springsteen (b. Bruce Frederick Joseph Springsteen, Sept. 23, 1949, Freehold, New Jersey) began playing the guitar in 1963. By 1965, he had joined the Castiles, with whom he recorded the demo "That's What You'll Get." After that group folded, in 1967, he spent the next several years performing on the New Jersey club scene with bands named Child, Steel Mill, and Dr. Zoom and the Sonic Boom. In 1971, he formed the Bruce Springsteen Band, which included several musicians who would later join him in the E Street Band.

In May 1972, Springsteen concluded a management deal with Mike Appel, signing the contract—as legend has it—on the hood of a car in an unlit parking lot. It was a relationship that would subsequently play a major, and damaging, role in the initial phase of his career.

At first, however, the results were fortuitous. Appel arranged for an audition with legendary producer John Hammond at Columbia Records. Hammond, who had discovered Bob Dylan, among many others, was impressed and immediately signed Springsteen to a long-term contract.

Springsteen's debut album, *Greetings from Asbury Park,* was released in January 1973, but the folk-oriented album failed on the charts.

TOP ALBUMS

BORN TO RUN (Columbia, '75, 3)
DARKNESS ON THE EDGE OF TOWN (Columbia, '78, 5)
THE RIVER (Columbia, '80, 1)
NEBRASKA (Columbia, '82, 3)
BORN IN THE U.S.A. (Columbia, '84, 1)
BRUCE SPRINGSTEEN & THE E STREET BAND LIVE/1975–85 (Columbia, '86 1)
TUNNEL OF LOVE (Columbia, '87, 1)

TOP SONGS

DANCING IN THE DARK (Columbia, '84, 2)
GLORY DAYS (Columbia, '85, 5)
BRILLIANT DISGUISE (Columbia, '87, 5)

Additional Top 40 Songs: 12

The Wild, the Innocent and the E Street Shuffle, released in November, was also a commercial disappointment, although it did gain a certain critical acclaim. But it was more rock-based than the first record and more accurately reflected the near-operatic scope and all-out energy of his live dates at the time, backed by an early incarnation of the E Street Band. After a performance in Cambridge, Massachusetts, critic Jon Landau wrote, "I saw rock and roll future—and its name is Bruce Springsteen." That review—apart from drawing attention to Springsteen—formed the basis for a friendship between the two that would expand into a professional relationship in the coming years.

The classic lineup of the E Street Band came together in August 1974, when drummer Max Weinberg and pianist Roy Bittan were added to the group, replacing Vini "Mad Dog" Lopez and David Sancious, respectively. The E Streeters by then included bassist Gary Tallent, keyboardist Danny Federici, and saxophonist Clarence Clemons (guitarist Steven Van Zandt, who had previously played with Springsteen, would be recruited in 1975). Springsteen and the group began recording the next album in 1975. He invited Landau to assist him as co-producer and alienated Appel in the process.

When *Born to Run* was released in September 1975, it was immediately hailed as a masterpiece, while reaching number three on the charts. Springsteen had become the one of the biggest names in rock. In October, he was featured on the covers of *Time* and *Newsweek* magazines. He and the band then embarked on a sold-out U.S. tour. But dissension was growing between Springsteen and Appel. The result was a series of lawsuits that precluded Springsteen from releasing new records until 1978.

His disputes with Appel resolved, Springsteen reemerged on the charts with the album *Darkness at the Edge of Town* in 1978 (with Landau now a full participant in Springsteen's career). The album's brooding tone and charging rock sound reconfirmed

Springsteen's status in the rock world—and charted at number five.

Success seemed to build on success. In 1980, *The River* topped the charts, and the sold-out tours continued. In 1982, Springsteen made a startling creative detour when he released *Nebraska*, an album of folk-based demos. With its ominous themes and stark, unadorned sound, it was a vast departure from his past work. Yet it charted at number three.

But both of those albums were merely the warmups for the main event. *Born in the U.S.A.* was released in 1984, selling 10 million copies and topping the charts for seven weeks. When Springsteen and the band went on tour that year, they played to full stadiums across the country and abroad.

His stature was such that in 1986, when he released a five-record compilation box set of stage performances, it stayed at Number One on the album charts for seven weeks.

But Springsteen began to retreat from the acclaim. In 1985, he married actress Julianne Phillips and focused on his personal life for a time.

Musically, his new life yielded the 1987 album *Tunnel of Love*, which took a notably more subdued approach. It, too, topped the charts.

Along the way, Springsteen became involved in numerous benefits and shows. Having participated in the 1979's No Nukes concert and 1985's Live Aid, Springsteen began to perform on shows and tours for the Rainforest Foundation and Amnesty International.

In 1989, he divorced Phillips and began a relationship with Patti Scialfa, who had been a backup guitarist-vocalist on a number of his tours. In 1992, he disbanded the E Street Band and simultaneously released the albums *Lucky Town* and *Human Touch*, on which he played most of the instrumental parts. When Springsteen toured that year with a new band, his devoted fans came out to hail their hero once again.

STEELY DAN

While Steely Dan nominally began as a five-piece group in 1973, it quickly evolved into a trio comprising keyboardist-vocalist Donald Fagen, bassist Walter Becker . . . and a recording studio.

With Fagen and Becker presiding over an illustrious array of session musicians and thoroughly peripheral group members, Steely Dan created a studio-perfect sound that was vastly successful during the 1970s and became something of a watershed in the development of rock.

Before Steely Dan, rock had enjoyed an estimable spontaneity and looseness and an air of youthful abandon and excitement; even producer Phil Spector and the Beatles had never relinquished such virtues in all their hours in the studio.

But Steely Dan changed all that. On songs such as "Reeling in the Years" and "Rikki Don't Lose That Number" and albums such as *Pretzel Logic* and *Aja*, Fagen and Becker created a sleek, seamless amalgam of rock, jazz, and pop that was as distinctive as it was painstakingly crafted.

More artisans than artists, Fagen and Becker made records with all the care and calculation of a fine watchmaker. There was never a note out of place, or a beat unconsidered, or a vocal, guitar, or keyboard part not performed to Fagen and Becker's unerringly exacting creative and technical standards.

In Steely Dan's records, form invariably followed

function—or at least proceeded hand-in-hand. The sound and the "chops" mattered as much as the music.

Perfectionists to the core, Fagen and Becker substituted studio types like drummer Bernard Purdie and guitarist Larry Carlton for group members when the latter proved unequal to the task of achieving the sound they had in mind or lacked the technical facility it required. Their entire creative process was subverted to that purpose, to the point that Becker himself was eventually replaced on bass by the likes of Chuck Rainey on later albums.

The duo's use of studio musicians was nothing new in rock. In fact, such legendary groups as the Byrds and the Kinks and scores of others had employed such musicians from time to time on their records. But Fagen and Becker took that practice to a new level. In so doing, they dissolved the crucial bond between individual rock musicians—with all their musical foibles and idiosyncrasies—and the identity of the group itself.

It was an approach to making rock that seemed to be validated, at least commercially, by Steely Dan's chart success. From 1973 to 1980, the group had six top 20 albums, three of which sold more than a million copies. A number of singles made the top 10. Moreover, this success was achieved without the tour support that the record business believed

was a basic necessity: Steely Dan rarely performed as a group onstage, with Fagen and Becker opting to spend most of their time in the studio.

And the music was not without its expressive charms. Fagen and Becker's vocals had a certain feeling, and their songs had intriguing harmonies and instrumental theme lines. The group's use of jazz phrasings and chord patterns on songs like "Deacon Blues" and "Aja" extended rock's musical vocabulary. And their use of studio musicians yielded some memorable, technically endowed solos.

But it was the sound itself and the way it was achieved that was Steely Dan's most significant contribution to rock. The group's success—commercially and, to an extent, musically—set an example of the way things should be done to scores of producers and artists who would subsequently come to equate the perfect record with a "perfect" studio sound.

Specifically, that sound would make its way into the records of such diverse rock acts as Paul Simon and the Doobie Brothers. The apex—if it can be referred to as that—of this approach was reached with Toto, a group that was made up entirely of session musicians, several of whom had contributed to Steely Dan records.

But in a broader context, Fagen and Baxter's

Steely Dan

methods would be embraced by scores of artists who would come to pursue technical expertise and a sleek studio sound at the expense of musical spontaneity, vivacity, and fervor. In time, much of rock would lose the energy and excitement that comes from inspired amateurs—like the Beatles and the Rolling Stones and the Who—who make music because they feel it. Instead, those amateurs would increasingly give way to trained professionals who had been paid to do it.

Fagen (b. Jan. 10, 1948, Passaic, New Jersey) and Becker (b. Feb. 20, 1950, New York) first met in 1967 while studying at Bard's College in New York state. By 1969, they had formed a songwriting partnership, and their initial effort was a score for the early Richard Pryor film *You Gotta Walk It Like You Talk It.*

They attempted to sell their songs to various New York publishers but were unsuccessful. Contemplating the formation of a group, they instead joined an outfit called Demian, with guitarist Denny Dias, in 1970. But in 1971, they quit to join the Jay and the Americans backup band. During that time, they met producer Gary Katz and guitarist Jeff "Skunk" Baxter (a former member of such Boston groups as Ultimate Spinach and the Holy Modal Rounders).

When Katz became a producer at Dunhill Records in Los Angeles, he hired Fagen and Becker as songwriters. That relationship soon developed into a recording contract for the duo, who invited Baxter, Dias, drummer Jim Hodder, and vocalist David Palmer to join them in a group. The name Steely Dan came from that of a device in the William Burroughs novel *Naked Lunch.*

The group proved to be an immediate success. Its debut album, *Can't Buy a Thrill,* was released in 1973 and charted at number 17. From the album, the single "Do It Again" made number six, and its follow-up, "Reeling in the Years," hit number 11. Shortly after the release of the album, Palmer quit the group and Fagen agreed to become the vocalist.

Later in the year, the group charted at number 35 with their second album, *Countdown to Ecstacy,* and they toured briefly in the U.K. and the U.S. But

when Fagen and Becker announced their retirement from the stage in 1974, Hodder and Baxter left the group, the latter subsequently teaming up with the Doobie Brothers. Drummer Jeff Porcaro (later to form Toto) and keyboardist-vocalist Michael McDonald were added to the ranks.

The group's success continued unabated. Its third album, *Pretzel Logic,* was released in 1974 and hit number eight on the charts. From that album the single "Rikki Don't Lose That Number" hit number four.

But Fagen and Becker's dominance of the group created dissension, and in 1975, Dias, Porcaro, and McDonald departed (the latter joining the Doobie Brothers). At that point, Fagen and Becker decided to proceed as a duo under the group's name and began to use session musicians on a full-time basis.

The subsequent albums *Katy Lied* (1975), *The Royal Scam* (1976), and *Aja* (1977), were all sleek, seamless affairs that did well on the charts: the latter peaked at number three and was a million seller. In 1981, Fagen and Becker released *Gaucho,* yielding the top 10 single "Hey Nineteen." Like all of its predecessors, the album was a technically refined amalgam of rock, jazz, and pop—a combination that the duo had virtually defined as their own.

But their success notwithstanding, Fagen and Becker called it quits in 1981. Fagen pursued a solo career that yielded the 1982 album *The Nightfly.* And Becker set up a studio in Hawaii and became a producer.

The duo reunited in 1987 to perform on the album *Zazu* by Rosie Vela. But speculation about a reformation of Steely Dan proved unfounded.

Fagen subsequently became the music editor of *Premiere* magazine and, in 1988, released the single "Century's End" from the film *Bright Lights, Big City.* He also participated in the 1991 all-star album, *New York Rock and Soul Revue—Live at the Beacon.*

In 1993, Fagen released the album *Kamikiriad,* and, wonder of wonders, Steely Dan reemerged to tour the U.S.

TOP ALBUMS

PRETZEL LOGIC (ABC, '74, 8)
KATY LIED (ABC, '75, 13)
THE ROYAL SCAM (ABC, '76, 15)
AJA (ABC, '77, 3)
GAUCHO (MCA, '80, 9)

Additional Top 40 Albums: 3

TOP SONGS

DO IT AGAIN (ABC, '72, 6)
REELING IN THE YEARS (ABC, '73, 11)
RIKKI DON'T LOSE THAT NUMBER
    (ABC, '74, 4)
PEG (ABC, '77, 11)
HEY NINETEEN (MCA, '80, 10)

Additional Top 40 Songs: 5

ROD STEWART

In June of 1968, guitar virtuoso Jeff Beck brought his new group to the U.S. for its debut tour. While rock fans were dazzled by Beck's instrumental wizardry and acrobatics, their attention was immediately drawn to the Jeff Beck Group's vocalist.

He was a scarecrow figure, with spiky, tousled hair, his skinny frame clad in an old T-shirt and crushed velvet pants. While Beck played in the spotlight, the vocalist often crouched behind an amplifier, swigging champagne from a bottle. As he moved about onstage, he held the mike stand above his head, leaned against it, twirled it about in his hands. And when he sang, he revealed a voice unlike any other.

Few fans who came to the shows of that first tour were familiar with the vocalist who was holding his own onstage with Beck. But they soon would. His name was Rod Stewart.

Over the course of his long career, Stewart would turn out to be one of rock's biggest stars and, in every sense, one of its true originals.

For a start, there was the Voice. Raw and raucous, warm and human, brawling and bluesy, Stewart's sound was immediately recognizable. Its gravelly coarseness had a quality that was almost pansexual in its allure and charm; in the late '60s it was referred to as "woman blues." Simply put, it was one of the most distinctive voices to emerge in the history of popular music.

And the irrepressible Stewart put it to good use. With the Jeff Beck Group on the 1968 album *Truth* and its 1969 follow-up, *Cosa Nostra—Beck Ola*, Stewart counterbalanced and urged on Beck's guitar solos with high moans, raspy commands, and rich, ebullient, blues-inflected whispers and shouts. During his tenure with the Faces, from 1969 to 1975, Stewart's brassy, bluesy vocals were the perfect complement to that group's slapdash, roughhouse rock sound, particularly on songs like "Stay with Me."

During his solo career, Stewart proved to be a vocalist—and composer—of exceptional range and insight. On his early albums, he created music that was warm and richly textured, with aspects of folk, rock, and blues blending without apparent effort into a singular and singularly entrancing sound. Vocally, he displayed an interpretive power that had few equals in rock.

But Stewart was more than a rock performer; he was also one of the scene's most ebullient personalities and bon vivants. The merest mention of his name conjured images of bouffant hairdos, ostentatious clothing, vintage cars, ravaged hotel rooms, and blondes, blondes, blondes. "Rod the Mod," it seemed, did have more fun.

His career with the Faces appeared to be one long party, onstage and off. Arrayed in their velvet garb, kicking soccer balls into the crowds, and supping fine wines onstage, he and his mates created the image of the rock group as a kind of club for wayward fops.

It was an image Stewart elevated to a new level in his solo work and in his personal life. He played golf in Spain with Sean Connery. He journeyed to Iceland to judge a beauty contest. An avid soccer fan, he recorded the 1974 album *Easy Easy* with the Scotland World Cup Soccer Squad. Moving to Los Angeles in 1975, Stewart became the epitome of the expatriate British rock idol, lolling about his mansion, bedecking himself in satins and scarves, entertaining a seemingly endless series of young women, including actress Britt Ekland, Alana Hamilton, and model Kelly Emberg (the latter hitting him with a

$25 million palimony suit in 1991). In 1990, he married another blonde: model Rachel Hunter.

Stewart's extracurricular activities were as much a part of his career—and his role in rock history—as his vocals and music. Like few other rockers before or after him, Stewart embraced and personified the rock ethos at its most flamboyant.

Stewart (b. Roderick David Stewart, Jan. 10, 1945, Highgate, London) emerged from the thriving British R&B scene of the early 1960s. After a period of busking in Europe in 1962, Stewart returned to England and hooked up with the Birmingham-based R&B group the Five Dimensions in 1963. The next year, he joined Long John Baldry's band, the

---

TOP ALBUMS

EVERY PICTURE TELLS A STORY (Mercury, '71, *1*)
NEVER A DULL MOMENT (Mercury, '72, *2*)
A NIGHT ON THE TOWN (Warner, '76, *2*)
FOOT LOOSE & FANCY FREE (Warner, '77, *2*)
BLONDES HAVE MORE FUN (Warner, '79, *1*)

Additional Top 40 Albums: 12

TOP SONGS

MAGGIE MAY (Mercury, '71, *1*)
TONIGHT'S THE NIGHT (GONNA BE ALRIGHT)
   (Warner, '76, *1*)
DA YA THINK I'M SEXY? (Warner, '78, *1*)
MY HEART CAN'T TELL YOU NO (Warner, '88, *4*)
DOWNTOWN TRAIN (Warner, '89, *3*)

Additional Top 40 Songs: 21

Hoochie Coochie Men, as a second vocalist. In October 1964, he released his debut record, a cover of the classic "Good Morning Little Schoolgirl," on the Decca label, but it failed to chart.

Over the course of the next two years, Stewart began to build a reputation in the burgeoning London blues scene. In 1965, he joined Steampacket, a group that also included vocalist Julie Driscoll, organist Brian Auger, bassist Rick Brown, and drummer Mickey Waller (with whom he would subsequently collaborate in the Jeff Beck Group). When Steampacket disbanded in 1966, Stewart teamed with keyboardist Peter Bardens, vocalist Beryl Marsden, guitarist Peter Green, and drummer Mick Fleetwood in the group Shotgun Express.

While neither of those acts was successful, Stew-

art began to gain recognition for his vocals. In time, he came to the attention of Beck, who was forming his own group after departing from the Yardbirds.

Stewart joined the Jeff Beck Group in 1967, along with bassist Ron Wood and drummer Waller. The group's U.K. debut in 1967 was something of a farce, with Stewart in particular drawing criticism. But when the group appeared in the U.S. in 1968, he was hailed by fans and critics as a new rock hero.

But he and the mercurial Beck soon began to have problems. And when the latter threatened to dismiss Wood from the group in 1969, Stewart and Wood both departed. Later that year, they joined the R&B-tinged pop group the Small Faces (who changed their name to the Faces). That same year, Stewart embarked on a solo career that he would pursue while maintaining involvement with the Faces until the breakup of that group in 1975. With the Faces and on his own, Stewart built an immense following that would eventually elevate him to the upper ranks of '70s rock stardom.

It was with the Faces that Stewart created his trademark image of the good-time, drink-besotted rocker, flouncing and strutting about onstage to the music of Wood (who had switched to guitar), drummer Kenney Jones, bassist Ronnie Lane, and keyboardist Ian McLagan. While the group's records were only moderately successful—its 1971 album *Long Player* charted at number 29, and the 1972 single "Stay with Me" peaked at 17—it became one of the most popular live acts of the early 1970s.

Stewart's solo career fared far better. While his 1969 debut record, *The Rod Stewart Album,* was a minor hit, its earthy blend of styles set the stage for a series of remarkable albums that would be the musical high points of Stewart's career. On 1970's *Gasoline Alley,* 1971's *Every Picture Tells a Story,* and 1972's *Never a Dull Moment,* the music ranged from folk-flavored, emotional ballads (like his cover of Tim Hardin's "Reason to Believe") to raucous rockers (like his 1971 hit single "Maggie May"). Along the way, the rough-hewn quality of his voice was notably downplayed, becoming warm and heartfelt on songs like "Gasoline Alley."

Those albums proved to be vastly popular. *Every Picture Tells a Story* topped the charts in the U.K. and the U.S., and *Never a Dull Moment* reached number two in the states. His somewhat lackluster 1974 album, *Smiler,* was a Number One hit in the U.K.

In 1975, Stewart quit the Faces to concentrate full-time on his solo career.

Rod Stewart

While none of his future records would approach the quality of his early '70s output, many were quite good and firmly established Stewart's status in the rock world. *Atlantic Crossing* (1975), *A Night on the Town* (1976), and *Foot Loose and Fancy Free* (1977) reached the upper levels of the U.S. charts. Along the way, Stewart released two singles that would become classics of his repertoire: 1976's

"Tonight's the Night" and 1978's "You're in My Heart (The Final Acclaim)."

But even as those songs built upon the sound he had created in the '70s, Stewart began to move in a new, pop-oriented direction. In 1978, he released the glitzy album *Blondes Have More Fun* and its disco single, "Da Ya Think I'm Sexy?" The album and the single topped the charts and widened Stewart's fame and fortune. But those records alienated older fans who began to think that Rod the Mod had finally sold out.

More trivial music followed. During the 1980s, Stewart released a series of rock-based albums—*Tonight I'm Yours* (1981), *Body Wishes* (1983), and *Out of Order* (1988)—that had little of the excitement and distinction of his older records. But his voice was still intact, as was the fire of old—at least on occasion. He reunited with Beck in 1984 on the wiry rocker "Infatuation" and again in 1985 for an inspired rendition of the classic "People Get Ready."

All of these records hit the upper levels of the charts, as did the 1991 album *Vagabond Heart*. In 1993, Stewart enjoyed one of the biggest hits of his career with the quasi-acoustic album *Unplugged . . . and Unseated*. Recorded as part of the MTV "Unplugged" series, the album hit the top 10 and sold more than a million copies. It inspired Stewart to revive his older, more folk-based style along with some of the hits of that era, a time when he and his music were a vital part of rock's evolution.

TALKING HEADS

Talking Heads was a
key group in the history of American rock and roll.
Artistic and intellectual, but at the same time funky and rocking,
the group combined these seemingly disparate aspects
into an intriguing whole that was entirely unique.

Emerging from New York's new wave scene of the later 1970s, Talking Heads eventually became one of the most popular rock acts of the '80s while never compromising its singular sound and vision.

The vision belonged to the group's enigmatic, eccentric leader, David Byrne. On record, Byrne's songs were infused with dense and notably obscure lyrical images of urban angst and wit, all set in the context of wiry, deconstructed, minimalistic rock. Onstage, Byrne set those songs on fire with quavering, hiccuped vocals and wild, almost spastic body language that not only diffused the songs' intellectualism but heightened it and made it all the more disturbing.

If the vision belonged to Byrne, the sound belonged, largely, to the rest of the group. Keyboardist Jerry Harrison punctuated Byrne's purposely simplistic songs and guitar work with stark, minutely constructed notes, phrases, and layers of chords that had an art-rock complexity and a garage-rock flimsiness. To this, drummer Chris Frantz and bassist Tina Weymouth added slamming, funky rhythms that propelled the songs and infused them with energy and excitement.

It was an oddly provocative and alluring creative package: Talking Heads records made you think, but they also had a good beat and you could dance to them.

It was this unlikely amalgam that, in time, made the group popular not only with rock's variant fringe but also with its mainstream.

Talking Heads was formed in 1974 by Byrne (b. May 14, 1952, Dumbarton, Scotland), Weymouth (b. Martina Weymouth, Nov. 22, 1950, Coronado, California), and Frantz (b. Charlton Christopher Frantz, May, 8, 1951, Fort Campbell, Kentucky). The three had met years earlier while they were students at the Rhode Island School of Design.

In October of that year, they moved to New York City and began rehearsing and writing songs, including one called "Psycho Killer" that would become one of the band's musical signatures. They took the name Talking Heads from a technical term used in television to describe a person talking on camera.

They began to build a reputation on the growing new wave scene that was flourishing in New York in the mid-1970s, opening for such acts as the Ramones at clubs like the legendary CBGB. In 1976, they recruited Harrison (b. Jeremiah Harrison, Feb. 21, 1949, Milwaukee, Wisconsin), who had formerly been a member of Jonathan Richman's proto-punk group, the Modern Lovers.

At the end of 1976, the group signed with the innovative Sire label and began recording its debut album. That album, *Talking Heads '77,* was released in October of the titular year and reached number 97 on the charts. With its tense and wiry sound and Byrne's maniacal vocals and hyperbolic imagery, the album was vastly different from the more predictable bashings of other New York groups of the time. But during its sessions the group clashed with producer Tony Bongiovi, and the musicians began to seek new

production guidance. That came in the person of avant-garde rock pioneer Brian Eno, whom the group had met while appearing in London in 1977. Eno was invited to produce their next album.

Released in July of 1978, *More Songs About Buildings and Food* was one of the most provocative records of the new wave era. Eno eschewed his usual electronic sound, providing instead a minimalistic setting that was the ideal complement for Byrne's dense lyrical tirades and the players' churning sound. From that album, the single "Take Me to the River" —a cover of Al Green's gospel-tinged R&B classic that underscored the group's affection for rhythm-based music—proved to be something of a hit, making number 26 on the charts. The single introduced Talking Heads to a broader-based rock following.

But the single was misleading. While the group adapted the song to its own distinctive, jittery form of rock, they did not pursue either a mainstream rock sound or fan base. Instead, their music grew increasingly dense, abstract, and lyrically intriguing on 1979's *Fear of Music* (also produced by Eno).

By that time, the group had been recording and touring almost constantly for several years, and in

1980, the members took a break. During this period, Byrne and Eno began to delve into African rhythms and the avant-garde, "chance" music of John Cage, facets of which made their way into their 1980 album *My Life in the Bush of Ghosts.*

Byrne began to incorporate the African rhythms and motifs of that album into the new songs he was composing for Talking Heads. When the group reconvened later in the year to record the material, they realized that they needed extra musicians.

The result was an expanded lineup that included bassist Busta "Cherry" Jones, vocalist Donette MacDonald, keyboardist Bernie Worrell, guitarist Adrian Belew, and percussionist Steven Scales. The new nine-piece lineup recorded the 1981 album *Remain in Light,* with Eno again producing.

With its complex rhythms and Byrne's by-then signature vocals, the record proved to be the group's most successful album to that point, reaching number 19 on the charts. The group also toured with its new lineup to increasing acclaim from critics and fans.

Along the way, the four original members began to pursue individual projects. Weymouth and Frantz (who had married in 1977) formed the group the Tom Tom Club, with which they would record and tour during the rest of the decade. Harrison released his first solo album, *The Red and the Black.* And Byrne composed the score for the Twyla Tharp ballet *The Catherine Wheel* (subsequently released on an album).

While it was otherwise engaged, the group released *The Name of This Band Is Talking Heads* in 1982, a compilation of live recordings from various phases of its career to that point.

The attention generated by that album set the stage for Talking Heads' emergence as one of the more popular rock acts of the decade. On its subsequent releases—*Speaking in Tongues* (1983), *Little Creatures* (1985), and *Naked* (1988)—the group returned to its original four-piece form and, mostly, its original sound. Songs such as 1983's "Burning Down the House" and 1986's "Once in a Lifetime" were arguably more sophisticated and refined than earlier work, but they contained the same musical and vocal elements that had distinguished the group from the start.

Along the way, Talking Heads released the exceptional live album *Stop Making Sense,* based on the Jonathan Demme film of the same title, since noted as one of the great rock concert movies. The group also performed the soundtrack for the Byrne-conceived 1986 film *True Stories,* an odd look at American culture. The film was very much the visual equivalent of Byrne's lyrics and songs: normalcy as refracted and reflected by his singularly skewed sensibilities.

Increasingly, those sensibilities distanced Byrne from the rest of the Talking Heads—or, at any rate, made the group an unworkable platform for his various projects. In 1988, the group was unofficially disbanded—placed on hold while the members resumed their individual careers. Weymouth and Frantz began touring and recording again with the Tom Tom Club. Harrison formed the group Casual Gods, which released an eponymous album in 1988.

Byrne began to pursue a wide range of projects. In 1985, he had collaborated with the theatrical pioneer Robert Wilson on the opera *The Civil Wars* (his incidental music for the opera was released on the 1985 album *Music for the Knee Plays*). Through the rest of the 1980s and into the '90s, Byrne followed various musical paths. In 1988, he co-composed the score for director Bernardo Bertolucci's film *The Last Emperor* and shared an Academy Award for that score with Ryuichi Sakamoto and Cong Su. In 1991, he composed an orchestral score for the film *The Forest.*

In addition to producing a series of albums, *Brazil Classics,* that documented the music of that country, he recorded *Rei Momo* (1989) and *Uh-Oh* (1992) in which he combined the funk and rock of his Talking Heads days with Latin-based rhythms and musical themes. While much of his later work often seemed more dilettantish than inspired, the range of his musical vision made him one of the more provocative rock performers of the time.

TOP ALBUMS

MORE SONGS ABOUT BUILDINGS
AND FOOD (Sire, '78, 29)
FEAR OF MUSIC (Sire, '79, 21)
REMAIN IN LIGHT (Sire, '80, 19)
SPEAKING IN TONGUES
(Sire, '83, 15)
LITTLE CREATURES (Sire, '85, 20)
TRUE STORIES (Sire, '86, 17)
NAKED (Sire, '88, 19)

Additional Top 40 Albums: 1

TOP SONGS

TAKE ME TO THE RIVER
(Sire, '78, 26)
BURNING DOWN THE HOUSE
(Sire, '83, 9)
WILD WILD LIFE (Sire, '86, 25)

JAMES TAYLOR

As the 1960s wound down and the communal spirit of the decade began to give way to the self-absorbed individualism of the "me" decade of the '70s, the seismic cultural shift was perfectly symbolized by the emergence of James Taylor.

While most of the rock heroes of the '60s, from John Lennon and Pete Townshend to Grace Slick and Mick Jagger, had made their names with groups (Dylan was a notable exception), Taylor was his own man. Singing his songs and playing his guitar, with an interchangeable group of studio musicians behind him, he was at the forefront of a new movement in music tagged with the label "singer-songwriter."

This movement, of which Taylor was unquestionably the leading exponent, was noted for its folky sound, introspective songs, and wholly sensitive demeanor: the solo artiste baring his (or her) soul in an individualistic display of musical and lyrical expression. It was a sound and image that proved to be perfectly in sync with the changing times.

Central to the power of Taylor's music was the way in which he skillfully and tastefully blended haunting melodies with lyrics that seemed to come straight from his tortured psyche. Those lyrics, with their offhanded and oblique references to personal friends and events, were given an emotional and eloquent rendering through his smooth but soul-inflected vocals.

With the release of the album *Sweet Baby James* in March 1970, Taylor became a leading pop-rock star of the new decade. The album hit number three on the *Billboard* charts (where it would reside for the next two years) and yielded a song, "Fire and Rain," that would become a pop-folk standard. Taylor made the cover of *Time* magazine in 1971, while his rendition of the Carole King song "You've Got a Friend" topped the charts. For that single he earned a Grammy for Best Pop Vocal Performance, Male, in 1972.

While other leading artists of the movement were also selling millions of records—King with her multi-platinum 1971 album *Tapestry* and John Denver with his country-folk hits like "Take Me Home, Country Roads"—Taylor stood apart from his counterparts. While his songs, like theirs, were melodic, accessible, and commercial, they were also endowed with humanity, wit, and a wry sense of self-deprecation. At one moment, on a song like "Fire and Rain," Taylor could display an aching feeling of loss and vulnerability. At the next, as on the riotous "Steamroller," he would mock his sensitivity, belting out down-home sexual double-entendres like a (faux) bluesman.

Taylor (b. May 12, 1948, Boston) had grown up in a musical family. His mother was a lyric soprano, and three of his siblings, Kate, Alex, and Livingston, would follow his lead in the singer-songwriter movement (but with much less musical or commercial success).

From his teen years, Taylor manifested emotional problems that would plague him during his career. At 17, he had himself committed to a mental institution because of severe depression. A year later, he moved to New York and joined a rock band, the Flying Machine, which had been formed by an old friend, Danny Kortchmar (an album of his work with this group, *James Taylor and the Original Flying Machine,* would be released in 1971). But in 1968 he left the group and moved to London.

Kortchmar had once been a backup musician for British Invasion duo Peter and Gordon, and he suggested that Taylor get in touch with Peter Asher, at the time an A&R man with the Beatles' new Apple label.

Taylor eventually signed with Apple and recorded his eponymous debut album, released in December 1968. The album, which included Paul McCartney and George Harrison on one cut, was largely ignored by the public, although it contained the future Taylor signature song "Carolina in My Mind."

But with a drug habit lingering, Taylor returned to the U.S. in 1969 and entered another mental institution. Asher left Apple at this time and also moved to the U.S., where he negotiated a deal between Taylor and Warner Bros. Taylor's first album with his new label would prove to be his breakout hit, *Sweet Baby James.*

In 1971, at the height of his popularity, Taylor met Carly Simon, an up-and-coming singer-songwriter. They were married by 1972, and soon began to record as a duo (in tandem with their solo careers). This new creative/personal collaboration yielded a 1974 hit version of Charlie and Inez Foxx's "Mockingbird," a fanciful blend of the folk-pop sound of Taylor and Simon and the R&B-based soul of the Foxxes.

That sound would increasingly inform Taylor's solo work. While never relinquishing his folk base, particularly on his albums, Taylor would release additional covers of R&B songs as the 1970s unfolded. These included a 1975 rendition of Marvin Gaye's "How Sweet It Is" and a 1979 version of the Drifters' "Up on the Roof." But Taylor didn't merely dabble in soul, blues, or rock. He infused them into

his folk-based music with an ease and assurance that made them seem wholly compatible. It was this breadth of musical vision, displayed on songs like 1977's "Your Smiling Face," that made him, as the years wore on, a songwriter in the truest sense.

And being a songwriter, he continued to do just that. By the mid-1970s, Taylor's popularity had reached its apex. But he kept on churning out album after album, from *In the Pocket* (1976), *Flag* (1979), and *Dad Loves His Work* (1981) to *That's Why I'm Here* (1986), *New Moon Shine* (1991), and others in between—all loaded with signature James Taylor songs.

And oddly, given the fact that his records were no longer reaching far into the charts, he continued to be a major concert draw, consistently performing to capacity crowds across the U.S. whenever he deigned to tour. When he performed a song like "Carolina in My Mind" (from that debut album of long ago), the years seemed to melt away and, nostalgia aside, the sheer grandeur of his artistry became overwhelmingly apparent. Perhaps that is why, while other singer-songwriters have receded into the realm of novelty and nostalgia, Taylor and his music have endured.

James Taylor

TOP ALBUMS

SWEET BABY JAMES (Warner, '70, 3)
MUD SLIDE SLIM AND THE BLUE HORIZON
   (Warner, '71, 2)
ONE MAN DOG (Warner, '72, 4)
GORILLA (Warner, '75, 6)
JT (Columbia, '77, 4)

Additional Top 40 Albums: 7

TOP SONGS

FIRE AND RAIN (Warner, '70, 3)
YOU'VE GOT A FRIEND (Warner, '71, *1*)
MOCKINGBIRD (Warner, '74, 5)
HOW SWEET IT IS (TO BE LOVED
   BY YOU) (Warner, '75, 5)
HANDY MAN (Columbia, '77, 4)

Additional Top 40 Songs: 10

TRAFFIC

·················

When the Spencer Davis Group hit the charts in 1966 with the top 10 hit "Gimme Some Lovin'," the rock world was astounded by the soulful vocals and bluesy organ refrains of its 18-year-old musical prodigy, Steve Winwood. But when Winwood quit in 1967, it was generally assumed he would build a new band around his immense vocal and instrumental talents. Instead he formed Traffic.

Far from being a mere backing band, Traffic proved to be one of rock and roll's great musical partnerships. With Winwood, drummer Jim Capaldi, guitarist Dave Mason, and reeds player Chris Wood combining their varied sensibilities and tastes on a wide range of songs and a vast array of instruments, Traffic created an entirely unique and unprecedented sound. That sound was an eclectic amalgam of numerous genres, from rock and folk to Motown soul, R&B, and jazz. But instead of reproducing these forms verbatim, Traffic insinuated their various aspects into its songs to pointedly creative musical ends. The result was expansive, all-encompassing, and innovative, leading the way to vast new areas of creative exploration in rock.

In addition to issuing the classic albums *Mr. Fantasy, Traffic,* and *John Barleycorn Must Die,* Traffic took rock to a new level of musicianship in its onstage performances. Moving about from keyboards and guitars to basses, flutes, and saxes, Winwood and Wood were among the first rock multi-instrumentalists. The group's performances also came with extended improvisational sections that were as much jazz as rock. The group's stage sound was displayed on two remarkable live albums, 1971's *Welcome to the Canteen* and 1973's *Traffic—On the Road.*

Over the course of its seven-year career, Traffic fielded various lineups, with Winwood, Capaldi, and Wood at their core. Winwood (b. May 12, 1948,

Birmingham, England) formed Traffic in 1967. Dave Mason (b. May 10, 1947, Worcester, England), a former roadie for the Spencer Davis Group, soon joined the ranks along with Wood (b. June 24, 1944, Birmingham) and Capaldi (b. Aug. 24, 1944, Evesham, England).

In a surprise move, and one that would become a part of the group's lore, Traffic immediately sequestered itself from the scene in a house in rural Berkshire and began to write songs and rehearse.

Amid much anticipation, the group's debut single, "Paper Sun," was released in July, offering the first taste of their wide-ranging sound. An overtly psychedelic record, with rolling vocal harmonies and complex layers of guitars, mellotrons, and sitars, "Paper Sun" became an anthem for London's version of the summer of love. But the record was also infused with Winwood's earthy, R&B-inflected vocals and the churning saxes of Wood winding their way through the colorful refrains and themes. "Sun" ultimately went to number five on the U.K. charts. The next single, Mason's "Hole in My Shoe," came with Mason's sandpaper vocals, Capaldi's compressed, rhythmically intricate drumming, and the taped sound of a young girl reciting poetry. It reached number five on the U.K. charts, and Traffic was established as a major force in British rock.

But in a development that would recur at various points during its career, Winwood and Mason began to have musical disagreements over the direction of

Traffic

Traffic's sound, and the latter departed the group at the end of the year.

In January of 1968, the group's debut album, *Mr. Fantasy,* was released and hit number five in the U.K. Originally titled *Heaven Is in Your Mind* in the U.S., it revealed the breadth of Traffic's collective musical vision. The group explored an almost Beatles-esque classicism on "No Face, No Name, No Number" and pursued a Latin course on "The Dealer." The album's title cut was a straightforward, three-chord ballad that turned into a dense rock jam, with Winwood's needle-nosed guitar leading the way. And on "Heaven Is in Your Mind," Wood spat out raspy sax lines that gave the rock song a belting jazz presence. The album was released in the U.S. in March and eventually reached number 88.

Subsequent albums were extrapolations on this wide-ranging approach. In September of 1968, Mason rejoined the group and contributed several songs to what would be its eponymous second album. Released in November, it was an exceptional record that included Mason's classic "Feelin' Alright" and the rolling, winsome country-folk song "You Can All Join In," along with Winwood and Capaldi's rocking "Pearly Queen" and the soul-strutting "Who Knows What Tomorrow May Bring." The album hit number 17 in the U.S. and number nine in the U.K.

While Traffic had enjoyed major pop success in its own country and had become something of an underground hit in the U.S., the centrifugal creative forces that had been at the core of its sound began to tear the group apart.

Traffic disbanded in January 1969 when Winwood left to form the supergroup Blind Faith with Cream's Eric Clapton and Ginger Baker. Despite its vast success, Blind Faith was short-lived. With its breakup later in the year, Winwood joined Ginger Baker's Air Force for a month and then left that group to pursue a solo career.

In February of 1970, Winwood began work on his first solo record, which he tentatively titled *Mad Shadows.* Dissatisfied with his attempts to play all of the instruments on the album, Winwood invited Wood and Capaldi to join him. Soon, Traffic was back together, and the result of their efforts was *John Barleycorn Must Die.* One of the finest albums in rock, it included a pioneering fusion of jazz and rock on "Glad" and "Empty Pages" along with the eloquent title track, an ancient British folk song on which the astounding Wood delivered a ravishing flute solo. The album also proved to be Traffic's breakout record in the U.S., hitting number five and generating legions of new fans. Their U.S. tour during the fall of 1970—for which they added Blind Faith's bassist Rick Grech—was equally successful.

But the group didn't capitalize immediately on its newfound popularity. Instead, Winwood, Wood, and Capaldi retreated from the scene once again, this time to Morrocco, where they spent the winter. In 1971, they reemerged with an expanded lineup that included Grech, percussionist Reebop Kwaku-Baah, and drummer Jim Gordon (formerly of Delaney and Bonnie and Friends and Derek and the Dominos). Mason re-joined, once again, and this lineup toured the U.K. later in the year, also recording the live album *Welcome to the Canteen*. But Mason departed at the end of the tour, and the rest of the group began to record the next Traffic album.

Released at the end of 1971, *The Low Spark of High Heeled Boys*, with its jazz-infused title cut, hit number seven on the U.S. charts and reaffirmed the group's status on the scene. But at the start of 1972, the new lineup splintered. Soon after that, Winwood contracted peritonitis and was forced to withdraw for a period of recuperation. Capaldi, meanwhile, began recording a solo album at Muscle Shoals studio in Alabama. While the album *Oh, How We Danced* failed on the charts, it generated a musical collaboration between Capaldi and the studio's legendary rhythm section of David Hood and Roger Hawkins. When Winwood recovered and Traffic resumed its career, they were recruited. (Muscle Shoals keyboardist Barry Beckett also joined the group for a world tour that year.)

The result of their work was the 1973 album *Shoot Out at the Fantasy Factory*, a fairly mundane rock effort that reached number six on the charts but was, creatively, a cut below Traffic's standards. By 1974, that lineup had disbanded and bassist Rosko Gee had joined. But Traffic had become mired in ennui, and its final album, *When the Eagle Flies*, was a lackluster, directionless set.

All four of Traffic's original members subsequently pursued solo careers that were greeted with varying degrees of acceptance. Wood recorded with several groups during the rest of the 1970s, but he finally faded from the scene (he died in 1983 from liver failure). Capaldi assumed a more pop-oriented stance, which he offered on such negligible albums as 1976's *Short Cut Draw Blood* and 1983's *Fierce Heart*.

Mason's career got off to a fine start with 1970's *Alone Together*, a remarkable album of folk and rock-based songs that hit number 22 on the charts. But his later records—including a 1971 collaboration with the Mamas and the Papas' Cass Elliot—were somewhat mediocre efforts that proved to be marginally successful. By the later '80s, his career had come to a standstill.

Winwood's career was just the opposite. It began in 1977 with the release of an eponymous album that created a stir among critics but was a modest commercial success. That changed in 1981, when *Arc of a Diver* made number three on the U.S. charts and yielded the hit single "While You See a Chance."

With its lithe, synthesizer-infused sound and Winwood's soulful vocals and instrumental solos, *Arc of a Diver* set the tone for the rest of the albums he would record into the '90s. The album also marked the start of a collaboration with lyricist Will Jennings, with whom Winwood would enjoy vast commercial success over the course of the rest of the decade.

While Winwood's career waned briefly in 1982 with the album *Talking Back to the Night*, it came roaring back in 1986 with the release of *Back in the High Life*. That album hit number three, sold over a million copies, and won Grammy Awards in 1987 for Record of the Year and Best Pop Vocal Performance, Male. In 1989, the album *Roll with It* hit Number One, as did the single of the same title. In 1990, *Refugees of the Heart* reached number 28.

While these records achieved a broad-based popularity that Traffic never reached, they were noteworthy more for Winwood's unparalleled vocals and his fine songs than for creative breathroughs on a par with those of Traffic in the 1960s.

TOP ALBUMS

TRAFFIC (United Artists, '68, *17*)
LAST EXIT (United Artists, '69, *19*)
JOHN BARLEYCORN MUST DIE (United Artists, '70, *5*)
WELCOME TO THE CANTEEN (United Artists, '71, *26*)
THE LOW SPARK OF HIGH HEELED BOYS (Island, '71, *7*)
SHOOT OUT AT THE FANTASY FACTORY (Island, '73, *6*)
TRAFFIC—ON THE ROAD (Island, '73, *29*)
WHEN THE EAGLE FLIES (Asylum, '74, *9*)

TOP SONGS

DEAR MR. FANTASY (United Artists, '68)
THE LOW SPARK OF HIGH HEELED BOYS (Island, '71)

U2
......

U2 appeared in the late 1970s as part of the new wave scene that emerged from the debris of the punk era. In the following decade the Irish group invaded the musical mainstream—with much of its new wave spirit intact—to become one of the most successful and important rock acts of its time.

The group's origins, and success, determined its significance. In fact, U2 didn't go to the mainstream as much as it forced the mainstream to come to it, accomplishing that feat by creating a sound that had the edge and energy of the new wave along with an instrumental sophistication and melodic grandeur that made it accessible to the vast rock marketplace. Arguably more than any other group—including Talking Heads—U2 made the new wave movement a major creative and commercial force.

U2 was formed in 1976 by vocalist Bono (b. Paul Hewson, May 10, 1960, Dublin, Ireland), guitarist the Edge (b. David Evans, Aug. 8, 1961, Dublin), bassist Adam Clayton (b. March, 13, 1960, Dublin), and drummer Larry Mullen (b. Oct. 31, 1961, Dublin). A fifth member, keyboardist Dick Evans, quit the group within months. Initially they were called the Hype but soon changed their name to U2.

The group began to perform on the local Dublin scene during 1977, gradually accruing a modest following. In 1978, U2 won a talent contest and subsequently auditioned for CBS Records in Ireland. With its popularity growing, the group released its debut record, "EP U2:3," which topped the Irish charts in 1979.

Over the next three years, U2 began to expand its reputation in the U.S. and the U.K. The seeds of the group's music—a sound that would come to full bloom later in the decade—were planted on the 1980 debut album, *Boy*. On songs such as "I Will Follow," U2 created a dense latticework of guitar chords and lines that were supplemented by the side bass motifs and spare, straightforward drumming. Above this sound, Bono's vocals provided a soaring, almost heroic, presence. It was a sound that was at once panoramic and stark, infused with the iconoclastic fervor of the new wave along with more traditional, timeless rock values.

Boy hit number 63 on the U.S. charts, and U2 began to tour constantly. Its second album, 1981's *October*, was modestly successful, but it added to the group's growing popularity.

That popularity expanded into the rock mainstream in 1983 when their third disc, *War*, charted at number 12 in the U.S. On that album, all of the group's musical signatures coalesced. The personal introspection of Bono's lyrics reached a new level of eloquence on songs like "New Year's Day," while his political sensibilities were expressed on the strident "Sunday, Bloody Sunday." The group's sound also assumed an expansiveness that was displayed in the melodic theme lines of the Edge's guitar and the way his chords interlocked with Clayton's bass lines and Mullen's drums (especially in the martial motif of "Sunday, Bloody Sunday"). With "New Year's Day" hitting number 53 on the U.S. singles chart, the album established U2 as a major force in the rock scene.

One of the hallmarks of U2's career was its ability to evolve musically while never relinquishing its core sound. With the crucial assistance of producers Brian Eno and Daniel Lanois, it did just that on

1984's *The Unforgettable Fire*. While the Edge's theme lines remained intact, as did Bono's emotional vocals, the group's music was rendered in a new, atmospheric setting that had both a gossamer lightness and a rock sturdiness, much of which came from the electronic effects directed by Eno. The result was a sprawling, complex instrumental grandeur exemplified by the song "Pride (In the Name of Love)." Dedicated to Martin Luther King Jr., "Pride" became one of the group's signatures, charting at number 33. Its sound was one the group would pursue during the rest of the decade.

U2 became one of the biggest touring acts of the time, with critics and fans hailing the group as one of the finest in rock. In 1985, *Rolling Stone* magazine dubbed U2 "The Band of the '80s," and its arena tour of the U.S. played to capacity crowds.

U2 began to assert an activist role that it continued over the course of the rest of its career. At the end of 1984, Bono and Clayton participated in the Band Aid single "Do They Know It's Christmas?" for the Ethiopian relief effort. The group also performed at the Live Aid concert in July 1985. In 1986, it joined Amnesty International's 25th anniversary tour. And that same year, it staged Self Aid in Dublin to benefit the unemployed.

With the release of *The Joshua Tree* in 1987, U2 finally moved into the top level of rock stardom while reaching the apex of its expansive sound. The album—one of the finest of the decade—was played

out on a vast musical canvas. Bono's vocals displayed a wide range of feelings and concerns, from the plaintive emotionalism of "With or Without You" to the raucous energy of "Bullet the Blue Sky" and the activist posturings of "Mothers of the Disappeared." Instrumentally, the group's dense, almost symphonic sound (played on guitar, bass, and drums) came with an intriguing array of textures and layers of harmonies and counter themes.

The world tour that accompanied *The Johua Tree* began in arenas but ended in stadiums as the album dominated the charts, holding the Number One position for nine weeks. The vast success of the album and tour subsequently landed U2 on the cover of *Time* magazine.

The curve of the group's career continued to rise inexorably in 1988. In February, *The Joshua Tree* won Grammy Awards for Album of the Year and Best Rock Performance by a Duo or Group with Vocal. The film of the world tour, *Rattle and Hum,* was released later in the year and proved to be a critical and commercial success. It yielded a two-record set of the same title, which topped the charts for six weeks, sold more than two million copies, and won two 1989 Grammy Awards for Best Rock Performance and Best Performance Music Video.

But the group's success had its downside. In the film, Bono could be seen posturing and posing like the rock star he had become. He also began to display the hubris that goes with that status. At a free show in San Francisco, Bono spray-painted a sculpture in a public park and then justified the act as artistic expression. He subsequently apologized, but it was obvious that the acclaim and adulation were becoming something of a problem, particularly for a group that had previously maintained its distance from the ego-driven excesses of the rock world.

Perhaps as a reaction to its success, U2 retreated from the scene for a time, touring sporadically and engaging in side projects. These included the Edge's score for the Royal Shakespeare Company's adaptation of the film *A Clockwork Orange* in 1990 and

Mullens's theme song for the World Cup soccer team. That same year, U2 contributed a version of the classic "Night and Day" for *Red Hot + Blue,* a set of all-star renditions of Cole Porter songs to benefit AIDS charities.

When U2 reemerged in 1991 with the album *Achtung, Baby,* the sound that it had pursued—and perfected on *The Joshua Tree*—had been largely abandoned. In its place was jagged, abrasive music that suggested that U2 was rebelling against itself. On songs like "The Fly" and the clangorous "Zoo Station," the metallic and abstract sound, created with the assistance of Eno and Lanois, was the polar opposite of the group's earlier melodicism and expansiveness.

U2's subsequent "Zoo TV" tour was as experimental as the album. Flanked by a complex array of video displays (designed by Eno) that flashed various images via the tour's satellite technology, and with six East German Trabant automobiles suspended over the stage, U2 seemed to be confronting its fans and itself with its new sound and imagery. When Bono came onstage in a gold suit and garish sunglasses, it was almost as if he were mocking the flashy rock star he had become.

U2 continued its new direction on the 1993 album *Zooropa*. The electronic sound and musical abstraction of *Achtung, Baby* was pushed to new extremes, with dark, brooding textures and lyrical images that were at once disturbing and exhilarating. The vocals of Bono and the Edge were at times almost garbled, and Eno's synthesizer chords and lines had an expressionistic eloquence.

Achtung, Baby and *Zooropa* amounted to one of the most astonishing volte faces by a major rock group since the Beatles. With these albums, U2 reasserted its ability to control and direct its musical destiny, its vast success notwithstanding. Indeed, the group, like the Beatles before it, was using that success as a support for its artistic freedom. Having created one of the grandest and most expressive sounds in rock during the 1980s, U2 was moving on to new creative territory.

TOP ALBUMS

WAR (Island, '83, *12*)
UNDER A BLOOD RED SKY (Island, '84, *28*)
THE UNFORGETTABLE FIRE (Island, '84, *12*)
THE JOSHUA TREE (Island, '87, *1*)
RATTLE AND HUM (Island, '88, *1*)

Additional Top 40 Albums: 1

TOP SONGS

WITH OR WITHOUT YOU (Island, '87, *1*)
I STILL HAVEN'T FOUND WHAT I'M
   LOOKING FOR (Island, '87, *1*)
WHERE THE STREETS HAVE NO NAME
   (Island, '87, *13*)
DESIRE (Island, '88, *3*)
ANGEL OF HARLEM (Island, '88, *14*)

Additional Top 40 Songs: 1

VAN HALEN

H eavy metal was rumbling along like a tank in the late 1970s, with groups such as Judas Priest and Black Sabbath stationed behind armored layers of beats and decibels. Suddenly, a group of brash newcomers from Los Angeles filled 'er up with high-octane riffs, put the pedal to the metal, and sent the machine racing ahead like a dragster. The group was Van Halen.

When their eponymous debut album was released in 1978, the world of metal was slammed back in its seat as it encountered the first revolution in its formulaic sound since the days of Led Zeppelin 10 years before.

To the primarily guitar-based metal world, the dizzying, wiry picking of Edward Van Halen (b. Jan. 26, 1957, Nijmegen, Holland) was a quantum leap of phenomenal proportions. It was as if all of metal's clichéd phrases had suddenly been speeded up and given an energy injection. Notes seemed to explode in all directions at once, with odd and angular screams and hammer-ons and harmonics issuing from his fretboard.

The group's hyperactive vocalist, David Lee Roth (b. Oct. 10, 1955, Bloomington, Indiana), couldn't sing his way out of a sheet-metal factory, but he had a hunky image and a wry wit that were perfect foils to Edward Van Halen's virtuosity. And with Edward's brother Alex (b. May 8, 1955, Nijmegen) pounding away on drums and Michael Anthony (b. June 20, 1955, Chicago) providing a rock-solid if unexceptional low end on bass, Van Halen—the group and the album—proved that a new metal age had arrived.

As if to confirm that, the album went on to sell two million copies and chart at number 19.

But if the sound was the first thing that turned metal heads, it wouldn't be the last.

From the start of its career, Van Halen was an exaggeration of the already-exaggerated metal ethos, and the exaggeration became more pronounced as the group—for wont of a better word—matured.

It began with the group's original name, Mammoth, which it used for a time after its lineup coalesced in 1974. It was a big name. And things proceeded to get bigger in every way.

The Van Halen brothers and Roth and Anthony toiled on the L.A. club circuit for several years, changing the group's name, in 1975, to Van Halen and accruing a following of thousands of local fans along the way. In 1976, Kiss bassist Gene Simmons heard the group at one of those clubs and offered to produce a demo based on live performances of the songs "Running with the Devil" and "House of Pain." But the demo was subsequently rejected by several major labels.

That situation changed in 1977 when Van Halen came to the attention of Warner. Bros. executive Ted Templeman, who saw them perform at the Starwood Club and immediately signed the group to that label.

In negotiating its record deal, Van Halen demanded complete artistic control . . . and a clause providing paternity insurance. Later, after Van Halen had attained platinum success, the group would make new and even more outlandish contractual demands, including an infamous concert rider that stipulated that M&M candies be provided backstage—with the brown ones specifically removed.

Meanwhile, *Van Halen II* was released in 1979. It sold five million copies and reached number six on the charts. The group's tours began drawing capacity crowds and the attention of the national media, whose interest was sparked by Van Halen's excessive offstage behavior.

Scores of smashed TV's and trashed hotel rooms later, Van Halen was writing a new chapter in the annals of rock touring. Tales of drug, alcohol, and groupie excess abounded. And new twists were written in: at the start of a July 4, 1979, concert at Anaheim Stadium, four Van Halen look-alikes were hired to parachute onto the field before the group's performance. Subsequent tours were titled "Invasion" and "Hide Your Sheep."

Amid the excess, Van Halen was transforming metal from a blues-based genre into a sleek, highly commercial amalgam of cranking rock and slick pop. Songs like "Running with the Devil," "Dance the Night Away," "Panama," and covers of Roy Orbison's "Pretty Woman" and the Kinks' "You Really Got Me" combined pounding beats, grandiose riffs, and vocal harmonies in an entirely new heavy metal alloy. A creative pinnacle was reached in 1984 with the single "Jump," a true rock masterpiece that came with an irresistible keyboard hook and one of the most inspired solos in the history of the electric guitar (Edward would rack up another memorable solo on Michael Jackson's 1983 hit "Beat It" from the latter's *Thriller* album). "Jump" topped the U.S. charts for five weeks.

Meanwhile, Van Halen also continued to thrive as a major concert act, becoming one of the preeminent touring draws of the era. In 1983, the group performed at the US Festival in San Bernardino, California, and earned a hefty $1 million for its work (a record fee at that point, and one that the event's organizer, Apple Computer founder Steve Wozniak, also reportedly paid to the festival's co-headliner, David Bowie).

While Edward Van Halen was the musical standout on record and onstage, it was Roth who, with his flowing blonde locks, onstage kick-jumps, and outrageous antics, proved to be the focus of the group's image. At various points on the group's tours, he also collapsed from exhaustion and was injured. During the taping of a performance on Italian television in 1980, he suffered various contusions and a concussion when he fell into a phalanx of stage lights while attempting a somersault.

Offstage, Roth was equally outlandish. In 1985, on a bet with Templeman, he drove across the U.S. in three days to meet up with the group at the MTV Awards. He also became involved in expeditions to New Guinea and Nepal and became an avid rock climber. And stories began to circulate about his penchant for writing songs in the back seat of his car while being driven around all night by his chauffeur.

Whether or not the many stories about him were true didn't really matter. To Roth, image was everything, and he became the symbol of the excesses that became an integral part of Van Halen's reputation.

Thus, when Roth announced that he was leaving the group in 1985, there was some question as to whether the group would continue; Warner Bros. reportedly advised the other members to drop the name Van Halen because of Roth's absence.

The group didn't bother.

Instead, while Roth pursued his solo career with his usual enthusiasm, Van Halen recruited singer-guitarist Sammy Hagar (formerly of Montrose and subsequently a solo metallist of minor stardom) to take his place, reportedly at the suggestion of the owner of a car repair shop frequented by Edward Van Halen and Hagar. It was an inspired choice. While Hagar couldn't sing any better than Roth, he proved equal to the task of maintaining his predecessor's braggadocio and hell-raising style.

Over the next few years, a rancorous rivalry developed between Roth and his former group. But success continued apace for both.

Roth's solo albums, 1985's *Crazy from the Heat,*

TOP ALBUMS

VAN HALEN II (Warner, '79, 6)
WOMEN AND CHILDREN FIRST (Warner, '80, 6)
FAIR WARNING (Warner, '81, 5)
DIVER DOWN (Warner, '82, 3)
1984 (MCMLXXXIV) (Warner, '84, 2)
5150 (Warner, '86, 1)
OU812 (Warner, '88, 1)

Additional Top 40 Albums: 1

TOP SONGS

JUMP (Warner, '84, 1)
WHY CAN'T THIS BE LOVE (Warner, '86, 3)
WHEN IT'S LOVE (Warner, '88, 5)

Additional Top 40 Songs: 11

Van Halen

1986's *Eat 'Em and Smile*, and 1988's *Skyscraper* (whose cover was a photo of Roth rock climbing in Yosemite National Park) made the upper reaches of the charts, along with an odd set of singles that included covers of the Beach Boys' "California Girls" and Al Jolson's "Just a Gigolo."

And Van Halen held up its end of the competition with such cheekily titled albums as 1986's *5150* (the code number used by the New York City Police for the criminally insane and the name of Edward Van Halen's home recording studio), 1988's *OU812,* and 1991's *For Unlawful Carnal Knowledge* (acronym intended). Singles such as 1986's "Why Can't This Be Love" and 1988's "Finish What Ya Started" were hits as well and proved that the group's sound had barely changed in the conversion from Roth to Hagar. Hagar, in fact as well as hype, seemed to fit perfectly into the Van Halen's traditional all-for-one

image. Onstage, they allowed him to perform his signature solo hit "I Can't Drive 55," a rather mundane effort that was hardly up to Van Halen's standards. And offstage, they seemed to make a point of doing things together. In 1989, the group's members opened their own club, the Cabo Wabo, in the Mexican resort town of Cabo San Lucas, where they were known to drop in from time to time and perform.

At the beginning of the 1990s, Roth's career began to fade somewhat. While his 1991 album *A Little Ain't Enough* charted at number 18, his tour of that year was cancelled due to poor advance ticket receipts. Increasingly, he began to retreat from the scene.

Van Halen's career, however, continued to flourish. Its 1993 concert album, *Live: Right Here, Right Now*, went platinum, marking another chapter in its remarkably successful and innovative career.

THE VELVET UNDERGROUND

The Velvet Underground
was a slap in the face to the era of peace,
love, and understanding.

Much of the rock world of 1967 was infused with a sense of idealism and spirituality. On the West Coast of the U.S., the "flower power" scene, with its hippies and psychedelic groups, was in full bloom. In England, the Beatles were singing "All You Need Is Love." Everywhere, rock artists and their followers were basking in the belief that they could transform the world into a better place. The Velvet Underground would have none of it.

Their debut album, *The Velvet Underground and Nico*, charted a new course in the rock of the time, one that was the very antithesis of the psychedelic age. Released in March 1967, the album came with a brazenly dark, spare sound and unsparing lyrical images that were polar opposites of the Beatles' grandiose visions and the effusive idealism of other rockers.

On songs such as "Sunday Morning," "I'm Waiting for the Man," and "There She Goes Again," the Velvets exuded a brooding, sullen sensibility that was utterly bleak in its view of reality.

While their counterparts in the psychedelic scene extolled the virtues and possibilities of mind-expanding drugs, the Velvets revelled in the numbing torpor and escape of "Heroin." While Eric Burdon sang of "warm San Francisco nights," they intoned "The Black Angel's Death Song." While seemingly the entire rock world of the time was getting back to basics and nature and meditation, the Velvets were hunkering down with the urban angst of their New York habitat.

Their music was equally uncompromising. Guitarist Lou Reed slashed out chords with a ferocious fervor, and his vocals had a sardonic, mordant edge. John Cale cut across the seams of the songs with the dense, angular phrases of his viola. Maureen Tucker—one of the first female drummers in rock—slammed out simplistic beats that propelled Cale's bass lines and Sterling Morrison's guitar counterpoints. And vocalist Nico wafted above it all with an ethereal sound and presence that were simultaneously decadent and disturbing.

The Velvets made something of a splash as part of Andy Warhol's scene in New York in 1966. But their sound and outlook were mostly shunned by the rock public of the time. By 1971, the original members of the group had departed.

But its lack of commercial success notwithstanding, the Velvet Underground had a vast and enduring impact on the course of rock music. Its deconstructed sound, based largely on Reed's churning chords and Tucker's primal rhythms, would be the building blocks of the London punks and the groups of the New York new wave scene, exemplified by Talking Heads, in the 1970s. The Velvets' abstract density and undiluted approach to rock would also be heard in the 1980s and '90s in various incarnations, from the noise experiments of Sonic Youth to the purposely simplistic bashings of the grunge groups of Seattle.

The Velvets' quasi-artistic aspects—largely supplied by Cale's stark, minimalistic keyboard and viola textures and Nico's mannered posturings—would also form the basis of the art rock of such '70s artists as Roxy Music and Brian Eno (who collaborated with Cale and Nico on various projects during the decade).

And as for the Velvets' bleak, pessimistic outlook, it, too, proved to be remarkably prescient. Long after the flower power era and ethos had wilted, the dark lyrical ruminations of the Velvet Underground would become all too relevant. In that sense, as

The Velvet Underground

much as in its music, the Velvet Underground was not of its time as much as ahead of its time.

The initial version of the Velvet Underground was formed in 1964, when Cale (b. Dec. 4, 1940, Garnant, Wales) teamed with Reed (b. Mar. 2, 1943, New York), Morrison, and drummer Angus MacLise. They used various group names—including, tellingly, the Primitives—before settling on the Velvet Underground, which they took from the title of a pornographic book.

The group performed in the underground New York art scene during the rest of the year (Cale had worked with avant-gardist La Monte Young before joining the Velvets). In 1965, they gained the attention of Andy Warhol, who became their manager of sorts and suggested they enlist Nico (b. Christa Paffgen, Cologne, Germany) as vocalist. MacLise quit because of this and was replaced by Tucker.

Warhol recruited the group to provide the music for *The Exploding Plastic Inevitable*, which was presented at a New York club in 1966. The event, a precursor of the "performance art" that would emerge in the late 1970s, was variously hailed and slammed by the critics. But it resulted in the group being signed by the MGM/Verve label later in the year.

Warhol's interest in the group began to wane, but for their debut album he produced a cover design—a banana on a white background—that was as elliptical and minimalistic as the music contained within. When *The Velvet Underground and Nico* was released in March 1967, it created a stir among rock cognoscenti but failed commercially.

The group had never been entirely in agreement about Nico's presence, and after the album was released, she was asked to leave. Continuing as a quartet, the group released *White Light/White Heat* in 1968, but it, too, proved to be too harsh and abstract for rock tastes of the time. Dissension had been growing between Cale and Reed, and in March of that year, the former quit the group to pursue a solo career. He was subsequently replaced by Doug Yule, formerly of the Grass Menagerie.

When the group's eponymous third album failed to chart in 1969, the Velvets were released by their record label. Signed to Atlantic, they continued to tour and record. But when the next album, *Loaded*, was released in 1970 without Reed's approval, he departed. By 1971, Morrison and Tucker had done the same. The Velvets continued with Yule as leader and various other musicians coming and going until the group folded in 1973.

Atlantic released *Live at Max's Kansas City* in 1972, a recording of the Velvets' last performance with Reed. In 1974, the album *1969 Velvet Underground Live* was released on Mercury.

Ironically, the Velvet Underground's most commercially successful album was 1985's *VU*, a set of "lost" studio tracks, which reached number 85 on the charts. Its success underscored the rock world's growing appreciation of the important role that the Velvet Underground had played in the evolution of the music. A similar compendium of additional tracks, *Another View*, appeared the next year.

Various members of the group subsequently pursued solo careers that were as intriguing as that of the Velvet Underground. Nico released a number of

---

TOP ALBUMS

THE VELVET UNDERGROUND AND NICO (Verve, '67)
WHITE LIGHT/WHITE HEAT (Verve, '68)
THE VELVET UNDERGROUND (MGM, '69)
LOADED (Cotillion/Atlantic, '70)
1969 VELVET UNDERGROUND LIVE (Mercury, '74)
VU (Polydor, '85)
ANOTHER VIEW (Polydor, '86)
LIVE MCMXCIII (Sire, '93)

---

albums, including 1974's *The End* (with Cale), 1981's *Drama of Exile* (a series of Reed and David Bowie covers), and 1985's *Camera Obscura* (also recorded with Cale). She died of a brain hemorrhage in 1988. Tucker was also active at various points. In 1989, she released *Life in Exile After Abdication,* which she recorded with Reed and Sonic Youth.

Not surprisingly, the two most prolific and creative former Velvets were the group's leaders, Cale and Reed. Their solo albums over the succeeding two decades illustrated the divergent leanings toward art and rock that had animated and defined the Velvet Underground's sound.

Cale's career was erratic but often inspired. His 1971 album *Church of Anthrax* was a provocative collaboration with minimalist composer Terry Riley, while 1972's *The Academy in Peril* displayed his classical predilections: the album was recorded with the Royal Philharmonic. During the middle 1970s,

Cale assumed various artistic guises. On the concert album *June 1st, 1974,* he teamed with Nico, Brian Eno, and Kevin Ayers on a terse art rock set. That same year, his album *Fear* came with a spare, rampaging sound that recalled his days in the Velvet Underground. By 1979, he had entered the punk–new wave world he had inspired, storming his way through jagged rock songs with a young group of mostly amateurish musicians. In 1982, he returned to his avant-garde sound on *Music for a New Society*. What may have been his finest music emerged at the beginning of the '90s. In 1990, he released the art rock album *Wrong Way Up*, a collaboration with Eno that came with intricate electronic flourishes and minimalistic, melodic songs. In the same year, he teamed with Reed on *Songs for Drella*, an oddly moving and affectionate tribute to Warhol.

While Cale pursued an overtly art rock course, Reed became the epitome of the *Rock 'n' Roll Animal* (an album he recorded in 1974). His eponymous debut album of 1970 had been mostly a set of songs he had written for the Velvet Underground. By 1972, with David Bowie acting as his producer, Reed had become a garish glam-rocker, intoning his monotonous paean to androgyny on the hit single "Walk on the Wild Side." The rest of the decade was spent thrashing about in various rock personae, from the proto-industrial noise of *Metal Machine Music* (1975) to the somewhat convoluted *The Bells* of 1979. By 1982, Reed had begun to mellow somewhat, exploring the doubts and questions of encroaching middle age on 1982's *The Blue Mask*. In 1989, the newly middle-aged Reed emerged with the masterful *New York,* an album that reconciled the sardonic edge of his rock sensibilities with a more mature expressivity. Reed's guitar and vocals had never sounded more assured, and his cynicism was tempered by a world-weary acceptance that gave songs like "Romeo Had Juliet" and "Dirty Boulevard" an almost charming presence. On 1992's *Magic and Loss,* he presented a dark and brooding but ultimately redemptive account of the deaths of two friends that was as inspiring and touching as any piece of music he had ever created.

In June of 1990, the original members of the Velvet Underground performed onstage together, for the first time since 1969, at the opening of a Warhol retrospective in Paris. They played "Heroin." In 1993, Cale, Reed, Morrison, and Tucker recorded a new live album.

THE VENTURES

For a brief time,
in the early 1960s, instrumental groups became
a force in rock. And the group that became the symbol
of them all was the Ventures.

Instrumental music never gained much currency in the world of rock and roll. Vocal heroes were the order of the day, and of the rock era. And what purely instrumental artists there were—with the exception of '50s guitar hero Duane Eddy—usually emerged as novelty acts with the odd and occasional signature hit.

With their 1960 debut single, "Walk—Don't Run," the Ventures established a new sound and stylistic approach in rock. Driven by charging beats and intense, wiry electric guitars and bass and shaped by a simple, direct theme line, "Walk—Don't Run" became the prototype for a new instrumental movement that stormed its way up the charts of the early '60s and inspired countless guitarists and groups of the time.

While a number of those groups would enjoy hits of their own, the Ventures were, by far, the most successful. They were also one of the most durable: over the course of their long career, which continued into the 1990s, the Ventures recorded over 50 albums.

Oddly, given the fact that their sound was exclusively instrumental, the Ventures were hardly virtuosos. Their songs and albums were simple and straightforward, and their playing was competent but little more. The Ventures didn't improvise; they didn't embellish the melodies of their songs with any technical flourishes or spectacular solos.

But they did create a monolithic sound that was smooth and sleek and indescribably "modern." Lead guitarist Nokie Edwards' theme lines had the twang of Eddy, but they were updated with echo and vibrato effects that gave them an edgy electricity (in 1963, he became the first guitarist in rock history to use a fuzz box, on the single, "The 2000 Pound Bee"). Rhythm guitarist Don Wilson, bassist Bob Bogle, and drummer Howie Johnson backed him with a wall of chords, beats, and rhythms that surged forward with a machine-like, incessant energy.

The Ventures also proved adept at making their music relevant for its time, by making records that latched onto prevailing trends and tastes. In 1962, they recorded the single "Twist with the Ventures" to capitalize on the dance craze that was sweeping the U.S. Albums like 1963's *Surfing*, 1965's *Ventures a Go-Go,* and 1967's *Guitar Freakout* indicated, by their titles, the ways in which the group remodeled its sound to adapt to the rock marketplace.

As an adjunct to this, the Ventures recorded a vast number of theme songs from films and television programs. Primarily released as singles, these included "(Theme from) Silver City," "Lolita Ya-Ya" (from the film *Lolita*), "Secret Agent Man," "Batman Theme," and the theme from "Hawaii Five-O."

But it didn't matter what the Ventures recorded. It was all filtered through the group's idiosyncratic style. Edwards' guitar would set up the melody, the other players would follow, and whatever it was that was being recorded would suddenly become a "Ventures" song—ironically, in much the same manner that a vocalist might put his or her interpretive stamp on a particular piece of music.

The group's sound was that distinctive.

It was also highly influential. The Ventures opened the floodgates for instrumental music in the early 1960s and inspired numerous surf-rockers like the Chantay's ("Pipeline"), the Marketts ("Surfer's

Stomp"), and the master of the surf guitar, Dick Dale, who, with the Del-Tones, gave the music a harder rock edge on "Let's Go Trippin'." One of the epochal moments of that movement came on the Surfaris' 1963 classic "Wipe Out," with its rolling, storming drum solo.

Less directly, the Ventures' driving sound made its way into that of the Who (whose drummer, Keith Moon, was a professed Ventures fan) and a number of garage-rock groups of the mid-1960s, including the Trashmen, the Wailers, and the Astronauts. The Ventures wiry, metallic rock was also a central ingredient in the music of late-'70s Los Angeles bands like the Go-Go's, among others.

Ultimately, the Ventures' music was more timely than timeless. But if it sounded somewhat dated, it was in the best sense of the word. Like tail fins or surf boards, the Ventures' records were emblematic of an era.

The Ventures were formed in Seattle in 1960, when Edwards (b. May 9, 1939, Tacoma, Washington) and Johnson (b. 1938, Washington) teamed with Bogle (b. Jan. 16, 1937, Portland, Oregon) and Wilson (b. Feb. 10, 1937, Tacoma). Originally calling themselves the Versatones, they released their debut single, "Cookies and Coke," on their own label, Blue Horizon, in February of that year. It gained the group a local following, but it failed to chart nationally.

Changing their name to the Ventures, the group released "Walk—Don't Run" in April. It, too, failed to chart. But when the single was subsequently released on the Dolton label—distributed across the U.S. by Liberty Records—it was an immediate success, hitting number two on the charts and selling more than a million copies. The Ventures then relocated to Los Angeles and began recording a new single. That record, a cover of the standard "Perfidia," charted at number 15 in January 1961 and was followed by a cover of the '50s R&B hit "Ram-Bunk-Shush," which hit number 29.

Those records set the tone for the group's music

and career. The Ventures were not as much interested in creating their own music as in bringing their sound to bear on songs that had been hits—and misses—for other artists, or that had been composed for films or television programs. Emblematic of this was the group's 1967 album *Golden Greats by the Ventures*, a compilation not of the Ventures' hits but of cover versions of other artists' material.

To the Ventures, it was the sound—not the songs —that mattered.

And the sound kept coming. While the Ventures did not return to the top 10 of the singles chart until their remake "Walk—Don't Run '64" hit number eight in 1964, they released a steady stream of records that gained the group an immense following and fared well commercially (in 1963, *The Ventures Play Telstar, The Lonely Bull* hit number eight on the album chart).

The group's lineup changed during this time. In 1962, Johnson was injured in an auto crash and was replaced by Mel Taylor on drums. In 1963, the group's twin lead guitar setup was shuffled, with Edwards assuming the lead role and Bogle switching from guitar to bass. For the rest of the 1960s, the Ventures maintained a constant presence on the album chart with 1964's *The Ventures in Space*, 1965's *The Ventures Knock Me Out!* and 1966's *Wild Things!* among others. Singles high points included a careening version of Richard Rodgers' classic "Slaughter on Tenth Avenue" in 1964 and their storming cover of the theme for TV's "Hawaii Five-O," the latter charting at number four in 1969.

While the group was superceded by the guitar virtuosos of the later '60s and by the increasing instrumental sophistication of much of the decade's rock music in general, it proved to be enormously important in the popularization of rudimentary music education. The Ventures inspired a generation of high school rockers to pick up a guitar—or a bass, or the drums—and play. In 1965, the group released the instructional album *Play Guitar with the Ventures*,

TOP ALBUMS

WALK DON'T RUN (Dolton, '60, *11*)
TWIST WITH THE VENTURES (Dolton, '62, *24*)
THE VENTURES PLAY TELSTAR,
    THE LONELY BULL (Dolton, '63, *8*)
WALK, DON'T RUN, VOL. 2 (Dolton, '64, *17*)
THE VENTURES A GO-GO (Dolton, '65, *16*)
HAWAII FIVE-O (Liberty, '69, *11*)

Additional Top 40 Albums: 10

TOP SONGS

WALK—DON'T RUN (Dolton, '60, *2*)
PERFIDIA (Dolton, '60, *15*)
WALK—DON'T RUN '64 (Dolton, '64, *8*)
HAWAII FIVE-O (Liberty, '69, *4*)

Additional Top 40 Songs: 2

The Ventures

THE VENTURES

that was wildly popular with aspiring teen musicians. It came with four Ventures hits, each of which was replicated on separate tracks with individual instruments lopped off. This allowed the listeners to perform their own solos, chords, and so forth—to literally play along with the Ventures. The record inadvertently anticipated the "interactive" technology that would ultimately emerge in the 1990s.

The Ventures continued their career into that decade with various instrumental configurations. In 1968, Edwards bowed out, and guitarist Jerry McGee was added. In 1969, the group became a quintet when it recruited keyboardist Johnny Durrill. Edwards rejoined in 1972 and departed again in 1985. By the '90s, the lineup included Bogle, Wilson, Taylor, and McGee.

While the Ventures' chart career had faded by 1972, the act continued to tour in the U.S. over the next two decades. In Japan, they became an immense concert draw and enjoyed a celebrity-like popularity. In 1981, the original members re-formed briefly and performed at various shows in southern California, which had become the scene of the surf revival movement.

THE WHO

The Who assaulted
the rock world in 1965 with an energy, violence,
and abandon that were astonishing.

Dressed in their mod gear and surrounded by mountains of amplifiers and drums, which they flagrantly demolished onstage, they created a rock sound that had never been heard before. It was a sound that, in time, would establish the Who as the third great group in the triumvirate of British rock, where they joined the Beatles and the Rolling Stones.

While the group's insouciant mod image and stage destructions instantly gained the attention of the rock scene, it was the evocative songs of the Who's leader and guitarist, Pete Townshend, and the overarching musical grandeur he created with vocalist Roger Daltrey, bassist John Entwistle, and drummer Keith Moon that would ultimately prove to be the basis of the group's renown.

Over the course of its long career, which reached into the 1990s, the Who created everything from groundbreaking songs to long, quasi-classical works that redefined the sound of rock even as they expanded the parameters of the form.

The Who's music was, at once, immediate and timeless. On early songs like "I Can't Explain" and "The Kids Are Alright," the group evoked the excitement and rebellious innocence of the mod era in ways that transcended that era. When Daltrey stuttered the words to "My Generation" in 1965, it was as if all the doubts and bravura of teen life were surging to the surface in a universal cry of defiance. "Hope I die before I get old," Daltrey sang. And with that single line, the song's composer, Townshend, expressed the ethos not only of the '60s but of young people anywhere, anytime.

But the Who was also one of the great innovative forces in the evolution of rock performance. Windmilling his arm and smashing his hand against his strings, Townshend created power chords that would be imitated by countless guitarists of future rock generations. On the early song "Out in the Street," his guitar "solo" consisted of the bleeping sound of his toggle switch altering the tone of his chords, which gave way to the slashing slide of his fingers down the length of the guitar neck.

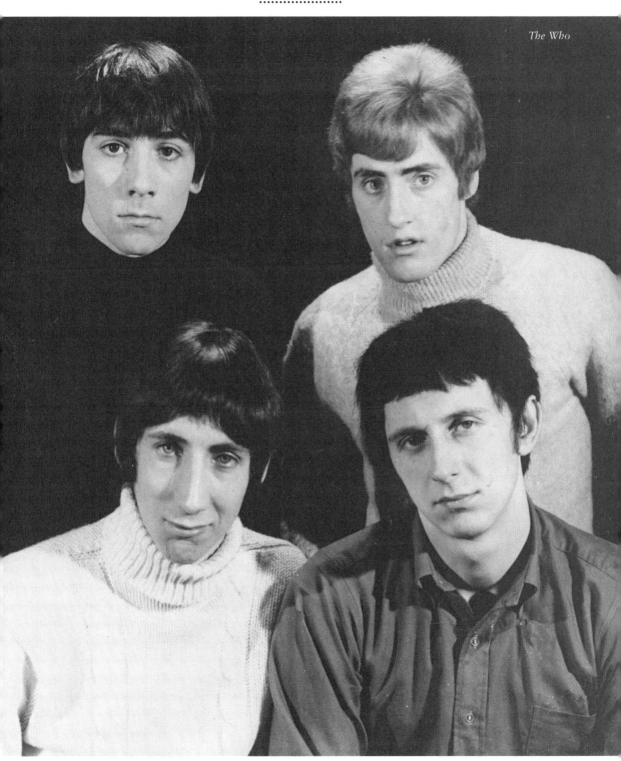

The Who

Moon and Entwistle countered and complemented Townshend's sonic tirades with innovations of their own. Surrounded by a gigantic drum kit—the like of which had never been seen before—Moon produced a series of thunderous rolls and flourishes that crossed the slamming style of rock with the dramatic accents of classical percussionists. Entwistle—one of the great virtuosos of his instrument in rock—moved the bass out from the background, playing lines that had the function, at times, of a lead guitar. On "My Generation," it was actually Entwistle's bass, not Townshend's guitar, that was given the solo role.

In the late 1960s—a time in which the album became the primary vehicle of expression for most rock groups—the Who was basically a singles band. While *The Who Sell Out*, of 1967, was a mildly intriguing concept album, with its interconnecting radio commercials and jingles, the group's major pieces during that phase of its career were songs like the rampaging "I Can See for Miles," the Bo Diddley–inflected "Magic Bus," and the oddly melodic "Pictures of Lily," the latter replete with the high, warbling vocal harmonies of Daltrey, Townshend, and Entwistle —another signature of the group's sound.

All of that changed with *Tommy*. Released in 1969, it was a vast, flowing work that combined the thematic and musical contrivances of grand opera with the sound and expressivity of rock. As such, it was the first so-called rock opera.

Townshend had experimented with the new form on the songs "A Quick One While He's Away" on the 1966 (U.S.) album *A Quick One (Happy Jack)* and "Rael" from *Sell Out*. Those experiments came to fruition with *Tommy*. The story of a "deaf, dumb, and blind boy" who became a pinball genius and was elevated to the level of spiritual leader, *Tommy* was Townshend's incisive depiction of the pretensions and lunacies of the rock world of the time. Musically, songs like "Pinball Wizard" and "I'm Free" had complex structures that were, nonetheless, grounded in the storming rock sound that he and the Who had pursued during their career.

That sound—augmented by more mature lyrical explorations of social and personal issues—reached its apex on the Who's defining masterpiece, the 1971 album *Who's next*.

While the Who went on to produce moments of excitement and eloquence, it never surpassed, or equalled, the brilliance of its music in the 1960s. Not that that was necessary. With its songs and performances of that era, the Who had created some of the finest rock of all time.

The Who began to form in 1962 when Daltrey (b. Mar. 1, 1945, Hammersmith, London) invited Entwistle (b. Oct. 9, 1944, Chiswick, London) to join his group the Detours. Townshend (b. May, 19, 1945, Chiswick), who had previously played in various groups with Entwistle while the two were students at Acton County Grammar School, was also recruited along with drummer Doug Sandom.

The group—subsequently changing its name to the Who—performed on the local rock scene for the next two years, during which time Sandom left and was replaced by Moon (b. Aug. 23, 1947, Wembley, London). In 1964, the group came to the attention of publicist Pete Meaden, who became its manager and introduced it to the thriving mod scene. At Meaden's suggestion, their name was changed to the High Numbers (mod slang for "style"), and they secured a recording contract with Fontana Records. Their debut single was "I'm the Face," a rewrite, by Meaden, of bluesman Slim Harpo's "Got Love If You Want It."

While the single failed, it generated interest in the mod scene and, more importantly, brought the group in contact with Kit Lambert and Chris Stamp (brother of actor Terence), who purchased the High Numbers' contract with Meaden and became its managers.

Lambert immediately assumed the role of mentor. He changed their name back to the Who and began to develop an op-art image that included a set of clothes—including Moon's "target" T-shirt and Townshend's Union Jack coat—that soon became the group's visual trademarks.

TOP ALBUMS

TOMMY (Decca, '69, 4)
LIVE AT LEEDS (Decca, '70, 4)
WHO'S NEXT (Decca, '71, 4)
QUADROPHENIA (MCA, '73, 2)
THE WHO BY NUMBERS (MCA, '75, 8)
WHO ARE YOU (MCA, '78, 2)
THE KIDS ARE ALRIGHT (MCA, '79, 8)
FACE DANCES (Warner, '81, 4)
IT'S HARD (Warner, '82, 8)

Additional Top 40 Albums: 3

TOP SONG

I CAN SEE FOR MILES (Decca, '67, 9)

Additional Top 40 Songs: 15

During a show at London's Railway Hotel in late 1964, Townshend inadvertently smashed his guitar into a low ceiling. When the crowd went wild, thinking it was part of the act, Moon capitalized on the reaction and demolished his drums. Lambert decided that the destruction should become a regular part of the group's performances, and the Who's legendary stage act was born.

In a similarly crucial move, Lambert gave Townshend two tape decks and suggested that he begin to write original songs.

The results of that suggestion proved to be fortuitous. In April 1965, the Townshend-composed single "I Can't Explain" was released and rose to number eight on the U.K. charts. It was followed by "Anyway, Anyhow, Anywhere," which made number 10 in June.

But a watershed—for the Who and for rock—occurred in November 1965, when Townshend's "My Generation" was released. It established the Who as one of the most important groups on the British rock scene while rising to number two on the singles chart. The accompanying debut album, *My Generation,* hit number five.

The group consolidated its position in the U.K. during 1966 with the singles "Substitute," which hit number five, and "I'm a Boy" which reached number two. But the group was still relatively unknown in the U.S.

That changed in 1967. In January, the Who made its U.S. stage debut at Murray the K's legendary "Music in the Fifth Dimension" shows in New York. Its subsequent performance at the Monterey Pop Festival in July finally brought the group to the attention of the broad U.S. public, and its single "Happy Jack" hit number 24 on the stateside charts.

Over the course of the next two years, the Who became a major rock act on both sides of the Atlantic, scoring major hits with "Pictures of Lily" and "I Can See for Miles." But during that time, Townsend began to expand his artistic vision and range. He also became a disciple of the Indian guru Meher Baba, whose teachings would have a crucial impact on his future work.

The culmination of his musical aspirations and Baba's influence came in 1969 with the release of *Tommy.* The album hit number four in the U.S., and the Who subsequently embarked on a tour at major opera houses around the world (including the Metropolitan in New York in 1970), performing full-length versions of the piece. Tommy would be Townshend's most enduring legacy: in 1975, director Ken Russell turned it into a garish film, and in 1992, Townshend revived it as a Broadway musical, which was greeted by vast acclaim, success, and several Tony Awards.

But the Who was still a potent rock group. And it proved as much on its 1971 album *Who's next.* Wielding synthesizers with the same abandon he had once reserved for his guitar, Townshend created complex, incessant, minimalist textures on songs like "Won't Get Fooled Again" and "Baba O'Riley"—arguably, the finest use of electronics in all of rock. He contrasted these smashing songs with others, like the boisterous "Goin' Mobile" and the aching ballad "Behind Blue Eyes," which, in combination with the rest, produced a summation of his creative vision.

From there, however, the group entered a long period of gradual but undeniable decline. While it continued to be one of the major rock acts of the time—on record and onstage—its subsequent releases began to reflect the artistic ennui of '70s rock in general and of the Who in particular. Mid-'70s albums of new material, like the 1973 rock opera *Quadrophenia* and 1975's *The Who by Numbers,* had their moments, but the freshness and force of the Who's early days were clearly on the wane. With the death of Moon in 1978, following the release of the album *Who Are You,* the group appeared to be on the verge of collapse.

It revived, temporarily, when ex-Faces drummer Kenney Jones was recruited later in 1978. But the 1981 album *Face Dances* was mostly a dull and remarkably lackluster effort, as was the group's final studio album, *It's Hard,* in 1982.

That year, the Who staged a "farewell" tour, then called it quits.

Townshend, Daltrey, and Entwistle pursued solo careers over the course of the rest of the 1980s. Daltrey and Entwistle released albums that were mediocre at best. But Townshend continued to produce work that was intriguing and provocative, particularly on albums like 1985's *White City,* 1989's *The Iron Man,* and 1993's *Psychoderelict.*

In 1989, the Who re-formed—with drummer Simon Phillips and an expanded instrumental lineup—and embarked on a major U.S. tour to commemorate the 20th anniversary of *Tommy.* In 1990, the group was inducted into the Rock and Roll Hall of Fame.

THE YARDBIRDS

I
n May of 1965,
the Yardbirds cut themselves loose from the R&B scene of London
and never looked back. With the release of the single "For Your
Love," the group embarked on a musical journey that would prove
to be one of the most adventurous and innovative in rock history
and one that would change the face of the music.

With its use of a harpsichord, bongos, and an exotic-sounding minor-keyed chord progression, "For Your Love" suggested that the Yardbirds had more on their minds than replicating the blues and R&B of the American masters. And indeed they did.

During the succeeding three years of their career, the Yardbirds became one of the first groups to freely experiment with non-rock musical forms, incorporating a vast range of ethnic idioms, guitar timbres, and vocal harmonies into their blues-inflected music. Their riff-based sound, propelled by guitar histrionics, also provided much of the basis for the heavy metal movement that emerged at the end of the 1960s, and specifically for the first definable heavy metal group, Led Zeppelin.

And in the mid-'60s, several of their songs, including "I'm a Man," "Heart Full of Soul," and "Shapes of Things," became signature hits of the time.

Over the course of its career, the group served as a platform for three guitarists who would subsequently play a pivotal role in the development of the instrument in rock: Eric Clapton, Jeff Beck, and Jimmy Page. These guitarists directed and shaped the group's sound—as well as that of much of the rock of the next two decades.

But the other members also played significant roles. Vocalist Keith Relf and bassist Paul Samwell-Smith provided much of the musical direction, suggesting many of the non-rock sources that were used in the songs. While rhythm guitarist Chris Dreja and drummer Jim McCarty primarily provided support, they freely participated in the group's experimental approach.

It was that approach that elevated the Yardbirds to a seminal role in the evolution of the music. With its pioneering sound and songs, the Yardbirds were one of the first groups to suggest that rock could, in fact, be more than rock. It could be an all-encompassing musical expression, not confined to any stylistic boundaries.

The group was initially formed in London in 1963 as the Metropolitan Blues Quartet with Relf (b. Mar. 22, 1943, Richmond, London), Samwell-Smith (b. May 8, 1943, Richmond), Dreja (b. Nov. 11, 1945, Surbiton, London), and guitarist Anthony "Top" Topham. They began to perform in the emerging R&B scene and subsequently changed their name to the Yardbirds.

Through these performances they came to the attention of Giorgio Gomelsky, who hired them as the house band of his Crawdaddy Club (replacing the Rolling Stones, who had begun to move out into the broad rock world). Topham left the group at that time and was replaced by Clapton.

Just as the Crawdaddy Club had proved to be the springboard for the Stones' career, the Yardbirds' stint had the same results. The group's nightly shows—soon to be called "rave-ups"—became one of the focal points of the scene. Gomelsky became the group's manager and producer, and he booked them on a U.K. tour backing blues legend Sonny Boy

The Yardbirds

Williamson at the end of 1963. This firmly established the group as one of the leading exponents of British R&B, and the tour would yield the 1966 album *The Yardbirds with Sonny Boy Williamson*.

At the start of 1964, Gomelsky secured a record deal with Columbia, and the group released its debut album, *Five Live Yardbirds,* in December. When the group performed on "The Beatles' Christmas Show," it was seen by songwriter Graham Gouldman (later of 10cc), who offered them his composition "For Your Love."

The group recorded the song and released it as its debut single in March 1965. While the record was an immediate success, reaching the top 10 in the U.S. and the U.K., its musical direction was one that Clapton did not agree with, and he left the group. Forced to find a new guitarist on short notice, the

---

TOP ALBUMS

For Your Love (Epic, '65)
Having a Rave Up with the Yardbirds (Epic, '65)
Over Under Sideways Down (Epic, '66)
The Yardbird's Greatest Hits (Epic, '67, 28)

TOP SONGS

For Your Love (Epic, '65, 6)
Heart Full of Soul (Epic, '65, 9)
I'm a Man (Epic, '65, 17)
Shapes of Things (Epic, '66, 11)
Over Under Sideways Down (Epic, '66, 13)
Happenings Ten Years Time Ago (Epic, '66, 30)

Yardbirds recruited Beck (b. June 24, 1944, Wallington, London) at the suggestion of Page, who had turned down an offer from the group.

The inclusion of Beck proved to be inspired. His innovative, virtuostic style was the perfect complement to the musical experiments the group was about to pursue.

Over the next two years, Beck and the Yardbirds created an astonishing body of work. It began with the group's next single, "Heart Full of Soul." Another Gouldman effort, the song was originally conceived by Relf and Samwell-Smith as an amalgam of pop and Indian music. But when a session with a sitarist failed to achieve the desired results, Beck offered to perform the song's theme line on the guitar. Simulating the sound of the sitar, Beck created a wiry, bending riff that was entirely revolutionary.

Released in June 1965, the record hit number two in the U.K. and number six in the U.S. and established the group's reputation as one of rock's leading innovators.

That reputation was solidified at the end of 1965 with the release of the (U.S.) album *Having a Rave Up with the Yardbirds.* Later viewed as one of rock's most important albums, *Rave Up* came with a vast range of new sounds. While its second side was devoted to live cuts from *Five Live Yardbirds* (recorded with Clapton), its first side came with songs that virtually redefined the parameters of rock. "Still I'm Sad" used a Gregorian chant melodic structure as the basis of the song's theme line. On "Mr. You're a Better Man than I," a lyrical protest against inequality, Samwell-Smith's bass line assumed a lead role that was quite new in rock. And on "Train Kept A-Rollin' " and "I'm a Man," the Yardbirds created the riff-based combination of blues and rock that was a direct precursor to heavy metal.

At the core of all the songs was Beck's guitar. Using distortion, power chords, and fleeting technical flourishes, Beck created a new lexicon for the instrument. In the process, he laid out the crucial role that the guitar—and the guitarist—would subsequently play in the evolution of the music.

The group's success, and its innovations, continued into 1966, with the singles "Shapes of Things" (containing a stupendous Beck solo) and "Over Under Sideways Down" reaching the upper levels of the charts.

But the Yardbirds were soon beset by defections. Samwell-Smith quit the group in June, to pursue a career as a producer. Page (b. Apr. 9, 1944, London) joined initially as bassist, but then assumed second-lead-guitar duties, with Dreja moving into the bass role. With Beck and Page on guitar, the group appeared in director Michelangelo Antonioni's film *Blowup,* performing the song "Stroll On" in one of the most exciting rock sequences in cinema history. The Yardbirds also recorded the storming single "Happenings Ten Years Time Ago," with the guitar duo creating a dense, abstract solo section of distorted lines and police sirens.

But the strains of touring proved too much for Beck, who quit the group in October 1966. Page moved into the lead guitar position, and he and the group began to experiment with new sound textures—including the bowed-guitar drones that were among his musical signatures—and an overtly effects-accented, psychedelic approach. The result of this was the 1967 album *Little Games* and its rhythmically charged title cut.

While the group had inspired a new generation of rock musicians with its innovative sound, by 1968 it was being increasingly superceded by groups like the Jimi Hendrix Experience and Cream (with Clapton) who were taking the Yardbirds' ideas to new technical and expressive levels. In July 1968, the Yardbirds disbanded.

The original members dispersed. Relf subsequently founded the group Renaissance, with whom he recorded until his death in 1976. Dreja became a photographer. McCarty played in various groups,

including Illusion (in the 1970s) and Regression (in the late 1980s). In 1983, Dreja, McCarty, and Samwell-Smith formed the group Box of Frogs with lead vocalist John Fiddler.

Following the Yardbirds' demise in 1968, Page attempted to recruit a new lineup, initially dubbed the New Yardbirds. They would ultimately attain vast popularity using the name Led Zeppelin.

In 1983, the Yardbirds' legendary guitar triumvirate convened onstage publicly for the first time when Clapton, Beck, and Page joined a star-studded group in a benefit performance for Ronnie Lane's ARMS charity at a show at London's Royal Albert Hall.

Y E S
....

The group that pioneered the progressive movement, along with some of its more inspired—and excessive—musical inclinations, was Yes.

With the release of the Beatles' *Sgt. Pepper's Lonely Hearts Club Band* in 1967, rock began to assume a new cachet. Paul McCartney stated at the time that rock had become the "classical music" of its time. His view seemed to be validated when the album was hailed as a musical masterpiece by critics and such classicists as Leonard Bernstein.

Inspired by this new perception—as much as by *Sgt. Pepper* itself—musicians began to create rock that was as grandiose as its new and exalted status. Thus, progressive rock was born.

Yes set the movement in motion and established the rules of what was to come. At every turn, Yes proclaimed its artistic intentions with grand flourishes and musical signatures. The group's music, for example, comprised intricate, classically inspired songs and extended improvisations that displayed an overt instrumental virtuosity and finesse.

The apex of that music—and the record that put the progressive movement on the commercial and creative map—was *Fragile*. On that 1972 album, vocalist Jon Anderson sang his quasi-poetic lyrics with the histrionics of a grand opera tenor. Guitarist Steve Howe, bassist Chris Squire, keyboardist Rick Wakeman, and drummer Bill Bruford created a sound that came with complex time signatures, vast and varied layers of chords and theme lines, and fleeting and remarkably agile solos that reflected classical approaches to form and content.

This high point notwithstanding, Yes also set the precedent for much of the musical excess and pretension that plagued the progressive movement. On albums such as 1972's *Close to the Edge,* Yes went over the edge, its classical ambitions pushed to the extreme. The group offered its immense and estimable instrumental talents as substitutes for substantive expression, while Anderson emoted his way through lyrics that were convoluted and overblown counterparts to the group's fanciful, quasi–science fiction record covers.

But even in its seemingly endless moments of excess, Yes expanded rock musicianship to new levels. And there was a grandeur of execution to the group's music that was impressive and that served as a model for subsequent progressive groups.

One of the best of them was King Crimson, whose long career—with guitarist Robert Fripp at its core—ranged from the flowing classicism of 1969's *In the Court of the Crimson King* to the metal-tinged, abstract onslaughts of 1974's *Red* and the minimalistic experiments of 1981's *Discipline.* Emerson, Lake and Palmer pushed progressive rock to its illogical extreme with its overblown interpretations of classical

TOP ALBUMS

FRAGILE (Atlantic, '72, *4*)
CLOSE TO THE EDGE (Atlantic, '72, *3*)
YESSONGS (Atlantic, '73, *12*)
TALES FROM TOPOGRAPHIC OCEANS
    (Atlantic, '74, *6*)
RELAYER (Atlantic, '75, *5*)
GOING FOR THE ONE (Atlantic, '77, *8*)
TORMATO (Atlantic, '78, *10*)
90125 (Atco, '83, *5*)

Additional Top 40 Albums: 4

TOP SONGS

ROUNDABOUT (Atlantic, '72, *13*)
OWNER OF A LONELY HEART
    (Atco, '83, *1*)

Additional Top 40 Songs: 3

works (including Mussorgsky's *Pictures at an Exhibition*) and such bombastic original efforts as 1971's *Tarkus*. The Canadian trio Rush highlighted the rock aspect of the progressive approach on albums like 1975's *Fly by Night* and 1977's *A Farewell to Kings,* which came with metal-inflected songs and lyrics that were the mystical equals of those of Anderson. Other lesser progressive groups, like the Yes/Crimson offshoot Asia and Todd Rundgren's Utopia, abounded in the 1970s and '80s, all with their own brands of instrumental wizardry and musical pretension.

Despite numerous defections and personnel realignments, Yes persisted and, at times, flourished into the '90s. In its more inspired moments, Yes created music that expanded the creative boundaries of rock. At its lower points, Yes proved just how musically regressive the progressive movement could be.

Yes began to take form in 1968 when Anderson (b. Oct. 25, 1944, Accrington, England) was introduced to Squire (b. Mar. 4, 1948, London) in a London nightclub. They were soon joined by keyboardist Tony Kaye, Bruford (b. May 17, 1948, London), and guitarist Peter Banks.

By 1969, the group had concluded a deal with Atlantic and released the single "Sweetness," which failed to chart. While the group's eponymous debut

Yes

album also proved to be a commercial disappointment, it established Yes's musical intentions, particularly on its hyperbolic interpretations of the Beatles' "Every Little Thing" and the Byrds' "I See You." The group's next album, 1970's *Time and a Word,* was an extension of its overtly classical sound, employing strings and sprawling instrumental sections.

Banks quit the group in 1970, and Howe (b. Apr. 8, 1947, London) was recruited as a replacement. His technical virtuosity added a new dimension to the group. On Yes's third effort, 1971's *The Yes Album,* Howe and Kaye wove dense, convoluted instrumental tapestries on songs such as "Yours Is No Disgrace," which had an almost baroque intricacy.

Just as the group's sound finally seemed to be coalescing, Kaye quit in 1971. But his replacement, keyboardist Rick Wakeman (b. May 18, 1949, London), proved to be even more in sync with the group's musical direction. A former member of the Strawbs (another progressive group, with traditional folk leanings), Wakeman shared Anderson's mystical sensibilities and persona. Like Howe, he was also a virtuosic musician, and the two began to create a symphonic sound in a rock context.

The result of their work, *Fragile,* proved to be a commercial and creative watershed, establishing Yes—and the progressive movement—in the broad rock marketplace. Fragile hit number four on the charts while its single, "Roundabout," reached number 13.

But Bruford quit in 1972 to join King Crimson. His replacement was Alan White (b. June 14, 1949, Durham, England), former drummer for the Plastic Ono Band.

By then one of the biggest rock acts of the time, Yes's grandiosity seemed to evolve in proportion to its popularity. The 1972 studio album *Close to the Edge* and 1973's triple record live set, *Yessongs,* were garish and self-indulgent yet at the same time vastly commercial: the former hit number three on the charts and the latter made number 12.

The success continued apace with the group's next album, 1974's *Tales from Topographic Oceans.* The album charted at number six, and the group toured before sold-out crowds in the U.S. (its shows augmented by amorphous, glowing forms that were drawn from the album's sc-fi cover by Roger Dean).

While the group had been reaching new commercial levels, Wakeman had been doing the same on his own with the 1973 solo album *The Six Wives of*

Henry the VIII and its 1974 successor, *Journey to the Centre of the Earth,* which charted at number three. Wakeman quit the group in 1974 to pursue his own career.

Swiss-born keyboardist Patrick Moraz was recruited as his replacement, and the group pressed on. Moraz brought a new, fusion jazz sound to Yes, which was heard on its 1975 album, *Relayer.* But when Wakeman rejoined the group in 1977, Moraz was released, and Yes retreated to its old ways and old sound on *Going for the One* and *Tormato.*

By the end of the 1970s, Yes's popularity was undiminished, even in the midst of the punks and new wave musicians who were rebelling against the progressive groups Yes epitomized. But it began coming apart, nonetheless. In 1980, Yes was rocked by the departures of Wakeman and Anderson.

But it temporarily rebounded with the enlistment of Trevor Horn and Geoff Downes, who had, ironically, made a name for themselves in the new wave scene as the Buggles. Horn and Downes pared down some of the group's more overblown aspects on the 1980 album *Drama.* But it was clear that the duo wasn't entirely compatible with Yes's sound or sensibility, and their collaboration was soon ended.

The group formally disbanded in 1981, but its career was hardly finished. The next year, Squire and White formed a new group, Cinema, with South African guitarist Trevor Rabin. Kaye soon came on board, and when Rabin's vocals proved inadequate, Anderson was invited to join. Renaming the group Yes, the group released the 1983 album *90125* (based on its international catalogue number). With a leaner, new wave–inspired sound, the album hit number five, and, propelled by the constant exposure of its video on MTV, the single "Owner of a Lonely Heart" topped the charts.

The group subsequently released the 1987 album *Big Generator.* In 1989, a new configuration of Anderson, Bruford, Wakeman, and Howe issued an album titled after their surnames; due to legal problems, they could not use the name Yes. When those problems were resolved in 1991, Yes reemerged with Anderson, Wakeman, Bruford, White, Kaye, Rabin, and Howe all joining forces for the "Yesshows" world tour and the album *Union.*

NEIL YOUNG

Neil Young staked his own claim to rock and roll and worked it like a mine.

Over the course of his long career, he created a vast array of songs and albums, some of which were nuggets, others simply fool's gold. Intuitively, he pursued various stylistic seams, some of which went nowhere and others that gave on to mother lodes of creativity and expression. Through the rich times and the lean, he was one of rock's true eccentrics and free spirits.

And he never stopped picking.

At the core of Young's musical vision was an overarching sense of independence. He defied expectations, trends, and tastes with an almost willful abandon. He was a rock hero, but one who didn't seem to pursue fame as an end in itself. His songs could be intensely personal or overtly political. He helped to define musical movements like folk-rock and the singer-songwriter scene and then abandoned them. And over the course of 25 years and 27 solo albums, he constantly made and remade his sound in flagrant, but notably directed, disregard for what his fans, critics, the culture, or his record labels seemed to want from him. From the melody-rich electric

Neil Young

songs of "Everybody Knows This Is Nowhere," Young journeyed, at various points in his career, through music that was country flavored (*Harvest*), punk inflected (*Rust Never Sleeps*), and techno-rock influenced (*Trans*).

Yet Young was never eclectic in the traditional sense. He didn't dabble in musical forms as much as exploit them to his own creative ends, much in the way a painter uses still lifes, portraits, and landscapes to achieve a particular expressive vision.

In fact, it never really mattered what specific style Young was pursuing at any given time. His high, frail, heartfelt vocals; jagged, brittle, furious guitar solos; and his eloquent acoustic work immediately stamped whatever he was doing with a sound and musical presence that were among the most memorable and recognizable in all of rock. And they did so whether he was performing as a solo artist or with such groups as Buffalo Springfield, Crazy Horse, and Crosby, Stills, Nash and Young.

Not all of Young's stylistic forays worked. But he never seemed daunted by his fallow periods. In fact, they were as much a part of his creative independence as the music of his more inspired moments. To Young, rock wasn't just a career; it was a sustaining passion.

Perhaps that was why Young was one of the few rock musicians able to transcend rock's oppressive obsession with youth. Into the 1990s, Young's performances, both onstage and on record, were endowed with an ageless quality. While he was clearly older than most contemporary rockers, it didn't seem to be an issue. It was the art—his art—that mattered.

Young (b. Nov. 12, 1945, Toronto, Canada) launched his career in 1963 with the Squires, with whom he performed in the Canadian folk scene (along with the likes of Stephen Stills and Richie Furay). In 1964, he relocated to New York and joined the Mynah Birds (fronted by Rick Matthews, who later gained fame as '80s funk star Rick James). The group's bassist, Bruce Palmer, invited Young to join him on a trip to Los Angeles in 1965, where they subsequently teamed with Stills, Furay, and drummer Dewey Martin in Buffalo Springfield.

When that group disbanded in 1968, Young began to pursue a solo career. His eponymous debut album was released in January 1969, but it failed to chart. Forming the group Crazy Horse (which included drummer Ralph Molina, guitarist Danny Whitten, and bassist Billy Talbot) later in the year, Young then released the album *Everybody Knows This Is Nowhere,* which yielded the signature songs "Cinnamon Girl" and "Down by the River" and eventually reached number 34 on the charts.

In July, Young was invited to join Crosby, Stills and Nash. A month later, the quartet delivered one of the musical high points of the Woodstock Festival. When their album *Déjà Vu* was released in March 1970, it was an immediate smash, topping the charts and becoming the biggest selling rock album of the year.

Young plunged into the political turmoil of the time when he wrote "Ohio," an angry response to the killing of four students at Kent State University in 1970. Released as a CSN&Y record, it charted at number 14.

While he had become a major rock star with CSN&Y, Young was intent on continuing his solo career. In September 1970, he released his third solo set, the folk-infused *After the Gold Rush,* with its haunting title cut and the raging rocker "Southern Man."

In 1971, he split from CSN&Y (although he would maintain an on-again, off-again professional relationship with that group and its members over the next 20 years).

The follow-up solo disc, 1972's *Harvest,* was an extension of the acoustic approach he had taken on his previous record. It included two of his most expressive songs, "Heart of Gold" and "Old Man." Released as a single, the former topped the charts, as did the album.

TOP ALBUMS

AFTER THE GOLD RUSH (Reprise, '70, 8)
HARVEST (Reprise, '72, 1)
TIME FADES AWAY (Reprise, '73, 22)
ON THE BEACH (Reprise, '74, 16)
AMERICAN STARS 'N BARS (Reprise, '77, 21)
COMES A TIME (Reprise, '78, 7)
RUST NEVER SLEEPS (Reprise, '79, 8)
LIVE RUST (Reprise, '79, 15)
TRANS (Geffen, '83, 19)

Additional Top 40 Albums: 7

TOP SONG

HEART OF GOLD (Reprise, '72, 1)

Additional Top 40 Songs: 2

But just as his career was reaching its peak, Young began to pursue new musical interests. The results, for the remainder of the 1970s, were uneven. There were inspired moments, like the tortured songs of 1975's *Tonight's the Night* and the dense imagery and rocking energy of *Zuma.* But Young also wandered aimlessly through albums such as 1974's *On the Beach* and 1978's *Comes a Time.* His 1974 film and album, *Journey Through the Past,* was a notably unfocused and lackluster career retrospective.

At the end of the decade, Young seemed revitalized. On 1979's *Rust Never Sleeps,* Young and the reunited Crazy Horse divided their time between storming, punk-inflected rockers and melodic, acoustic ballads. A film of the same title and a subsequent concert album, *Live Rust,* reaffirmed Young as one of the most inspired rock musicians of the time.

But just as he had done at the height of his career, Young again seemed to veer off track. 1980's *Hawks and Doves* and its 1981 successor, *Re-ac-tor,* were energetic but directionless records. The electronic experiments of 1982's *Trans* were intriguing, as were the rockabilly stomps of 1983's *Everybody's Rockin'* and the country sounds of 1985's *Old Ways.* But 1986's *Landing on Water* was another mundane affair.

Young rebounded in the late 1980s with one of his most remarkable records. Summoning the jagged intensity of *Rust* and augmenting it with the emotion of his folk era, Young (again with Crazy Horse) issued *Freedom* in 1988. From that album, "Rockin' in the Free World" emerged as, arguably, the finest song of his career.

As Young made his way into the 1990s, he continued to demonstrate his passion and independence. *Ragged Glory* of 1990 was a musical extension of *Freedom,* while 1991's *Weld* was an exercise in noisy, abstract rock that was similar to the music of Sonic Youth (who had opened for him on a tour that year). And in 1993, he released *Harvest Moon,* a set of winsome and melodic ballads that recalled the *Harvest* album.

THE YOUNG RASCALS

Along with the Righteous Brothers, the Young Rascals introduced the power of soul—soul music, that is— to the world of rock and roll.

While the Righteous Brothers came first, they maintained a certain distance from rock, opting instead for grandiose ballads and Phil Spector's walls of sound. The Young Rascals charged full-bore into their music with a soulful fervor and rocking energy that was the first true marriage of the two musical forms.

It was an enormously influential sound that, in time, would form the basis for the songs and styles of "blue-eyed soul" acts like Hall and Oates in the 1970s and the soul-flavored songs of Billy Joel, Paul Young, and others in the '80s. On a broader level, the Young Rascals' use of soul-inflected vocals, harmonies, and rhythms in a rock context would inspire countless artists who were not specifically a part of the blue-eyed soul movement.

With their first major hit, 1966's "Good Lovin'," the Young Rascals immediately established their signature sound. Propelled by Gene Cornish's saw-toothed guitar chords, drummer Dino Danelli's pounding rock beats, and the soulful vocal harmonies of Brigati, Cornish, and keyboardist Felix Cavaliere, "Good Lovin' " defied simple categorization: it was as much rock as soul, and vice versa. And it pointed to an entirely new creative path for rock music.

While the group's vocals were undeniably rooted in soul, its instrumental sound was a revolutionary blend of soul and rock signatures. Pumping out rolling chords and high, wailing notes from the keyboard of his Hammond B3 organ, Cavaliere conjured images of soul man Booker T. Jones and R&B/jazz master Jimmy Smith. Cornish countered with raw, abrasive chords and lead lines on his gui-

tar, giving the sound its rock-tinged feels and textures. Danelli's drumming combined the energy of basic rock beats with the syncopation and rhythmic strut of soul drummers like Al Jackson of the MG's. The apex of this sound came on the group's third hit, "You Better Run," with Cavaliere's organ phrases suspended as if in mid-air above Cornish's slashing chords, while Brigati shouted out rhythmic asides.

In true '60s fashion, the Young Rascals did not adhere to the sound they created. Their music evolved over the course of the rest of the decade, assuming a more pop and R&B-oriented flavor as their artistic vision became more expansive. The 1967 hit "Groovin' " had a lush, lugubrious quasi-Latin feel that came with simmering rhythms and rich layers of vocal harmonies, congas, a piano, vibes—and bird calls. That same year, "How Can I Be Sure" had an overtly pop sound augmented by a refrain that had traces of the themes and rhythms of the hits written by Burt Bacharach and Hal David.

Even as it evolved, the group never neglected the soul that was at the core of their music. Later hits like 1968's "A Beautiful Morning" and "People Got to Be Free" were filled with the idealism of the Aquarian Age, but they were also infused with the lithe soul that had grounded the music of the Young Rascals from the start.

In 1964, Cavaliere (b. Nov. 29, 1944, Pelham, New York), Brigati (b. Oct. 22, 1946, Garfield, New Jersey), and Cornish (b. May 14, 1945) split from Joey Dee and the Starliters to form their own group, which they called the Rascals. They were soon joined by Danelli (b. July 23, 1945, New York), who had previously played with jazz titan Lionel Hampton.

The group became the house band at the Barge, a fashionable floating nightclub off the coast of Southampton, Long Island, in July 1964. Cavorting about the stage in knickerbocker pants and Little Lord Fauntleroy shirts, they stormed their way through R&B classics like "Mustang Sally," immediately establishing themselves as a standout sight and sound on the local scene.

Their shows at the Barge gained the attention of New York promoter Sid Bernstein, who became their manager. Famous in rock history as the promoter of the Beatles' Shea Stadium concert, Bernstein booked the group—which by that time had become the Young Rascals—to open the show. He also concluded a deal with Atlantic Records.

TOP ALBUMS

COLLECTIONS (Atlantic, '67, *14*)
GROOVIN' (Atlantic, '67, *5*)

The Rascals:
ONCE UPON A DREAM (Atlantic, '68, *9*)
TIME PEACE/THE RASCAL'S GREATEST HITS
  (Atlantic, '68, *1*)

Additional Top 40 Albums: 2

TOP SONGS

GOOD LOVIN' (Atlantic, '66, *1*)
GROOVIN' (Atlantic, '67, *1*)
A GIRL LIKE YOU (Atlantic, '67, *10*)
HOW CAN I BE SURE (Atlantic, '67, *4*)

The Rascals:
A BEAUTIFUL MORNING (Atlantic, '68, *3*)
PEOPLE GOT TO BE FREE (Atlantic, '68, *1*)

Additional Top 40 Songs: 7

The group's debut single, "I Ain't Gonna Eat Out My Heart Anymore," was released in January 1966. It was in the Righteous Brothers mode, with vocalist Eddie Brigati baring his soul on a grand and glorious ballad. Heavily supported by R&B stations across the U.S., it hit number 52 on the charts and established the Young Rascals' blue-eyed soul sound long before the term was coined. That sound rampaged the charts during the rest of the year. In April, "Good Lovin' " hit Number One, and in July, "You Better Run" made the top 20. The group's eponymous debut album reached number 15 that same month, and in October, the single "Come on Up" hit number 43.

The group's success continued in 1967. The

Motown-inflected single "I've Been Lonely Too Long" peaked at number 16 in March, while the group's second album, *Collections,* reached number 14. The group also began to revise and expand its sound, the result being the single "Groovin'," which topped the charts in May, selling more than two million copies. The album of the same title, including the group's next hit, "A Girl Like You," hit number four in September.

Inspired—like nearly every other act in rock—by the Beatles' *Sgt. Pepper's Lonely Hearts Club Band* album, the Young Rascals began to evolve, musically and personally. Cavaliere became a disciple of Indian guru Swami Satchidananda, and the rest of the group became involved in the Integral Yoga Institute. The next album, *Once Upon a Dream,* was a concept piece, as much pop as soul in sound.

In line with its new approach, the group dropped the "Young" from its name, becoming the Rascals in May 1968. But its new name and sound notwithstanding, the group continued its well-established chart success. That same month, its new single "A Beautiful Morning" hit number three and passed the million sales mark. In August, the romping "People Got to Be Free" topped the charts for five weeks,

also selling one million copies. And in September, the album *Time Peace/The Rascal's Greatest Hits* topped the charts.

The group continued its musical evolution on the 1969 album *Freedom Suite,* a sprawling concept record that included a more expansive instrumental sound. It hit number 17 on the charts.

But dissension was growing in the group, and in 1970 Brigati quit to pursue a career as a studio musician. Following the chart failure of the group's 1971 album *Search and Nearness,* Cornish also departed. Guitarist Buzzy Feiten, bassist Robert Popwell, and vocalist Ann Sutton were recruited by Cavaliere and Danelli, but when 1972's *The Island of Real* also proved to be a commercial disappointment, the group disbanded.

Cavaliere pursued a career as a producer (his credits including Laura Nyro), and he released an eponymous solo album in 1974. Danelli and Cornish formed the group Fotomaker in 1978, which released three albums. Danelli subsequently joined Steve Van Zandt's group, Little Steven and the Disciples of Soul.

In 1988, Cavaliere, Cornish, and Danelli regrouped and embarked on the "Good Lovin' '88" tour.

The Young Rascals

FRANK ZAPPA

Over the course of Frank Zappa's long career, it sometimes seemed as if he had become a rock musician through some monumental miscalculation, or perverse design.

Humorist, satirist, avant-garde classicist, sociopolitical polemicist, "freak"—Zappa was all of these and more at various times, with rock being the glue that held them all together.

With his group the Mothers of Invention in the 1960s, and later, during the lengthy solo phase of his career, Zappa created a vast and immensely varied body of work that had few equals in rock, even as it extended the boundaries of the music and pointed to new realms of creative expression.

Musically, Zappa had as much in common with classical composers and jazz musicians as he did with the rock and blues masters. The dense, abstract collages of sound pioneered by his hero, French avant-gardist Edgard Varèse, were core components of much of his work, particularly the symphonic sections of his 1967 album *Lumpy Gravy*. His use of random noise and extramusical sound on albums like *Uncle Meat* recalled that of John Cage. And on pieces such as "Peaches en Regalia" (from *Hot Rats*) he displayed an affinity for the musical wit and charm of Erik Satie. On later sets like *Orchestral Favorites* and *London Symphony Orchestra*, Zappa created modern classical music that was guided and directed by his rock sensibilities.

Similarly, Zappa's use of the technical and improvisational aspects of jazz could be heard in the charging fusion music of albums like *Chunga's Revenge* and *The Grand Wazoo*. But, as in his more classically oriented music, Zappa directed his jazz to rock ends, with beats (if not time signatures) and energy that jazz in its purer forms had never really employed.

There were also numerous creative digressions. The album *Sheik Yerbouti* mocked disco, while *You Are What You Is* took on everything from arena rock to the Doors with savage, satirical sideswipes. These later albums and others contained overt examples of the biting humor and commentary that were at the core of all of Zappa's music and that reinforced his image as an outsider moving around in the rock world.

It was this role, which he seemed to revel in, that made Zappa rock's first—and arguably greatest—observer-participant. With his scathing, sardonic wit and incisive mind, he continuously picked apart the foibles of rock music and its surrounding culture. On his early masterpieces *Absolutely Free* and *We're Only in It for the Money*, Zappa wove a dense tapestry of songs, noise, and orchestrated voices while attacking the strictures of "straight society" along with the superficiality and greed of the rock world (the latter album came with a garish cover that parodied that of the Beatles' *Sgt. Pepper* album).

These were themes he would return to again and again. On *Ship arriving too late to save a drowning witch*, he and his daughter Moon Unit joined together on the single "Valley Girl" to satirize the vacuous speech and mindset of the female mall denizens of southern California (the song became an artifact of modern culture and, ironically, a top 40 hit in 1982).

But Zappa was more than an outsider, just as his musical eclecticism, satirical wit, and overt eccentricity were more than the ramblings of an exhibitionistic dilettante. As a composer, Zappa insinuated rock signatures into new and alien contexts that redefined their simplicity and power. On the song "Plastic People" (from *Absolutely Free*), he opened with a salvo of "Louie Louie" chords, then contrasted them with the furious, atonal abstractions of free jazz. On

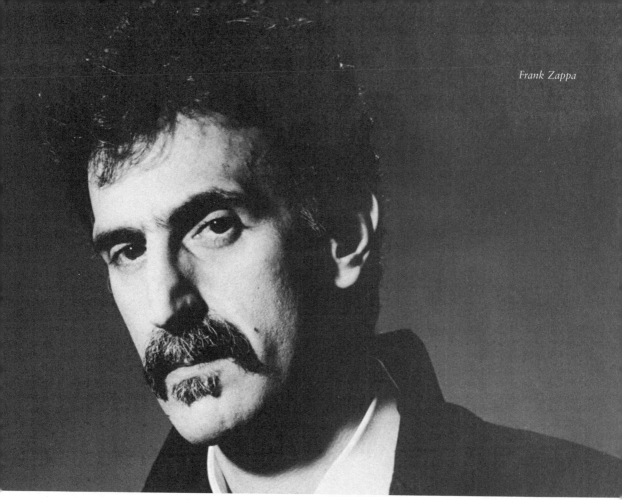

Freak Out, Zappa interspersed scary, maniacal rock songs like "Help I'm a Rock" with sections that came with a babble of voices and extraneous noises—a soundtrack for a world gone berserk. Art had rarely imitated life more incisively.

At times, the satire and musical technicality became overbearing. Zappa's wit seemed strained, sophomoric, and ultimately tasteless on such albums as *Joe's Garage, Act I* and *Tinsel Town Rebellion*. Similarly, some of his 1970s recordings—*Overnight Sensation* and *Apostrophe* among them—seemed merely facile displays of his compositional skills and musical silliness.

But when the wit and musical daring coalesced, Zappa created a sound world all his own, one that reflected the absolute artistic freedom and all-encompassing range that his singular genius demanded.

Zappa (b. Francis Vincent Zappa, Jr., Dec. 21, 1940, Baltimore, Maryland) moved to southern California with his family in 1950. During the subse-quent decade he played in various high school bands, one of which, the Blackouts, included Don Van Vliet (who, renamed Captain Beefheart, would collaborate with Zappa later in his career).

By the start of the 1960s, Zappa had become a composer. He scored various B movie soundtracks, including those for the films *The World's Greatest Sinner* and *Run Home Slow*. With his friend Ray Collins, he co-composed the doo wop song "Memories of El Monte," which was recorded by the Penguins. In 1964, he was arrested and subsequently served a brief stint in jail for recording a mock pornographic tape for an undercover vice squad policeman.

During this period, he performed with the groups the Masters and the Soul Giants. In 1964, the latter became the Muthers, the lineup including Collins (vocals), Elliott Ingber (guitar), Roy Estrada (bass), Jimmy Carl Black (drums), and Zappa (guitar and vocals). Renaming themselves the Mothers, the group began an engagement at the Whisky A-Go-Go club in Hollywood in 1965, where it soon developed a devoted base of fans (who called themselves "freaks").

The Mothers were signed by the MGM/Verve label in 1966. But the company immediately became uncomfortable with the name and suggested that it be changed to the Mothers of Invention. The group then released its debut album, *Freak Out*, in July.

A two-record set, *Freak Out* was a watershed. With its discordant, atonal songs contrasted with more straightforward numbers like "Ain't Got No Heart," it was, to say the least, a departure from anything that had previously been issued under the label of rock. Zappa's satirical lyrics were something

---

TOP ALBUMS

WE'RE ONLY IN IT FOR THE MONEY (Verve, '68, 30)
THE MOTHERS/FILLMORE EAST—JUNE 1971
   (Bizarre, '71, 38)
OVER-NITE SENSATION (DiscReet, '73, 32)
APOSTROPHE(') (DiscReet, '74, 10)
ROXY & ELSEWHERE (DiscReet, '74, 27)
ONE SIZE FITS ALL (DiscReet, '75, 26)
SHEIK YERBOUTI (Zappa, '79, 21)
JOE'S GARAGE, ACT I (Zappa, '79, 27)
SHIP ARRIVING TOO LATE TO SAVE
   A DROWNING WITCH (Barking P., '82, 23)

TOP SONG

VALLEY GIRL (Barking P., '82, 32)

---

of a revelation, with their calls for artistic and social freedom and their attacks on bourgeois complacency. The album's title soon became a part of the lexicon of the counterculture.

The next two albums, *Absolutely Free* and *We're Only in It for the Money* reflected a continuation and expansion of that sound and point of view. Zappa's tirades and parodies grew more intense, as did the dense mix of classical, jazz, and rock sounds.

While the group was becoming something of an icon on the underground scene, Zappa was moving on to other projects. In 1968, he released the largely instrumental album *Lumpy Gravy*. In 1969, he formed his own label, Bizarre/Straight Records, for which he began to record such fringe rock acts as Captain Beefheart and the fledgling Alice Cooper.

That same year, he and the Mothers released an affectionate and parodistic paean to early rock and

doo wop, *Cruisin' with Ruben and the Jets*. Then, in a dizzying turnaround, they issued the mixed media and musical experiments of *Uncle Meat*. But in October of 1969, Zappa decided to pursue a solo career and disbanded the Mothers of Invention. (He would subsequently employ various members on later albums and would re-form the group as a performing unit for sporadic tours during the 1970s.)

The initial phase of his solo career produced some of his finest music. Albums such as 1970's *Hot Rats* and *Chunga's Revenge* and 1972's *The Grand Wazoo* and *Waka Jawaka* were inspired amalgams of Zappa's jazz and classical signatures set in a rock context. During that period, he performed onstage with John Lennon and Yoko Ono at the Fillmore East (captured on Lennon's album *Some Time in New York City*). And in 1972, Zappa released the film *200 Motels*, in which he parodied the Mothers and their milieu with the same savagery he had brought to his lampoons of the rest of the rock and roll world.

But as the 1970s progressed, Zappa's music and wit became increasingly self-parodistic. A few high points, like 1975's *Bongo Fury* (recorded with Captain Beefheart) were offset by albums like *Apostrophe*, in which Zappa seemed to be packaging his strangeness into a commecial product. That album, in fact, was his only top 10 hit.

From the later 1970s into the '80s, Zappa's music was uneven. The virtuosic classicism of 1979's *Orchestral Favorites* was contrasted by the silly humor of 1981's *Tinsel Town Rebellion*. *The Man from Utopia*, from 1983, was mundane and directionless, while 1986's *Jazz from Hell* was a fascinating display of Zappa's instrumental wizardry; the latter album won a 1987 Grammy Award for Best Rock Instrumental.

Zappa began to expand his efforts, musically and politically, as time went on. In 1983, he made his conducting debut, performing music by Varèse and Anton Webern with the chamber group the San Francisco Music Players. In the later 1980s, he became a tireless crusader and proponent of artistic freedom, waging a verbal war with the Parents Music Resource Center. In 1990, referring to himself as a "trade consultant," Zappa conferred with Czech president Vaclav Havel in Prague. Zappa later claimed that Havel was a fan who had stated his particular affection for the album *Bongo Fury*.

Zappa died on December 4, 1993 after an extended battle with prostate cancer.

INDEX

PHOTO CREDITS

ABOUT THE AUTHOR

Photo: Leslie Sumrall

Harry Sumrall grew up playing rock and roll in the late 1960s in Houston (where he once performed in a club with Lightnin' Hopkins). He subsequently pursued a career as a composer in Washington, D.C. He has written for the *Washington Post, The New Republic, The New Grove Dictionary of American Music,* and other publications. He is currently a music critic for the *San Jose Mercury News,* and his work appears regularly on the Knight Ridder News Service. He lives in San Francisco with his wife, Leslie, and his son, Sam.